SPLENDOUR OF EARTH

SPLENDOUR OF

EARTH

AN ANTHOLOGY OF TRAVEL

COMPILED BY

MARGARET S. ANDERSON

Lately Fellow of Girton College and Lecturer in
Geography, University of Cambridge

1954

LONDON

GEORGE PHILIP AND SON LIMITED

30-32 FLEET STREET LONDON EC4

ANNOUNCEMENT

This book is Copyright in the United Kingdom of Great
Britain and Northern Ireland and in Berne Convention
countries. Apart from any use specifically permitted under
the Copyright Act of 1911 no portion of it may be reproduced by any process without written permission.
Enquiries should be addressed to the publishers.

PRINTED IN GREAT BRITAIN BY GEORGE PHILIP AND SON LIMITED

PREFACE

This anthology was in galley proof when Mrs. Anderson died. It was complete but without the title, the introduction, or the maps. Among her papers were found the titlepage, parts of several manuscript drafts of an introduction, a few regional maps and some incomplete index maps. The index maps published in the book were drawn before her originals were found and have been used because they differed but little from her own. She evidently intended to include, to quote her own words, "maps of out of the way parts of the world treated scurvily in the atlases, reference maps to help the reader find his bearings in descriptions full of names, and just maps for their own sake", but she did not leave sufficient material for us to make the maps she had in mind. Her own introduction has been printed, incomplete and unpolished as it is, since it states more clearly than we can do her purpose in making this anthology, and explains her selection of the passages.

The two sonnets that follow were also found with other poems in manuscript. They were printed in the *Girton Review*, 1952, and by permission of the Mistress and Fellows they are reprinted here as they seem to us to express perfectly the attitude to Nature that gave character to all Margaret Anderson's work.

Cambridge, 1954

J. B. M.
A. A. L. C.

THE ANDES

Where the tall Andes lift a giant stair
Above the cold Pacific, there are high
Pale plains where jewel-green oases lie;
And great snow capped volcanoes stand in air
Shadowed at dawn, at sunset rosy-fair:
Around their feet, below the burning sky,
The everlasting mists of ocean lie,
Veiling the beaches in their wet grey hair.

And in that country is the peace of dreams
Peace cool and welcome as the phantom rain
Over the foothills, or as icy streams
Threading the green oases on the plain
Peace all-enfolding as the mist and sand
Lapping the mountains of that naked land.

February, 1949   **M. S. A.**

PLANTING A TREE

Not here for centuries the winds shall sweep
Freely again, for here my tree shall rise
To print leaf-patterns on the empty skies
And fret the sunlight. Here where grasses creep
Great roots shall thrust and life run slow and deep:
Perhaps strange children, with my children's eyes
Shall love it, listening as the daylight dies
To hear its branches singing them to sleep.

O kindly earth, accept this little tree:
Guide its blind rootlets groping in the soil,
Let warm rain bathe it softly: let there be
No pale insidious fungus to despoil.
Men will need beauty in the times to be
Let this tree's beauty be a gift from me.

January, 1950   M. S. A.

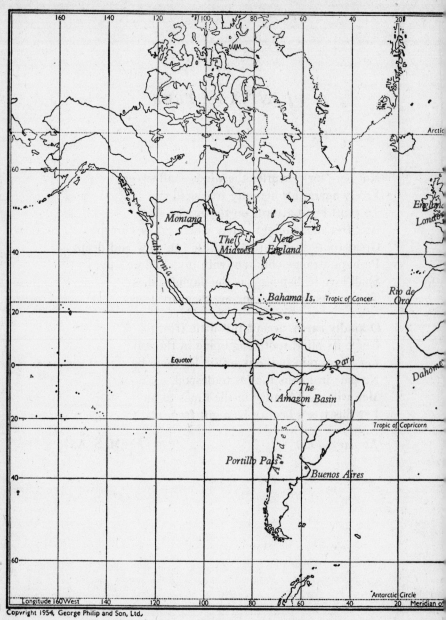

Map 1. CLIMATE AND WEATHER: showing regions

sub-regions and places referred to in the excerpts.

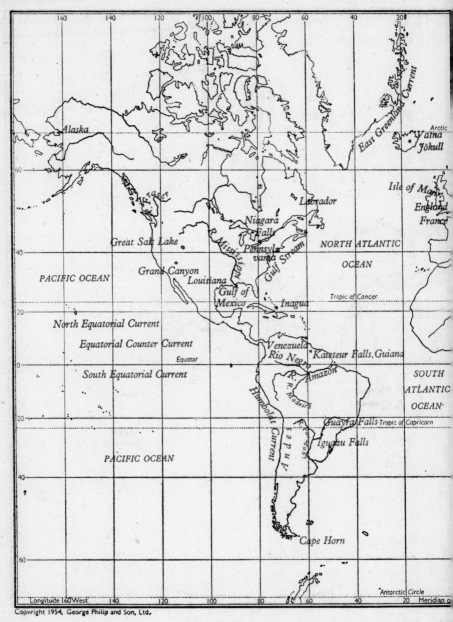

160   140   120   100   80   60   40   20

Alaska

East Greenland Current

Arctic
*Vatna
Jökull*

60

Fraser

Isle of M

*England
France*

Labrador

Great Salt Lake

*Niagara
Falls*

40

Grand Canyon

R. Mississippi

*Pennsyl-
vania*

NORTH ATLANTIC

PACIFIC OCEAN

Louisiana

Gulf Stream

OCEAN

*Gulf of
Mexico*

Tropic of Cancer

20

Inagua

North Equatorial Current

Equatorial Counter Current

Venezuela
Rio Negro • *Kaieteur Falls, Guiana*

Equator

0

South Equatorial Current

R. Amazon

R. Madeira

SOUTH

ATLANTIC

OCEAN

Humboldt Current

20

Guayra Falls Tropic of Capricorn

Iguazu Falls

Andes

PACIFIC OCEAN

40

60

Cape Horn

Antarctic Circle

Longitude 160 West   140   120   100   80   60   40   20   Meridian o

Map 2. WATER AND ICE: showing regions, sub

x

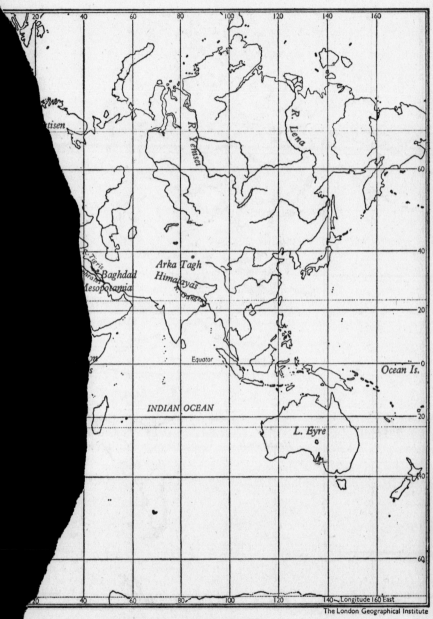

The London Geographical Institute

...ns and places referred to in the excerpts.

Map 3. Islands, Rocks and Desert: showing reg...

Copyright 1954, George Philip and Son, Ltd.

CONTENTS

PAGE

EARTHQUAKES, VOLCANOES AND HOT SPRINGS

MOUNTAINS AND PLATEAUS

CONTENTS

xxi

AUTHOR'S INTRODUCTION

Few of us will ever see for ourselves the Grand Canyon of the Colorado, the Painted Desert, dark Amazon, daughter of the Andes, the Mountains of the Moon, or the Valley of Ten Thousand Smokes —we must rest content with the written word, a photograph or two, and perhaps a travel film. This book has been compiled to provide a few descriptions as aids to the imagination. For I do firmly believe that no deadly accurate, purely technical description can bring vividly to life a mountain, a great river, or even a climate, can make it our own to love and remember, as an imaginative description by a great writer can do. "Etna, that wicked witch", says D. H. Lawrence, "resting her thick white snow under heaven and slowly, slowly rolling her orange coloured smoke" – is there not something there that you will never get from a sheaf of photographs, and "Etna, a great lava dome or shield, through which a central funnel may be maintained, and above which a debris-built cone may rise, built by occasional explosive eruptions"? We must have the technical descriptions: our mental picture without them would be as fluid and formless as honey without comb. But technicalities alone are comb without honey; we need imagery, ideas, beautiful words well used to give full enjoyment and appreciation.

In compiling this book my first and most important rule has been to choose only accounts that give something more to stimulate the imagination than will be found among ordinary text-books. The second rule, seldom broken, has been that every account quoted must be a recognizable account of real physical features in a real place. It has thus been possible to plot the sites of most of them fairly closely on the index maps, and they can be used if need be to illustrate the physical geography of a particular continent or country directly. The third rule was that no account should be put in unless vividly written, filling the mind with coloured pictures clear cut as jewels. This rule I have not been able to keep entirely because it has clashed with another very important requirement, namely, that the book should contain a complete set of descriptions of all standard physical features and all parts of the world, of climate of every type, and all the winds and currents, mountains, seas and rivers that we meet in the atlas. Stevenson, Kipling, D. H. Lawrence and a few other great authors write exact and brilliant descriptions of things, scenery and places, such as I have sought in accordance with my rules, but they suffer as we do from the inability to see in one lifetime more than a tithe of the world's riches. Hence to complete the set I have had to use many descriptions by writers with a less superb command of words and less forceful style and imagery. Often indeed I have fallen back on plain straightforward accounts by eyewitnesses, written with hardly a flicker of the bright flame of language to kindle fires in the mind. But if style cannot stimulate, matter may; when quoting less vivid writers I have tried to find accounts of features viewed from new angles or through strange eyes to stir the sluggish fancy and make us realize anew the unending wonder and beauty of the world. Lastly, I have so far as possible avoided using accounts written by well-known geographical authors and the great travellers, for most geographers read their writings and use their accounts already: I have tried instead to use literary authors and some of the less famous travellers whose works are often neglected.

I owe a deep debt of gratitude to the authors and their publishers for permission to quote from their writings in a context for which these passages were never intended; I owe a yet deeper one to the authors for the many hours of delight that they have given me while compiling this book. It is my sincere hope that I may be able to repay a small part of this debt by helping to make their work more widely known. I hope that those who read this book, appreciating the artistry of the authors quoted, will go to the originals and read them in full. They will find, as I have done, unfailing delight in journeying in imagination in such good company across the wide seas and great continents.. . . . .

M. S. A.

Circa June, 1952

CLIMATE

CLIMATE

Equatorial Climate

MID-ATLANTIC

THE WIND came from nowhere, because there was nowhere for it to come from. That was the odd thing about it. For its point of departure, if it had one, was somewhere just ahead of us below the skyline ; but there was nothing there. That was quite undeniable. Had we not been engaged for days in proving that there was nothing there ? We had been driving steadily towards it in the hope, presumably, of finding something ; but it was something like a week since there had been anything at all for us to look at. There was still the sea, of course. That perfect colour would have drawn thousands to a beach to look at it ; but such colours are not visible from any coast. For they can only be distilled from deep-sea waters by the deep light of mid-ocean, where there is nothing to cast any shadow. The tone, if one must find a name for it, was blue ; but it was a blue that soared far beyond the reach of adjectives ; and it gleamed deepest where it was jewelled with the leaping diamonds from our cutwater, and our creamy wake lay gracefully across it like a Court lady's train. We moved across it, fixed centre of a moving circle, under the sky ; and that, if one must find a name for it, was blue as well. But the sky's blue was different from the sea's, since it was pure light—except, of course, when it put on all its jewels after dinner and swept overhead in black and silver. The still ship moved on between sea and sky, and the invisible wind blew steadily from nowhere.

Such winds have a peculiar power to irritate. I have known a wind that blew from nowhere in the heart of Africa and grew almost maddening after three days of its invisible presence, as the tall palms of the oasis dipped and bowed to one another and the sand borne upon its wings blurred the hard outline of the Atlas. The desert wind of the Sahara drives upon the nerves ; and the sea-wind of the Equator has something of that irritant effect. For it is a little trying to be played upon so steadily by something quite invisible that comes from nowhere. There was

3

indubitably nothing there. Indeed, to all appearances there would never be anything again in the vast emptiness of sea and sky. It was just an airy and disused store-room where one might store a continent, and it had somehow got forgotten. One had always read that the Equator was an imaginary line ; but one had never dreamt that it could be quite so imaginary as this. Yet from some unseen point in the blue in front of us the world began to curve towards another Pole and the vast paradox of the Southern Hemisphere commenced. That was another world, where travellers moved southward to escape the heat or travelled north into the glare of tropical plantations. The ship moved slowly on ; and the uncomfortable wind of the Equator blew steadily along the shaded decks.

(*Equator; 30°W.*) (Philip Guedalla : *Argentine Tango*.)

Equatorial Climate

AMAZON BASIN : A DAY AT PARA IN 1848

WE USED to rise soon after dawn, when Isidoro would go down to the city, after supplying us with a cup of coffee, to purchase the fresh provisions for the day. The two hours before breakfast were devoted to ornithology. At that early period of the day the sky was invariably cloudless (the thermometer marking 72° or 73° Fahr.) : the heavy dew or the previous night's rain, which lay on the moist foliage, becoming quickly dissipated by the glowing sun, which rising straight out of the east, mounted rapidly towards the zenith. All nature was fresh, new leaf and flower-buds expanding rapidly. Some mornings a single tree would appear in flower amidst what was the preceding evening a uniform green mass of forest—a dome of blossom suddenly created as if by magic. The birds were all active ; from the wild-fruit trees, not far off, we often heard the shrill yelping of the Toucans (*Ramphastos vitellinus*). Small flocks of parrots flew over on most mornings, at a great height, appearing in distinct relief against the blue sky, always two by two, chattering to each other, the pairs being separated by regular intervals ; their bright colours, however, were not apparent at that height. After breakfast we devoted the hours from 10 a.m. to 2 or 3 p.m. to entomology ; the best time for insects in the forest being a little before the heat of the day.

4

The heat increased rapidly towards 2 o'clock (92° and 93° Fahr.), by which time every voice of bird or mammal was hushed ; only in the trees was heard at intervals the harsh whirr of a cicada. The leaves, which were so moist and fresh in early morning, now become lax and drooping ; the flowers shed their petals. Our neighbours, the Indian and Mulatto inhabitants of the open palm-thatched huts, as we returned home fatigued with our ramble, were either asleep in their hammocks or seated on mats in the shade, too languid even to talk. On most days in June and July a heavy shower would fall some time in the afternoon, producing a most welcome coolness. The approach of the rain-clouds was after a uniform fashion very interesting to observe. First, the cool sea-breeze, which commenced to blow about 10 o'clock, and which had increased in force with the increasing power of the sun, would flag and finally die away. The heat and electric tension of the atmosphere would then become almost insupportable. Languor and uneasiness would seize on everyone ; even the denizens of the forest betraying it by their motions. White clouds would appear in the east and gather into cumuli, with an increasing blackness along their lower portions. The whole eastern horizon would become almost suddenly black, and this would spread upwards, the sun at length becoming obscured. Then the rush of a mighty wind is heard through the forest, swaying the tree-tops ; a vivid flash of lightning bursts forth, then a crash of thunder, and down streams the deluging rain. Such storms soon cease, leaving bluish-black motionless clouds in the sky until night. Meantime all nature is refreshed ; but heaps of flower-petals and fallen leaves are seen under the trees. Towards evening life revives again, and the ringing uproar is resumed from bush and tree. The following morning the sun again rises in a cloudless sky, and so the cycle is completed ; spring, summer, and autumn, as it were, in one tropical day. The days are more or less like this throughout the year in this country. A little difference exists between the dry and wet seasons ; but generally, the dry season, which lasts from July to December, is varied with showers, and the wet, from January to June, with sunny days. It results from this, that the periodical phenomena of plants and animals do not take place at about the same time in all species, or in the individuals of any given species, as they do in temperate countries. Of course there is no hyberna-tion ; nor, as the dry season is not excessive, is there any summer torpidity as in some tropical countries. Plants do not flower or shed their leaves, nor do birds moult, pair, or breed simultaneously. In Europe, a woodland scene has its spring, its summer, its autumnal and its winter aspects. In the equatorial forests the aspect is the same or nearly so every day in the year : budding, flowering, fruiting and leaf-shedding are always going on in one species or other. The activity of birds and insects proceeds without interruption, each species having its own separate times ; the colonies of wasps, for instance, do not die off annually, leaving only the queens, as in cold climates ; but the succession of generations and colonies goes on incessantly. It is never either spring, summer, or autumn, but each day is a combination of all three. With the day and night always of equal length, the atmospheric disturbances of each day neutralizing themselves before each succeeding morn ; with the sun in its course proceeding mid-way across the sky, and the daily temperature the same within two or three degrees throughout the year—how grand in its perfect equilibrium and simplicity is the march of Nature under the equator !

(*2°S; 48°30′W.*)

(Henry Walter Bates : *The Naturalist on the River Amazons.*)

Tropical Climate

FRENCH INDO-CHINA

UNFORTUNATELY the very convenient and comfortable wooden rest-house, situated just opposite the steps of the causeway that leads over the moat to Angkor Vat, and thus affording the visitor such wonderful views of stone tower and corridor and trees, of elephants and water-lilies, of gryphons and fan-headed serpents, had this year not opened its doors, owing, it was said, to an ingenious change of tactics on the part of its many scorpions. The only permanent residents of all the hotels here, these ingenious little creatures had learnt now to hide under shady ledges in the bathrooms, in order suddenly to spring out at the gallop and sting their unsuspecting victims with the greatest possible verve and venom.

First, therefore, I went to an inn, one of many, in Siemréap itself. But, though for these latitudes it was comfortable (and in these latitudes, because of the heat, the word *comfortable* of neces-

6

sity implies what would be considered extreme discomfort else-where ; darkness, bare, cold floors, and beds and pillows so hard that they might be made of stone), the scent of that Malay dish I have mentioned, prepared from decaying fish, hung too hauntingly in the streets of a night and early morning, distilled by the cool air, and obliged me to move out of the town to a large new hotel, a mile or so away in the direction of the ruins. Here I obtained a fine room, a mosquito net in perfect order (rare in a hotel anywhere), a bathroom, and a distant view of the towers of Angkor Vat swelling high above palm trees and jungle. . . . But my bathroom, too, possessed its peculiarities ; every time I turned on the water, I found the bath lined—absolutely black, no inch of white showing through—with insects ; species that were new to me and the very sight of which would, I suspect, have warmed the heart of an entomologist. One sort, I remember, consisted of little jack-in-the-boxes about an inch long : they were full of fun, and would stay quite still till you came near, when they would jump right up to the ceiling in one bound—an amazing perform-ance, as though a man were to leap to the top of Mont Blanc—and buzz and whirr and bang and titter in a thousand different ways.

* * * * *

. . . After leaving church, we repaired immediately to the temple in the town ; a building which consisted of red, wooden columns supporting a winged roof. Screens of rush lattice hung from the pillars, but the sunlight, by this time strong as steel, soon found the chinks in this armour. Further, the entire population of Siemréap seemed to be pressed into this space or clustered together just outside it, impeding the entry of the air, and talking, groaning, singing, beating gongs and drums and thrumming upon stringed instruments to its heart's content.

By now the heat was reaching its climax, slowing down even the tempo of the service, and as, sometimes, a gust of fiery air would be wafted in, it brought with it the drone of the countless winged creatures under the tall palm trees outside. . . . Indeed, as we left, the insects appeared to be holding a midday service of their own, such were the shrill and wiry crepitations, deep drummings and intonings ; a busy, reverent but rather meaning-less sound of buzzing, and of castanetted whirring, twang and jangle, very similar to the music we had just heard performed.
(13°N; 104°E.)   (Osbert Sitwell : *Escape with Me!*)

Tropical Climate

DAHOMEY

THE CLIMATE is in general healthy, and, near the coast, not too hot, the average temperature being about 80 deg. F., while on the Gambia it is about 100 deg. F. This is owing to the exposure of the Bights to the cooling influence of the sea breeze. The season may be divided into four quarters—viz., the *summer*, the *rains*, the *autumn*, and the *harmattan*. The summer generally commences in March, when the heat is greater than at any other season, the maximum being attained about two o'clock in the afternoon. This is the season for dysentery and the unpleasant sensation known as prickly heat. The prevailing winds in March in the morning are easterly, and during the day south-westerly, while in April westerly and south-westerly winds blow throughout the day and night. The heat at night is intense, the perspiration reeking from every pore ; the thermometer being often up to 96 deg. F.

In May the first rains commence, the season always being marked out by violent storms known as *tornadoes*, a corruption of the Portuguese *travado*, a thunderstorm. At this season the atmosphere contains a maximum of ozone. The occurrence of a tornado is always heralded by certain premonitory symptoms. The weather immediately preceding is generally very hot ; but as the storm brews a cold wind springs up, bringing with it a peculiar hazy appearance of the atmosphere. Soon a solitary white cloud is observed high up in the heavens, which gradually extends in an easterly direction, and at the same time assumes the form of an arch stretching over a fourth part of the horizon and shrouding it in a gloom like a funeral pall. The breeze has by this time given way to an unearthly calm, while all nature seems hushed in anticipation of some impending catastrophe. The silence is oppressive ; not a leaf moves, and the insect world itself is awed into perfect stillness. Even the clamour of the market-women is subdued with the continued sensation of apprehension and reverence for the strife of the elements.

Suddenly a vivid flash of lightning rends the sky, followed by a tremendous crash as if the heavens were destroyed. A rushing sound succeeds, and in a moment the fierce breath of the tornado is upon us, sweeping everything before it, unroofing houses, tearing

8

up trees, and whirling tiles and slates from the roofs of the more substantially-erected houses. Oftentimes the flimsy structures of bamboo erected in the bush are carried away entire, and the whole atmosphere becomes filled with ruin. Huge rain drops follow, which, after pausing for a time as if to gather strength, descend in a furious deluge, resembling a vast sheet rather than a succession of drops of water. The gullies in the streets are soon impetuous torrents, bringing down quantities of the red soil. This heavy rain lasts about a quarter of an hour, and is followed by a gradually diminishing shower, until in about an hour from the first flash, the sun is again shining, and a dark cloud far away to leeward and a few distant mutterings of thunder are the only aërial signs of the tempest.

After the tornado the air is most refreshingly cool and exhilarating, the thermometer not unfrequently falling fifteen degrees during its continuance. Should a vessel be unfortunately taken unprepared by one of these violent whirlwinds, her masts must inevitably go by the board or she will be capsized.

In June, there is a short interval of fine weather, followed by the latter rains in July and August. The temperature in these months is at its lowest, averaging 65 degrees Fahrenheit. As a rule more rain falls at new and full moon, when more than 18½ inches have been recorded in twenty-four hours.

In August, terrific thunderstorms occur, the effects of which are often very destructive. The Whydahs put themselves under the protection of *Khevyosoh*, the lightning god, by making presents to the fetiche priests. Mosquitoes and sandflies abound in this season, so tormenting to the sleeper as to put him into a high fever ere the morning, while the new comer is especially selected as a victim. At Badagary, the natives frequently bury themselves in the sand, and even then their blood-thirsty tormentors will find them out. Tobacco smoke, and green wood burning with a smoke thick enough to choke any other creature, only appear to give an additional whet to their appetite. I have been told that a mixture of tar and oil smeared over the body will prevent their onset ; but, ugh ! the remedy is as bad as the disease. There appears to be only one preventive, and that is a sure one—don't go where they exist.

In September the unhealthy autumnal season sets in, the exodus of the rain being accompanied by a series of tornadoes and severe thunderstorms, as at the change of the monsoon in the East Indies. Vegetation is now in full swing, fruits and grain are gathered, the harvest often yielding a hundred fold to the rude cultivation, and a few leaves wither and fall to the ground. Decomposition is likewise rife ; and stimulated by heat and moisture, malaria is developed in profusion, the fruitful parent of fever. Guinea worm is also troublesome, and in countries where it is endemic, goitre commences.

November generally goes out with the commencement of the Harmattan, which usually lasts about three months. The term is said to be derived from the Fantee *aharaman*, to blow, and *ta*, grease ; because at this season the air is so dry and parching that the natives preserve the skin from cracking by copious applications of grease, generally the commonest of European pomades, odoriferous with the vilest patchouli. The Harmattan is called Yeou, and is supposed to be a deity who is allowed to visit the world at certain seasons. He has a keeper, Yeouhuntoh, who, before releasing his charge, oils his body to protect it from the Yeou, and then opens the gate of the cave within which the Dahoman Æolus is confined. This wind blows along the whole northern shores of the gulf of Guinea, being strongest on the western coast, and gradually diminishing in intensity as we approach the head of the Gulf. Its approach is generally foretold by a thick fog, which often extends ten miles out to sea, and is known to European residents on the coast as the "smokes". The smokes are not, however, dull brown like a London fog, but pure white, the sun sometimes appearing at mid-day with a white light like that of the full moon. The dry parched breath of the Harmattan coming from the north-east licks up every trace of moisture. The leaves of the trees droop, and drying up become crisp, thereby being prevented from breeding malaria by their putrefaction. All young plants are dried up ; the long grass withers and becomes converted into hay, and is then fired by the natives to ensure a fresh crop in the following rains. Even evergreens suffer from the effect of the moisture-devouring wind, their leaves becoming flaccid and easily reduced to dust by the fingers. The earth cracks, and doors and furniture split and open out, warping into grotesque shapes. The effect upon the system is unpleasant ; the skin chaps, and the face has the feeling of being drawn up. The lips are parched and the skin peels off them,

10

while an intolerable thirst can scarcely be allayed by the most copious potations of iced claret. The Harmattan usually blows for two or three days at a time, and is succeeded by an interval of perhaps a week of winds from the south or west. The Harmattan is a cold, dry wind, and its season is justly considered to be the healthiest on the coast. Fevers are of rare occurrence, all malignant diseases abate, small-pox quickly heals, and gout and rheumatism disappear. In the intermediate days between the Harmattan the weather is usually hot, with a strong wind blowing from the south-west. The dry sensation disappears, and if a person is subject to fever it will make its appearance, but in a very mild form. People are seen walking about with their clothes wrapped closely around them to protect themselves from the chilling effect of the wind, and children suffer from severe colds. The Europeans often call the Harmattan the " Doctor ", from its beneficial results; for sometimes a person, who appears to be at death's door before it commences, will immediately revive under its exhilarating influence.

The sea-breeze usually commences about ten o'clock in the morning, beginning at south-east and gradually veering to south-west, from which quarter it blows during nine months in the year. In the dry summer season it is often a stiff gale about sundown.

The current along the coast sets to the south-east, but often after a heavy tornado it will run to the westward for two or three days, during which time vessels bound to windward take advantage of its favourable influence to aid them against the prevalent westerly winds.

The surf always beats furiously along the whole coast, but during the prevalence of the rains it is terrific. The dull booming roar is carried inland for many miles by the sea-breeze, and communication between the vessels and the shore is sometimes cut off for days together. Of course, should a vessel be so unfortunate as to get within its influence she is speedily reduced to splinters. On such occasions she becomes the property of the King, the hapless sailors being scarcely allowed to take their clothing. Not unfrequently the priests assemble on the beach to sacrifice, or " make fetiche " as it is called, in order that the gods may be induced to send a vessel ashore.

(7°N; 2°E.)   (J. A. Skertchley : *Dahomey as it is*, 1874.)

Monsoon Climate

INDIA : CANARA FOREST, SAHYADRI RANGE

OF OUR three seasons, my favourite is, and always has been, the monsoon. It is the time of refreshing, and all nature rejoices in it, and I rejoice with nature. What the spring is to northern latitudes, the monsoon is to us. I do not mean that spring has no place in the Indian calendar. That mysterious influence which comes with the returning sun, and, undiscerned by eye or ear, awakens the earth, visits us too. Then

" The wanton lapwing gets himself another crest,"

and if a fuller crimson does not come upon the robin's breast, it is because in this country that is not the region in which his crimson is situated ; but he and the other birds break out into song and begin to build their nests, the trees bud, and many gay butterflies awaken to life. But in our spring-tide vivifying heat is divorced from refreshing moisture, so that half nature, instead of being warmed to life, is scorched to death. True, the Banian tree, whose roots reach down into the secret chambers of the earth, comes out in bright array, and the Mango buds and blooms ; but the grass, packed in dust above and below, cannot rouse itself to the call of spring, and the fields grow only more dusty and more dry. Our spirits are like the grass and seemed to be packed in dust. The cattle wander about like shadows and grow visibly leaner every day, envying the serpent for the curse that lies on him. He only of living things has enough and to spare. So I say, our true spring, the beginning of our year, the birthday of nature, is not in March, but in June. Let it be ushered in with salvoes of artillery and a carnival of the elements, or let it leak in silently during the night and greet us in the morning, the effect is the same. The leaves of the trees are washed, the dust on the roads is laid, and the spirits of man and beast participate in the baptism.

Scarcely has the earth sent up the incense of its gratitude to heaven when a thousand activities are awakened within it of which we shall soon see the outward signs.

Within a few days of the first rain the air is full of Dragon Flies, crossing and re-crossing, poised motionless for a moment, then darting away with that mingled grace and power which among the winged things of this world is, I think, unmatched. Where they come from I cannot tell, but anyone may read the meaning

12

of their presence in the air. Dragon-flies are the swallows of the insect world, and their prey is the Mosquito, the Gnat, the Midge, the Fly of every size and hue. These swarms, therefore, tell us, that the moistened surface of the ground, with its mouldering leaves and sodden grass, its mouldy bark and decaying refuse, has become one vast incubator teeming with every form of ephemeral life. Many another indication of the same kind will catch the observant eye.

The roadside rivulets are full of little Fishes, arrived from I know not where, to grow fat on the Earthworm and the Mole Cricket borne helplessly along by the sweeping flood. When night comes on, great Moths fly past, and " the Beetle wheels his droning flight." The Fireflies also light their lamps and hold their silent concerts, the occupants of each tree flashing in unison and making sheet lightning in the woods. And what shall I say of the garden Bugs on the dinner table and the Blister Beetles and the squeaking Green Crickets ? And what of the Musk-rats which come in to eat them ?

This is *par excellence* the season for rambling abroad. At every turn there is something new to see. Out of earth and rock and leafless bough the magic touch of the monsoon has brought life and greenness. You can almost see the broad-leaved vines grow and the twining creepers work their snaky way, linking tree to tree and binding branch to branch.

There is another feature of the monsoon which has a wonderful charm for me. I mean the clouds. Many Englishmen never throw off the bondage of their old English feelings, and a cloudy day depresses them to the last. Such conservatism is not in me. After the monotony of a fierce sun and a blue sky and a dusky landscape quivering in the dim distance, I cry welcome to the days of mild light and green earth and purple hills coming near in the clear and transparent air. And later on, when the monsoon begins to break up and the hills are dappled with light and shade, and dark islands move across the bright green sea, the effect on my spirits is strangely exhilarating. Why is it that so few of our Indian painters have given us monsoon scenes ?

In candour it must be admitted that the monsoon brings with it some inconveniences ; but they are for the most part connected with our civilisation. Books grow limp and their backs come off, leprosy attacks gloves and all manner of silk and satin finery, a marvellous forest of mould springs from the bodies of the tiniest butterflies in my collection, cheroots grow too damp to smoke, rats infest the house, and basins and soup-plates stand about on the carpet to catch the drops from the leaky roof. The ants, which stand next to us in point of civilisation, evidently suffer in much the same way. The water has got into their under-ground houses flooding the cellars and nurseries, wetting their stores of grain and drowning a good number of babies. All day long they are busy repairing or checking the ravages of the flood.

But the prime inconvenience of monsoon weather is independent of civilisation : the fear of getting wet is universal. The gentleman runs because the rain will spoil his clothes, but the coolie runs as fast because he has none. And when you realise that at this time birds of all kinds and the majority of wild beasts, not to speak of flimsy butterflies and moths, live and sleep in the open air, you cannot help wondering how they manage. My sympathies go especially with the monkeys. When the pitiless rain is pouring hour after hour, and the water is streaming down the trees, and the branches are all nasty and slimy, and every shake brings down a redoubled shower from the leaves, I wonder where the poor monkeys are and what they are doing. Are they all huddled together, with their heads buried in each other's bosoms, and the water spouting from their long tails ?

Many birds, too, lay their eggs during the first and heaviest month of rain, and sit in open nests day and night, pelted with drops almost as big as their heads. It is true that the feathers of birds, oily and smooth and arranged one over another like tiles, with an under-layer of soft, warm down, form a costume for all weather, to which the art of man has never been able to make any approach ; and the combination of long hair and short wool which forms the fur of many beasts is nearly as good ; but a bird or beast can be wet to the skin when the station doctor is registering ten inches in twenty-four hours.

And what of the bats, Flying Foxes for instance, which hang with their feet up and their heads down ? The fur of bats, we know, is different from that of all other animals, and forms a most interesting object under the microscope ; but what is the advantage of that if it slopes the wrong way for keeping out the rain ? It is nothing short of a scandal to Darwinism that bats have not long since reversed their fur.

*　　*　　*　　*　　*

14

For the last two months the rain has been simply ridiculous. Last week the weather did seem to vacillate for a few days, but I rashly planned an excursion for Gunputtee day, and the deluge returned with renewed resolution. We have had nearly eleven feet already, but the total up to date goes on rising at the rate of several inches a day. The people say that this rain is particularly good for the crops, and so I find it. The crops of mould and mildew have grown rank beyond all precedent. If I neglect my library for a few days a reindeer might browse upon the lichens that whiten my precious books. The roots of these vegetables, penetrating the binding, disintegrate the glue underneath, so that the books gradually acquire a limp and feeble-minded aspect, and presently the covers are ready to come away from the bodies ; and the rain has undoubtedly some effect of the same kind on ourselves. How is it possible to keep up any firmness of mind or body in such weather ? It is too dark to do anything inside the house and too wet to do anything out of it.

(20°30′N; 76°E.)   (E. H. Aitken : *A Naturalist on the Prowl.*)

Desert Climate
EGYPT : KHARGA OASIS

THE FIRST summer in Kharga was rather a shock ; though I had been in Egypt for over four years and had experienced what I considered quite unpleasant heat during the war in Sinai and also in the Western Desert, I had no idea what a southern oasis could do in the way of sending up the mercury till I experienced it. We got our first really hot day in March coming back from Dakhla in an old box Ford, and I shall not forget it as long as I live. The day before we started I had some idea we were in for a bad *khamsin* (hot wind from the south) and we started from Dakhla at 4 a.m.—by 10 a.m. we were half-way between the two oases in the most stark and ghastly desert with the temperature registering 120° in the shade. The wind was blowing hard from the south and felt exactly like a blast from a furnace, and all the metal work of the car was so hot it nearly seared one's fingers when one touched it.

This spell of hot weather occurred in early April when Cairo and the northern part of Egypt is only just beginning to warm up, and by May I realized what the oasis could do in the way of heat.

15

At 6 a.m. in the morning the mercury stood at 98°, and this being the cool of the day the house was then shut right up until evening, so that coming in from the glare and heat at mid-day one got the impression—a totally false one—that the house was cool. At mid-day one saw the most ghastly sight I have ever seen and that was a bright patch of sunlight in the fireplace caused by the sun shining straight down the chimney.* A warm red glow from a fireplace in mid-winter is one of the pleasantest things I know, but a staring yellow patch of sunlight where the glowing coals ought to be, lightening up the gloom of a darkened room that is pretending to be cool, has a most grisly effect.

During the whole of the day the temperature remained at from 110° to 115° with a hot wind. At 6 p.m. the wind dropped and it seemed to get hotter till 11 p.m. when the wind started again, feeling quite as blistering and unpleasant as it had been at mid-day. It was quite impossible to sleep, and I used to walk about on the verandah throwing water on the mosquito-curtains in a vain attempt to bring down the temperature and do something to moisten the intense dryness that caused the tables and chests of drawers in the house to split with loud reports. At about 2 a.m. there was a slight but appreciable cooling off and one could usually get to sleep then till 5.30 a.m. when the heat of the newly-born sun awoke one to another day of hell.

(25°30′N; 30°40′E.)   (C. S. Jarvis : *Three Deserts*.)

Desert Climate

THE RED SEA

AT NIGHT the heat lay over the Red Sea in clouds almost palpable. Everything you touched, the walls, the switch for the electric light, the sheets on the bed, the glass of water beside it on the table, was warm, and sleep was out of reach. In those hours it was impossible not to wonder if any country, even China itself, could repay such a journey. . . . I lay, turning from side to side in my bunk in the illogical effort by so doing to escape the heat (which now entered at the port-hole like the gusts from a machine for drying the hair at a barber's shop).

(Osbert Sitwell : *Escape with Me!*)

*Kharga is in Lat. 25° 26′ N, and therefore the sun at midsummer would be about two degrees from the zenith at noon.

Cold-water Coast Climate: Coastal Sea Fogs

CALIFORNIA

ONE SUNDAY morning, about five, the first brightness called me. I rose and turned to the east, not for my devotions, but for air. The night had been very still. The little private gale that blew every evening in our canyon, for ten minutes or perhaps a quarter of an hour, had swiftly blown itself out; in the hours that followed not a sigh of wind had shaken the treetops; and our barrack, for all its breaches, was less fresh that morning than of wont. But I had no sooner reached the window than I forgot all else in the sight that met my eyes, and I made but two bounds into my clothes, and down the crazy plank to the platform.

The sun was still concealed below the opposite hilltops, though it was shining already, not twenty feet above my head, on our own mountain slope. But the scene, beyond a few near features, was entirely changed. Napa valley was gone; gone were all the lower slopes and woody foothills of the range; and in their place, not a thousand feet below me, rolled a great level ocean. It was as though I had gone to bed the night before, safe in a nook of inland mountains, and had awakened in a bay upon the coast. I had seen these inundations from below; at Calistoga I had risen and gone abroad in the early morning, coughing and sneezing, under fathoms on fathoms of grey sea vapour, like a cloudy sky—a dull sight for the artist, and a painful experience for the invalid. But to sit aloft one's self in the pure air and under the unclouded dome of heaven, and thus look down on the submergence of the valley, was strangely different and even delightful to the eyes. Far away were hilltops like little islands. Nearer, a smoky surf beat about the foot of precipices and poured into all the coves of these rough mountains. The colour of that fog ocean was a thing never to be forgotten. For an instant, among the Hebrides and just about sundown, I have seen something like it on the sea itself. But the white was not so opaline; nor was there, what surprisingly increased the effect, that breathless, crystal stillness over all. Even in its gentlest moods the salt sea travails, moaning among the weeds or lisping on the sand; but that vast fog ocean lay in a trance of silence, nor did the sweet air of the morning tremble with a sound.

As I continued to sit upon the dump, I began to observe that this sea was not so level as at first sight it appeared to be. Away in the extreme south, a little hill of fog arose against the sky above the general surface, and as it had already caught the sun, it shone on the horizon like the topsails of some giant ship. There were huge waves, stationary, as it seemed, like waves in a frozen sea ; and yet, as I looked again, I was not sure but they were moving after all, with a slow and august advance. And while I was yet doubting, a promontory of the hills some four or five miles away, conspicuous by a bouquet of tall pines, was in a single instant overtaken and swallowed up. It reappeared in a little, with its pines, but this time as an islet, and only to be swallowed up once more and then for good. This set me looking nearer, and I saw that in every cove along the line of mountains the fog was being piled in higher and higher, as though by some wind that was inaudible to me. I could trace its progress, one pine tree first growing hazy and then disappearing after another ; although sometimes there was none of this fore-running haze, but the whole opaque white ocean gave a start and swallowed a piece of mountain at a gulp. It was to flee these poisonous fogs that I had left the seaboard, and climbed so high among the mountains. And now, behold, here came the fog to besiege me in my chosen altitudes, and yet came so beautifully that my first thought was of welcome.

The sun had now gotten much higher, and through all the gaps of the hills it cast long bars of gold across that white ocean. An eagle, or some other very great bird of the mountain, came wheeling over the nearer pine-tops, and hung, poised and something sideways, as if to look abroad on that unwonted desolation, spying, perhaps with terror, for the eyries of her comrades. Then, with a long cry, she disappeared again towards Lake County and the clearer air. At length it seemed to me as if the flood were beginning to subside. The old landmarks, by whose disappearance I had measured its advance, here a crag, there a brave pine tree, now began, in the inverse order, to make their reappearance into daylight. I judged all danger of the fog was over. This was not Noah's flood ; it was but a morning spring, and would now drift out seaward whence it came. So, mightily relieved, and a good deal exhilarated by the sight, I went into the house to light the fire. (*38°30'N; 123°W.*)

(Robert Louis Stevenson : *The Silverado Squatters.*)

Continental Climate

THE MIDDLE WEST

OF ALL the regions of the United States, the Midwest has what seems both to Americans and to other visitors the most unkind climate and the most inclement weather. That probably explains one of the general practices of the better-off, and one of the general aims of those hoping to get rich enough, which is to leave the Midwest at least twice every year on vacation. Many of them ultimately retire altogether from it. In every case the aspirants make for the sun in winter, for dryness at all times, and for a temperate zone in retirement. Lest I be thought grimly facetious, or just an Englishman preoccupied with that English weather which has been one of the stock American vaudeville jokes for three generations, let me develop this point.

It is the core of the Midwest which has the worst weather : the area east of the Mississippi including the northern halves of Illinois, Indiana, and Ohio, the Michigan peninsula, and southern Wisconsin. This is the coastal area of the Great Lakes, which here exercise an attraction on the transcontinental lines of temperature and pressure and form a kind of water pocket around which the great winds sweep snow, rain, and cold spells.

Dwellers in the belt that runs from Milwaukee to Chicago, the big cities along the Indiana-Michigan coastal rim, Detroit, Toledo, Cleveland, Erie, and Buffalo and a long way inland, during the ferocious winters are weighed down by a cold humidity and blasted by icy winds reaching gale dimensions. They are snowed-in frequently by blizzards that blacken noonday and paralyse all forms of traffic. They are exposed to the packing of snow into miniature but almost as deadly Himalayas of solid black ice on every path from the home driveway to the side-walks of the metropolis. Blizzards snow-in the suburbanites to this day ; and the normal snows are heavy enough to make shovelling and cleaning, overshoes and snowboots, an indispensable part of every midwesterner's winter. Rare, indeed, in any winter in this wide core of the Midwest is an ideal winter-sports day : clear, dry air, bright blue skies, hard, strong sun, no wind, and zero or sub-zero temperature. When such a day dawns, everyone talks about it : commuters and housewives and store-keepers and schoolchildren.

In defense against the bitter winds and cold the Midwest has developed artificial heating in its houses, offices and vehicles to a point at which its people are alternately baked and frozen a dozen times a day. It is not fantastic to suppose that this contributes to that extraordinarily widespread Midwest affliction known as " sinus trouble," and it certainly contributes to the pallor of the people in winter, just as the equally savage summer sun, the wind, and the extreme variations of natural and artificial temperatures contribute to the more numerous lines and wrinkles of Midwest faces.

In this core of the Midwest there is no spring—a significant natural phenomenon which may account for at least one big gap in the romantic literature and poetry of the Midwest. Winter lasts, solid and remorseless, from Thanksgiving to March. Then it often begins to relent for a tempting few days which fool plants and people alike. Next, the fierce solidity of winter gives way to chill, howling winds, torrents of rain which seem as if they should be falling at another season in the tropics, a long period of ground frosts, and day temperatures in the forties and fifties. At this time the thaw and the rains swell the big Midwest rivers into floods which devastate the countryside far down the rivers and outside the region and drown or render homeless hundreds and sometimes thousands of people.

This inclement spell generally lasts well into May or even the beginning of June—making both the fierce and the milder portions of winter into one season of six or seven months' duration. Then, the trees and plants and birds having crept gradually and imperceptibly into a chill, bedraggled version of spring, suddenly the gales abate overnight. Meanwhile the sun has long been fooling everyone by clambering stoically up to the summit of the heavens for almost half the year, but with the benefit of light alone. Equally suddenly he now explodes in heat ranging between 80° and 100°. (Republicans will not quickly forget their Chicago Convention of 1944!) Frosts in May, 100° in June, are more regular than irregular. Flowers, shrubs, birds, and mankind drink in the sun for an ecstatic week or two ; the grass and the leaves are spring-green for only two or three weeks in the year ; and then " summer has set in with its usual severity ".

" Severity " is the word. When the summer heavens are not as brass, which they are for periods of a few days and often for weeks at a time, they pile up with majestic and terrifying cumulations of rain and thundercloud. The summer storms provide, with the star-spangled moonless nights of winter and fall, the most majestic display of the Midwest heavens in the entire year. Then the Midwest becomes tropical. Nowhere in the so-called temperate zone—from which I think the Midwest should be forever excluded—do you encounter such thunder and lightning, such torrential rains, such an opening of the fountains of the great deep. The temperature often does not fall. Instead a steamy, clammy heat pervades everything. The storms are over as quickly as they begin, but meanwhile much of the topsoil in garden and field alike has gone down to the rivers and oceans—unless the owner has level land, or has drained, terraced, or plowed by contour, or repaired the gullies on his land. Out comes the sun again and with methodical cynicism proceeds to bake the remaining topsoil to terra cotta. This then cracks into new fissures, eagerly expecting the next waterspout to widen them.

The dust, too, comes from the topsoil, whipped up in the remoter areas of the Midwest by the little embryonic " twisters " or whirlwinds which, drunkenly, waltz across the fields like pillars of cloud by day, or blown off by the sudden blasts which precede and follow the savage summer storms.

In the country the summer means dust : dust which permitted, and in many parts still permits, the poorer children to walk safely and comfortably barefoot into the pages of the Midwest's folklore, thus establishing an almost necessary qualification for the childhood of Midwestern presidential candidates. The sidewalks of the towns in summer are as uncomfortable to rapidly tiring feet in all-too-light footgear as they are in winter to ankles, when the surface is knobbed and craggy with black ice.

In high summer come the insects—flies, mosquitoes, winged bugs of every shape and colour—all of them " bigger and better " than in Europe—which necessitate the ubiquitous wire-screen doors and windows. This also necessitates the semi-annual chore of paterfamilias, who has to put the screens up and take them down—unless he is one of the five per cent who live in town apartments offering janitor service or are rich enough to employ gardeners or hired men. It is impossible to sit in a Midwest garden in summer because of the insects, except for two weeks in May or June.

21

Summer, too, conditions the household appliances : iceboxes ; that figure of smoking-room folklore, and favorite of all children, the ice-man ; automatic refrigerators, which betray their origin by still being called ice-boxes ; and the new deep-freeze repository either at home or at a central store of private lockers. Suburban and country folk take to that most civilized institution of the Midwest summer, the sleeping porch, wire-screened on three sides. But even then the nights are treacherous for parent and child alike. Frequently the tropical storms break in the wee, sma' hours ; the rain is blown in ; the lightning and thunder wake the sleeper ; and what begins as a welcome drop in temperature for man and beast quickly degenerates into a deathtrap by way of pleurisy or pneumonia. The temperature first yields, then falls, then drops, then plummets downward. Again paterfamilias or materfamilias plods around, this time closing windows and covering the awakened children. In the morning, heavy-lidded and loath to part from sleep, they find the sun beating down with refreshed zeal upon a porch well on the way to becoming a Black Hole of Calcutta.

When storms do not vary the monotony of heat and humidity, night succeeds night in a remorselessly growing tedium of rising temperature, and sleep comes ever more and more slowly to a humanity already exhausted, worn, and dehydrated by the rigors of successive brazen days. What winds or breezes then blow come from the Great Plains to the west, sweeping across half-parched prairies, more suggestive of a prairie fire than of the frolic wind that breathes the spring or summer's gentle zephyr.

Another trick of the Midwest summer and early fall is to bring out the grasses and weeds whose pollenation causes thousands of sufferers from hay fever and other allergies to spend agonising days and weeks. The newspapers print the day's pollen count on the front page—sure sign of its general importance ! The worst sufferers can be seen wearing a kind of gas mask that makes them look like Martians. Those prone to the ubiquitous sinus trouble are also among the sufferers. Thus is the prairie revenged on the children of its destroyers !

Yet the Midwest has one season which, though only of two months' duration, goes some of the way to redress the over-weighted balance of wicked winters and savage summers. It is the fall. From mid-September to mid-November, with short interruptions of chilly, rainy days, the Midwest gets its only temperate period of the year. It is much finer, much more beauful, than what is conventionally called " Indian summer." The days are warm and the nights cool, with occasional light frosts gradually becoming more intense. The foliage slowly takes on those remarkable shades and colors which make the fall in America and Canada unique in the whole world. " Great clouds along pacific skies " rarely explode into the wrathful and regular thunderstorms of summer. The last tiring insects become fewer and lazier. The skies become more brightly blue than at any other time of the year.

Paterfamilias takes down his screens, puts up storm windows and rakes leaves. The air is mildly imbued with the thin and acrid smell of wood smoke. The winds are tamed ; the dust dies out of the atmosphere ; and the only real breezes of the year gently rustle the long, crackling, dried-out leaves of corn on the stalks. Berries of all kinds and colors deck the hedges and shrubberies. The very heart of the city becomes finally comfortable. Over all, a different suffused light from the sloping sun strikes street and building, forest and field, in a strange way, throwing shadows into unexpected places and illuminating what for most of the year lay in shadow. The sunsets, always imposing in the Midwest, now reach their majestic climax. Homeward-bound commuters see the red sun making the west look like that " dark and bloody ground " whence the Midwest itself sprang. The fruit is picked, bottling goes on in kitchens or basements, and late root vegetables alone are left in the fields or gardens. And so imperceptibly, but with the logic of seasons and Nature and the pioneers' history, the Midwest draws toward that peculiarly American family festival of Thanksgiving to the accompaniment of the first flurries of new snow.

(*Approx. 42°N; 86°W.*)   (Graham Hutton : *Midwest at Noon.*)

Continental Climate

CANADA

A warm rain whispers, but the earth knows best
and turns a deaf ear, waiting for the snow,
the foam of bloom forgotten, the rolling crest
of green forgotten and the fruit swelling slow.

The shearing plow was here and cut the mould
and shouldered over the heavy rain-soaked lands,
letting the hot breath out for the quiet cold
to reach deep down with comfort in its hands.
The sap is ebbing from the tips of the trees
to the dry and secret heart, hiding away
from the blade still green with stubborn memories ;
down in the roots it closes the door of clay
on grief and growing and this late warm rain
babbling false promises in the pasture lane.

> (Kenneth Leslie: *By Stubborn Stars*.)

Climates

EUROPE

NORTH OF the Alps, the everlasting winter is interrupted by summers that struggle and soon yield ; south of the Alps, the everlasting summer is interrupted by spasmodic and spiteful winters that never get a real hold, but that are mean and dogged. North of the Alps, you may have a pure winter's day in June. South of the Alps, you may have a midsummer day in December or January or even February. The in-between, in either case, is just as it may be. But the lands of the sun are south of the Alps, for ever.

> (D. H. Lawrence : *The Phœnix*.)

Temperate Climate : Rain

ENGLAND

Desolate

From the sad eaves the drip-drop of the rain !
The water washing at the latchel door ;
A slow step plashing by upon the moor !
A single bleat far from the famished fold ;
The clicking of an embered hearth and cold ;
The rainy Robin tic-tac at the pane.

" So as it is with thee
Is it with me,
So as it is and it used not to be,
With thee used not to be,
Nor me."

24

So singeth Robin on the willow tree,
The rainy Robin tic-tac at the pane.

Here in this breast all day
The fire is dim and low,
Within I care not to stay,
Without I care not to go.
A sadness ever sings
Of unforgotten things,
And the bird of love is patting at the pane ;
But the wintry water deepens at the door,
And a step is plashing by upon the moor
Into the dark upon the darkening moor,
And alas, alas, the drip-drop of the rain !
(Sydney Dobell: *Lyrics from England in Time of War*.)

Temperate Climate: Cold

ENGLAND

NOW the moment people wake in the morning, they perceive
the coldness with their faces, though they are warm with their
bodies, and exclaim " Here's a day ! " and pity the poor little
sweep, and the boy with the water-cresses. How anybody can
go to a cold ditch, and gather water-cresses, seems marvellous.
Perhaps we hear great lumps in the street of something falling ;
and looking through the window, perceive the roofs of the neighbouring houses thick with snow. The breath is visible, issuing
from the mouth as we lie. Now we hate getting up, and hate
shaving, and hate the empty grate in one's bedroom ; and water
freezes in ewers, and you may set the towel upright on its own
hardness, and the window-panes are frost-whitened, or it is foggy,
and the sun sends a dull, brazen beam into one's room ; or, if it
is fine, the windows outside are stuck with icicles ; or a detestable
thaw has begun, and they drip ; but, at all events, it is horribly
cold, and delicate shavers fidget about their chambers looking
distressed, and cherish their hard-hearted enemy, the razor, in
their bosoms, to warm him a little, and coax him into a consideration of their chins. Savage is a cut, and makes them think
destiny really too hard.

25

Now breakfast is fine ; and the fire seems to laugh at us as we enter the breakfast-room, and say " Ha ! ha ! here's a better room than the bed-chamber ! " and we always poke it before we do anything else ; and people grow selfish about seats near it ; and little boys think their elders tyrannical for saying, " Oh, *you* don't want the fire ; your blood is young." And truly that is not the way of stating the case, albeit young blood is warmer than old. Now the butter is too hard to spread ; and the rolls and toast are at their maximum ; and the former look glorious as they issue, smoking, out of the flannel in which they come from the baker's ; and people who come with single knocks at the door are pitied ; and the voices of boys are loud in the street, sliding or throwing snow-balls ; and the dustman's bell sounds cold ; and we wonder how anybody can go about selling fish, especially with that hoarse voice ; and schoolboys hate their slates, and blow their fingers, and detest infinitely the no-fire at school ; and the parish-beadle's nose is redder than ever.

Now sounds in general are dull, and smoke out of chimneys looks warm and rich, and birds are pitied, hopping about for crumbs, and the trees look wiry and cheerless, albeit they are still beautiful to imaginative eyes, especially the evergreens, and the birch with boughs like dishevelled hair. Now mud in roads is stiff, and the kennel ices over, and boys make illegal slides in the pathways, and ashes are strewed before doors ; or you crunch the snow as you tread, or kick mud-flakes before you, or are horribly muddy in cities. But if it is a hard frost, all the world is buttoned up and great-coated, except ostentatious elderly gentlemen, and pretended beggars with naked feet ; and the delicious sound of " All hot " is heard from roasted apple and potato stalls, the vendor himself being cold, in spite of his " hot," and stamping up and down to warm his feet ; and the little boys are astonished to think how he can eat bread and cold meat for his dinner, instead of the smoking apples.

Now skaters are on the alert ; the cutlers' shop-windows abound with their swift shoes ; and as you approach the scene of action (pond or canal) you hear the dull grinding noise of the skates to and fro, and see tumbles, and Banbury cake-men and blackguard boys playing " hockey ", and ladies stand shivering on the banks, admiring anybody but their brother, especially the gentleman who is cutting figures of eight, who, for his part, is admiring his own figure. Beginners affect to laugh at their tumbles, but are terribly angry, and long to thump the bystanders. On thawing days, idlers persist to the last in skating or sliding amidst the slush and bending ice, making the Humane-Society-man ferocious. He feels as if he could give them the deaths from which it is his business to save them. When you have done skating, you come away feeling at once warm and numb in the feet, from the tight effect of the skates ; and you carry them with an ostentatious air of indifference, as if you had done wonders ; whereas you have fairly had three slips, and can barely achieve the inside edge.

Now riders look sharp, and horses seem brittle in the legs, and old gentlemen feel so ; and coachmen, cabmen, and others, stand swinging their arms across at their sides to warm themselves ; and blacksmiths' shops look pleasant, and potato shops detestable : the fishmongers' still more so. We wonder how he can live in that plash of wet and cold fish, without even a window. Now clerks in offices envy the one next the fireplace ; and men from behind counters hardly think themselves repaid by being called out to speak to a countess in her chariot ; and the wheezy and effeminate pastry-cook, hatless and aproned, and with his hand in his breeches-pockets (as the graphic Cruikshank noticeth in his almanac) stands outside his door, chilling his household warmth with attending to the ice which is brought him, and seeing it unloaded into his cellar like coals. Comfortable look the Miss Joneses, coming this way with their muffs and furs ; and the baker pities the maid-servant cleaning the steps, who, for her part, says she is not cold, which he finds it difficult to believe.

Now dinner rejoiceth the gatherers together, and cold meat is despised, and the gout defieth the morrow, thinking it but reasonable on such a day to inflame itself with " t'other bottle " ; and the sofa is wheeled round to the fire after dinner, and people proceed to burn their legs in their boots, and little boys their faces ; and young ladies are tormented between the cold and their complexions, and their fingers freeze at the pianoforte, but they must not say so, because it will vex their poor comfortable grand-aunt, who is sitting with her knees in the fire, and who is so anxious that they should not be spoilt.

Now the muffin-bell soundeth sweetly in the streets, reminding us, not of the man, but his muffins, and of twilight, and evening, and curtains, and the fireside. Now playgoers get cold feet, and invalids stop up every crevice in their rooms, and make themselves worse ; and the streets are comparatively silent ; and the wind rises and falls in moanings ; and fires burn blue and crackle ; and an easy chair with your feet by it on a stool, the lamp or candles a little behind you, and an interesting book just opened where you left off, is a bit of heaven upon earth. People in cottages crowd close to the chimney, and tell stories of ghosts and murders, the blue flame affording something like evidence of the facts.

The owl, with all her feathers, is a-cold,

or you think her so. The whole country feels like a petrifaction of slate and stillness, cut across by the wind ; and nobody in the mail-coach is warm but the horses, who steam pitifully when they stop. The " oldest man " makes a point of never having " seen such weather." People have a painful doubt whether they have any chins or not ; ears ache with the wind ; and the wagoner, setting his teeth together, goes puckering up his cheeks, and thinking the time will never arrive when he shall get to the " Five Bells."

At night, people get sleepy with the fireside, and long to go to bed, yet fear it on account of the different temperature of the bedroom ; which is furthermore apt to wake them up. Warming-pans and hot-water bottles are in request ; and naughty boys eschew their night-shirts, and go to bed in their socks.

" Yes," quoth a little boy, to whom we read this passage, " and make their younger brother go to bed first."

(Leigh Hunt : *Essays:* "A 'Now': Descriptive of a Cold Day".)

Temperate Climate : Fog
ENGLAND

In the room the women come and go,
Talking of Michelangelo.

The yellow fog that rubs its back upon the window-panes,
The yellow smoke that rubs its muzzle on the window-panes,
Licked its tongue into the corners of the evening,
Lingered upon the pools that stand in drains,
Let fall upon its back the soot that falls from chimneys,
Slipped by the terrace, made a sudden leap,
And seeing that it was a soft October night,
Curled once about the house, and fell asleep.

(T. S. Eliot : from *The Lovesong of J. Alfred Prufrock.*)

28

Temperate Climate : Frost

ENGLAND

THE WINTER was long and hard. I made many observations on freezing. For instance the crystals in mud.—Hailstones are shaped like the cut of the diamonds called brilliants.—I found one morning the ground in one corner of the garden full of small pieces of potsherd from which there rose up (and not dropped off) long icicles carried on in some way each like a forepitch of the shape of the piece of potsherd it grew on, like a tooth to its root for instance, and most of them bended over and curled like so many tusks or horns or—best of all and what they looked likest when they first caught my eye—the first soft root-spurs thrown out from a sprouting chestnut. This bending of the icicle seemed so far as I could see not merely a resultant, where the smaller spars of which it was made were still straight, but to have flushed them too.—The same day and others the garden mould very crisp and meshed over with a lace-work of needles leaving (they seemed) three-cornered openings : it looked greyish and like a coat of gum on wood. Also the smaller crumbs and clods were lifted fairly up from the ground on upright ice-pillars, whether they had dropped these from themselves or drawn them from the soil : it was like a little Stonehenge.—Looking down into the thick ice of our pond I found the imprisoned air-bubbles nothing at random but starting from centres and in particular one most beautifully regular white brush of them, each spur of it a curving string of beaded and diminishing bubbles.—The pond, I suppose from over pressure when it was less firm, was mapped with a puzzle of very slight clefts branched with little twigs : the pieces were odd-shaped and sized—though a square angular scaping could be just made out in the outline but the cracks ran deep down through the ice markedly in planes and always the plane of the cleft on the surface. They remained and in the end the ice broke up in just these pieces.

(*The Notebooks and Papers of Gerard Manley Hopkins*.)

Sub-polar Climate

SIBERIA

SHUT OFF by mountain-chains from the warmer currents of air coming from the south and the south-east, and exposed to the Arctic winds from the north, this immense country has the severest climate in the world, with an extreme temperature varying between $+103°$ and $—93°$ Fahrenheit. The winter commences early. The smaller rivers and the numberless lakes—of which there are said to be 100,000—begin to freeze in September. In the first or second week of October the whole country is covered in snow. The cold increases day by day. The mean temperature of October and November varies between $+5°$ and $—22°$ Fahr.; in the months of December, January and February between $—13°$ and $—40°$ Fahr.; and in March and April between $—14°$ and $—22°$ Fahr. In the middle of the winter the temperature may remain for weeks together below the freezing-point of mercury, and at times will sink to 80° below zero Fahr. Such a low temperature gives a keen and penetrating sharpness to the air, and all life seems to have congealed. The Yakut winter does not rage and roar, as does that of northern Europe, but suppresses all motion. Neither the sun, which only for a few hours appears above the horizon, nor the earth, which is frozen to an unknown depth and in the summer melts only two or three feet, can withstand its power. The constantly growing cold compresses the air more and more, until it finally threatens, as it were, to suffocate all life beneath its weight. The strongest currents of air from the Arctic sea, from the Pacific, or from the immense continental regions lying to the south are unable to move this inert and compressed mass of air. The heaviest storms powerlessly rebound from it, and, so to speak, become bound at its feet, being cooled down and assimilated in their turn into the colossal frost-mass, which is sufficient to cool all Siberia during the whole year. This incubus, as with justice it may be termed, lies immovable over the whole country for weeks and months, and if the dry and compressed air did not itself somewhat hinder the radiation of heat, all life would perish beneath the colossus.

All moisture is pressed out of the atmosphere by this terrible cold, becomes crystallized, and fills the air as a thin, frosty fog, making the moon appear as if surrounded by a silvery ring. And when a faint milky or silvery phosphorescence shines from the polar ice, and the many-coloured flames of the aurora borealis suddenly appear, then the frost is reaching its climax. Perhaps from an instinctive knowledge of the approach of still greater cold, or more probably frightened at the sight of this phenomenon, the Yakut sledge-dogs unite in raising a protracted and hideous howl, which ceases only when the last flames of the northern lights have disappeared. Then every living sound ceases and silence as of the grave prevails, the Yakuts shovel more snow about their huts, and even the smoke has hard work to go up through the chimney and rises only a few feet above the roof.

But the stillness is only apparent. The snow does not creak, it grates and squeaks under foot, and rings like metal ; the breath congeals and falls to the ground in the shape of fine ice-crystals. The deep silence of the night is broken only by weird and hideous sounds resembling long-drawn-out moanings and howlings, with now and again a sudden thunder as of a cannonade, from the bursting ice and the rending of the frozen earth.

In the lakes which do not freeze to the bottom, the ice attains a thickness of 10 feet ; in the rivers still more. The ice becomes as hard as stone, its splinters cut the hands like a knife, and if a hard-tempered axe is directed against the stem of a tree its edge breaks into fragments.

(67°N; 134°E.) (J. Stadling : *Through Siberia.*)

Sub-polar Climate

SIBERIA

THE NEXT day it was —70°C (—94°F), which was perfectly unbearable. When I came out of the house, such clouds of steam escaped with me through the door that it looked as if the vestibule was on fire behind my back. I felt the cold so acutely in my nose and throat that I did not dare to breathe, and expected that if I inhaled the air freely I would share the fate of the cock who had escaped on the previous day from the priest's hen-coop and had fallen down stone dead after having flown for about fifteen yards. In my ears I heard all the time a sound as of a trickle of corn, produced by the freezing of one's own breath into hoar-frost ; this music was locally called " star-whisper " and only occurred when the thermometer was below —60°C

(—75°F). The hard snow of the road did not rustle, but cracked. All the trees were covered with a white layer, so thick that even a bit of straw was as big as a finger and the woods seemed to be clothed with white foliage. The dogs' nostrils emitted such dense steam that they were like fire-breathing dragons and smoke curled up from their coats. Out of my sleeves rose whiffs of vapour which looked as if I had hidden a lighted cigarette in them, like a naughty schoolboy. The air was absolutely quiet and the smoke rose up out of the chimneys in straight columns, widening out at the top from the accumulation of consecutive puffs. The sky was greenish-blue and the glare of the snow was unbearable. The stillness was complete, nothing stirred, even the dogs did not bark. (*63°30′N; 141°E.*)

(Alexander Polovtsoff : *Wyna: Adventures in Eastern Siberia*).

Sub-polar Climate
NORWAY

EVERYWHERE on the earth there are hours around mid-day when the whole world seems flat, sober, and rather uninteresting, most probably because the sun stands high in the sky and throws only short shadows ; these never make objects plastic enough. Here in the North it is different ; here the sun is always so low down near the horizon that objects cast shadows in a long and rich manner as they do with us towards the end of the day ; as they do with us when the magic hours of the late afternoon are reached, when the light turns golden, and the shadows lengthen, and objects recede further away, stand out in finer outline, and with more relief than in the white and perpendicular heat of the day ; and you see, extremely sharply, every dear feature on the face of the earth, but with the seducing and sublime detachment of distance. The northern day has the finesse of the fifth hour ; and if I might choose, well then, I say, give me the northern light.

* * * * *

I could no longer trace it with my finger on the map ; I don't know exactly which way we sailed, and where we anchored ; wait a bit, it was Honningsvåg, one of the most forsaken human habitations in the world, and then again Hammerfest, and Kvalsund, where we landed at zero hour, and not even the children and perhaps nobody was asleep, such a terribly white, such a ghastly clear daylight there was ; and then came Vargsund, as smooth as oil, and then again Tromsø, but it is not that that muddles me ; it was the sky, and the sea, those changing and endless days without dusk, nights or dawns ; there time is abolished, that's all. There time doesn't flow, but it is spilt, without banks like a sea ; and it mirrors in itself the course of the sun and the pilgrimage of the clouds, but it does not progress with them, and does not flow away ; here only the watch on the wrist with needless eagerness, and ridiculous tick, measures the time that does not exist. It is as strange and confusing as if space were distorted and there were no difference between above and below ; one might even grow accustomed to this, but at the beginning one feels as little at home in it as in another world.

Tenderly, with golden obliquity the sunshine glides over the round shoulders and the steep brows of the mountain ; it may be two o'clock in the morning, or five in the afternoon, it is just the same, and in fact, my friend, it does not matter ; you sleep, or you don't sleep, that also does not matter when for once you are beyond time. Even the food on the boat will not take you away from the immutability of time ; all the time *smorgås*, and again *smorgås*, all the time salt meat and fish, and brown goat's cheese with syrup, whether it is breakfast, supper, or dinner ; I let my watch run down, and I let day, year, and century, slip out of my mind ; what use is it for man to know the minute or hour if he lives in eternity ?

Here there is no night, and there is not even day ; here are only the morning hours, when the sun is still low, all golden with the dawn and silvery with the dew, the fine, sparkling sun of early day ; and then without a break came the hours of late afternoon, when the sun is already low, turning gold with the sunset, already purple and misty with the sweet melancholy of evening. It is only morning without beginning passing over into evening without end, and never does the high bright arch of the steep noon raise its vault aloft, and the golden evening without an end in the fiery midnight dissolves into the silvery morning without a beginning, and it is again day : a Polar day, an enormous day, a day spun out of nothing but its first and last hours.

(Hammerfest: 68°40'N; 23°30'E.)

(Karel Čapek : *Travels in the North.*)

Mountain Climate
THE ANDES

THERE could be no more convincing proof that mountain sickness is not due to fatigue than is furnished by the passengers who daily reach altitudes of about 15,000 feet by train. A vivid account has been given by Haldane and his colleagues* of the condition of the tourists who were conveyed to the summit of Pike's Peak during the stay there of the party. Even more convincing, if possible, is the exhibition which daily takes place at Ticlio the highest point of the Central Railway of Peru. It would seem that here the effect of the rare atmosphere is more immediate than at Pike's Peak, for this there may be several reasons. In the first place, the altitude is somewhat higher being just short of 16,000 feet at the highest point (15,885 feet to be exact), in the second place, the train conveys not merely tourists whose object is to ascend the mountain, but all and sundry—men, women and children who are crossing the Andes in the course of their business, and in the third place, the train when on its journey east comes up the whole way from the sea level in less than twelve hours. Unlike ascents on the Alps, the element of cold may be ruled out as constituting a possible cause of the sickness of the passengers who reach Ticlio for the trains are warmed to a very comfortable temperature. It must be admitted that when first I passed over this summit I was occupied in keeping very quiet lest I should be sick myself—an effort which proved to be abortive, for while I was not actually sick in the train, the crisis came two or three hours later when I left the train at an altitude of 12,000 feet. On the occasion of my second crossing I was in a better position to observe my neighbours, looking out at Ticlio I saw the most astonishing spectacle ; all along the train from the windows of the carriages occupied by οἱ πολλοί, a row of heads protruded from the windows—the outward and visible sign of a single purpose, that of regurgitation.

(*11°30'S; 76°W*.)

(Joseph Barcroft : *The Respiratory Function of the Blood*.)

*Douglas, Haldane, Henderson & Schneider : Phil. Trans. Roy. Soc. B. CCIII 185 1912

Mountain Climate

THE ANDES

IN THE previous chapter, when speaking about the physical characteristics of the mountain dwellers, I made a passing reference to the colour of their faces and said that I would reserve the matter for future discussion. I do not mean, in using the phrase " the colour of the natives ", any allusion to whether they are a black, a white or a yellow race, but my only concern is whether they are pale or flushed, whether as the phrase runs " they have any colour in their cheeks," and if so whether it is the fresh colour of a healthy person or whether their cheeks are of a blue tinge such as is seen in middle-aged or elderly persons suggesting heart pathology. Keen as was our interest in the colour of the natives, we were at first almost more concerned about our own. All the way up in the railway one might have seen us examining the tint of the flesh beneath our finger-nails. In this matter we were somewhat fortunate for accompanying us was Dr. Crane the Chief Medical Officer of the Cerro de Pasco Company. He had come down from Oroya only two days before and was on his way back. He therefore was a person thoroughly acclimatised to life "on the Hill," and he formed an excellent standard for comparison. It was evident that at any altitude from 8,000 to 16,000 feet our finger-nails were bluer than his. This phenomenon has been noticed by many observers. The difficulty in its interpretation heretofore has been that most of the previous ascents have involved the transition from a warm to a cold climate, and that therefore it has been difficult to know how much of the blueness of the skin and nails has been due to cold and how much to deficiency of oxygen in the blood. I remember on arrival at Col d'Olen calling attention to the colour of my finger-nails, only to be told that the bluish tint was not the effect of altitude but of frost.

In Peru, however, there could be no question of that kind as we went up to 15,800 feet in a heated car. Even so two facts were apparent : firstly that all our nails and cheeks were bluer than at sea-level and secondly that those of the party were bluer than those of Dr. Crane.

After two days' stay at Oroya the difference disappeared and our nails were much like those of the doctor's, but in each case the colour was not the same as at sea-level.

At Cerro de Pasco (14,000 feet) the abnormality of colour was more striking than at Oroya and was general, being obvious both amongst the residents of Anglo-Saxon extraction and the Cholos. Many of the latter were of a very ruddy appearance, but their cheeks were more a plum colour than a red. This is true even of the children.

In any interpretation of this phenomenon it must be borne in mind that these people have many more corpuscles in their blood than have normal people. Even down here such a person— a polycythaemic as he is called—has a typically bluish appearance, but there was abundant evidence that the colour was not due to the stagnant circulation of the polycythaemic but to a deficiency of oxygen in the blood. In the first place, if oxygen was given to such a person to breathe his face changed in colour in a matter of a few seconds, and in the second place, we had the opportunity on seeing the phenomenon disappear on descent from the " Hill " in a time so short that the number of corpuscles could not have been greatly changed. There was at Cerro an engineer whose cheeks were of a very high colour ; on the mountains he had a purple, almost apoplectic appearance. Such a general appearance has been known to result from alcoholic excesses. He came down to Lima in the train with us, and when we saw him about half-way down quite a new vision burst on our eyes. Here was a man with the fresh, rosy complexion of a child, a man whose skin was so delicate that the colour conferred upon it by the blood in its capillaries was shown up to perfection. To say that he was a " cross between a chameleon and a barometer " would be un-dignified, so I shall avoid the phrase and adopt some more lengthy way of expressing my meaning which is that just as the chameleon passes through all the shades of one particular colour, say from light yellow to dark brown, or from light green through dark green to something nearly approaching black, so this man passed from a purple to a bright pink, the blue tinge which he had at Cerro becoming less and less accentuated with each thousand feet which he descended.

(*11°30'S; 76°W.*)

(Joseph Barcroft : *The Respiratory Function of the Blood.*)

Mountain Climate

THE ANDES : PORTILLO PASS, CHILE

UNDER THE diminished pressure, of course water boils at a lower temperature ; in consequence of this the potatoes after boiling for some hours were as hard as ever ; the pot was left on the fire all night, but yet the potatoes were not softened. I found out this, by overhearing in the morning my companions discussing the cause ; they came to the simple conclusion that " the cursed pot (which was a new one) did not choose to boil potatoes ".

(30°30'S; 70°20'W.)   (Charles Darwin : *The Beagle Diary*.)

Mountain Climate

THE LOWER animals also feel the influence of rarefied air. When we put a dog under the pneumatic bell, the fleas jump out from under its hairs, and restlessly seek to escape, a sign that they, too, experience discomfort from the change of pressure.

(Angelo Mosso : *Life of Man on the High Alps*.)

Mountain Climate

THE ALPS

Hints to Lady Pedestrians

THE FIRST thing in order, if not in importance, which must be thought of by a lady intending to make long Alpine expeditions, is the dress which she is to wear when on the mountain. This is a more serious consideration than might at first be supposed, as not only should she aim at presenting as much as possible a tidy appearance on all occasions, but also must she endeavour to have clothes which will protect her effectually from extremes of heat and cold, and which will not impede her movements more than can be helped, in situations where great exertion and activity are required. A great deal of her comfort and enjoyment will depend on her costume being suitable and well selected.

To begin with her hat ; it ought to be light, large, slightly mushroom-shaped to shade the eyes, lined with some thick white material to protect the head from the sun's rays, and trimmed simply, in a manner to bear rain without being spoiled. White

Indian muslin is convenient for this purpose, as it can be taken off and washed as often as necessary, but when a veil is worn along with it, it looks a little clumsy ; a small silk scarf, or a piece of black ribbon looks better, and is not much the worse for a wetting. The hat should be firmly attached to the head with strong elastic, to prevent its slipping back or over the eyes in the high winds so often encountered at great elevations ; above all things it should not press on the forehead ; nothing is more tiring to the head than the continued stress of a hat, which has often to be worn for twelve or fourteen hours at a time.

Plenty of blue gossamer should be taken, as the veil so constantly worn will have to be often renewed. The parasol should be large, as it must serve also for an umbrella, light, not to attract the sun, and lined with a dark colour to give shade ; blue is the best, as it does not fade, and is pleasant to the eyes. A veil will afford sufficient protection to the face so long as a parasol can be used along with it, but on rocks, snow slopes, or glaciers, it is often impossible to hold up the latter, and then the veil must be discarded, and the mask adopted in its place, which should be made either of soft linen, or of cambric doubled, and may be of the simplest construction, two holes for the eyes, and one for the mouth, being all the features required. This rather absurd-looking disguise is absolutely necessary to those who wish to preserve the skin of their faces whole ; one day spent without it on snow or ice, and the consequence is a face of the deepest crimson, embossed with large white blisters, painful to the owner, and hideous to all beholders. No lady, however devoid she may be of vanity or personal attractions, would like to present such a spectacle, and the only safeguard against it lies in the use of a linen mask. Care should be taken to make it large and long, so that it may cover the throat also, or else a scarlet rim will mark the place where the neck-handkerchief has ceased to afford protection. A pair of blue glasses or spectacles must always be worn while on snow, to protect the eyes from inflammation.

All the clothing should be of wool ; the thinnest and softest materials may be used, but in situations where great heat is sometimes followed immediately by intense cold, any other substance causes a chill, and is both uncomfortable and unwholesome. The dress and jacket should be of a woollen texture, capable of bearing sun and rain, without either fading or shrinking ; Scotch tweed or homespun are good, but they must not be too heavy ; grey, brown, or black and white, are the best colours to use, and all superfluous trimmings, such as fringes, frills, etc., should be avoided. A waterproof is indispensable.

(The Hon. Frederica Plunket : *Here and There Among the Alps*.) 1875.

4

WEATHER

WEATHER

Frost

What swords and spears, what daggers bright
He arms the morning with ! How light
His powder is, that's fit to lie
On the wings of a butterfly !
What milk-white clothing he has made
For every little twig and blade !
What curious silver work is shown
On wood and iron, glass and stone !

" If you, my slim Jack Frost, can trace
This work so fine, so full of grace,
Tell me," I said, " before I go—
Where is your plump young sister, Snow ? "

(W. H. Davies.)

Snow

London Snow

When men were all asleep the snow came flying,
In large white flakes falling on the city brown,
Stealthily and perpetually settling and loosely lying,
   Hushing the latest traffic of the drowsy town ;
Deadening, muffling, stifling its murmurs failing ;
Lazily and incessantly floating down and down :
   Silently sifting and veiling road, roof and railing ;
Hiding difference, making unevenness even,
Into angles and crevices softly drifting and sailing.
   All night it fell, and when full inches seven
It lay in the depth of its uncompacted lightness,
The clouds blew off from a high and frosty heaven ;
   And all woke earlier for the unaccustomed brightness
Of the winter dawning, the strange unheavenly glare :
The eye marvelled—marvelled at the dazzling whiteness ;
   The ear hearkened to the stillness of the solemn air ;
No sound of wheel rumbling nor of foot falling,
And the busy morning cries came thin and spare.

Then boys I heard, as they went to school, calling,
They gathered up the crystal manna to freeze
Their tongues with tasting, their hands with snow-balling ;
    Or rioted in a drift, plunging up to the knees ;
Or peering up from under the white-mossed wonder,
" O look at the trees ! " they cried, " O look at the trees ! "
    With lessened loads a few carts creak and blunder,
Following along the white deserted way,
A country company long dispersed asunder :
    When now already the sun, in pale display
Standing by Paul's high dome, spread forth below
His sparkling beams, and awoke the stir of the day.
    For now doors open, and war is waged with the snow ;
And trains of sombre men, past tale of number,
Tread long brown paths, as toward their toil they go :
    But even for them awhile no cares encumber
Their minds diverted ; the daily word is unspoken,
The daily thoughts of labour and sorrow slumber
At the sight of the beauty that greets them, for the charm they
    have broken.
(51°30′N; Long. 0°.)   (Robert Bridges.)

Snow

The Snowflake

Before I melt
Come, look at me !
This lovely icy filigree !
Of a great forest
In one night
I make a wilderness
Of white :
By skyey cold
Of crystals made,
All softly, on
Your finger laid,
I pause, that you
My beauty see :
Breathe, and I vanish
Instantly.   (Walter de la Mare.)

Snow

CHINA : PEKIN

I HAVE been fortunate enough to see the Forbidden City under snow, and it was a sight unforgettably lovely. The huge buildings floated upon clouds, were borne up by them, like the Hospital of St. John the Baptist (the only building said to have been designed by El Greco himself) in the master's famous picture of Toledo and the landscape surrounding it. The glory that shone from the ground (for it seemed now as if more light came up from the earth than down from the sky) imparted a brilliance beyond belief to the interiors, to the great red pillars, up the length of which golden dragons clawed their way, to doors and frescoed walls ; and still more glittering was it outside, where it reverberated up against the flashing eaves which supported the quilted tents of snow covering the roofs. Below, the white terraces were now whiter still, beneath their soft loads of swansdown : and this expanse of whiteness still further exaggerated the size of hall and of court. Even the moats beyond were padded out of sight, the canals extinguished ; and in the gardens, the dark foliage of cypress and cedar made startling patterns, of lace and fans and cubist needles, over the light ground. From the walk round the top of the Guard-House, floating high above walls and roof—a walk, like that in the gallery of an Italian Romanesque cathedral, just wide enough for one person—the more distant towers and gateways of the Forbidden City appeared sombre and isolated by this whiteness. . . . But astonishing as were the reversals of appearance undergone by the great buildings, it was the delicacy of the nearer details that, by this new emphasis placed upon them, triumphed ; the flowers painted upon a shutter, the bird or crag upon a panel, were now luminous and melting as the snow itself.
(40°N; 116°30′E.)   (Osbert Sitwell : *Escape with Me!*)

Snow

NEW ENGLAND

FOR UNDISTRACTED people winter is one long delight of the eye. In other lands one knows the winter as a nuisance that comes and goes, and is sorely man-handled and messed at the last. Here it lies longer on the ground than any crop—from

November to April sometimes—and for three months life goes
to the tune of sleigh-bells, which are not, as a Southern visitor
once hinted, ostentation, but safeguards. The man who drives
without them is not loved. The snow is a faithful barometer,
foretelling good sleighing or stark confinement to barracks. It
is all the manure the stony pastures receive ; it cloaks the ground
and prevents the frost bursting pipes ; it is the best—I had almost
written the only—road-maker in the States. On the other side
it can rise up in the night and bid the people sit still as the
Egyptians. It can stop mails ; wipe out all time-tables ;
extinguish the lamps of twenty towns, and kill man within sight
of his own door-step or hearing of his cattle unfed. No one who
has been through even so modified a blizzard as New England
can produce talks lightly of the snow. Imagine eight-and-forty
hours of roaring wind, the thermometer well down towards zero,
scooping and gouging across a hundred miles of newly fallen snow.
The air is full of stinging shot, and at ten yards the trees are invisible. The foot slides on a reef, polished and black as obsidian,
where the wind has skinned an exposed corner of road down to
the dirt ice of early winter. The next step ends hip-deep and over,
for here an unseen wall is banking back the rush of the singing
drifts. A scarped slope rises sheer across the road. The wind
shifts a point or two, and all sinks down, like sand in the hour-
glass, leaving a pot-hole of whirling whiteness. There is a lull,
and you can see the surface of the fields settling furiously in one
direction—a tide that spurts from between the tree-boles. The
hollows of the pasture fill while you watch ; empty, fill, and dis-
charge anew. The rock-ledges show the bare flank of a storm-
chased liner for a moment, and whitening, duck under. Irrespon-
sible snow-devils dance by the lee of a barn where three gusts
meet, or stagger out into the open till they are cut down by the
main wind. At the worst of the storm there is neither Heaven
nor Earth, but only a swizzle into which a man may be brewed.
Distances grow to nightmare scale, and that which in the summer
was no more than a minute's bare-headed run, is half an hour's
gasping struggle, each foot won between the lulls. Then do the
heavy-timbered barns talk like ships in a cross-sea, beam working
against beam. The winter's hay is ribbed over with long lines of
snow dust blown between the boards, and far below in the byre
the oxen clash their horns and moan uneasily.

The next day is blue, breathless, and most utterly still. The farmers shovel a way to their beasts, bind with chains their large ploughshares to their heaviest wood-sled and take of oxen as many as Allah has given them. These they drive, and the dragging share makes a furrow in which a horse can walk, and the oxen, by force of repeatedly going in up to their bellies, presently find foothold. The finished road is a deep double gutter between three-foot walls of snow, where, by custom, the heavier vehicle has the right of way. The lighter man when he turns out must drop waist-deep and haul his unwilling beast into the drift, leaving Providence to steady the sleigh.

In the towns, where they choke and sputter and gasp, the big snow turns to horsepondine. With us it stays still : but wind, sun, and rain get to work upon it, lest the texture and colour should not change daily. Rain makes a granulated crust over all, in which white shagreen the trees are faintly reflected. Heavy mists go up and down, and create a sort of mirage, till they settle and pack round the iron-tipped hills, and then you know how the moon must look to an inhabitant of it. At twilight, again, the beaten-down ridges and laps and folds of the uplands taken on the likeness of wet sand—some huge and melancholy beach at the world's end—and when day meets night it is all goblin country. To westward, the last of the spent day—rust-red and pearl, illimitable levels of shore waiting for the tide to turn again. To eastward, black night among the valleys, and on the rounded hill slopes a hard glaze that is not so much light as snail-slime from the moon. Once or twice perhaps in winter the Northern Lights come out between the moon and the sun, so that to the two unearthly lights is added the leap and flare of the Aurora Borealis.   (Rudyard Kipling : *Letters of Travel*.)

Glazed Frost or Silver Thaw

DENMARK

And yet, but lately, have I seen ev'n here
The winter in a lovely dress appear.
Ere yet the clouds let fall the treasur'd snow,
Or winds begun thro' hazy skies to blow ;
At evening a keen eastern breeze arose,
And the descending rain unsully'd froze.

Soon as the silent shades of night withdrew,
The ruddy noon disclos'd at once to view
The face of Nature in a rich disguise,
And brighten'd every object to my eyes :
For every shrub, and every blade of grass,
And every pointed thorn, seem'd wrought in glass ;
In pearls and rubies rich the hawthorns show,
And thro' the ice the crimson berries glow ;
The thick-sprung reeds, which watery marshes yield,
Seem'd polish'd lances in a hostile field.
The spreading oak, the beech, the towering pine,
Glaz'd over in the freezing ether shine ;
The frighted birds the rattling branches shun,
Which wave and glitter in the distant sun.
When, if a sudden gust of wind arise,
The brittle forest into atoms flies ;
The crackling wood beneath the tempest bends,
And in a spangled shower the prospect ends.

(*Approx* : *56°N; 10°W.*)   (Ambrose Phillips.)

Ice Storm

NEW ENGLAND

IN JANUARY or February come the great ice-storms, when
every branch, blade, and trunk is coated with frozen rain, so
that you can touch nothing truly. The spikes of the pines are
sunk into pear-shaped crystals, and each fence-post is miraculously hilted with diamonds. If you bend a twig, the icing cracks
like varnish, and a half-inch branch snaps off at the lightest tap.
If wind and sun open the day together, the eye cannot look
steadily at the splendour of this jewelry. The woods are full
of the clatter of arms ; the ringing of bucks' horns in flight, the
stampede of mailed feet up and down the glades ; and a great
dust of battle is puffed out into the open, till the last of the ice
is beaten away and the cleared branches take up their regular
chant.

(Rudyard Kipling : *Letters of Travel.*)

Rime

(1869.) Nov. 17 there was a very damp fog, and the trees being drenched with wet a sharp frost which followed in the night candied them with ice. Before the sun, which melted the ice and dried the trees altogether, had struck it I looked at the cedar on the left of the portico and found every needle edged with a blade of ice made of fine horizontal bars or spars all pointing one way, N. and S. (if I am not mistaken, all on the S. side of the needles). There was also an edging of frost on the clematis up the railings and, what is very striking, the little bars of which the blades or pieces of frost were made up though they lay all along the hairy threads with which the seed-vessels of the clematis are set did not turn with their turnings but lay all in parallels N. and S.

(*The Notebooks and Papers of Gerard Manley Hopkins.*)

Thaw

CANADA

Procrastination fumbles
    Every frond
Of forest-snow ; across
    The frozen pond

The plane of sunlight scrapes
    Concealment thin,
On north-banks cuts away
    Each ravelin.

The tooth of April chumbles
    In the mud,
Razing history where
    A footstep stood ;

The crusted runnels sag
    Beneath the weight
Of sun ; the brittle drifts
    Disintegrate.

Abrupt, the cables of
    The landscape lapse,
The hidden girders of
    The frost collapse

And like a blast of gold,
  A clarion,
A thousand startled waters
Take the sun.
> (Ralph Gustafson : *Flight into Darkness*.)

Clouds

NORWAY : VESTERÅLEN

VESTERÅLEN is a place prolific with dried cod and clouds ; when we arrived there young clouds were just being hatched out. At such times a wisp of fog begins to rise from a rock crater, it climbs speedily higher and gets caught on the top of the mountain ; there for a time it flutters like a flag, it shakes itself out, unfolds ; after that it detaches itself, starts on its journey, and sprinkles a handful of rain on the steely sheet of the sea. At times like that in our country the meteorological stations report that a depression is approaching. And again at another time a small white cloud floats in the sky, it gets caught on a mountain peak, and it cannot get any further ; it would like to get loose, it struggles but maybe it develops a tear, or something ; it begins to droop and deflate, and slowly it sinks, it settles down on the mountains like a heavy feather-bed, it rains down over them, something like a thick broth, or cream, and then languidly, miserably and hopelessly, it dissolves into misty rags. This is the way of the world when one is unmindful of the mountain peaks. But these misty shreds recover again in the lap of the mountains ; they begin to ascend rapidly, and so on ; in Vesterålen, in Iceland, in Greenland, and in other places, this is how clouds are formed.
> (Karel Čapek : *Travels in the North*.)

Mist

SWITZERLAND : GENEVA

IN THE autumn, when the fogs prevail, it is often a thick drizzling mist in Geneva, and nothing visible, while on the mountain tops the air is pure and the sun shining. On such a day as this, when the children of the mist tell you that on the mountains it is fair weather, you must start early for the range nearest Geneva, on the way to Chamouny, the range of the Grand Salève, the base of which is about four miles distant, prepared to spend the day upon the mountains, and you will witness one of the most singular and beautiful scenes to be enjoyed in Switzerland.

The day I set out was so misty that I took an umbrella, for the fog gathered and fell like rain, and I more than doubted whether I should see the sun at all. In the midst of this mist I climbed the rocky zigzag half hewn out of the face of the mountain, and half natural, and passing the village that is perched among the high rocks, which might be a refuge for the conies, began toiling up the last ascent of the mountain, seeing nothing, feeling nothing, but the thick mist, the veil of which had closed below and behind me over village, path, and precipice, and still continued heavy and dark above me, so that I thought I should never get out of it. Suddenly my head rose above the level of the fog into the clear air, and the heavens were shining, and Mont Blanc, with the whole illimitable range of snowy mountain tops around him, was throwing back the sun ! An ocean of mist, as smooth as a chalcedony, as soft and white as the down of the eider-duck's breast, lay over the whole lower world ; and as I rose above it and ascended the mountain to its overhanging verge, it seemed an infinite abyss of vapour, where only the mountain tops were visible, on the Jura range like verdant-wooded islands, on the Mont Blanc range as glittering surges and pyramids of ice and snow. No language can describe the extraordinary sublimity and beauty of the view. A level sea of white mist in every direction, as far as the eye could extend, with a continent of mighty icebergs on the one side floating in it, and on the other a forest promontory, with a slight undulating swell on the bosom of the sea, like the long smooth undulations of the ocean in a calm.

Standing on the overhanging crags, I could hear the chime of bells, the hum of busy labour, and the lowing of cattle buried in the mist, and faintly coming up to you from the fields and villages. Now and then a bird darted up out of the mist into the clear sun and air, and sailed in playful circles, and then dived and disappeared again beneath the surface. By and by the wind began to agitate the cloudy sea, and more and more of the mountains became visible. Sometimes you have a bright sunset athwart this sea of cloud, which then rolls in waves burnished and tipped with fire. When you go down into the mist again, and leave behind you the beautiful sky, a clear bracing atmosphere, the bright sun and the snow-shining mountains, it is like passing from heaven to earth, from the brightness and serenity of the one to the darkness and cares of the other. The whole scene is a leaf in nature's book, which but few turn over ; but how rich it is in beauty and glory, and in food for meditation, none can tell but those who have witnessed it. This is a scene in Cloud-land, which hath its mysteries of beauty that defy the skill of the painter and engraver.

(46°10′N; 6°10′E.)

(George B. Cheever : *Wanderings of a Pilgrim in the Shadow of Mont Blanc.*)

Tropical Rain

RHODESIA

IN MAY, June, July, and August, as well as in October, I can, from personal experience, vouch for the fact that here it rains almost every afternoon. Sefari life is none the worse for such a rainfall, indeed, in many ways it makes the hunting better, as tracking can be done and camps made, when during a rainless period it would be difficult to hunt or camp. The flowers, too, are out, mushrooms grow (which, in a land where there are no vegetables, is important), and the country is green and lovely. The day's work can be done before the afternoon storm rolls up. Indeed, I much prefer the rainy season for hunting. Its one and only drawback is the difficulty that sometimes arises in saving your headskins. The rain, in East Africa, comes in a way all its own. Probably you notice a little cloud, and not a very dark one, that circles round half the horizon for an hour or more. " It may rain," you say, " but it won't be much. There is clear sky all round the cloud, and beneath it. If it does come, it will quickly rain itself out." Still, on it comes, and it seems to grow bigger as it moves, and as its fringes draw over you it begins to rain—rain hard, big, heavy drops, every one of which hits, as they come, and you feel them land with a cool pat, and sink in. Then, in some unaccountable way that little cloud spreads itself out, and the rain now pours down in a deluge. In our land such a torrent would quickly empty any cloud. But in Africa clouds must be thicker through, than they are wide ; and from some higher source, that we below them cannot see, they can spread themselves out, as though they held water in a funnel and not in a saucer, and grow thicker and darker as they pour, from somewhere, the water down. Once they come they do not seem, as ours do, to drift aside, but wait on you and over you, and pour and pour, hour after hour, till all the level ground is deep in standing water.

(W. S. Rainsford : *The Land of the Lion.*)

Tropical Rain

INDIA : QUETTA

FOR FIVE months there was no rain. All day the sky was stainless blue, growing gradually a little bleached as the sun drained away its colour. All night the stars shone brilliant and undimmed by any cloud. The colour faded from the flowers, from the leaves, even, it seemed, from the very earth. The troops of tall hollyhocks that stood clustered in every watercourse of every garden, growing there unsown like weeds but far more welcome, turned gradually pale and faint. Mohan and his assistant, a stupid but sturdy coolie engaged to help him while so much watering was necessary, toiled from dawn till sunset with the dripping tins of water, wearing smooth tracks in the dust with their shuffling feet.

And then one morning there appeared in the sky a very little cloud. While we were at breakfast it grew until it had covered half the sky. Darker it grew every moment, ominous and brooding, until with a sudden roar the storm broke, crashing down upon the tin roof until even Simon the stout-hearted began to yell, because he had forgotten what rain was like, and had, in any case, never known such rain as this. The verandah was crowded with humble and apologetic passers-by who had rushed there for shelter. Two policemen hobnobbed with a durzi, a tonga driver, and the water jemadar, who remarked that it was a pity this was our day for having water, when we might now have even more than we required for nothing.

Mohan, with loincloth plastered to his skinny little person, flitted here and there with a spade, digging new channels to release the floods from his most precious beds, which had become a series of ponds. Steam rose from the warm earth, and with it a moist, fresh smell of wet grass and thirsty dust. One could almost hear the parched roots drinking greedily of the fountain that poured down, chanting rhythmically among the leaves, beating upon the roof, from which it poured down in a gleaming curtain, to bespatter the roses in the border. The ditches were brimming over, and flowed on to the roads and gardens. Our lawn was a lake whereon the ducks swam gloriously, mocking the draggled and resentful hens.

After half an hour the downpour ended as suddenly as it had begun ; the clouds swept away, the sun reappeared, and lit up a thousand waterfalls that glittered upon the sides of the mountains. We could hear a roar of water where a spate had turned the dry watercourse that scarred the maidan at the end of the road into a raging torrent.

Packing ourselves, Nannie, Jeremy, and Simon into the car we set out to survey the neighbourhood. The Cavalry mess was a sight to see, and as it was a well-known target for floods most of Quetta's population seemed to be seeing it. A foot or so of mud and water had rushed through one door and out of the opposite one, while the startled inmates took refuge upon tables. Unfortunately though all the water had gone it had left behind it most of the mud—a costly day for the Cavalry, as apart from the damage to be made good they must have spent a small fortune in giving drinks to commiserating visitors.

The streets of the bazaar were a series of lakes and pools. Flower beds had been transported on to roads, and manure heaps into drawing-rooms. The whole country was seamed with glittering ribbons of water, and torrents leaped down the precipices of the hills. Loveliest of all was the smell of the wet earth : in England one takes that for granted, but there the smell of storm upon dry dust was like a miracle. All the parched earth, exhausted air, shrivelled trees and flowers were like so many sponges, eagerly sucking up the moisture, and I could even feel my skin growing softer and my hair less brittle.

" Just fancy," Nannie said, " if we went on like that in England about nothing but a drop of rain ! "

(30°N; 67°E.)   (Leonora Starr : *Colonel's Lady.*)

The Burst of the Monsoon

INDIA

OFFICIALLY the rains are due on the fifteenth of June. That year they never broke until the first of July, and the heat was awful. I had not felt a spot of rain since my arrival in India the previous November. Every day one would see dust storms in the distance ; leaden clouds with dark pencil lines leading to the earth looking like cascades of rain ; nothing but shadows. With the gathering of clouds, the heat became yet more oppressive ; it was bottled up ; the air was stagnant. A P.W.D. officer joined me for the last few days of my stay. We slept in the open, of course. The sheets were so hot and the pillows so soaked in our perspiration that we had to turn them two or three times in the night. Even in the morning the ground was hot to the bare feet. The clouds grew bigger and darker in hue as we watched them anxiously, hoping for the long-delayed rain.

I remember on the first of July walking from the railway station back to the rest-house, and passing over the causeway that spanned the small *nala*. How absurdly large it looked in that sun-scorched land of withered grasses and leaves ! It was a mockery to suppose that water ever flowed along that course, or ever would.

At midday the sun went out and the heat became almost worse. But there was a change. There was something new in the midday wind. It was still a scorching blast, it still made the window-panes of the rest-house unbearably hot, but there was a damp feeling of softness in the air, a perspiring greasy feeling. We heard thunder, but that was nothing new. Thunder had mocked us loudly for the last week. The Deputy Commissioner opened the door, letting in the blast of a furnace. We protested loudly.

" Here it comes," he said, leaving the door wide open. Hitherto we had only opened it at night to let in the less hot air to be bottled up in the morning for the day's use. Now he left it wide open. More, he opened the window. Going out into the verandah, we heard a dull rumbling roar. The higher hills were covered with cloud and a strong wind blew from them towards us. It was heavily charged with moisture and there was the rank smell of rain on parched earth. One or two large drops flicked the dust in

55

front of the rest-house. There was the roar of close thunder, and suddenly the rain came down in bucket-loads. Never before had I seen such a downpour. It continued till nearly sundown, and in the great stillness of the evening, when the fury of the storm had passed away, we went towards the railway station. We only got half-way, the causeway had disappeared under a raging torrent of dark muddy water.

In the space of a few hours the country had changed from a land scorched and arid with a shade temperature of over 120° Fahr. to one of flowing rivers and floods and a temperature of about 70° Fahr.

That night we dined in the verandah listening to an orchestra of frogs that croaked and squeaked their joy in the marsh below us. Heaven knows that we wanted the rain, but our prayers could have been nothing to those of the frogs now proclaiming their thanks to heaven.

Next day the waters had subsided enough for us to reach the railway station and take train for Balaghat.

A month later the meteorological department in Simla published the monsoon forecast !

(22°N; 80°E.) (James W. Best : *Forest Life in India*.)

Desert Rain

EGYPT : KHARGA OASIS

IT NEVER rains in Kharga, or hardly ever ; and when I arrived there had not been a shower for twenty-five years. I, however, caused a tremendous downpour and I am willing to undertake to supply rain to waterless districts as a profession, but the method employed is expensive. The architect arrived one day with thirty tons of cement to start new buildings ; the cement was unloaded on to the platform and the architect asked that waterproof sheets should be placed over it to protect it from rain.

" That's quite all right," I said, " there hasn't been rain here in the lifetime of man," and that night we had a cloudburst and thirty tons of cement set into solid blocks in its sacks. And, as far as I know, it has not rained there since.

(25°30'N; 30°40'E.) (C. S. Jarvis : *Three Deserts*.)

Pampero (Line-squall of Cold Front)

ARGENTINA : BUENOS AIRES

OVER the city the sky turned black abruptly. Buildings, masts, and funnels were sharply outlined on a leaden ground ; and an unpleasant wind went roaring down the narrow streets. It swept every corner with the uncomfortable thoroughness of a machine-gun barrage ; and there were corners everywhere, since cities built on a rectangular ground-plan consist principally of corners. Then the rain arrived. It came as though it felt it would not be able to stay long and was determined to say as much as possible before it left. But it soon became apparent that it found our company so congenial that it had quite decided, abandoning all other engagements, to spend the day with us ; and all that afternoon it rained with a demented energy. The rain fell as though the air had turned to water ; it came from all directions ; as the wind drove it home, we began to understand why the Professor in " Sylvie and Bruno " had worn umbrellas round his boots as a precaution against horizontal rain. And even when it condescended to rain vertically it rained in ways that we had never seen at home, since most of it appeared to come from underfoot. There were occasional defects in the paving of that southern city, and the rain made the most of them. Lakes appeared in fashionable streets ; the pavement outside expensive mansions in the best French style developed uncomfortable watersheds in systems of sub-Alpine complication ; and callers leaping out of cars were drenched from the knees down before they reached the front-door bell. Inside the house a charming hostess eyed her streaming visitors and, pointing to the window where a black sky was still pouring its tropical deluge on Buenos Aires, made them feel quite at home by murmuring politely, " Como Londres ".

" Yes," they replied with perfect chivalry, " just like London."
(34°30′S; 58°30′W.)   (Philip Guedalla : *Argentine Tango*.)

Thunderstorm

Call the cows home!
Call the cows home!
Low'ring storm clouds
Hitherward come ;
East to West
Their wings are spread ;
Lost in the blue
Is each heaven-high head ;
They've dimmed the sun ;
Turned day to night ;
With a whistling wind
The woods are white ;
Down streams the rain
On farm, barn, byre,
Bright green hill,
And bramble and brier,
Filling the valley
With glimmer and gloom :
Call the cows home !
Call the cows home !

(Walter de la Mare : Bells and Grass.)

Thunderstorm

ENGLAND

JULY 22.—Very hot, though the wind. which was south, dappled very sweetly on one's face and when I came out I seemed to put it on like a gown as a man puts on the shadow he walks into and hoods or hats himself with the shelter of a roof, a penthouse, or a copse of trees, I mean it rippled and fluttered like light linen, one could feel the folds and braids of it—and indeed a floating flag is like wind visible and what weeds are in a current ; it gives it thew and fires it and bloods it in.—Thunderstorm in the evening, first booming in gong-sounds, as at Aosta, as if high up and so not reechoed from the hills ; the lightning very slender and nimble and as if playing very near but after supper it was so bright and terrible some people said they had never seen its like. People were killed, but in other parts of the country it was more violent than with us. Flashes lacing two clouds above or the cloud and the earth started upon the eyes in live veins of rincing or riddling liquid white, inched and jagged as if it were the shivering of a bright riband string which had once been kept bound round a blade and danced back into its pleatings. Several strong thrills of light followed the flash but a grey smother of darkness blotted the eyes if they had seen the fork, also dull furry thickened scapes of it were left in them.

(*The Notebooks and Papers of Gerard Manley Hopkins.*)

Hailstorm

MONTANA

SHE HAD never worked like this ; she had never known what it was to work like this, but the joy of the achievement, the beauty of the glistening rows of shocks which huddled so close together was a constant urge for her to hurry.

Several times she looked at the horizon for smoke. She had heard of prairie fires and she knew that if there were one the wheat would go up like tinder. But the sky was crystalline beneath the blazing sun.

At eleven o'clock she saw, far to the southwest, the beginning of a fleecy cloud which hugged the foothills. She knew what time it was because John came around then and she asked him, for she felt that it was almost time to feed the baby again. He pulled his father's old key winder out of his overall pocket and told her. " There're no better watches made nowadays than this one," he said. " Pa carried it fifty years, and it never missed a beat nor a minute one way or another."

She fed the baby and came back to the field for an hour before it was time for dinner. Then she went to the house and sat down while John and Jimmie watered and fed the horses, because she felt that she could not stand on her feet another minute. Pauline was crying, but Anna did not hear. Her senses were numbed. After a while John and Jimmie came into the house and she watched them as they washed their faces and hands in the granite-ware washbasin. Mrs. Thurman bustled ponderously about the room complaining of the heat which penetrated the tar-paper shack and stayed there. But Anna did not feel it or anything but the relaxation of tired muscles.

"You better take it easier this afternoon," John said. "We can't have you getting sick on us."

She tried to smile at him, but even her face was tired. Then for a moment or two she lost consciousness, only to be rudely awakened by Mrs. Thurman's voice with just a touch of acid in it saying: "I said, Anna, that your dinner was ready for you."

She got up listlessly and started to sit down at the table, but she heard John's voice from the porch: "Look here, all of you, what a funny cloud. Come here."

She did not want to go outside to see any cloud. She had seen some strange ones in Wisconsin, clouds which suddenly developed funnels that reached down from a mile overhead, and picked up barns with livestock in them and houses with live people in them and whirled them round and round and crumpled them like soda crackers in a closing fist. No, she had seen plenty of clouds, and she was too tired to look at any more. Besides, it couldn't be a cyclone, for people had told her there were no cyclones in Montana.

So she sat down and stared at the food before her—salt pork and boiled potatoes, boiled cabbage, boiled onions, and radishes. She was so tired that she was not hungry, and only toyed with the portion she piled on her plate. When John came in he said: "Remember that cloud this morning? Well, it's bigger now, piled up white like a snowbank, and the sun's drawing water through it. You ought to see it."

She tried to eat, but she couldn't and pushed back from the table and went out onto the porch. There seemed to be a slight movement in the air, and she beat it into a breeze with a palm-leaf fan. She walked to the corner of the house and looked toward the southwest. John was right—it was a strange cloud. She could not remember ever seeing one just like it. Funny, that the sun should be drawing water in the middle of the day, but there were long slashes of white in the grey curtain which swept earthward from the cloud itself, like strands of white in long, straight grey hair. Over there somewhere, not five miles away, men were working on the roadbed of the branch line which the Great Northern was putting through between Billings and Great Falls. John had been told on his last trip to Billings that trains would be running within the next six months.

As she waited there was a rumble like a lonely train heard afar off. Anna listened to distinguish the sound. But it was like nothing she had ever heard here before. She said, " John, come here."

He came to her, wiping his mouth with the sleeve of his shirt. She said, " Do you hear anything ? "

He listened carefully and she strained her ears. She could hear the horses pawing in the stalls, the squawking of the chickens about them, and the cattle bawling and stamping underneath the shed which John had built them for protection from the sun near the well. " No, I don't hear anything unusual," he said. " What did you think it was ? "

She said : " Never mind. It was nothing—just my nerves."

He looked at her as if he did not understand her, and shook his head. " I guess I'll finish my dinner. Don't you want anything at all ? "

" No. You go back and finish. I'll just sit here a while."

But she could not take her eyes off the cloud which grew astonishingly and swept like a great broom across the prairie. To her left lay the field of grain, perhaps a sixth of it in bundles, and a small portion of that piled in shocks. She wondered vaguely if rain would damage the portion that lay on the ground, but she knew they could do nothing now. If it rained it would have to rain—that was all there was to it.

Before John and Jimmie and Mrs. Thurman had finished their meal she was sure of the noise, but she had no idea what it was. It seemed to be inside her head, like the roaring of her own blood. It was all about her, but always growing louder and louder. When John came back to the stoop she said : " I do hear something now, no question about it."

He came to her quickly and looked westward. Yes, he could hear it, too. He sniffed the air. " It's going to rain, I guess. Maybe I better take the canvases off the binder so they won't get wet."

Anna watched him run to the binder which he had left a dozen rods from the house. It had begun to smell like rain for sure, but Anna had never heard a rain cloud make a noise like that. It was now almost like thunder which rolled ceaselessly. She thought that perhaps it had been thunder all along, for at least in the bright daylight she could detect long forks of lightning flickering within the protection of the cloud itself. After each flash the rumble was a little louder, until finally the sun was blanketed from sight, and the cloud commenced to rush faster and faster straight toward the centre of the Rim.

John had trouble with the canvases, and before he finished the wind had begun to blow so hard that Anna went into the shack. She was a little afraid of lightning, but she thought if she could not see it she would not mind.

" Is it going to storm, Anna ? " Mrs. Thurman asked.

" I'm afraid so."

" Well, thank goodness we didn't wash today."

Unconsciously Mrs. Thurman had raised her voice to be heard above the rumble, and when John came in with Jimmie he shut the door. " We're going to have a jim-dandy," he said. " Listen to that wind ! "

But as he said it the wind stopped, as if somebody had suddenly shut off a great fan. " That's funny," he said. " Maybe we're not going to get it after all."

Anna sat in a chair beside the baby's crib, and Jimmie had crawled onto the bed. Mrs. Thurman sat on her cot, because she wanted to get away from the windows and the stove during an electrical storm, while John stood in the center of the room. He started to walk to the door when there came a crash like a stone dropped from a great height.

Anna sat up straight, the blood drained from her face leaving it ashen beneath the sunburn. She said, " *My God—oh, my God!*" stood up, and picked up her baby. She said, " Come here, Jimmie, come to your mother ! "

Jimmie ran to her questioningly and, grasping her skirt in his hand, looked up at her face which wore a far-away expression, as if she understood a great many things he did not understand.

Then there was another crash, louder than the first, and another and another, and suddenly it was dark, the gloom in the cabin eerie as the bombardment on the thin roof.

They knew what it was now—hail ; but it was hail like none they had ever seen or heard. John opened the door and stood looking out at his field, where balls of ice as big as hens' eggs were falling. Over his shoulder he said, " What do you suppose this will do to the wheat, Anna ? "

She did not answer. The baby in her arms had commenced to cry again, awakened by the thunder on the roof which grew steadily louder. She suddenly realized that she was not hearing the baby, and she looked down at Jimmie who pulled at her skirt but did not open his mouth.

And then came the full fury of the storm. Like a million guns exploding at once and constantly the hail shelled the roof. In all the world there was nothing but sound, stifling, pressing in, beating, pounding, shattering sound. They were all inside a drum and the devil was beating a tattoo. Anna held her breath for a minute and did not realize it, did not know what she was doing. She had taken both hands now and pressed them over the crying baby's ears, for she was afraid the thundering roar might injure the child's sensitive membranes.

She was afraid, too, that the roof would collapse. It did not seem possible that the flimsy boards could withstand such brutal shelling. John came to her, and she saw that tears were running down his face, that his mouth was open wide and round and trembling and that he was crying like a child. He screamed at her, and it was almost funny, because she could not hear him, but his lips formed the words, " The wheat ! The wheat ! "

She could not think of the wheat now. She could not think at all. She had only one sense, and that was hearing, for her whole being was filled with that blatant, ear-splitting cacophony. No, she could not think about the wheat now. If they lived through it, if the roof did not fall in, that would be enough.

Streams of water poured through the roof, but Anna watched it in dumb contemplation. Then she saw Mrs. Thurman scuttling about, setting milk pans and dishes to catch the streams. She yelled, " Stop it ! Never mind ! " but Mrs. Thurman could not hear her and went on. The storm broke through new crevices faster than Mrs. Thurman could take care of the old ones.

From the time the first hailstone broke on the roof until the storm began to subside it could not have been more than ten minutes, and from then until the sun again broke through the cloud which still roared eastward it was but another ten minutes. Yet so complete, so ravishing had been its domination that Anna fell weak and depleted into the rocking chair. The cushion was soaked with ice water, but Anna could not rise. Only now did she cry, and she looked up through her tears to see long rays of sunlight streaming through knotholes in the roof. The tar-paper covering was, of course, pulverized and the punishing percussion of the hail had knocked the round pine knots out of the timber.

Half a dozen or more of them lay about the floor of the shack in pools of water.

She knew without John's telling her what had happened in the field. He rushed out as soon as the cloud had passed and Jimmie followed him, leaving Anna alone with her baby and Mrs. Thurman. Anna pressed her hands to her temples which throbbed now that the storm had passed as if the blood would crack through. Mrs. Thurman stood in the doorway.

" Poor boy. Poor boy," she sighed. " I'm afraid this will just about finish him."

" Don't—please ! " Anna moaned. She did not think she could stand any more, and yet she knew that she must, that she must for one thing go to John now. She got up with Pauline and started to lay her in the crib, but it was wet and soggy, so she handed her silently to Mrs. Thurman and went out through the door.

She had known vaguely the damage the storm must have caused, still the sight shocked her. For something whispered to her that perhaps, after all, the crop would not be utterly ruined, there might be some way in which it could be salvaged. But her first look shattered any faint hope she had harbored. The field, a half-hour earlier a golden fulfillment of their year's toil, was now a tangled mass of wet straw. Here and there a few strands stood pitifully beheaded—like tree trunks after a battle. The binder which had been at the edge of a forest of wheat with its sickle eating into the harvest, now stood desolate in the middle of the plain. And over the whole landscape were the grey hailstones, melting and glistening like sapphires in the sun which shone again as brightly as it had before.

(*46°N; 109°W.*)   (Dale Eunson : *Homestead.*)

WINDS

Trade Winds

THE BAHAMAS

I SLEPT most of the night on the hard rock and wakened several hours before dawn. . . . The moon was still high in the heavens and was flooding the world with cold blue light. The Pleiades flared in a scattered mass low on the horizon ; the planet Jupiter stared unwinkingly out of the dark background of infinite space ; in the north the pole star glittered faintly, half hidden in the sea haze ; around it revolved the tremendous galaxy of a million solar systems. The great sombre ocean stretched darkly away into the night, suggested rather than revealed by the soft loom of the moonlight on its surface ; it gave the sensation of a great sleeping monster whose rhythmic breathing was audible as low, deep thunder. The waves rumbling against the island's barrier were not visible, but they filled the air with guttural sobbing, a subdued moaning that began heavily and then faded into an audible sigh. The earth seemed divided between two great and tremendous powers, one which was firm and stable, the other surging and fluid. Swelling behind these forces was the sound of another, and seemingly all-pervading, energy.

This third force seemed to come out of the emptiness of outer space ; the wail of its pressure dominated the whole of existence. It did not rise and fall in rhythmical sequence like the surf but maintained a constant tenor, a deep, organ-like lamentation that swept on and on in constant reiteration, never ceasing. The sound was the howl of the trade winds as they poured over the earth in a continuous stream. I had never noticed it quite like that before. The entire firmament seemed alive and on the move ; the slight pocket of still air behind the mound of boulders where I lay accentuated, by contrast, the sense of power flowing by on all sides. The earth was being washed by a vast river of rushing gas—intangible, invisible but none the less potent.

By listening intently I could separate the hundred components that combined to make up the majestic sound. There were weird soft whistles, countless hundreds of them, so low as to be barely audible, ranging in scale as the pressure fluctuated slightly, the rending of air as it was torn into fragments over needle-sharp spires of hard stone, over the sponge-like encrustations of weather-decayed coral; close upon these low flute notes was a faint pattering that at first was indefinable. It was composed of billions of mote-proportioned explosions, Lilliputian particles of sound that broke in swelling crescendos of rhythm through the medley of other tones. I lay listening a long time before I was able to place them; then suddenly recollection came to me; I heard this once before in a golden wheat-field just before the August harvest; the sound was the tapping of millions of grass plants in the wind, the tiny clatter of blade against blade, of stem against stem, bending and straightening, nodding one blade to another. Turning, I verified it immediately. In the moonlight were the shadowy patches of beach grass, swirling, alternately lightening and darkening as they were pressed close to the earth and released again.

From higher in the air came a sweet, tuneful whispering, that before this night I had associated with only one scene. By half closing my eyes I found myself transported thousands of miles away; the tropical vegetation melted away and I was lying in a forest of great pines, the whisperings were the breeze sounds filtering between the needles, the sighing that with increase of wind becomes great roaring moans and then subsides again to gentle singings. It was the voice of evergreens talking one to the other, confiding secrets of the good rich earth, of the dry carpets of smooth brown needles, of sky-topping clouds and of warm rain. Then presently, and at first all but unnoticeable, came another rustling, impinging slowly on the ear, becoming perceptible only after it made itself known. Even more vividly than the pine-whispering, this new sound brought memories of the north country flooding back to mind. It was a murmur akin to the swishing of old silk and taffeta, and, briefly, I thought of Victorian ladies clad in multi-hued petticoats moving in old-fashioned parlours. But this memory vanished swiftly, and once again the green pines dominated the scene. Except this time the air was not warm, but was frosty and cold. Down through the interstices of the sombre needles were drifting swirling clouds of tiny white motes, the falling of new snow. The gyrating horde of six-shaped crystals danced across the clearings and fell on the carpet of dead leaves. Their falling and bumping against the dried vegetation combined in a mysterious murmuring that ran up and down between the aisles of the trees.

I opened my eyes once more. The same trade wind that was bringing the rollers in was drifting the beach sand, rolling the countless grains up and down the beach, tumbling them into one another, piling them into drifts and sweeping them on again. The sound was not snow, but the movement of tropical beach sand that was causing this whispering, billions of infinitesimal sounds accumulating one upon the other, the noise of grain against grain, of lime rasping against lime. The wind was blowing the sand, tearing the island apart, building it up, scouring the slopes of the dunes, etching graven lines in the soft rock.

Gaunt and dark in the moonlight, the ghostly silhouettes of a thousand thorn trees crouched blackly against the luminous sky. From these came the tones that I had mistaken for the whisperings of the pines. These trees had all grown to an equal height, stretching supplicating fingers to the heavens, and then like old men had all become bowed—curtsying evenly in one direction— pointing to the west. They seemed to suggest that in that direction moved the stream of life. Vainly their branches had sought to resist the current, growing in normal tree fashion until the uppermost twigs emerged from the still zone close to the earth, and felt for the first time the ceaseless pressure of the moving river. Then slowly they had turned, bent by a force greater than themselves, turned and followed the lines of least resistance. Life flowed all in one direction.

I rose from my shelter and stepped out into the stream. Its force was surprising. While I had slept the trades had increased in intensity until they were blowing half a gale ; the loose fabric of my shirt and trousers fluttered in the breeze ; the temperature was slightly cool and I shivered. Striding down to the water I stopped at the edge and listened. Here, too, the air was alive with sound, with the liquid splash of wave on wave, the sing of salt spray. But these sounds were mostly farther out, and I remembered that I was still in the lee, and that the full power of the wind would not become apparent until I passed a headland called Polacca Point a few miles up the coast. Returning to the shelter, I gathered together the contents of my two bags, ate another tin of beef, and set out again determined to cover a few miles before the heat of day.

From that hour early in the morning the wind became a personal enemy, a hostile and relentless antagonist which gave no peace, chilling my body when I slept at night huddled behind a rock, catching up the shimmering heat waves during the day, blasting them against my face and forehead, singing, howling, whistling. I could escape the sun by hiding beneath the trees or crawling in the shade of boulders ; the wind granted no amnesty. Eddying, swirling, it worried me endlessly ; drifting sand covered my bags when I set them down, the tiny grains filtered into my food, making it gritty ; my clothes flapped ceaselessly, breaking my rest, irritating me during the day. Not for an hour, not for so much as a minute, did it slacken. In my hut back in Mathewtown I had been conscious of the trades in a vague sort of way : they whistled through the palmettos and rustled the grasses in the clearing, but behind the snug walls of my home the wind did not exist ; I could sleep, eat and live unmolested. The clearing was in a semi-vacuum, its position in the lee of the island sheltered it from all but the most violent gusts. The trades roared overhead and then passed on out to sea again.

Inagua lies squarely in the path of the trades. These winds at times blow incessantly for weeks, at others fall to near calm or gentle zephyrs, more often they are vigorous and gale-like. Usually they increase and decrease in intensity, slowly building up velocity over several days, holding it for long or short periods and then gradually waning again. My exploration of the island was in a period of increasing intensity.

About dawn I passed the last of the lee. From Polacca Point the coast swings southwards in a long sweeping bay known as the Bight of Ocean. Polacca Point was visible long before I reached it, by the curtain of white spray surging up from the windward side. There was no sheltering reef to guard the coast from the onslaughts of the huge swells that were running ; the bottom dropped straight down for fifty or sixty feet ; the water hit the blank wall with nothing to slow its impact ; white sheets of dazzling foam shot skywards and were whipped into long streamers by the wind. The roar could be heard for miles.

(21°N; 73°30'W.)   (Gilbert C. Klingel : *Inagua*.)

Tramontana and Scirocco : Red Rain

ITALY : CAMPANIA

UNAVOIDABLY one learns to take an interest in the winds hereabouts, seeing that these Siren regions are fanned by every breath of Heaven. In summer it is a simple matter ; sea-breeze by day and land-breeze by night, stepping into each other's shoes with praiseworthy regularity ; but later on things become complicated, and the catalogue of local winds swells to a formidable size. The northern *tramontana* which closes the pores (speak not of love to these folk when the *tramontana* blows), and the scirocco* that relaxes them, are the best known, but not the most popular ; the latter may well have increased since ancient times, perhaps on account of the deforestation of northern Africa, else the Romans, who had absurdly sensitive skins and nerves, would have execrated it even more than they did.

Blue-black tints and crisp waves prevail during the *tramontana*; an " honest " wind, because, blowing off the land, it is debarred from becoming dishonest so near the shore. The scirocco's tints are green and yellow, and it has no pretensions to honesty—its wintry convulsions are sometimes so violent that the salty spray is carried far inland, and can be tasted in secluded orchards on the last remaining figs. But perhaps this is cloud-work, for when the delirium is at its height, the clouds often descend and join the fun, tempting the waves to meet them half-way. When these waterspouts, careering distractedly over the waste, break, the clouds cling to what they can of the nether element and bear it away with them on their aerial voyages.

The great storm of 1343, described by Neapolitan chroniclers and in one of Petrarca's letters, blew from this quarter ; it destroyed shipping and villages, swallowing what little was left of Amalfi (for that town had been reduced to a fragment before Mola da Tramonti wrote his chronicle in 1149), obliterating landmarks all along this coast, and thrusting even rivers, like the Sebeto, from their courses. Intense darkness fell over the land during those awful days, and turned men's minds to thoughts of prayer.

I can remember a scirocco phenomenon equally unearthly,

---

*Graglia's Dictionary of Italian distinguishes between *siròcco* or *scilòcco*, the south wind or sirocco, and *scirócco*, the south-east wind.

perhaps, in appearance. At that time, too, our hearts were some-what perturbed; things had happened; there had been wars and assassinations of kings, and it was feared, by the simpler sort, that retribution was due. A sultry afternoon was drawing to its close, and I had been observing a small cloud that emerged above the sky-line. It was round as a disc, of ruddy hue, and in texture so compact and un-ethereal as to appear solid. Slowly it grew, and never changed its shape; an hour passed; it gradually expanded into a monstrous peony upon the firmament and, instead of drifting as clouds do, seemed rather to be pushed forwards mechanically from behind the scenes. Its uncommon shape and colour, its spasmodic growth, began to attract attention; we herded together and found ourselves watching its movements not without uneasiness. Suddenly, after an unusually vigorous jerk, the cheering sun was effaced, blotted out behind the curtain, leaving the world in a dim roseate fog. The change was dis-quieting, and there fell upon us the hush of an eclipse. Then it rained in big, warm drops. I looked at my hand—blood!

"Male pioggia, signore," said an old man, hurrying past me. *Male:* that was the word—an evil rain.

Next morning trees and flowers were smeared over with an incrustation of mud, and sprightly white-stuccoed houses splotched with brown. And presently wise men came with microscopes and chemical paraphernalia; they analysed a speck of the deposit of the blood-rain and found in it plant-spores from the Sahara and animalcules of a thousand kinds—a whole world in miniature, fallen in a raindrop from the sky. . . .

(40°40′N; 14°30′E.)   (Norman Douglas : *Siren Land.*)

Khamsin Wind
EGYPT

GOING OUT one morning, I met unexpectedly the scorching breath of the Khamsin wind, and fearing that I should faint under the infliction, I returned to my rooms. Reflecting, however, that I might have to encounter this wind in the Desert, where there would be no possibility of avoiding it, I thought it would be better to brave it once more in the city, and to try whether I could really bear it or not. I therefore mounted my ass, and rode to old Cairo and along the gardens by the banks of the Nile. The wind was hot to the touch, as though it came from a furnace;

it blew strongly, but yet with such perfect steadiness that the trees bending under its force remained fixed in the same curves without perceptibly waving ; the whole sky was obscured by a veil of yellowish grey that shut out the face of the sun. The streets were utterly silent, being indeed almost entirely deserted ; and not without cause, for the scorching blast, whilst it fevers the blood, closes up the pores of the skin, and is terribly distressing therefore to every animal that encounters it.

(30°N; 31°E.) (Kinglake : *Eothen.*)

Hot Wind

AUSTRALIA

THIS DAY we had an instance of the sirocco-like wind of Australia, which comes from the parched deserts of the interior. While riding I was not fully aware, as always happens, how exceedingly high the temperature was. Clouds of dust were travelling in every part, & the wind felt like that which has passed over a fire. I afterwards heard the thermometer out of doors stood at 119° and in a room in a closed house at 96°.

(Approx : 34°S; 150°30'E.) (Charles Darwin : *The Beagle Diary.*)

Simoom

LIBYA

THE NATIVES and the observant can foretell the coming of the sandstorm at least one day, often several days, ahead. Unfailing symptoms tell of its approach. The air becomes sultry and oppressive ; a light, grayish or reddish vapour obscures the sky ; and there is not a breath of wind. All living creatures suffer visibly under the gradually increasing sultriness ; men grumble and groan ; the wild animals are shyer than usual ; the camels become restless and cross, jostling one another, jibbing stubbornly, even lying down on the ground. The sun sets without any colour ; no red-glow fringes the evening sky ; every light is veiled in a vaporous shroud. Night brings neither coolness nor refreshment, rather an aggravation of the sultriness, the lassitude, the discomfort ; in spite of all weariness one cannot sleep. If men and beasts are still able to move, no rest is taken, but they hurry on with the most anxious haste as long as the leader can see any of the heavenly bodies. But the vapour becomes a dry fog, obscuring one constellation after another, hiding moon and sun, though in the most favourable conditions these may be visible, about half their normal size, pale in colour and of ill-defined contour.

Sometimes it is at midnight that the wind begins to raise its wings ; more commonly about noon. Without a watch no one could tell the time, for the fog has become so thick that the sun is completely hidden. A gloomy twilight covers the desert, and everything even within a short radius is hazy and indistinct. Gently, hardly perceptibly the air at length begins to move. It is not a breeze, but the merest breath. But this breath scorches, pierces like an icy wind into bone and marrow, producing dull headache, enervation, and uneasiness. The first breath is followed by a more perceptible gust, equally piercing and deadening. Several brief blasts rage howling across the plain.

It is now high time to encamp. Even the camels know this, for no whip will make them take another step. Panic-stricken they sink down, stretch out their long necks in front of them, press them closely on the sand, and shut their eyes. Their drivers unload them as rapidly as possible, build the baggage into a barricade, and heap all the water-bags closely together, so as to present the least possible surface to the wind, and cover them with any available mats. This accomplished, they wrap themselves as closely as may be in their robes, moisten the part which surrounds the head, and take refuge behind the baggage. All this is done with the utmost despatch, for the sandstorm never leaves one long to wait.

Following one another in more rapid succession, the blasts soon become continuous, and the storm rages. The wind roars and rumbles, pipes and howls in the firmament ; the sand rushes and rages along the ground ; there is creaking and crackling and crashing among the baggage as the planks of the boxes burst. The prevailing sultriness increases till the limit of endurance seems all but reached ; all moisture leaves the sweat-covered body ; the mucous membranes begin to crack and bleed ; the parched tongue lies like a piece of lead in the mouth ; the pulse quickens, the heart throbs convulsively ; the skin begins to peel, and into the lacerations the raging storm bears fine sand, producing new tortures. The sons of the desert pray and groan, the stranger murmurs and complains.

The severest raging of the sand-storm does not usually last long, it may be only for an hour, or for two or three, just like the analogous thunderstorm in the north. As it assuages the dust sinks, the air clears, perhaps a counter-breeze sets in from the north ; the caravan rearranges itself and goes on its way.

(Alfred Edmund Brehm : *From North Pole to Equator*.)

Harmattan

RIO DE ORO

BEFORE we reached Cape Blanco we had our experience with that mystery of nature to which the natives of the African coast have given the name of Harmattan. This is the wind that during the winter months comes suddenly on the coast and the sea from the eastward. It is a wind that has travelled over the millions of square miles of the driest region on earth. In its sweep over unbroken territory it has caught up volumes of finely divided sand, which it carries out to sea. One morning our wind shifted, coming out of the east. By noon our weather looked more fantastic than usual. The haze about us was closer, thicker, less white. It seemed as though the light of even the tropic sun was diminishing, and it set early, a dull red ball sinking into a purple haze like a glowing ingot being quenched in a bath of oil. You expected it to hiss as it sank from sight. Night came, but with it no cool breeze or heavy tropic dews. The hot, dry wind continued. Our lips felt dry and our throats parched ; our feet began to grate upon the deck. We wiped up and washed down as usual, but in a few hours everything you touched, the brasswork, the hatch covers, the steering wheel itself, was gritty again. We were passing through a light sandstorm, though we were many miles out to sea, far out of sight of land even if our visibility had not been cut off by the smoky haze that hung around us. It was as though Africa were too powerful a continent to be bounded by a mere ocean. She had put out fingers across the sea to draw us within the circle of her influence.

Our Harmattan cleared up shortly, but sometimes these winds blow for days and the coast is shrouded in darkness. It is dangerous then for vessels to approach the shore, as though there were a heavy fog.

(*Approx : 22°N; 17°W*.)   (Leonard Outhwaite : *Atlantic Circle*.)

Dust Storm

TUNISIA

WAKING at dawn, I looked out of the window. We were in the desert. On either side of the railway an immense plain, flat as Holland, but tawny instead of green, stretched out interminably. On the horizon, instead of windmills, a row of camels was silhouetted against the grey sky. Mile after mile, the train rolled slowly southward.

At Tozeur, when at last we arrived, it had just finished raining— for the first time in two and a half years—and now the wind had sprung up ; there was a sandstorm. A thick brown fog, whirled into eddies by the wind, gritty to the skin, abolished the landscape from before our smarting eyes. We sneezed ; there was sand in our ears, in our hair, between our teeth. It was horrible. I felt depressed, but not surprised. The weather is always horrible when I travel.

Towards evening the wind somewhat abated ; the sand began to drop out of the air. At midday the brown curtain had been impenetrable at fifty yards. It thinned, grew gauzier ; one could see objects at a hundred, two hundred yards. From the windows of the hotel bedroom in which we had sat all day, trying—but in vain, for it came through even invisible crannies—to escape from the wind-blown sand, we could see the fringes of a dense forest of palm trees, the dome of a little mosque, houses of sun-dried brick and thin brown men in flapping night-shirts walking, with muffled faces and bent heads, against the wind, or riding, sometimes astride, sometimes sideways, on the bony rumps of patient little asses. Two very professional tourists in sun helmets—there was no sun— emerged round the corner of a street. A malicious gust of wind caught them unawares ; simultaneously the two helmets shot into the air, thudded, rolled in the dust. The too professional tourists scuttled in pursuit. The spectacle cheered us a little ; we descended, we ventured out of doors.

(*34°N; 8°E.*)   (Aldous Huxley : *The Olive Tree*.)

Föhn

SWITZERLAND : ALPS OF CANTON URI

I AWOKE next morning to see a little rectangle of grey sky framed by the window ; and arose to find the hut enveloped in mist and a light granular snow falling. It was a dismal outlook, but the Swiss, with the confidence born of his past experiences in this district, assured me that the sky would clear. He was right. A few minutes later the mist parted and rolled slowly back.

But it was an ominous dawn. An ocean of mist that stretched northwards as far as the eye could see concealed all but the summits of the higher peaks ; the hut stood just above it and was now and again enveloped in its sluggish waves. The sky immediately overhead was no less ominous—a pale moistful sky branded with fiery clouds—whilst oily masses of grey cloud were slowly pouring over the ridges in the south. A cloud sea with a clear sky above it often presages good weather, but taken in conjunction with higher cloud formations it is more often than not a forerunner of bad weather.

. . . The rising sun did something to soften the scowl in the weather and at 8 a.m. I decided to start for the Clariden Pass. If bad weather developed, as seemed probable, I could return to the Clariden hut ; if not I should continue and descend to the Maderanerthal.

. . . I had not been going long, and had covered not more than a quarter of the distance to the hut, when I became aware of a sudden change in the air. So far it had been quiescent with a suspicion of frost in it, but now I felt light puffs of wind against my cheek and puffs of astonishing warmth. It was as though I was standing in the cold on the threshold of a house and someone opened the door letting out the warmth of the house into my face. It was the Föhn wind.

I halted ; once again I had to make a decision, and this time it was one on which rested my immediate safety. If I retreated it would not take me as long to regain the trough by which I had descended as it would take to reach the hut, but the trough, situated as it is between the glacier and the slopes of the Düssistock, is a perfect avalanche trap. I might find temporary refuge on the glacier by chancing its crevasses, but there was a strong possibility that the Föhn preceded bad weather, in which case retreat over the Clariden Pass was not a pleasant prospect. I might descend to the sloping shelf which I could now see below me, but on this there would be a risk of being overwhelmed by an avalanche from above, whilst my position as regards the weather would force an eventual ascent of the steep slopes to the Hüfi hut. The last possibility was of finding a ridge which might afford protection from the avalanches which must fall directly the Föhn had melted the crust on the snow. The mind works quickly in moments of emergency, and it was only a matter of seconds before I decided to advance at the best possible speed on the assumption that half an hour would see me at the hut and that the snow would remain safe that long. In spite of subsequent events, I believe this to have been the best decision.

As I laboured across the slopes, putting all I knew into the speed that meant safety, the puffs of warm air increased to stronger blasts, and they were not warm, they were hot ; they might have blown for hundreds of miles over a sun-scorched desert, and the temperature shot up like the mercury of a thermometer in the mouth of a man with tropical fever. Never have I experienced so sudden a rise of temperature on a mountain, and never have I seen safe snow change to unsafe snow so quickly. In a few minutes the crust had gone, the snow was clinging in masses to the under-surface of my ski, and the threat of avalanches was apparent.

I removed my ski, not only because their cutting action was more likely to detach an avalanche than the disturbance caused by walking, but because the man on foot has a better chance of surviving an avalanche than a man on ski, as ski tend to drag the ski-er beneath the surface of the avalanche, besides spraining or breaking the legs.

As I bent down to remove my ski I heard from somewhere the long-drawn-out thunder of an avalanche.

Progress on foot was hard work ; I sank knee-deep into the soft snow at every step, whilst here and there were concealed cavities in which I wallowed and floundered up to the waist. The slope was steep and I had to carry my ski under one arm. I turned an ill-defined shoulder, and the hut, which had been out of sight after the initial corner, came into view. It was only two hundred yards away, and I looked at it gratefully, promising myself that in a few minutes I should be off these abominable snow-slopes and in safety.

To reach it involved crossing the steepest slope I had yet encountered. I had taken a few steps on this when I heard a sudden sharp hissing sound like an angry serpent. Two hundred feet above me an avalanche was starting. A little coverlet of snow resting on a rock slid off on to the slope beneath ; it set a small ball of snow rolling ; this gathered mass and impetus ; it attained to the dimensions of a cartwheel, then burst into fragments ; each fragment augmented itself, then burst to form other fragments. It was the matter of a second or so for this to happen. The main body of the snow-slope was unable to withstand the weight of these charging masses of snow, it began to slide as one compact wave, a wave which widened rapidly as the snow on either side was gathered up, so that the track of the avalanche was in the form of an inverted V.

I remember saying out loud : " Now you're for it." I said this quite calmly and with a curious feeling of detachment, an unhurried acceptance of fact as though this was merely the culminating incident in some badly played drama in which I was the principal actor. I have had this feeling of detachment before in moments of danger ; one stands outside oneself, viewing dispassionately the impending dissolution of the physical entity.

This strange feeling lasted for a mere fraction of a second. Then I saw that there was a chance of escaping the avalanche by running forward. I dropped one ski, but for some reason I cannot explain clung on to the other, and floundered desperately through the soft snow. As I laboured thus I looked up and saw the avalanche sweeping downwards towards me. It must have approached quickly, yet it seemed deliberate and unhurried as though assured of its strength and certain of its prey. It missed me ; there was nothing to spare ; one block of sodden snow on the fringe of it caught the end of the ski I was carrying and drove it against my hip, inflicting a nasty bruise. Then, to my surprise, it stopped about fifty feet lower where the slope for some yards eased off slightly in angle. Why it stopped I do not know, as the slope at this point was still steep. Possibly the snow there had frozen more firmly and the Föhn had not yet entirely softened the crust on it, so that, instead of amalgamating with the avalanche, it offered a determined resistance to it. It was quite a small avalanche not more than twenty yards broad, and I doubt if it would have killed me, but it would most likely have injured me, which would have been worse. The ski I had dropped had been caught by it. I decided I must recover it, so I descended to the head of the avalanche. There, after some minutes of searching, I saw one end of it, and managed to dig it out from beneath the sodden blocks of snow which were piled three or four feet deep.

If the snow was not yet ready to slide *en masse*, it was only a matter of minutes before it would be sodden through and through ; then the whole slope might go.

A few minutes later, panting from exertion, I stood in safety on the ridge, where stands the Hüfi hut. Never have I felt anything so honest and comforting as the stone steps leading up to the threshold of the hut.

Entering the hut, I unloosed the shutters and immediately sought for the emergency provisions. They were on a shelf—a large tin labelled *Notproviant* (emergency food) filled with maize and several dozen Maggi soup packets. A dull diet, I reflected, but sufficient for a fortnight or more if the weather made it impossible to descend to Amsteg within the next three days. Later, in a cupboard, I discovered some provisions left by a former party—a small cube of dried bacon, half a tin of drinking chocolate, and a packet of Brazilian maté—a queer place in which to find this exotic beverage. Being thus assured of the wherewithal of life in the event of being marooned, I lit the stove, donned some dry underclothing and had some lunch. As I ate there came the roar of an avalanche from the slopes I had traversed, but I did not even bother to glance in their direction, and it was not until hunger and thirst had been assuaged and my pipe lit that I went outside.

There was a drizzle of hail falling, but now and again the sun glanced through the mists. It was still amazingly hot—so hot that for some time I sat on the steps in my shirt-sleeves.

Avalanches were now falling every few seconds, and within an hour the sound of them was so continuous that not a second's silence was detectable. Never have I seen or heard so many avalanches.

The south-facing snow-slopes had slid off long ago under the influence of the sun, but up to date the north-facing slopes had remained *in situ*. This was the first great Föhn, and it was bringing down these slopes wholesale.

There must be many who wonder how the enormous accumulations of winter snow are cleared away ; they would not have done so had they seen that afternoon's work. I had only to close my eyes to imagine myself in the midst of some Alpine battle area, for never have I listened to such a volleying and thundering. From the cliffs of the Düssistock alone there was a continuous fusillade of minor snow avalanches and ice fragments, and farther down the valley larger masses were falling over the line of cliffs above the steeply sloping terrace along which I must go to reach the Maderanerthal, sweeping the terrace and finally pouring over the lower cliffs on to the floor of the valley. Frozen waterfalls augmented by winter frosts into columns of ice hundreds of feet high and weighing hundreds of tons, were torn loose, and every few minutes the slopes above the upper cliffs slid bodily to destruction over the cliffs in cataracts that must have weighed thousands of tons.

Even greater were the avalanches that fell into the cloud-filled Maderanerthal, from the Oberalpstock. These were the *grund lawinen* (ground avalanches), monsters weighing tens of thousands of tons and descending for thousands of feet past the snow-line into the valley pastures.

It was an interesting and unusual experience to watch in perfect safety a natural bombardment greater than any I could have believed possible, even taking into account the extraordinary rise in temperature. Several times avalanches rushed down on either side of the ridge on which stands the hut, and my track across the slopes was repeatedly swept. As to the route from the hut to the Maderanerthal, there were few sections of it that were not visited by avalanches from the Düssistock.

Meanwhile, both above and below the hut, the mists born of the warm Föhn wind gathered more densely. I watched them anxiously, for I had no desire to be confined to the hut for several days, possibly a week or more if snow fell to any depth. I saw how the cloud sea covering the Maderanerthal advanced like a tide until it filled the gorge below and even stretched an occasional tentative finger of mist upwards to the hut. Then it retreated, but presently surged back until it had almost recovered its lost ground, when it halted and lay sullen and quiescent without further movement. Above, long silvery cloud Zeppelins swam in the few pools of blue between formless masses of grey mist centred on the Düssistock and the range bounding the southern side of Maderanerthal. It was only in the west that there was a hint of better weather conditions, and occasionally the clouds lifted sufficiently to disclose a clear line of limpid blue sky and peaks shining in sunlight.

Long I sat outside the hut watching the interplay of the weather, the struggle for supremacy of the forces that would determine the fate of the morrow, but it was not until late in the afternoon, when I was having my tea, that the struggle was decided, and I came outside to see the blue pools widening and the declining sun shining serenely with a new-found power.

During this evening period the avalanche bombardment reached an intensity exceeding anything that had gone before. The range of cliffs extending westwards from the crest of the Düssistock smoked, rumbled and roared, and the noise of the falls reverberated along the opposite precipices of the Scheerhorn and Ruchen. I could see the torrents of snow falling one after another, darting in streams down the gullies or licking like dragon tongues over the cliffs. So insignificant did all but the largest avalanches appear against the precipices that, had it not been for their noise, I should never have suspected their weight and power.

The sun sank lower ; the clouds melted swiftly ; for the first time the graceful peak of the Windgälle appeared ; the cloud sea retreated steadily down the Maderanerthal ; and between its thinning waves I could discern snow-covered pastures and smoky grey forests.

The sun vanished behind a level cloudbank. With its departure there came a chill to the air. Forces were at work stifling the Föhn. And the avalanche barrage ceased, not suddenly, but gradually, first of all from the lower levels, then from the vicinity of the hut, and lastly from the peaks. An invisible and caressing hand reached upwards, stilling little by little the commotion of the hills. There were seconds between the avalanches, then minutes, then one last rumble high up, then silence absolute and complete.

(46°45'N; 8°50'E.)   (F. S. Smythe : *An Alpine Journey.*)

Winter Wind

CHINA : PEKING

THE FLATNESS of the plain which surrounds Peking is broken in a few instances by little rolling hills that, bare and brown, resemble in the winter vast tumuli, and in the narrow clefts between them are hidden many dying temples. Sometimes, when the golden dust-clouds whirl across Eastern Asia from the Gobi Desert, and an icy wind insinuates a layer of dust between the pages of every book in the house, it seems, if you go in their direction, as though these buildings must have been translated into heaven, as if the crumbling stone and brick must have ascended in the cloud of its own disintegration and there been assembled again among the blue distances and snowy peaks that are today obscured. A thick golden haze blurs the outline of roof and wall and tree until you are a few yards off them. . . . Such a day it was when, on the advice and in the company of a great friend who lives in Peking, we set off one afternoon on an expedition, the object of which, buried among these tomb-like hills and now so seldom visited, is yet quite near the city in space, though many hundreds of years, it seems, removed from it in time, and, therefore, perhaps, so difficult to find : Kang T'ieh Miao, the Temple and Refuge of the Palace Eunuchs.

No road led to it, that much we knew. So, leaving Chang's motor at the roadside (today he had not accompanied us), we started to walk over these small, dry, rounded hills in the whistling, frosty wind—or rather, winds ; for two systems of dust fought and swooped in the air, throwing into action squadron after squadron of flying particles, one the invasion launched from the Gobi Desert, the other, defensive, rising from the ground itself. Yet, through the cold, stinging bombardment of these atoms upon our faces, the sun, a golden fleece that showed but dimly, yet shone, unexpectedly, a little warm. Only in the valleys, round sheltered corners, was it possible to speak : elsewhere your breath was wrung from you, your words were snatched from your mouth in the act of talking. . . .

(40°N; 116°30'E.)　　　　　(Osbert Sitwell : *Escape with Me!*)

Buran

CENTRAL ASIA : TARIM BASIN

FROM KOSH-LENGHER it is reckoned one and a half days' journey to the beginning of the desert proper, which is known under the names of Takla-makan, Jallat-kum, and Adam-öllturgan-kum, or the Sand that Slayeth Men.

This region is characterised by a strictly continental climate, that is the winters are harsh and the summers oppressively hot. The burans begin to blow towards the end of March, and continue till the close of summer. It is estimated, that there are on an average fifteen " black burans " every year. They almost always occur in the afternoon, scarcely ever in the morning or during the night. As a rule, they only last about an hour, and are rather more frequent from the west than from the east. Their violence is almost inconceivable ; they drive across the open, level plains with a force that is absolutely irresistible. Sheep grazing around the villages are sometimes swept bodily away, or get separated from the rest of the flock in the dust-haze. This has given rise to certain peculiar local enactments : for instance, if a sheep goes astray from the flock when the weather is still and fine, then the shepherd is responsible, and must make good the loss to the owner of the sheep, but if a sheep gets lost during a storm, then no man is responsible. If straying sheep do damage to a man's field or crop, and the mischief is done in fine weather, the owner of the sheep must recompense the injured party ; but not if the mischief is done during a buran or under cover of the haze of a dust-storm.

The custodian of the serai told me, that ravens and other birds are often blown by unusually violent burans all the way from Kargalik to Guma, or from Guma to Kargalik, and not seldom are dashed against larger fixed objects and killed. The following legend illustrated the effect which these wind-storms produce upon the native imagination. Many hundred years ago a holy man dug a well near the station of Chullak, which is now completely filled up again with sand. When the holy man got down about eighty fathoms, the earth opened underneath him and vomited forth a terrific wind, which swept the holy man right up to heaven, and since that time all the winds and storms have come out of that well. Another apothegm is more rational, in

that it is based upon actual observation. For instance, it is said, that if the last buran came from Kargalik, then the next will come from Guma ; but that it is either the same buran going back again, or else one that is hurrying to find the first.
(38°N; 78°E.)   (Sven Hedin : *Through Asia.*)

Whirlwinds and Dust-Devils

NORTHERN RHODESIA

SEPT. 18. The season of dust-devils has started. They are usually born in a little whirl of leaves on open ground exposed to the full heat of the sun—often where the grass has been freshly burnt. They say that if you pop a waste-paper basket over the devil at this stage you can kill him dead. No doubt you can, but I, for one, can never remember to carry a waste-paper basket with me.

The devil grows with lightning speed. In a few seconds he is roaring through the bush at ten miles an hour or more, towering fifty feet in the air and growing all the time, whirling leaves and sticks and coal-black dust and bending the tallest trees.

The natives call him "Mbidzi," and turn him aside by pointing their thumbs at him. I always do this, too, and it always works, especially if you lick your thumb.

I once saw the Governor's party at a military review hilariously routed by Mbidzi. He whirled their plumed helmets high into the air like thistledown. Of course, they had gloves on, or perhaps they didn't know about pointing the official thumb.

Mbidzi treated us to a magnificent exhibition today. I reached camp at one o'clock and found it had been pitched in a garden on an open hillside. Just as we came near Mbidzi sprang up at the other end of the garden and came roaring straight for the tent. We all stuck out our thumbs and held our breath. He went between the tent and the kitchen, contenting himself with smothering all our belongings, including lunch, with a layer of leaves and ash. Already a hundred feet high, coal black, and ten feet in diameter, he rushed towards the village.

" If," said Kachaje, " he meets a man he will carry him away."

Two women, carrying pots of water on their heads, were straight in his path. We held our breath—again. I saw them point, and Mbidzi passed them by. Did I detect disappointment in Kachaje's eye ? He was looking his most piratical.

85

" If," he said hopefully, " he goes through the village he will
carry some roofs away."

But, alas for Kachaje, Mbidzi would not play. He missed the
village by twenty yards.

When I looked again, ten minutes later, he was like a waterspout on the horizon—thin and clear-cut, five hundred feet or
more in height, with his head almost touching the clouds.

(Kenneth Bradley : *The Diary of a District Officer*.)

Willy-Willy

SOUTH AUSTRALIA

AFTER a month or two among the stations on either side
of the Broken Hill line, I wandered off into other parts of the
State. When I returned to the North-east summer had unsheathed
its sword. One afternoon (filling in time before being picked up
by a car which was to take me out to a station some distance
from the railway) I sat on the top of a hill and looked over what
must have been one of the most ill-treated areas in the district.
It was so denuded, so utterly barren and bare, that the few living
shrubs seemed quite out of place. There was not a cloud in the
sky, and not a movement in the air ; and on every side twisted
red dust columns crept about the plain. At one time over a
dozen were in sight.

Willy-willies usually appear on windless days. This puzzled
me greatly until the cause of the phenomenon was explained to
me. On a hot still day the air immediately above the ground will
be heated by contact with, and reflection from, the earth, and
will tend to rise up through the cooler layers above. The diffusion
will be more rapid in some spots than in others ; and here upward-
rushing currents will develop. Just as water escaping down a
waste-pipe of a wash-hand basin gets into a whirl, so these air
currents take on a spiral twist ; and this sucks up the dust and
débris until a solid-looking column hundreds of feet high is formed.

The power of a willy-willy is amazing. I know, because I have
been in the middle of one. It was just such a day as this—
scorching and still ; and I had been helping a man put up a
windmill. We were resting from our labours, and the billy was
on the boil. I had been reading the instructions about the oiling
of the mill, and was holding the printed folder in my hand. I

remember my companion had just made the delightful statement that he hated shaving at that time of year, because you felt every one of the six legs of the flies which walked over your face, when I noticed that the foliage of some trees about fifty yards away suddenly began to dance and toss in a most unnatural fashion. I simply could not understand it ; for, as I say, there was not a breath of wind. The branches heaved more and more wildly, and a cloud of dust rose up between the trunks and started to move in our direction. I hardly had time to pull my hat over my face before the willy-willy hit us. Some seconds of mad confusion followed ; and when I deemed it safe to open my eyes, the dust column was a hundred yards away. In it was entangled most of the litter which had been lying about from the unpacking of the windmill parts ; while the lubrication brochure, which had slipped out of my hand when I grabbed my hat, was floating like a little white butterfly high up in the sky. A pair of eagles, which had been circling overhead for the last half-hour, were apparently so smitten with curiosity that they swung over to investigate it.

(Francis Ratcliffe : *Flying Fox and Drifting Sand.*)

Waterspouts

WEST AFRICA

THUS, WHEN Mermoz first crossed the South Atlantic in a hydroplane, as day was dying he ran foul of the Black Hole region,* off Africa. Straight ahead of him were the tails of tornadoes rising minute by minute gradually higher, rising as a wall is built ; and then the night came down upon these preliminaries and swallowed them up ; and when, an hour later, he slipped under the clouds, he came out into a fantastic kingdom.

Great black waterspouts had reared themselves seemingly in the immobility of temple pillars. Swollen at their tops, they were supporting the squat and lowering arch of the tempest, but through the rifts in the arch there fell slabs of light and the full moon sent her radiant beams between the pillars down upon the frozen tiles of the sea. Through these uninhabited ruins Mermoz made his way, gliding slantwise from one channel of light to the next, circling round those giant pillars, in which there must have rumbled the upsurge of the sea, flying for four hours through these

*The Doldrums, or equatorial low-pressure belt.

corridors of moonlight toward the exit from the temple. And this spectacle was so overwhelming that only after he had got through the Black Hole did Mermoz awaken to the fact that he had not been afraid.

(Antoine de Saint-Exupéry : *Wind, Sand and Stars*. Translated by Lewis Galantière.)
(*Approx : 5°N; 15°W.*)

Typhoon

PHILIPPINES

ON LAND also the typhoon was a fearful thing. No one who has not been through it can appreciate it. The impressive thing is the way the wind increases, increases, and increases until it seems impossible that it can blow harder—and then it does. One particular typhoon I was able to watch from the reasonably safe doorway of a strong stone house. It was as though I were looking at the stage of a theatre. I alone was motionless. Huge trees would be lifted up, roots and all, and go sailing off into the atmosphere. Small houses dashed after them. In the harbour, steamers of ten thousand tons, with noses pointed frantically at the open sea, with the anchors out and steaming full speed ahead, were piled stern foremost on top of the breakwater. Street cars left the tracks ; down went the wires. Sheets of corrugated iron roofing soared through the air, sometimes cutting off the arms or legs of desperately hurrying pedestrians seeking shelter.

Then in the midst of the wildest confusion came the ominous dead calm, which marked the so-called centre of the typhoon. But the quiet was only momentary. The other edge arrived, the wind reversed, and everything movable went roaring back again.
(*Approx. 15°N; 121°E.*)   (Victor Heiser : *A Doctor's Odyssey.*)

Typhoon

CHINA SEA

AT ITS SETTING the sun had a diminished diameter and an expiring, brown, rayless glow, as if millions of centuries elapsing since the morning had brought it near its end. A dense bank of cloud became visible to the northward ; it had a sinister dark olive tint, and lay low and motionless upon the sea, resembling a solid obstacle in the path of the ship. She went floundering towards it like an exhausted creature driven to its death. The coppery twilight retired slowly, and the darkness brought out overhead a swarm of unsteady big stars, that, as if blown upon, flickered exceedingly and seemed to hang very near the earth. At eight o'clock Jukes went into the chart-room to write up the ship's log.

He copied neatly out of the rough-book the number of miles, the course of the ship, and in the column for " wind " scrawled the word " calm " from top to bottom of the eight hours since noon. He was exasperated by the continuous, monotonous rolling of the ship. The heavy inkstand would slide away in a manner that suggested perverse intelligence in dodging the pen. Having written in the large space under the head of " Remarks " " Heat very oppressive", he stuck the end of the penholder in his teeth, pipe fashion, and mopped his face carefully.

" Ship rolling heavily in a high cross swell," he began again, and commented to himself, " Heavily is no word for it." Then he wrote ; " Sunset threatening, with a low bank of clouds to N. and E. Sky clear overhead."

Sprawling over the table with arrested pen, he glanced out of the door, and in that frame of his vision he saw all the stars flying upwards between the teak-wood jambs on a black sky. The whole lot took flight together and disappeared, leaving only a blackness flecked with white flashes, for the sea was as black as the sky and speckled with foam afar. The stars that had flown to the roll came back on the return swing of the ship, rushing downwards in their glittering multitude, not of fiery points, but enlarged to tiny discs brilliant with a clear wet sheen.

Jukes watched the flying big stars for a moment, and then wrote : " 8 P.M. Swell increasing. Ship labouring and taking water on her decks. Battened down the coolies for the night. Barometer still falling." He paused, and thought to himself, " Perhaps nothing whatever'll come of it." And then he closed resolutely his entries : " Every appearance of a typhoon coming on."

* * * * *

Jukes was as ready a man as any half-dozen young mates that may be caught by casting a net upon the waters ; and though he had been somewhat taken aback by the startling viciousness of the first squall, he had pulled himself together on the instant, had called out the hands and rushed them along to secure such openings about the deck as had not been already battened down earlier in the evening. Shouting in his fresh, stentorian voice, " Jump, boys, and bear a hand ! " he led in the work, telling himself the while that he had " just expected this."

But at the same time he was growing aware that this was rather more than he had expected. From the first stir of the air felt on his cheek the gale seemed to take upon itself the accumulated impetus of an avalanche. Heavy sprays enveloped the *Nan-Shan* from stem to stern, and instantly in the midst of her regular rolling she began to jerk and plunge as though she had gone mad with fright.

Jukes thought, " This is no joke." While he was exchanging explanatory yells with his captain, a sudden lowering of the darkness came upon the night, falling before their vision like something palpable. It was as if the masked lights of the world had been turned down. Jukes was uncritically glad to have his captain at hand. It relieved him as though that man had, by simply coming on deck, taken most of the gale's weight upon his shoulders. Such is the prestige, the privilege, and the burden of command.

Captain MacWhirr could expect no relief of that sort from any one on earth. Such is the loneliness of command. He was trying to see, with that watchful manner of a seaman who stares into the wind's eye as if into the eye of an adversary, to penetrate the hidden intention and guess the aim and force of the thrust. The strong wind swept at him out of a vast obscurity ; he felt under his feet the uneasiness of his ship, and he could not even discern the shadow of her shape. He wished it were not so ; and very still he waited, feeling stricken by a blind man's helplessness.

To be silent was natural to him, dark or shine. Jukes, at his elbow, made himself heard yelling cheerily in the gusts, " We must have got the worst of it at once, sir." A faint burst of lightning quivered all round, as if flashed into a cavern—into a black and secret chamber of the sea, with a floor of foaming crests.

It unveiled for a sinister, fluttering moment a ragged mass of clouds hanging low, the lurch of the long outlines of the ship, the black figures of men caught on the bridge heads forward, as if petrified in the act of butting. The darkness palpitated down upon all this, and then the real thing came at last.

It was something formidable and swift, like the sudden smashing of a vial of wrath. It seemed to explode all round the ship with an overpowering concussion and a rush of great waters, as if an immense dam had been blown up to windward. In an instant the men lost touch of each other. This is the disintegrating power of a great wind : it isolates one from one's kind. An earthquake, a landslip, an avalanche, overtake a man incidentally, as it were—without passion. A furious gale attacks him like a personal enemy, tries to grasp his limbs, fastens upon his mind, seeks to rout his very spirit out of him.

Jukes was driven away from his commander. He fancied himself whirled a great distance through the air. Everything disappeared—even, for a moment, his power of thinking ; but his hand had found one of the rail stanchions. . . . It seemed to him he remained there precariously alone with the stanchion for a long, long time. The rain poured on him, flowed, drove in sheets. He breathed in gasps ; and sometimes the water he swallowed was fresh and sometimes it was salt. For the most part he kept his eyes tight shut, as if suspecting his sight might be destroyed in the immense flurry of the elements. When he ventured to blink hastily, he derived some moral support from the green gleam of the starboard light shining feebly upon the flight of rain and sprays. He was actually looking at it when its ray fell upon the uprearing sea which put it out.

* * * * *

He waited. Before his eyes the engines turned with slow labour, that in the moment of going off into a mad fling would stop dead at Mr. Rout's shout, " Look out, Beale ! " They paused in an intelligent immobility, stilled in mid-stroke, a heavy crank arrested on the cant, as if conscious of danger and the passage of time. Then, with a " Now, then ! " from the chief, and the sound of a breath expelled through clenched teeth, they would accomplish the interrupted revolution and begin another.

There was the prudent sagacity of wisdom and the deliberation of enormous strength in their movements. This was their work— this patient coaxing of a distracted ship over the fury of the waves and into the very eye of the wind. At times Mr. Rout's chin would sink on his breast, and he watched them with knitted eyebrows as if lost in thought.

The voice that kept the hurricane out of Jukes's ear began : " Take the hands with you . . . , " and left off unexpectedly.

" What could I do with them, sir ? "

A harsh, abrupt, imperious clang exploded suddenly. The three pairs of eyes flew up to the telegraph dial to see the hand jump from FULL to STOP, as if snatched by a devil. And then these three men in the engine-room had the intimate sensation of a check upon the ship, of a strange shrinking, as if she had gathered herself for a desperate leap.

" Stop her ! " bellowed Mr. Rout.

Nobody—not even Captain MacWhirr, who alone on deck had caught sight of a white line of foam coming on at such a height that he couldn't believe his eyes—nobody was to know the steepness of that sea and the awful depth of the hollow the hurricane had scooped out behind the running wall of water.

It raced to meet the ship, and, with a pause, as of girding the loins, the *Nan-Shan* lifted her bows and leaped. The flames in all the lamps sank, darkening the engine-room. One went out. With a tearing crash and a swirling, raving tumult, tons of water fell upon the deck, as though the ship had darted under the foot of a cataract.

Down there they looked at each other, stunned.

" Swept from end to end, by God ! " bawled Jukes.

She dipped into the hollow straight down, as if going over the edge of the world. The engine-room toppled forward menacingly, like the inside of a tower nodding in an earthquake. An awful racket, of iron things falling, came from the stokehold. She hung on this appalling slant long enough for Beale to drop on his hands and knees and begin to crawl as if he meant to fly on all fours out of the engine-room, and for Mr. Rout to turn his head slowly, rigid, cavernous, with the lower jaw dropping. Jukes had shut his eyes, and his face in a moment became hopelessly blank and gentle, like the face of a blind man.

At last she rose slowly, staggering, as if she had to lift a mountain with her bows.

Mr. Rout shut his mouth ; Jukes blinked ; and little Beale stood up hastily.

"Another one like this, and that's the last of her," cried the chief.

He and Jukes looked at each other, and the same thought came into their heads. The Captain ! Everything must have been swept away. Steering gear gone—ship like a log. All over directly.

" Rush ! " ejaculated Mr. Rout thickly, glaring with enlarged, doubtful eyes at Jukes, who answered him by an irresolute glance.

The clang of the telegraph gong soothed them instantly. The black hand dropped in a flash from STOP to FULL.

" Now then, Beale ! " cried Mr. Rout.

The steam hissed low. The piston-rods slid in and out. Jukes put his ear to the tube. The voice was ready for him. It said : " Pick up all the money. Bear a hand now. I'll want you up here." And that was all.

*　　*　　*　　*　　*

Jukes on coming out of the alleyway found himself up to the neck in the noisy water. He gained the bridge, and discovered he could detect obscure shapes as if his sight had become preternaturally acute. He saw faint outlines. They recalled not the familiar aspect of the *Nan-Shan*, but something remembered—an old dismantled steamer he had seen years ago rotting on a mudbank. She recalled that wreck.

There was no wind, not a breath, except the faint currents created by the lurches of the ship. The smoke tossed out of the funnel was settling down upon her deck. He breathed it as he passed forward. He felt the deliberate throb of the engines, and heard small sounds that seemed to have survived the great uproar : the knocking of broken fittings, the rapid tumbling of some piece of wreckage on the bridge. He perceived dimly the squat shape of his captain holding on to a twisted bridge-rail, motionless and swaying as if rooted to the planks. The unexpected stillness of the air oppressed Jukes.

" We have done it, sir," he gasped.

" Thought you would," said Captain MacWhirr.

" Did you ? " murmured Jukes to himself.

" Wind fell all at once," went on the Captain.

After the whisper of their shouts, their ordinary tones, so distinct, rang out very loud to their ears in the amazing stillness of the air. It seemed to them they were talking in a dark and echoing vault.

Through a jagged aperture in the dome of clouds the light of a few stars fell upon the black sea, rising and falling confusedly. Sometimes the head of a watery cone would topple on board and mingle with the rolling flurry of foam on the swamped deck ;

93

and the *Nan-Shan* wallowed heavily at the bottom of a circular cistern of clouds. This ring of dense vapours, gyrating madly round the calm of the centre, encompassed the ship like a motion-less and unbroken wall of an aspect inconceivably sinister. Within, the sea, as if agitated by an internal commotion, leaped in peaked mounds that jostled each other, slapping heavily against her sides ; and a low moaning sound, the infinite plaint of the storm's fury, came from beyond the limits of the menacing calm. Captain MacWhirr remained silent, and Jukes' ready ear caught suddenly the faint, long-drawn roar of some immense wave rushing unseen under that thick blackness, which made the appalling boundary of his vision. . . .

Captain MacWhirr had gone into the chart-room. There was no light there ; but he could feel the disorder of that place where he used to live tidily. His armchair was upset. The books had tumbled out on the floor : he scrunched a piece of glass under his boot. He groped for the matches, and found a box on a shelf with a deep ledge. He struck one, and puckering the corners of his eyes, held out the little flame towards the barometer whose glittering top of glass and metals nodded at him continuously.

It stood very low—incredibly low, so low that Captain MacWhirr grunted. The match went out, and hurriedly he extracted another, with thick, stiff fingers.

Again a little flame flared up before the nodding glass and metal of the top. His eyes looked at it, narrowed with attention, as if expecting an imperceptible sign. With his grave face he resembled a booted and mis-shapen pagan burning incense before the oracle of a Joss. There was no mistake. It was the lowest reading he had ever seen in his life.

Captain MacWhirr emitted a low whistle. He forgot himself till the flame diminished to a blue spark, burnt his fingers and vanished. Perhaps something had gone wrong with the thing !

There was an aneroid glass screwed above the couch. He turned that way, struck another match, and discovered the white face of the other instrument looking at him from the bulkhead, mean-ingly, not to be gainsaid, as though the wisdom of men were made unerring by the indifference of matter. There was no room for doubt now. Captain MacWhirr pshawed at it, and threw the match down. . . .

When Captain MacWhirr came out on deck, which he did

brusquely, as though he had suddenly become conscious of having stayed away too long, the calm had lasted already more than fifteen minutes—long enough to make itself intolerable even to his imagination. . . .

A hollow echoing noise, like that of a shout rolling in a rocky chasm, approached the ship and went away again. The last star, blurred, enlarged, as if returning to the fiery mist of its beginning, struggled with the colossal depth of blackness hanging over the ship—and went out.

" Now for it ! " muttered Captain MacWhirr. . . .

The ship laboured without intermission amongst the black hills of water, paying with this hard tumbling the price of her life. She rumbled in her depths, shaking a white plummet of steam into the night, and Jukes' thought skimmed like a bird through the engine-room, where Mr. Rout—good man—was ready. When the rumbling ceased it seemed to him that there was a pause of every sound, a dead pause in which Captain MacWhirr's voice rang out startlingly.

" What's that ? A puff of wind ? "—it spoke much louder than Jukes had ever heard it before—" On the bow. That's right. She may come out of it yet."

The mutter of the winds drew near apace. In the forefront could be distinguished a drowsy waking plaint passing on, and far off the growth of a multiple clamour, marching and expanding. There was the throb as of many drums in it, a vicious rushing note, and like the chant of a tramping multitude.

Jukes could no longer see his captain distinctly. The darkness was absolutely piling itself upon the ship. At most he made out movements, a hint of elbows spread out, of a head thrown up.

Captain MacWhirr was trying to do up the top button of his oilskin coat with unwonted haste. The hurricane, with its power to madden the seas, to sink ships, to uproot trees, to overturn strong walls and dash the very birds of the air to the ground, had found this taciturn man in its path, and, doing its utmost, had managed to wring out a few words. Before the renewed wrath of winds swooped on his ship, Captain MacWhirr was moved to declare, in a tone of vexation, as it were : " I wouldn't like to lose her."

He was spared that annoyance.

(*Approx. 15°N; 112°E.*)   (Joseph Conrad : *Typhoon.*)

95

OCEANS AND SEAS

OCEANS AND SEAS

Ocean

It dreams in the deepest sleep, it remembers the storm last
    month or it feels the far storm
Off Unalaska and the lash of the sea-rain.
It is never mournful but wise, and takes the magical misrule of
    the steep world
With strong tolerance, its depth is not moved
From where the green sun fails to where the thin red clay lies on
    the basalt
And there has never been light nor life.
The black crystal, the untroubled fountain, the roots of endurance.
                      (Robinson Jeffers : *Cawdor*.)

The Sea's Edge

THE BAHAMAS : INAGUA

WITH A tremendous heave I hoisted the eighty-pound helmet
on my head and settled it on my shoulders. It was so top-heavy
that I staggered and nearly fell. The native boy that I hired for
the task started the pump, and, like a drunken man, I felt my
way across the padded algae and stepped into the first gradient
of the slope. The foam whirled slightly about my knees and then
about my hips. In a second I had advanced to my shoulders, and
the intolerable weight was suddenly lifted. Once more I assumed
control of my feet. I paused a moment at eye height gazing at
the strange sight of a world divided in half, and enjoying the
unusual perspective of being exactly at the level of the water.
Most impressive was the definiteness of the division ; above was
dry air and sunshine, all the familiar sights, flowers and white
clouds ; below was a strange blue cosmos of tumbled rocks, vague
shadows and dancing bubbles. The surface was as rigid a barrier
for most life as if it had been made of hard metal instead of the
light-transmitting, yet opaque, film that it appeared from beneath.
    The amount of life that clung to the film itself was surprising.
On the upper side it was dusted with yellow grains of pollen

drifted from the bushes on shore, and with down and winged seeds that had floated too far on the trades. There were also a few dead bugs, the frayed and broken wings of a butterfly, and some beetle elytra, little else. For the land creatures the top of the sea was death and failure. But a mere fraction of an inch beneath, the reverse was true ; the under film was a marine maternity ward. For clinging to the burnished ceiling was a host of just-created things : baby fishes scarcely a quarter of an inch in length, transparent as glass and as helpless as the current-swirled plankton ; microscopic lacy crustaceans aglow with jets or iridescent colour ; round globular pelagic eggs with long filaments and dark specks of nuclei ; small blobs of pulsating jellies just released from their rock-dwelling, hydroid-like, animal-flower parents ; and other myriads too small to be identifiable to the naked eye, but made apparent by the rays of sunlight they caught and refracted. This final yard of open sea before the beginning of dry land was a veritable hatchery of sea-life.

(21°N; 73°30′W.) (Gilbert C. Klingel : *Inagua.*)

The Sea

WHAT I most love in the sea is its silence : a sentence that may sound strange till it is closely considered. For the loud noises that a man at sea remembers are not of the sea itself—no, not even in a gale of wind—but of battle between the wind and what it encounters : rigging or the ship's side, or canvas, or the play of a loose rope ; the pouring of water taken in over the lee or the strain of timbers. The sea of itself is more reserved in its expression and, if it be alone in its vastness, lives in its own communion.

Because the sea lives (while the land lies inert) we cannot think of it as dumb : nor is it. But it speaks in a veiled fashion as do the oracles of the Gods, whereof it is one, the most universal and the most august of the oracles : and indeed the oracles of which we read were mostly not far from the salt and the air of the waves.

* * * * *

The shores are sounding things ; but only because they are limits and bonds, not part of the Strength of Ocean. We, being creatures of the land, mostly know Ocean from his beaches or even louder steeps and stones ; the tall cliffs that stand up to the surge and re-echo the fierce come and go of a swirl over uncovering rocks, or (rare but best remembered) the tremendous booming of the rollers through half-drowned caverns swallowing the rising tide. But the sea, absolute in its unchallenged majesty, disdains to shout and clamour ; it proclaims its advance, strength and volume not by battle cries. A comber in deep water not far from land is awful in the might of its advance ; it rears into the sky and fills it, overhanging the hollow like a doom ; but it does not threaten audibly. The sweeping crest charges over as might a line of cavalry, but without thunder ; it resolves into a seething which barely hisses over the slope it had threatened and it dies in long streaks of almost silent foam.

When a man lying to, or barely making way up into the weather, has had a score of such liftings, his craft beneath him dipping and rising again, what stands in his mind when he looks back in memory upon the passage is not a fury but a ride repeated unceasingly as rank on rank of the successive ridges pass and slide below ; and in most waters the days on which even so much of speech from the water reaches him are few. The greater part of his time at sea lacks even so much of any sound. There is for most of his voyage little answer from the Great Companion and no conversation but the murmur of water moving by, or, when he is working forward, the chatter of the perpetual wave at the bows when the water falls to either side before the stem and the ship sails on.

*　　*　　*　　*　　*

Now if even in storm the sea makes less of cry or hail than any other creature in activity, in all other moods it gives out no voice at all. We may imagine its breathing but we hear none ; though the large heave of it is the heave of a living breast. The sea contemplates itself and is content with that endless self-neighbour-hood. On which account, I suppose, it is that you will hardly find any man bound to a seafaring life but has something profound about him, more than landsmen have. He is clasped all round about by an immeasurable companion he can neither escape nor would do so, for the sea conditions him, and makes him, and is with him all his hours—even on land, if he has known the sea long enough for the sea to have formed him.

All will discover, on examining their memories, that Silence, like her brother Darkness, is enhanced and framed by slight exceptions. Darkness to be felt must be what John Milton called

101

the abysmal gloom, " darkness visible." So also Silence is framed and underlined by the least sounds accompanying it ; and the sea is the more silent for the hidden murmur of it, the half-heard hint of small foam whitening in the night for a moment and the whisper of a chance air that is lost as it comes.

(Hilaire Belloc : *The Silence of the Sea, and other Essays.*)

Ocean : The Pacific
Chart of the Pacific

This paper flatness, yellow-isled and neat,
with parallel, meridian complete,
is not the Pacific. Here is not the sting
of blown spume hurtling in the face, the ring
of anchor-links against the chocks, the slosh
surging on tilted deck, the phosphor wash
streaming astern, or the small voice of bells
tinkling the sea's half-hours, between the swells.
The sea is no dead thing of deftly drawn
latitudes, longitudes, but live as dawn
and cruel as absolute zero ; it is kind
as food, and as indifferent as the stars
that weave cold-patterned webs between the spars.

(Clifford Gessler : *The Leaning Wind.*)

Ocean : The Pacific
Continent's End

At the equinox when the earth was veiled in a late rain, wreathed
with wet poppies, waiting spring,
The ocean swelled for a far storm and beat its boundary, the
ground-swell shook the beds of granite.

I gazing at the boundaries of granite and spray, the established
sea-marks, felt behind me
Mountain and plain, the immense breadth of the continent,
before me the mass and doubled stretch of water.

I said : You yoke the Aleutian seal-rocks with the lava and coral
sowings that flower the south,
Over your flood the life that sought the sunrise faces ours that has
followed the evening star.

102

The long migrations meet across you and it is nothing to you, you
have forgotten us, mother.
You were much younger when we crawled out of the womb and
lay in the sun's eye on the tideline.

It was long and long ago ; we have grown proud since then and
you have grown bitter ; life retains
Your mobile soft unquiet strength ; and envies hardness, the
insolent quietness of stone.

The tides are in our veins, we still mirror the stars, life is your
child, but there is in me
Older and harder than life and more impartial, the eye that
watched before there was an ocean.

That watched you fill your beds out of the condensation of thin
vapour and watched you change them,
That saw you soft and violent wear your boundaries down, eat
rock, shift places with the continents.

Mother, though my song's measure is like your surf-beat's ancient
rhythm I never learned it of you.
Before there was any water there were tides of fire, both our
tones flow from the older fountain.
(Robinson Jeffers : *Roan Stallion, Tamar and other Poems.*)

Sea and Ocean : the Gulf of Mexico and the Atlantic

GETHIN DAY would sit for hours at the very tip of the ship,
on the bowsprit, looking out into the whitish sunshine of the hot
Gulf of Mexico. Here he was alone, and the world was all strange
white sunshine, candid, and water, warm, bright water, perfectly
pure beneath him, of an exquisite frail green. It lifted vivid wings
from the running tip of the ship, and threw white pinion-spray
from its green edges. And always, always, always it was in the
two-winged fountain, as the ship came like life between, and
always the spray fell swishing, pattering from the green arch of
the water-wings. And below, as yet untouched, a moment ahead,
always a moment ahead, and perfectly untouched, was the lovely
green depth of the water, depth, deep, shallow-pale emerald above
an under sapphire-green, dark and pale, blue and shimmer-green,
two waters, many waters, one water, perfect in unison, one

moment ahead of the ship's bows, so serene, fathomless and pure and free of time. It was very lovely, and on the softly-lifting bowsprit of the long, swift ship the body was cradled in the sway of timeless life, the soul lay in the jewel-coloured moment, the jewel-pure eternity of the gulf of nowhere.

And always, always, like a dream, the flocks of flying fish swept into the air, from nowhere, and went brilliantly twinkling in their flight of silvery water wings rapidly fluttering, away, low as swallows over the smooth curved surface of the sea, then gone again, vanished, without splash or evidence, gone. One alone like a little silver twinkle. Gone! The sea was still and silky-surfaced, blue and softly heaving, empty, purity itself, sea, sea, sea.

Then suddenly the faint whispering crackle, and a cloud of silver on webs of pure, fluttering water was soaring low over the surface of the sea, at an angle from the ship, as if jetted away from the cut-water, soaring in a low arc, fluttering with the wild emphasis of grasshoppers or locusts suddenly burst out of the grass, in a wild rush to make away, make away, and making it, away, away, then suddenly gone, like a lot of lights blown out in one breath. And still the ship did not pause, any more than the moon pauses, neither to look nor catch breath. But the soul pauses and holds its breath, for wonder, wonder, which is the very breath of the soul.

All the long morning he would be there curled in the wonder of this gulf of creation, where the flying fishes on translucent wings swept in their ecstatic clouds out of the water, in a terror that was brilliant as joy, in a joy brilliant with terror, with wings made of pure water flapping with great speed, and long-shafted bodies of translucent silver like squirts of living water, there in air, brilliant in air, before suddenly they had disappeared, and the blue sea was trembling with a delicate frail surface of green, the still sea lay one moment ahead, untouched, untouched since time began, in its watery loveliness.

* * * * *

(*They call at Havana and continue.*)

* * * * *

The next morning they woke to greyness, grey low sky, and hideous low grey water, and a still air. Sandwiched between two greynesses, the long, wicked, old ship sped on, as into death.

104

" What has happened ? " Day asked of one of the officers.
" We have come north, to get into the current running east.
We come north about the latitude of New York, then we run due
east with the stream."

" What a wicked shame ! "

And indeed it was. The sun was gone, the blueness was gone, life
was gone. The Atlantic was like a cemetery, an endless, infinite
cemetery of greyness, where the bright lost world of Atlantis is
buried. It was December, grey, dark December on a waste of
ugly, dead-grey water, under a dead-grey sky.

And so they ran into a swell, a long swell whose oily, sickly
waves seemed hundreds of miles long, and travelling in the same
direction as the ship's course. The narrow cigar of a ship heaved
up the upslope with a nauseating heave, up, up, up, till she
righted for a second sickeningly on the top, then tilted, and her
screw raced like a dentist's burr in a hollow tooth. Then down she
slid, down the long, shivering downslope, leaving all her guts behind
her, and the guts of all the passengers too. In an hour, everybody
was deathly white, and sicklily grinning, thinking it a sort of joke
that would soon be over. Then everybody disappeared, and the
game went on : up, up, up, heavingly up, till a pause, ah !—then
burr-rr-rr ! as the screw came out of the water and shattered every
nerve. Then whoo-oosh ! the long and awful downrush, leaving
the entrails behind.

She was like a plague-ship, everybody disappeared, stewards
and everybody. Gethin Day felt as if he had taken poison : and he
slept—slept, slept, slept, and yet was all the time aware of the
ghastly motion—up, up, up, heavingly up, then ah ! one moment,
followed by the shattering burr-rr-rr ! and the unspeakable
ghastliness of the downhill slither, where death seemed inside the
entrails, and water clattered like the after-death. He was aware
of the hour-long moaning, moaning of the Spanish doctor's fat,
pale Mexican wife, two cabins away. It went on for ever. Everything went on for ever. Everything was like this for ever, for ever.
And he slept, slept, slept, for thirty hours, yet knowing it all,
registering just the endless repetition of the motion, the ship's
loud squeaking and chirruping, and the ceaseless moaning of the
woman.

Suddenly at tea-time the second day he felt better. He got up.

The ship was empty. A ghastly steward gave him a ghastly cup of tea, then disappeared. He dozed again, but came to dinner.

They were three people at the long table, in the horribly travelling grey silence : himself, a young Dane, and the elderly, dried Englishwoman. She talked, talked. The three looked in terror at *Sauerkraut* and smoked loin of pork. But they ate a little. Then they looked out on the utterly repulsive, grey, oily, windless night. Then they went to bed again.

The third evening it began to rain, and the motion was subsiding. They were running out of the swell. But it was an experience to remember.

(*Approx. 24°N; 90°W. and 40°N; 50°W.*)

(D. H. Lawrence : *Phoenix.*)

Warm Current : the Gulf Stream

I

WE STEAM under the colossal span of the mighty bridge ; then for a little while Liberty towers above our passing,—seeming first to turn towards us, then to turn away from us, the solemn beauty of her passionless face of bronze. Tints brighten :—the heaven is growing a little bluer. A breeze springs up . . .

Then the water takes on another hue : pale-green lights play through it. It has begun to sound. Little waves lift up their heads as though to look at us—patting the flanks of the vessel, and whispering to one another.

Far off the surface begins to show quick white flashes here and there, and the steamer begins to swing. . . . We are nearing Atlantic waters. The sun is high up now, almost overhead : there are a few thin clouds in the tender-coloured sky—flossy, long-drawn-out, white things. The horizon has lost its greenish glow : it is a spectral blue. Though the sun shines hot the wind is cold : its strong irregular blowing fans one into drowsiness. Also the somnolent chant of the engines—*do-do, hey ! do-do hey !*—lulls to sleep.

. . . Towards evening the glaucous sea-tint vanishes—the water becomes blue. It is full of great flashes, as of seams opening and reclosing over a white surface. It spits spray in a ceaseless drizzle. Sometimes it reaches up and slaps the side of the steamer with a sound as of a great naked hand.

II

Morning : the second day. The sea is an extraordinary blue— looks to me something like violet ink. Close by the ship, where the foam-clouds are, it is beautifully mottled—looks like blue marble with exquisite veinings and nebulosities . . . . Tepid wind, and cottony white clouds—cirri climbing up over the edge of the sea all around. The sky is still pale blue, and the horizon is full of a whitish haze.

. . . A nice old French gentleman from Guadeloupe presumes to say this is not blue water ; he declares it greenish (*verdâtre*). Because I cannot discern the green, he tells me I do not yet know what blue water is. *Attendez un peu !* . . .

. . . The sky tone deepens as the sun ascends—deepens deliciously. The warm wind proves soporific. I drop asleep with the blue light in my face,—the strong bright blue of the noonday sky. As I doze it seems to burn like a cold fire right through my eyelids. Waking up with a start, I fancy that everything is turning blue, myself included. " Do you not call this the real tropical blue ? " I cry to my French fellow-traveller. " *Mon Dieu ! non,*" he exclaims, as in astonishment at the question ; " this is not blue ! " . . . What can be *his* idea of blue, I wonder !

Clots of sargasso float by—light yellow sea-weed. We are nearing the Sargasso-sea—entering the path of the trade-winds. There is a long ground-swell, the steamer rocks and rolls, and the tumbling water always seems to me growing bluer ; but my friend from Guadeloupe says that this colour " which I call blue " is only darkness—only the shadow of prodigious depth.

III

Morning of the third day. Same mild, warm wind. Bright blue sky, with some very thin clouds on the horizon—like puffs of steam. The glow of the sea-light through the open ports of my cabin makes them seem filled with thick blue glass . . . It is becoming too warm for New York clothing . . .

Certainly the sea has become much bluer. It gives one the idea of liquefied sky : the foam might be formed of cirrus clouds compressed,—so extravagantly white it looks today, like snow in the sun. Nevertheless, the old gentleman from Guadeloupe still maintains this is not the true blue of the tropics !

... The sky does not deepen its hue to-day : it brightens it ;—the blue glows as if it were taking fire throughout. Perhaps the sea may deepen its hue ;—I do not believe it can take more luminous colour without being set aflame . . . I ask the ship's doctor whether it is really true that the West Indian waters are any bluer than these. He looks a moment at the sea, and replies, " *Oh* yes ! " There is such a tone of surprise in his " oh " as might indicate that I had asked a very foolish question ; and his look seems to express doubt whether I am quite in earnest . . . I think, nevertheless, that this water is extravagantly, nonsensically blue !

. . . I read for an hour or two ; fall asleep in the chair ; wake up suddenly ; look at the sea,—and cry out ! This sea is impossibly blue ! The painter who should try to paint it would be denounced as a lunatic . . . Yet it is transparent ; the foam-clouds, as they sink down, turn sky-blue,—a sky-blue which now looks white by contrast with the strange and violent splendour of the sea color. It seems as if one were looking into an immeasurable dyeing vat, or as though the whole ocean had been thickened with indigo. To say this is a mere reflection of the sky is nonsense !—the sky is too pale by a hundred shades for that ! This must be the natural color of the water,—a blazing azure,—magnificent, impossible to describe.

The French passenger from Guadeloupe observes that the sea is " beginning to become blue."

IV

And the fourth day. One awakens unspeakably lazy ; this must be the West Indian languor. Same sky, with a few more bright clouds than yesterday ;—always the warm wind blowing. There is a long swell. Under this trade-breeze, warm like a human breath, the ocean seems to pulse,—to rise and fall as with a vast inspiration and expiration. Alternately its blue circle lifts and falls before us and behind us ;—we rise very high ; we sink very low,—but always with a slow, long motion. Nevertheless, the water *looks* smooth, perfectly smooth ; the billowings which lift us cannot be seen ;—it is because the summits of these swells are mile-broad,—too broad to be discerned from the level of our deck.

. . . Ten A.M.—Under the sun the sea is a flaming, dazzling

lazulite. My French friend from Guadeloupe kindly confesses this is *almost* the color of tropical water. . . . Weeds floating by, a little below the surface, are azured. But the Guadeloupe gentleman says he has seen water still more blue. I am sorry,—I cannot believe him.

(From 40°30'N; 74°W to 25°N; 75°W.)

(Lafcadio Hearn : *Two Years in the French West Indies*.)

Cold Current: the Humboldt Current

SOUTH AMERICA

MORNING was unusually clear. Before us lay the panorama of one of Nature's great pranks. To the east lay Malpelo Point. Here ended the limitless jungle coast that stretched to the north along the shores of South America, and on and on the length of Central America : a practically unbroken jungle coast of dank mangrove swamps and savannahs, from Malpelo Point over there—low and green against the mist-shrouded hills—all the way to North America. It was the edge of one of the greatest jungles of the world that we gazed upon. But marvellous to behold : it ended there with a sharp finality that was hard to believe. To the south of the point there was no more green. It was as though the Supreme Power had made a mark across the land, and said to the jungle : " Beyond here you shall not pass ! "

The same land, the same hills, rolled on to the south. The same Gulf bathed the shores. But the jungle and all vegetation ended, giving way to an arid desert, a rainless coastal belt thirty miles wide that stretched on into the south for nearly two thousand miles to the forests of southern Chile. Off this coast the Humboldt Current reigned supreme. The Humboldt Current—beginning and end of all interest in this coast. The Humboldt Current— cause of the impoverishment of the west coast of the continent and one of the greatest sources of natural riches anywhere, responsible for one of the greatest field laboratories of science in the world. The scientist can find a lifetime of work in the Humboldt, and a lifetime of interest. The Humboldt gets in your blood, and well it might—for it is the most exciting of all the great ocean currents.

The Humboldt comes direct from the Antarctic and wells up against the continental shelf of South America way down south of latitude 40 south, and urged by the prevailing southerly winds of the coast follows the trend of the land northward in a great belt a hundred to a hundred and fifty miles wide, until after two thousand miles it reaches the westernmost extremity of the continent, Pariñas Point. Here the main body of the current turns off to the north-west through equatorial waters to the Galapagos, and loses itself in the vastness beyond. A lesser branch continues northwood from Pariñas, affecting slightly the waters off the coast of Ecuador and Colombia. All through the main body of the current it retains amazing antarctic qualities, due of course to its cold waters. That great observer, Alexander von Humboldt, whose name has been given to the current, first noticed the thick invisible plant life in the stream, and the hordes of smaller fishes which lived upon it, and the myriads of larger fishes and seabirds which preyed on the small fry, and connected this all with the low temperature of the waters off the coast. The prodigal chain of life in the Humboldt finds its ultimate source in the astonishing profusion of microscopic marine plants or diatoms. These tiny organisms are the fundamental food supply of all the creatures of the sea, and at second hand of the birds of the air above it. We, on the *Svaap*, often sailed through vast soupy areas actually coloured red from the masses of this microscopic life.

Thus the chain of life : The Humboldt provides the basic elements of nourishment for living things in the form of the chemical results of decomposed matter. Nature provides the microscopic plants like the diatoms, capable of absorbing this material and preparing it for consumption by higher life. The smaller fish and crustaceans then come along and browse on the plentiful nourishing diatoms and grow fat. And the chain is well under way. The small fish multiply in unbelievable numbers and cover the surface waters of the current with their vast seething schools, pursued relentlessly by larger fish and sea lions. And thus the stage is set for the enormous flocks of sea birds, the most spectacular emblem of the waters of the Peruvian coast. They hover in clouds over the Humboldt by day, and blacken the coastal islands by night. They pursue the constantly migrating hordes of fish up and down the coast, but remain always within the confines of the current, growing to maturity, mating, raising their young, and finally dying here : the birds of the Humboldt Current. The sea birds gather and breed in fantastic numbers on the island rookeries, where they deposit their excrement which hardens and becomes guano. Man comes along after a while and digs up the vast accumulation, rich in nitrates, and ships it to his agricultural regions where it is used as fertilizer to raise abundant crops to nourish man. The larger fish in a more direct way go to nourish man, after having themselves consumed the small fish and thus the original chemical substances. Thus the fundamental chemicals in the sea, via the microscopic plants of algæ and diatoms, go to nourish man in the end or perhaps not in the end, for I suppose some at least, of the same elements, find their way back into the sea eventually and there is neither ending nor beginning, but a continuous cycle.

Suppose you went south to the Bahamas for your vacation, and saw polar bears lumbering over the white sandy cays, or killing with their lightning paws the colourful fishes of the coral lagoons. Or suppose I wrote in this book that I was capsized in the Gulf of Panama by a herd of walrus. Yet it is no more fantastic to find albatross rookeries in the Galapagos in sight of the equator itself, or penguins, or sea lions, both of which are also found there and in the islands of Peru—in fact all along the Humboldt Current. This unbelievable range for creatures of the antarctic is due to the cold waters of the Humboldt. The surrounding sea is the luscious warm Pacific, whose waters in these latitudes average perhaps 80° Fahrenheit. You can loll all day in the Pacific of these latitudes and feel no chill. And the mainland coast is also tropical. But in between runs this great ocean river, a hundred miles or more in width—20 degrees colder than the warm waters it thrusts aside. Dive into the water here and you soon come back aboard. And so, along this long ocean highway, creatures of the far south have found their way to the equator. Through countless generations they have adapted themselves to their new surroundings and have prospered. But they are still creatures of the far south to me—creatures of a land of snow and ice and glaciers, and as such they enriched those days and nights for me as we lay in equatorial waters, which became my equatorial antarctica.

... The night mist hung over the land but did not fall to the sea. The moon shone through a golden archway in a bank of clouds. Ashore, miles of twinkling lights along the coast : and inland, the lights of the oil wells. The cold of the Humboldt crept into our bones. Ahead, glowing on the surface of the sea a lone steady light guided us south. It was Pariñas, the western extremity of the continent. At two in the morning we passed Pariñas. From its black rocks came the bellowing of " lobos", the sea lions that would be with us from now on. The coast dropped away to the eastward. Down there lay the Straits, and Cape Horn. Some day perhaps . . . we would see the rest of that coast that sloped away from Pariñas, a thin black strip in the moonlight . . . white mist hanging low.

Another day. Another night—forging steadily south into the current. This night the wind brought us the smell of the guano of Lobos, fifty miles away, which is my long-distance smelling record. The fog came down thick and heavy and it was colder than ever. The cabin thermometer registered sixty degrees. All night through the fog came splashings and breathings. As dawn came, and I could see in a little mist-bounded circle around me, the first life I saw was a whale who came very close, breathing, then threw up his barn door tail and dived under us. Other whales near by. The mist thinned a little—and there all around us on the uneasy oily waters lay a fleet of fishing boats, and a small steamer, uncertain of her position, steering uncertainly back and forth waiting for visibility. At ten-thirty the gentle morning breeze sprang up from the south and cleared the air. There was no land in sight, but we were in a new world.

The sea itself was a Neptune's broth of undulating red—alive with the microscopic plant life that enriches the Humboldt. Vast areas here and there were churned to a froth where tremendous schools of small fish (we later learned they were anchovies) were attacked from below by rushing hordes of larger fish and lobos, and from above by hysterical flocks of birds who threw themselves into the churning mess until the water was alive with the anchovies, larger fish, and birds. In between the areas of carnage the surface of the sea was coated with white acres of fresh droppings from other gorged flocks that hovered overhead. We could see no land, but we knew the bird islands were close at hand. The birds about us were new to us. The great Humboldt pelican, so different from the little brown tropical pelican of Panama, Ecuador, and elsewhere. Streaming flocks of cormorants. Javelin-like piqueros. The gulls that followed our wake were Antarctic gulls, new to us. The flying fish were gone, and the rays and the tropical birds we knew so well : the magnificent fork-tailed man-o'-war, the lovely bo'sun bird . . . these had strayed down with us into the thinning waters of the Humboldt along the coast as far as Peru. But now we were in the real domain of the current and they were with us no longer.

We were fifty miles offshore, but dozens, almost hundreds of little Peruvian fishing boats with their Arabian dhow sails were about us—little open boats, not fit for heavy weather. A little water and food aboard—fifty miles offshore ! But they have nothing to fear. Nature here is kind. The land breeze at night takes them out part way, the virazon* carries them where they want to go in the fishing grounds, and will bring them home again. Never a strong offshore wind to bring danger. Never a storm to upset the plan of their lives. For all days are alike in the Humboldt . . . the gentle night wind, the morning calm, misty, with a dreamy mirage quality like the Arabian coast of the Red Sea, then the virazon—always from southerly quarters—starting unassuming enough, but working up to considerable proportions in the afternoon, reefing strength at times, and then the peaceful calm of the evening. The fishing boats often stay out for days, working constantly to windward when they can, to balance the current, drifting to a sea anchor occasionally, when it is calm or when the virazon blows too strong. They often fish by night when the sea is calm—drawing their seines around the fiery phosphorescent areas of fish. And then when they are ready they lift their sails and slant away across the current back home again with holds full of drying fish. Theirs is a strange, calm, placid life, filled with a sureness unknown to most fishermen the world over. Like a cog partaking of the regularity of a well-oiled mechanism, they have fitted themselves into the scheme of things, perfectly in tune with their world.
(*4°S; 82°W to about 8°S; 80°W.*)

> (William Albert Robinson : *Voyage to Galapagos*).

Warm Current : the Equatorial Current
PACIFIC OCEAN : OCEAN ISLAND

OCEAN ISLAND lies only fifty-two miles south of the equator, and in the full rush of the equatorial current, which, streaming across the mid-Pacific from east to west, runs past the island

*Sea-breeze.

with a varying strength of from one to three miles an hour. . . .

There can be no reasonable question as to the origin of the native population of Ocean Island. They come from the central islands of the Gilbert Group, most probably drifted away from thence by the current, which, running at its strongest, would carry them over the 240 miles which separate the islands from Abemama in about four days. Since Ocean Island is high, compared to any land in the Gilbert Group, and would be visible from a canoe for about sixteen miles, it is probable that it has been the saving of many a lost crew of natives, who used to be carried away by the equatorial current in incredible numbers. During a year, 1896 to 1897, in which I lived on two of the Gilbert Islands, almost under the equator, no less than twenty-seven natives were lost from these two islands alone in this fashion, nor were any of them ever heard of again. The names of the present inhabitants of Ocean Island are purely Gilbertine in form, . . . and one name seems to be very significant. It is that of a woman, Nei Tematemaimarawa, or " Miss the Corpse from the Sea".
(*1°S; 170°E.*) (*Blackwood's Magazine*, No. MCXLI: "Ocean Island")

The Tide : Tidal Currents
THE BAHAMAS : INAGUA

THE FLOWING of a tide to anyone familiar with the sea, and with the least grain of perception, is an impelling and inspiring event. The tides of time are discernible only from a distance, but the surging of a sea tide is a potent and tangible happening. Perhaps the inexorable character of a tide is its impressive quality, but I think the emotional response to the occurence goes deeper than that. The newly-formed embryo of a human being bearing its tell-tale marks of ancient gill clefts harks back to the time when our ancestors, no matter how far removed, strove and battled fin and tail with the tide. If you have never leaned over a ship's rail and watched the soft swirl and eddy of the tide-urged water flowing past a rudder, you cannot fully appreciate what I mean. If you have, and were at all aware, you will know that the sight of a moving tide is a stimulating experience.

Here at my typewriter, far from the flow of moving water, the feel of a tide is a difficult emotion to catch and imprison on a sheet of paper. If a tide boomed and crashed like the surf it would not be so hard. But a tide is *silent* ; it cannot be heard except faintly when interrupted by a rudder or a ship's bow ; it cannot be smelled nor touched. A tide is best seen though it is more readily *sensed* than visualized. Its very vastness makes it difficult to grasp. In my mind's eye I see barren sand-bars lying idle in the sun with fiddler crabs moving about, or boats lying on their bellies in the sand ; I picture seaweeds trailing toward the mouth of a river, or whirlpools eddying about a buoy and I say " this is a tide." But it is not. These are only small manifestations of a tide. A complete tide is a stupendous awakening, a gargantuan breathing of the whole ocean, or a monstrous wave running the circuit of the earth extending from pole to pole. It is a swelling giant that sends millions of creeping fingers into the hollows of the land, bringing life to those hollows and as regularly withdrawing it again. A tide is the pulsing bosom of our planet. The Norsemen grasped the idea better than we when they believed it to be the breathing of the earth-serpent, Iörmungander, a monster so enormous that it encircled the globe and held its tail in its mouth to make room for that appendage.

> " Beneath the lashings of his tail
> Seas, mountain high, swelled on the land."

It was a tide that wrecked me on Inagua when I thought all danger from the ocean was past, and it was to the tide that I turned for one of the most entertaining days I spent on that island. Near Mathewtown, toward the south and in the direction of the opening of the Windward Passage, the coast of Inagua makes a last turn before sweeping away in a long spit toward the desolate frozen sand-dunes of the weather side of the island. At the last point of the turn the rock cliffs by the settlement crumble away, and a little beyond, the interminable arcs of the barrier reef take up their existence and fling away toward the infinite horizon. Here the full force of the tide, sweeping in twice a day from the wastes of the Atlantic Ocean and from the turbulent deeps of the blue Caribbean, meets in a boiling mass of currents and counter-currents. When all the remainder of the coast was calm and smooth this point was flecked with foam and with the peculiar lapping waves of tide-rips. The diving at this rendezvous of the seas promised to be good, so I lugged the heavy helmet with its hose and line down to a little shelf on the very edge of the breakers. Instead of diving from a boat I decided to crawl from dry land to the depths on foot, so that I might experience the full sensation of the transition from dry to wet and examine the structure of the cliff wall and its life on the way. A small oblique opening in the sloping rock made an easy entering wedge without making it necessary to battle the full force of the surf.

Swiftly I dropped into the wedge and entered the frothing line of bubbles. These hurled about in all directions, and I had to seize a rock to keep from being smashed against the sheer wall. The waves retreated and came plunging in again, forcing me to cling tightly, digging in toes and fingers like one of the *Grapsus* crabs against the swirling retreat. Six times I crouched against the onslaughts before there came a lull and I was able to step lightly into space and float downwards to a ledge eight or nine feet below. I had hardly landed when the seventh wave came in and I had to fall on my knees to keep a firm hold. Once more there came a period of quiet and again I jumped, pausing momentarily on a round mound of meandrina before I gave a final seven-league step and landed thirty feet below the surface on the level white sand at the base of the cliff that was the foundation of Inagua.

Catching my balance and my breath I looked about. Seaward a smooth plain of dazzling white sand levelled off into a blue immensity, dipping slightly at the point where it went out of vision. To the right the south-westernmost crags of the island lay piled in gigantic fashion, torn loose in great blocks by some heavy force. On the left a similar but smaller bluff jutted out into the azure world.

In order to take in the entire vista of the base of an island resting on its bed of sand, I moved forward toward the open plain and stepped from the shelter of the twin bluffs. Instantly and unexpectedly, I was met by a blast of water that threw me off my feet, rolling and twisting on my side over the smooth sand bottom. My helmet filled with bitter salt water. I gasped for breath and fought to stand erect. With a jerk I came to the end of the light rope that I was trailing between my fingers, then was startled to find myself yanked off my feet, and streamed out on the end of the line like a rag in the breeze. Fortunately my flight into open water brought me erect again, and with a final splash the liquid subsided in the helmet so that I was able to catch my breath once more. The savage current caught my lightly balanced body, swooped it in a great arc nearly to the surface, swirled me toward the shore, where it slackened and let me drop again on the sand.

Then I became aware that beyond the shelter of the crags a great assortment of objects was floating by at a dizzy rate. I had noticed them before but they had made no impression. Between the cliffs the current was barely perceptible except as a cool back eddy from the main stream. Once more I tried to breast the flow but was thrust back as if by a heavy hand. There was a solidity to the pressure that was unequalled by any other flow of energy with which I have experience. Wind in a violent storm pushes and buffets one about, but water moving at one-twentieth the speed of a gale of wind would level everything in its path and tear up the ground besides.

The sand out in the swath of the tide was moving too. Close to the bottom the grains were rolling and bumping, creating small dust storms—a strange phenomenon under water—and long curving ridges and valleys a foot or more in depth which formed in endless parallel arcs at right-angles to the course of the water. On a larger scale they were precisely like the smaller ripples seen on the mud-bars when the tide is out. The whole ocean bottom seemed on the move, as though it were alive and were creeping toward an unknown destination.

Crouching in the shelter of the outermost boulder, I made myself comfortable and sat down to contemplate this stupendous event. For it was exactly that. All along the hundreds of miles of coast all over the world this same action was taking place. Great rivers of liquid were surging past thousands of headlands into bays, creeks, rivers and lagoons, over shallow bars and in the hollows of deep channels, rolling countless sand grains and bringing oxygen, food, life and death to millions of swarming creatures. I remembered another tide I had watched in the murky green waters of the Chesapeake Bay in Maryland. In comparison to this Inaguan tide it was a dull, slow affair, but before I was through witnessing it from the windows of a steel cylinder hung from a barge anchored in the mouth of the Patuxent River near Solomons Island, I was completely overwhelmed at the mass of life it had brought past my small sphere of vision. The Chesapeake tide, however, had none of the gigantic sweep and force of this Inaguan occurrence. It was a small-scale flow, performed in a landlocked bay. This, of Inagua, was a full-fledged deep-sea current with the pressure of two immense oceans forcing it on. While I watched, it increased

117

in intensity until even the backwaters of my quiet eddy began to circle and tug at my bare flesh. The algæ on the outer rocks were all streamed in one direction, straining at their fastenings as though they would momently tear loose. There was none of the gentle swaying and graceful undulations of the sea-fans that I had seen on the reef. The actions of the marine plants and organisms gave the impression that a vast underwater hurricane was brewing, and that they would all be shorn away into the blue abyss beyond. Some of them had been pulled from their anchorages, for large heads of orange-coloured algæ went swirling past and were lost in the haze. Clinging to one of them was the curved, ringed torso of a spotted sea-horse and the saffron-coloured carapace of a small crab. They were battling bravely to maintain their positions on the rotating fronds, but they were probably going to a certain death. By this time the chill of moving water began to penetrate every fibre of my being. Some of the current seemed to be welling up from the depths, for it carried bands of warm and cold. As the tide increased the cold became more pronounced until I was shivering. So I called a recess for a half-hour.

When I again dropped below a great change had taken place. The current had become so violent that I had difficulty in keeping my position, even in the shelter of the boulders. Practically all the fish had disappeared. Those that were still about were swimming close to the rocks or were snuggled down in depressions where they were slowly undulating their tails. . . . The water had become a veritable avalanche and its speed was so great that even the fish did not consider it prudent to fight against it, but took refuge in a philosophical retreat.

I did not descend again until just a few minutes before the tide began to change. The water which had flowed so swiftly before was barely moving. It was nearing the full flood. The aqueous dust storms had all subsided and the limit of visibility had extended thirty feet or more. Only the long curving rows of sand ripples remained to remind one of the deluge. I could stand without danger of being swept away.

In ten minutes all motion ceased and a perfect calm settled over everything, except at the surface where the waves still rolled over the rocks. The greatest change, however, was in the fishes. They no longer hung hidden in deep holes or lay quiescent in hollows on the bottom. The grunts were back again from their indefinite errands, though the amber-jacks that pursued them did not return. Most of the fish were busily feeding.

For a half-hour the water at the base of the submarine cliff remained quiet and motionless. The fishes glided about, moving and turning in an easy, effortless way. Then faintly, imperceptibly, the tide began to swing. At first I did not notice it, so gently did it start. But soon I became aware that the algæ no longer drooped listlessly. They began to point their delicate fronds in the direction of the distant and invisible island of Mariguana. I noticed that the sea-fans on the rocks were bending too, and that, unlike the sea-fans on the great reef, they were all aligned at right-angles to the shore instead of parallel to it. Here the tide, not the surf, was the dominating force. Out on the sand the long ripples began to re-form, reversing the position of their slopes, gradual on the upstream side, steep on the lee. The parrots, demoiselles, and other rock-feeding species began to drift over to the sheltered side of the boulders, where they temporarily resumed their interrupted feeding. The easy relaxation of the past half-hour began to disappear. The underwater gale was approaching, and in preparation the fishes, and even some of the invertebrates, including a half-dozen wandering hermit-crabs, began to vanish into little holes or fissures where they drifted into that wide-awake yet apparently restful sleep of the creatures without eyelids. I could not help but wonder what sort of perilous life the creatures of this outermost point must lead, for ever hedged in by marauding, patrolling enemies, limited above by the boiling surf, and twice daily forced to battle, or sustain, an almost irresistible deluge of flooding water. I was reminded of the people of Flanders, or of Alsace, who are periodically overwhelmed by floods of conquest or counter-conquest, who bravely or hopefully continue living there, building new homes to replace those destroyed by shells or gutted by flames, and who after a time see them destroyed once more, and are faced with the necessity of doing it all over again. Yet the comparison is not a completely true one, for a sea-tide is a river of life, not of death, a manifestation of nature which is a normal state of affairs for millions of creatures all over the world.

(*21°N; 73°30'W.*)   (Gilbert C. Klingel : *Inagua.*)

The Tide

GERMANY : ELBE ESTUARY

SO BEHOLD us, then, at eight o'clock on October 5th, standing down the river towards the field of our first labours. It is fifteen miles to the mouth ; drab, dreary miles like the dullest reaches of the lower Thames ; but scenery was of no concern to us, and a south-westerly breeze blowing out of a grey sky kept us constantly on the verge of reefing. The tide as it gathered strength swept us down with a force attested by the speed with which buoys came in sight, nodded above us and passed, each boiling in its eddy of dirty foam. I scarcely noticed at first—so calm was the water, and so regular were the buoys, like milestones along a road—that the nor-thern line of coast was rapidly receding and that the " river " was coming to be but a belt of deep water skirting a vast estuary, three—seven—ten miles broad, till it merged in open sea.

" Why, we're at sea ! " I suddenly exclaimed, " after an hour's sailing ! "

" Just discovered that ? " said Davies, laughing.

" You said it was fifteen miles," I complained.

" So it is, till we reach this coast at Cuxhaven ; but I suppose you may say we're at sea ; of course that's all sand over there to starboard. Look ! Some of it's showing already."

He pointed into the north. Looking more attentively I noticed that outside the line of buoys patches of the surface heaved and worked ; in one or two places streaks and circles of white were forming ; in the midst of one such circle a sleek mauve hump had risen, like the back of a sleeping whale. The tide whirled us down, and, our straining canvas aiding it, we were soon off Cuxhaven, which crouched so low behind its mighty dyke, that of some of its houses only the chimneys were visible. Then, a mile or so on, the shore sharpened to a point like a claw, where the innocent dyke became a long, low fort, with some great guns peeping over ; then of a sudden it ceased, retreating into the far south in a dim perspective of groins and dunes.

We spun out into the open and leant heavily over to the now unobstructed wind. The yacht rose and sank to a little swell, but my first impression was one of wonder at the calmness of the sea, for the wind blew fresh and free from horizon to horizon.

" Why, it's all sand there now, and we're under the lee of it,"

said Davies, with an enthusiastic sweep of his hand over the sea
on our left, or port, hand. " That's our hunting ground."

* * * * *

The yacht was motionless, and the water round her visibly
lower. Petulant waves slapped against her sides, but, scattered as
my senses were, I realised that there was no vestige of danger.
Round us the whole face of the waters was changing from moment
to moment, whitening in some places, yellowing in others, where
breadths of sand began to be exposed. Close on our right the
channel we had left began to look like a turbid little river ; and
I understood why our progress had been so slow when I saw its
current racing back to meet the Elbe. Davies was already below,
laying out a more than usually elaborate lunch, in high content of
mind.

" Lies quiet, doesn't she ? " he remarked. " If you *do* want a
sit-down lunch, there's nothing like running aground for it."

* * * * *

The yacht lay with a very slight heel (thanks to a pair of small
bilge-keels on her bottom) in a sort of trough she had dug for
herself, so that she was ringed with a few inches of water, as it
were with a moat.

For miles in every direction lay a desert of sand. To the north
it touched the horizon, and was only broken by the blue dot of
Neuerk Island and its lighthouse. To the east it seemed also to
stretch to infinity, but the smoke of a steamer showed where it
was pierced by the stream of the Elbe. To the south it ran up to
the pencil-line of the Hanover shore. Only to the west was its
outline broken by any vestiges of the sea it had risen from. There
it was astir with crawling white filaments, knotted confusedly at
one spot in the north-west, whence came a sibilant murmur like
the hissing of many snakes. Desert as I call it, it was not entirely
featureless. Its colour varied from light fawn, where the highest
levels had dried in the wind, to brown or deep violet, where it was
still wet, and slate-grey where patches of mud soiled its clean
bosom. Here and there were pools of water, smitten into ripples
by the impotent wind ; here and there it was speckled by shells
and seaweed. And close to us, beginning to bend away towards that
hissing knot in the north-west, wound our poor little channel,
mercilessly exposed as a stagnant, muddy ditch with scarcely
a foot of water, not deep enough to hide our small kedge-anchor,

which perked up one fluke in impudent mockery. The dull, hard sky, the wind moaning in the rigging as though crying in despair for a prey that had escaped it, made the scene inexpressibly forlorn.

Davies scanned it with gusto for a moment, climbed to a point of vantage on the boom, and swept his glasses to and fro along the course of the channel.

" The only way to learn a place like this," he shouted, " is to see it at low water. The banks are dry then, and the channels are plain."

(53°50′N; 8°30′E.)   (Erskine Childers : *The Riddle of the Sands*.)

Sea-Ice and the Polar Current

EAST GREENLAND

OUR IDEAS regarding the origin, formation and course of drift ice were at that time, i.e. in 1882, still very defective. The voyage of the " Fram " in 1893–1896 was the main factor in giving us the more complete knowledge of its entire life history that we now possess.

It is formed on the surface in the Polar Sea and the Northern Arctic Sea. It is in constant drift over those waters, and later on melts in the sea. Large quantities of drift ice are borne away by wind and current from the sea north of Siberia, Bering Strait and Alaska, over the sea around the North Pole, and to the north of Franz Josef's Land and Spitzbergen. They then come south through the opening between Greenland and Spitzbergen, and borne by the the East Greenland Polar current they drift past Jan Mayen, as a rule between the latter and the east coast of Greenland.

In these southern latitudes the temperature becomes too high for the ice during the summer, so that it melts more and more the farther it proceeds to the south. The stream of ice, therefore, becomes narrower by degrees. It continues southward through Denmark Strait between Greenland and Iceland, where it meets the warmer water of the Atlantic. The Polar Current narrows, the masses of ice become smaller, and steadily diminish in width along the southern east coast of Greenland.

The last remnant of this drift ice bends round Cape Farewell, and to the west and north-west along the south-west coast of Greenland.

During the whole of its long voyage, for five or six years, from the Siberian Sea and the regions north of Bering Strait and Alaska, to the southern point of Greenland, the drift ice undergoes constant changes. It is formed, grows, is broken up, is massed together by wind and current, it diminishes in size and finally disappears.

These masses of ice are formed out at sea, whether the latter be shallow or deep, and they do not to any appreciable extent come from the land or from the sea near the coasts.

As regards ice-bergs, i.e. those originating in glaciers, there are practically none in the whole of the Polar Sea. They are first met with off the east coast of Greenland, where they enter the sea from the enormous glaciers that rise from the huge Inland Ice.

Some icebergs are also formed from the glaciers of Spitzbergen, Franz Josef's Land and Nova Zembla, but they are not large, and as a rule are not encountered outside the neighbourhood of those countries. They rarely join the ice masses in the East Greenland Polar Current.

There is also relatively speaking no large quantity of river ice in the Polar Sea. It is true that every summer large quantities of ice are carried out into the sea from the Siberian rivers, but these are quite small as compared with the immense tracts of Polar ice. In addition, a great deal of river ice melts in summer in the sea near the coast of Siberia, where there is then open water at a great distance from land.

When autumn approaches and the sun sinks lower in the heavens, the open parts of the sea in these northern regions become covered with ice. As by degrees the sun sinks, and darkness begins to fall upon those vast tracts of sea, and the long clear Polar night slowly deepens, the surface of this covering of ice constantly radiates heat into space, and the formation of ice rapidly augments. But the newly formed covering of ice on channels and open spaces is broken into pieces by wind and tide ; and by violent pressure is jammed together and piled up into hummocks and ridges, whilst at other times or in other places large open spaces and channels like open lakes are formed in the ice. But this open water is soon covered again by thick new ice, which in the course of a day or a night may increase many centimetres in thickness, and after a few hours will bear a man.

This ice is again broken up and once more massed together.

Open water is once more formed and this again is covered with ice, and the process thus continues day after day, week after week, throughout the winter.

Sometimes there is a lull for long periods, and the new ice which is formed on the open spaces has time to grow thick and strong into huge surfaces that are not easily broken up when the pressure is resumed.

Whilst all this is going on the masses of ice are constantly drifting and zig-zagging as they slowly proceed month after month, year after year, across the Polar Sea.

In winter the drift snow is blown across the surface of the ice, and is collected by the rough surface of the ridges and hummocks, and little by little it is packed together by the wind and becomes hard. The snow thus helps to level out these ridges and hummocks, but as only a little snow falls in the cold Polar atmosphere, there is not sufficient to form a smooth covering, nor are snow storms very violent or frequent in the Polar seas. On the other hand, towards the periphery of the latter there may be heavier snow-falls and higher winds.

In summer the sun shines upon the surface of the ice and first melts the snow, and then large parts of the ice itself, especially of the ridges and hummocks, which thereby become smaller and more rounded.

On account, however, of the low temperature long retained by the ice in the deeper strata beneath the surface, new layers of ice are still formed on the under surface and this may continue into the summer. Early in autumn the temperature again falls, the melting on the surface ceases and the cold begins to penetrate the ice, which in the course of the winter again increases in thickness.

When the snow melts on the surface of the ice and also when the upper layers of ice melt, there are formed on the floes large pools of almost fresh water, and from these sealers and whalers obtain their supplies of water both for cooking and drinking and also for their engines if they do not use sea water in them.

In the manner described above, by freezing on the under side, mostly in winter and spring, and melting on the upper surface every summer, the ice lives on year after year. In these immense fields of drifting ice we therefore find ice-floes of all ages, from the newly frozen ice on the open channels, which is perhaps only an

124

inch thick and will scarcely bear the weight of a man, to the huge floes several years old, and the enormous hummocks that may rise fifteen or twenty, sometimes, perhaps, even twenty-five or thirty feet above the water, and which go down one hundred and fifty or two hundred and at times two hundred and thirty, or perhaps two hundred and sixty feet below the surface of the water.

The older the ice becomes in those northern Polar seas, the thicker it grows, and by direct freezing, without the floes being jammed together or piled up on one another, they may after three or four years become ten feet thick, or possibly even more. But not all the floes or ordinary Polar ice are so thick, since the majority are of more recent formation. On the other hand, many floes consist of piled up ice, and may then be much thicker.

As by degrees the ice reaches the gap between Greenland and Spitzbergen and farther south, it is driven towards the west along the coast of Greenland. This is due to the rotation of the earth, which causes all currents in the northern hemisphere to be deflected towards the right, the more markedly so the farther northward we proceed. In the course of its drift southward, therefore, a broad belt of Polar ice follows the banks of the coast of Greenland.

But besides this ice which comes from the north, large masses of ice are formed in these regions between Spitzbergen, Iceland and Greenland, and these may cover the sea to a wide extent east of the edge of the true Polar ice.

Of course there may also be found scattered amongst this ice older floes and hummocks which have come from farther north, but the real Polar ice, the élite of the Polar current, is not encountered in great masses until we come farther in towards the east coast of Greenland.

In the formation of the younger ice on the outskirts of the Polar Current in the sea between Spitzbergen and Jan Mayen and Iceland, there enters a new factor that does not play any part farther north in the Polar Sea. This is the swell which comes rolling up from the open sea in through the ice, and which little by little is subdued by the floes, so that it is no longer noticeable at some distance in from the edge of the ice. This movement breaks up the ice into floes.

If we go far in, where the movement of the sea does not reach, the floes may be of huge dimensions, perhaps half a mile or more in length, and this is what sealers call " unbroken ice."

But the farther we proceed towards the outer edge, the smaller the floes become, and out there when the sea is in movement they are broken up and smashed against each other into a brash of ice that may cover the sea for a great distance outwards. This brash breaks the movement of the sea, and as by degrees the belt becomes broader, it protects the ice within against attack. In winter or spring, when it is cold, this brash again freezes into a firm covering, as soon as the sea becomes quiet.

We must not think of the edge of the drifting masses of ice as a straight line. It may of course be so to a certain extent, when wind and sea pack the ice tightly together, and it may then be difficult for vessels to penetrate into the ice. But if it is calm or the wind comes from the ice, the latter slowly moves outward. Promontories of floes creep out to sea, and deep bays are formed. Long open lanes and channels may appear in the ice, and " streams " may be torn quite loose and driven out to sea as separate fields of ice in strips that usually consist of small, comparatively thin floes that little by little are broken up by the waves into brash. But into all these bays and open lanes, and through these promontories, the sealer forces his way in order to find seals.

(Fridtjof Nansen : *Hunting and Adventure in the Arctic*.)

Icebergs
OFF CAPE HORN
" Cutty Sark," 1892, homeward bound from Australia

GOOD WEATHER did not last. Almost at once, an icy, clinging fog enveloped the ship. Sharp lookout was kept ; and several gigantic icebergs were sighted, drifting past in giant procession. It grew very cold—and we apprentices had reason to know it, handling the board-stiff canvas with our broken nails. Sleet and snow whipped the ship steadily ; and through the thick white flakes and the drifting spume we got terrifying glimpses of constant lines of bergs, standing high above our 150-feet topmast and completely dwarfing us, there being sometimes thirty or more in sight on each side at once.

The slapping green sea struck the sides of the bergs, some of which were 400 feet high (an average church spire is about 60 feet), and burst into fountains of sea and foam that shot up with intolerable concussion far above the top of the dark ice.

Modern huge Atlantic liners heave-to when icebergs are sighted, but we averaged 200 miles a day. The weather got worse and worse, but grim old Captain Woodget kept the canvas on her, and we swept southward steadily. He never left the deck. He seemed to dispense with sleep, and we trusted him, even with those immense mountains of ice crowding, like silent nightmare giants, all about us in the impenetrable fog.

It was a weird experience, going to the top of the mainmast into that clammy whiteness, sitting astride a yard yawing to and fro, unable even to see one's own hands, and pressed in by a silence broken only by the thunder of the seas on our hull, and the terrifying explosions and crackings, like stupendous crackling laughter, from icebergs shoving up beside us but quite invisible.
. . . In the midst of a great school of them, drifting on mysterious courses to uncharted fairy ports, hurrying on their way, now the top of this one gleaming like a single legendary diamond high above the fog, now a stupendous dark forefoot, sharp as a battleship's ram, stretching suddenly out from the clammy mists towards our frail side (and it was a touch from just such a frozen claw that later ripped the steel side clean out of the " unsinkable " ocean mammoth, *Titanic*), now on this side, now on that, our cockleshell boat twisted and fled like a minnow among the feet of a hurrying mob of sea-gods.

And, with the very voices of sea-gods, the vast bergs crackled and gobbled and thundered ; you could hear the breakers booming in their great caverns, and against their slippery sides, and the intolerable roaring of enormous waterfalls racing endlessly down from their pinnacles as they melted, and crashing tirelessly into the heaving sea.

Sometimes the sounds resembled great salvoes of artillery. At other times there would re-echo what seemed like the rattle of volleys of musketry from ghostly icemen fighting to the death. Again, the noise would growl past like sudden thunder. And then, in the midst of all, some twist of the helm, or a trick of the blanketing fog, would bring us to a pool of silence more ghastly and unnatural than all.

Some of the bergs, as they flashed past us, blinding bright in a sudden flicker of the Polar sun, rose in indescribably beautiful

127

fretted forms, like the ice-castles of the ancient Northern legends, and one looked for fairies and mermaids and white trolls dancing there. Others lumbered sullenly by like walking hills helplessly following a wicked wizard who had enchanted them into ever-lasting greenish darkness.

At one o'clock that day we passed a great berg that Captain Woodget wrote down in the ship's log to be over 1,000 feet out of the water. That meant that its total depth was about 10,000 feet—*three times the size of Snowdon, and a third the height of Mount Everest.*

We sailed *6 miles* along the side of the big berg, and Woodget entered that too. How long it was we never knew; as soon as the water was open enough we sheered thankfully away from it, and, for the first time that morning, we began to draw breath that did not come in uneasy and frozen gulps.

Woodget took several bearings of that floating world of ice, and estimated that, on one side, it was *19 miles long.*

I have never since felt the relief I experienced when we turned away from that big berg. Crowding silently in behind us along the narrow passage we had sailed had come a school of smaller bergs—smaller, but any one of them would have ripped the side out of *Cutty Sark* like paper. There was no turning back for us. If the ice had not cleared ahead we were all dead men.

As it was we were almost frozen men, the cold was so deadly and overwhelming.

When we were through at last we left behind us a sea of floating islands of ice many miles across. No one ever knew what had occurred in the silent, vasty solitudes of the Antarctic. Evidently a whole continent of ice had come adrift somewhere, and broken up, before nosing its way northwards; how we ever emerged from it all, it would take a better story-teller than I to explain. (*Approx. 55°S; 75°W.*)

(Captain G. Purssey Phillips : *Two Million Miles on Salt Water.*)

The Sea : Wave-action

AUG. 10th.—I was looking at high waves. The breakers always are parallel to the coast and shape themselves to it except where the curve is sharp however the wind blows. They are rolled out by the shallowing shore just as a piece of putty between the palms whatever its shape runs into a long roll. The slant ruck or crease in them shows the way of the wind. The regularity of the barrels surprised and charmed the eye ; the edge behind the comb or crest was as smooth and bright as glass. It may be noticed to be green behind and silver white in front : the silver marks where the air begins, the pure white is foam, the green solid water. Then looked at to the right or left they are scrolled over like mouldboards or feathers or jibsails seen by the edge. It is pretty to see the hollow of the barrel disappearing as the white combs on each side run along the wave gaining ground till the two meet at a pitch and crush and overlap each other.

About all the turns of the scaping from the break and flooding of the wave to its run out again I have not yet satisfied myself. The shores are swimming and the eyes have before them a region of milky surf but it is hard for them to unpack the huddling and gnarls of the water and law out the shapes and the sequence of the running : I catch however the looped or forked wisp made by every big pebble the backwater runs over—if it were clear and smooth there would be a network from their overlapping, such as can in fact be seen on smooth sand after the tide is out ; then I saw it run browner, the foam dwindling and twitched into long chains of suds, while the strength of the backdraught shrugged the stones together and clocked them one against another.

Aug. 16th.—We rose at four when it was stormy and I saw duncoloured waves leaving trailing hoods of white breaking on the beach. Before going I took a last look at the breakers, wanting to make out how the comb is morcelled so fine into string and tassel, as I have lately noticed it to be. I saw big smooth flinty waves, carved and scuppled in shallow grooves, much swelling when the wind freshened, burst on the rocky spurs of the cliff at the little cove and break into bushes of foam. In an enclosure of rocks the peaks of the water romped and wandered and a light crown of tufty scum standing high on the surface kept slowly turning round : chips of it blew off and gadded about without weight in the air. At eight we sailed for Liverpool in wind and rain. I think it is the salt that makes rain at sea sting so much. I did not look much at the sea : the crests I saw ravelled up by the wind into the air in arching whips and straps of glassy spray and higher broken into clouds of white and blown away. Under the curl shone a bright juice of beautiful green. The foam exploding and smouldering under water makes a chrysoprase green. (*Isle of Man.*)

Aug. 13th.—Heavy seas : we walked along the seawall to the Kennaway Tunnel to watch them. The wave breaks in this order—the crest of the barrel " doubling " (that, a boatman said, is the word in use) is broken into a bush of foam, which, if you search it, is a lace and tangle of jumping sprays ; then breaking down these grow to a sort of shaggy quilt tumbling up the beach ; thirdly this unfolds into a sheet of clear foam and running forward in leaves and laps the wave reaches its greatest height upon the shore and at the same time its greatest clearness and simplicity ; after that, raking on the shingle and so on, it is forked and torn and, as it commonly has a pitch or lurch to one side besides its backdraught, these rents widen : they spread and mix and the water clears and escapes to the sea transparent and keeping in the end nothing of its white except in long dribble bubble-strings which trace its set and flow.—The shore here is not pebbly but sand and in some places a fine red grit hardly to be called sand, when wet of a rich maroon, fallen from the red cliffs, which are richly tapestried with bramble, traveller's-joy I think, and ivy and other things. The colour of the breakers registered the nature of the earth they were over—mostly brown, then a wandering streak or stain of harsh clayey red.   (*Teignmouth.*)

(*The Notebooks and Papers of Gerard Manley Hopkins.*)

Waves

LOOKING AT the combers from below I was interested to observe that it was the wave form that moved, not the water itself ; the great bulk of the liquid seemed to throb forward slightly, but always came back to its original station. I ascertained this by watching some floating bumpers* that hung close to the watery ceiling. Only in the last few yards did the inverted wave-mounds fling themselves in their entirety at the cliff. In the open the wave-shapes advanced ceaselessly ; their power seemed to be transmitted from particle to particle, but the particles remained in their relative positions. Were this not so the destruction that would be wreaked on the land would be so tremendous that the islands and the continents would be quickly eaten away.

(*21°N; 73°30'W.*)   (Gilbert C. Klingel : *Inagua.*)

*Bumpers : A species of fish.

ISLANDS

Coral Atolls

Where the sea-egg flames on the coral and the long-backed
breakers croon
Their endless ocean legends to the lazy, locked lagoon.
(Rudyard Kipling : *The English Flag.*)

" Delectable mountains hung in air, and far-seen islands that
shine like jewels in the circumambient waste."
(Dr. L. P. Jacks : *Among the Idol-makers.*)

AS IF beaten flat by the tremendous sun, the atolls hug the sea.
A ship may pass within a few miles of many of them without
sighting them, and years may pass before some of them are
visited, save by fishermen blown from their courses or inhabitants
of more frequented islands in search of sea-birds' eggs. Tiny and
unregarded, these little worlds bask in the sun as the years pass
over leaving them virtually unchanged.
(Clifford Gessler : *The Leaning Wind.*)

Coral Atoll: the Milli Atoll

MARSHALL ISLANDS

THE NAME Atoll is of Maldive origin. The potentate who rules
over that group styles himself " Sultan of the Thirteen Atollons
and Twelve Thousand Isles." In one sense the title is only a mild
Oriental exaggeration, each Atollon consisting of a salt-water
lagoon and a number of islets—sometimes a very large number—
strung together at irregular intervals on the narrow surface of
the surrounding coral reef. The islet-covered reef hems in the
deep lagoon which it has cut off from the surrounding ocean. Its
characteristic features are the steepness and great depth of the
reef-walls, and the narrowness, flatness, and low level of the
islets formed upon its surface. Few lagoons are less than ten miles
long and three or four miles broad. The majority are much larger,
some being of great size. The lagoon of Naira in the Paumotus is
described by Dr. Dana as fifty miles long and twenty broad. The

Buster did not call at Naira, but did so at Milli (in the Marshall Archipelago), which will be a good illustration of one of these larger lagoons.

The Milli atoll, about thirty miles long and twelve to fifteen broad, cannot be seen from a ship's deck in the clearest weather at a greater distance than ten to twelve miles. Even then it is only the tops of the tall cocoanut-trees on the islets that are visible. The land is about twelve feet above the sea, as a rule, but in some parts a few feet higher. Approaching Milli, the long line of breakers is discerned as the ocean beats with fury upon the outer edge of the massive reef. A narrow brown line gradually coming into view, marks the belt of shallow water, a couple of hundred yards wide, covering the surface of the reef between the breakers and the white beaches of pure coral sand which border the little islets on the reef. The houses of the natives, picturesque and cool, soon peep out from the thick green cocoanut groves. Walk straight through these groves for 150 to 300 yards as the case may be, and you will have crossed the island and find yourself in face of the deep blue water of the lagoon, with another intervening brown belt of shallow water similar to that on the ocean side of the reef.

The reef which encloses the Milli lagoon is still bare, at intervals, to the extent probably of a third of its area. Rarely are these intervals fordable on any lagoon reef as the sea rolls over them freely into the enclosed area. On the other two-thirds of the Milli reef the ocean has formed, from coral *débris*, many islets varying in length but seldom attaining 300 to 500 yards at their greatest breadth. So near the level of the ocean and covered with stately palms whose crested heads tower above the few trees that find a home among them, the islets scattered on the reef between the deep blue ocean on the one side and the deep blue lagoon on the other, lie like a chaplet of emeralds set in a sapphire sea. The beauty of the coral gardens formed in the clear pools on the seaward face of a reef has been often described. Assuming every shape of miniature shrub and tree and with fish of dazzling colour and of varied hue darting to and fro among the branches, these fairylike gardens, once seen, can never be forgotten. But they are not common, and can only exist in clear deep pools with a perennial supply of the freshest and purest sea-water pouring into them.

The narrowness of the land makes the climate of these islands cool and, for a tropical latitude, delightful. Truth compels me to add that thing of beauty though it be, a lagoon island has drawbacks even from an æsthetic point of view. There are no hills, no valleys, no running streams, no land birds, very few flowers and none of the features which in other lands stimulate the imagination and make life beautiful. The effect is shown by their barrenness in tradition and legend so plentiful among the same races inhabiting the high volcanic islands.

In his natural state, the wants of the lagoon islander are few. For food there is always the cocoanut, and in the larger the breadfruit and Jack fruit ; while all have the Pandanus of which the natives are extremely fond. The singular cones of the Pandanus are chewn for the sweet juice, or the substance, extracted by maceration, is formed into long bands which make a not unpleasant confection. The sea and the lagoon abound with fish, tasteless and insipid to the inhabitants of a colder clime but regarded by these people as delicious and often eaten raw when caught. They have their feasts of turtle and, on the whole, lead a joyous, contented life, marred only by failures in the cocoanut crop, by the tyranny and cruelty of a chief, or by the ravages of fell disease.

Civilized or uncivilized, the water question must become a serious one on these low flat islands. Ponds are dug out of the coral rock or hollows cut in the cocoanut trees and the rain is collected in them. The rocky ponds are also used as bathing places and the natives drink the water without, it is said, suffering the ill effects which a European would anticipate. Groups of all ages and both sexes may be seen disporting themselves in these stagnant pools and occasionally one of the number will sweep the scum from the surface and drink a handful of the dirty tepid fluid below. Some day, fever and dysentery will avenge poor outraged nature but no instance of mischief has yet been known. The purifying character of the limestone may have something to do with past immunity, but the conditions of life—the food, clothing, and personal habits—have within the last few years much changed among these people. Their chief drink has hitherto been the cool and bright fluid contained in the green cocoanut ; but the enormous numbers so used materially affected the production of copra, only to be made from the ripe nut in which the fluid is neither so abundant nor palatable. Hence, the use of water is becoming more common and the erection of cisterns to hold a proper supply will be one of the first economical and sanitary reforms to be undertaken.

(Frederick J. Moss : *Through Atolls and Islands in the Great* *(6°N; 172°E.)*   *South Sea*, 1889.)

Coral Atolls

SOUTH PACIFIC

IN NO quarter are the atolls so thickly congregated, in none are they so varied in size from the greatest to the least, and in none is navigation so beset with perils, as in that archipelago that we were now to thread. The huge system of the trades is, for some reason, quite confounded by this multiplicity of reefs ; the wind intermits, squalls are frequent from the west and south-west, hurricanes are known. The currents are, besides, inextricably intermixed ; dead reckoning becomes a farce ; the charts are not to be trusted ; and such is the number and similarity of these islands that, even when you have picked one up, you may be none the wiser. The reputation of the place is consequently infamous ; insurance offices exclude it from their field, and it was not without misgiving that my captain risked the *Casco* in such waters.

For a few days we sailed with a steady trade, and a steady westerly current setting us to leeward ; and toward sundown of the seventh it was supposed we should have sighted Takaroa, one of Cook's so-called King George Islands. I slept that night, as was then my somewhat dangerous practice, on deck upon the cockpit bench. A stir at last awoke me, to see all the eastern heaven dyed with faint orange, the binnacle lamp already dulled against the brightness of the day, and the steersman leaning eagerly across the wheel. " There it is, sir ! " he cried, and pointed in the very eyeball of the dawn. For a while I could see nothing but the bluish ruins of the morning bank, which lay far along the horizon, like melting icebergs. Then the sun rose, pierced a gap in these *débris* of vapours, and displayed an inconsiderable islet, flat as a plate upon the sea, and spiked with palms of disproportioned altitude.

So far, so good. Here was certainly an atoll ; and we were certainly got among the archipelago. But which ? And where ? The isle was too small for either Takaroa : in all our neighbour-

hood, indeed, there was none so inconsiderable, save only Tikei ;
and Tikei, one of Roggewein's so-called Pernicious Islands, seemed
beside the question. At that rate, instead of drifting to the west,
we must have fetched up thirty miles to windward. . . . Tikei
our island turned out to be ; and it was our first experience of
the dangerous archipelago, to make our landfall thirty miles out.

The sight of Tikei, thrown direct against the splendour of the
morning, robbed of all its colour, and deformed with disproportioned trees like bristles on a broom, had scarce prepared
us to be much in love with atolls. Later the same day we saw under
more fit conditions the island of Taiaro. *Lost in the Sea* is possibly
the meaning of the name. And it was so we saw it ; lost in blue
sea and sky : a ring of white beach, green underwood, and
tossing palms, gem-like in colour ; of a fairy, of a heavenly
prettiness. The surf ran all around it, white as snow, and broke
at one point, far to seaward, on what seems an uncharted reef.
There was no smoke, no sign of man ; indeed, the isle is not
inhabited, only visited at intervals.

The night fell lovely in the extreme. After the moon went down,
the heaven was a thing to wonder at for stars. And as I lay in
the cockpit and looked upon the steersman I was haunted by
Emerson's verses :

> " And the lone steersman all the night
> Sails astonished among stars."

By this glittering and imperfect brightness, about four bells in
the first watch we made our third atoll, Raraka. The low line
of the isle lay straight along the sky ; so that I was at first
reminded of a towpath, and we seemed to be mounting some
engineered and navigable stream. Here and there, but rarely,
faint tree-tops broke the level. And the sound of the surf accompanied us, now in a drowsy monotone, now with a menacing swing.

By daylight on the 9th we began to skirt Kauehi, and had
now an opportunity to see near at hand the geography of atolls.
Here and there, where it was high, the farther side loomed up ;
here and there the near side dipped entirely and showed a broad
path of water into the lagoon ; here and there both sides were
equally abased, and we could look right through the discontinuous
ring to the sea horizon on the south. Conceive, on a vast scale,
the submerged hoop of the duck-hunter, trimmed with green
rushes to conceal his head—water within, water without—you

have the image of the perfect atoll. Conceive one that has been partly plucked of its rush fringe ; you have the atoll of Kauehi. And for either shore of it at closer quarters, conceive the line of some old Roman highway traversing a wet morass, and here sunk out of view and there re-arising, crowned with a green tuft of thicket ; only instead of the stagnant waters of a marsh, the live ocean now boiled against, now buried the frail barrier. Last night's impression in the dark was thus confirmed by day, and not corrected. We sailed, indeed, by a mere causeway in the sea, of nature's handiwork, yet of no greater magnitude than many of the works of man.

The isle was uninhabited ; it was all green brush and white sand, set in transcendently blue water ; even the cocoa-palms were rare, though some of these completed the bright harmony of colour by hanging out a fan of golden yellow. For long there was no sign of life beyond the vegetable, and no sound but the con-tinuous grumble of the surf. In silence and desertion these fair shores slipped past, and were submerged and rose again with clumps of thicket from the sea. And then a bird or two appeared, hovering and crying ; swiftly these became more numerous, and presently, looking ahead, we were aware of a vast effervescence of winged life. In this place the annular isle was mostly under water, carrying here and there on its submerged line a wooded islet. Over one of these the birds hung and flew with an incredible density like that of gnats or hiving bees ; the mass flashed black and white, and heaved and quivered, and the screaming of the creatures rose over the voice of the surf in a shrill clattering whirr. As you descend some inland valley a not dissimilar sound announces the nearness of a mill and pouring river. Some stragglers, as I said, came to meet our approach ; a few still hung about the ship a we departed. The crying died away, the last pair of wings was left behind, and once more the low shores of Kauehi streamed past our eyes in silence like a picture. I supposed at the time that the birds lived, like ants or citizens, concentred where we saw them. I have been told since (I know not if correctly) that the whole isle, or much of it, is similarly peopled ; and that the effervescence at a single spot would be the mark of a boat's crew of egg-hunters from one of the neighbouring inhabited atolls. So that here at Kauehi, as the day before at Taiaro, the *Casco* sailed by under the fire of unsuspected eyes. And one thing is surely true, that even on these ribbons of land an army might lie hid and no passing mariner divine its presence.

By a little before noon we were running down the coast of our destination, Fakarava : the air very light, the sea near smooth ; though still we were accompanied by a continuous murmur from the beach, like the sound of a distant train. The isle is of a huge longitude, the enclosed lagoon thirty miles by ten or twelve, and the coral tow-path, which they call the land, some eighty or ninety miles by (possibly) one furlong. That part by which we sailed was all raised ; the underwood excellently green, the topping wood of cocoa-palms continuous—a mark, if I had known it, of man's intervention. For once more, and once more unconsciously, we were within hail of fellow-creatures, and that vacant beach was but a pistol-shot from the capital city of the archipelago. But the life of an atoll, unless it be enclosed, passes wholly on the shores of the lagoon ; it is there the villages are seated, there the canoes ply and are drawn up ; and the beach of the ocean is a place accursed and deserted, the fit scene only for wizardry and shipwreck, and in the native belief a haunting ground of murderous spectres.

By and by we might perceive a breach in the low barrier ; the woods ceased ; a glittering point ran into the sea, tipped with an emerald shoal, the mark of entrance. As we drew near we met a little run of sea—the private sea of the lagoon having there its origin and end, and here, in the jaws of the gateway, trying vain conclusions with the more majestic heave of the Pacific. The *Casco* scarce avowed a shock ; but there are times and circumstances when these harbour mouths of inland basins vomit floods, deflecting, burying, and dismasting ships. For, conceive a lagoon perfectly sealed but in the one point, and that of a merely navigable width ; conceive the tide and wind to have heaped for hours together in that coral fold a superfluity of waters, and the tide to change and the wind fall—the open sluice of some great reservoirs at home will give an image of the unstemmable effluxion.

We were scarce well headed for the pass before all heads were craned over the rail. For the water, shoaling under our board, became changed in a moment to surprising hues of blue and grey ; and in its transparency the coral branched and blossomed, and the fish of the inland sea cruised visibly below us, stained and striped, and even beaked like parrots. I have paid in my time to

139

view many curiosities ; never one so curious as that first sight over
the ship's rail in the lagoon of Fakarava. But let not the reader
be deceived with hope. I have since entered, I suppose, some
dozen atolls in different parts of the Pacific, and the experience
has never been repeated. That exquisite hue and transparency
of submarine day, and these shoals of rainbow fish, have not
enraptured me again.
(17°S; 146°W.)   (Robert Louis Stevenson : *In the South Seas.*)

Coral Atoll

LATITUDE 14:09 SOUTH

You ask me what it was like to be in that country
and I answer : The wind leaned always on the land
out of the sea, and life looked toward the sea.
It was good, there, to walk into morning
fresh as that wind : the tall, sea-leaning fronds
clashing aloft, and the clean new sunlight
washing the sanded street. And in that country
the tide of noon flowed gently up between
the houses plaited of leaves. Deep pools of shade
lay boldly-patterned and velvet-dark ; the mats
were kind to our bodies as the afternoon
ebbed gently. And at dark the fires of husk
glowed in the coral dooryards ; the low moon
hung melon-coloured, and the night was sown with stars.

Then dancing feet stirred pebbled sand, and all the songs
were love-songs. It was good as drink to rest
on the smooth mat when the cool-fingered evening
crept softly out of the sea. There was peace in that far country
where wind of night was a long caress to the sleeper—
and all the stars over that country were kind.

(Clifford Gessler : *The Leaning Wind.*)

Raised Atoll: Henderson Island
SOUTH PACIFIC

IN THE seagoing vocabulary of the Pacific there are three kinds of islands—high, low, and makatea. High and low islands are what their names imply: hilly or mountainous ones, usually of volcanic origin, and coral atolls, which are low and almost flat. A makatea island is an atoll that has been raised, so that it stands up well out of the sea and has been exposed to erosion. Any sailor of those seas will tell you that it's a difficult kind of island.

For the weather gnaws at the surface and the sea nibbles at the shore, forming a cavern-punctured coastline and an interior wilderness of jagged pinnacles and deep pits studded with murderous spears of razor-edged rock. The mixture of decomposed coral and the deposits of birds often forms an extraordinarily rich soil—indeed, several makatea islands, including the one named Makatea, north of Tahiti, are " mines " of commercial phosphate. The vegetation on such an island often forms an almost impenetrable jungle, hiding the pitfalls that lurk in the uneven surface of the land.

Such an island is Henderson. It rises eighty to a hundred feet from the sea, in a wedge-shaped mass about five miles long, tapering from a width of two and half miles at the north to a point at the south. Grayish cliffs gird it nearly all the way around, broken only by two narrow sandy beaches toward the north, one of them situated in a small cove, partly sheltered from the swells that were still mounting high as the *Islander* approached.

A few coconut palms stood in tropical disorder near the cove. At the top of the cliffs a dense wall of jungle barred the way, so thick that our party literally cut their way at every step. The botanists led, swinging with heavy cane knives and laying the course by a compass. So dense was the forest that, even on so small an island, one could have lost one's way. Zimmy climbed a tall tree, in an effort to get some general idea of the terrain, but the vegetation was so thick that he could not see the ground.

Nevertheless there were some barren areas—fantastic deserts where the bare gray makatea rose in pinnacles and spires, among six-foot pits whose bottoms and sides were eroded into sharp ridges and projections. These stalagmites, if one may call them that, rang like metal when one tapped on them with a knife blade or a stone.

Toward the interior the land sloped downward into a shallow bowl that marked the site of the vanished lagoon—now such a wilderness as I have just described. More than one pair of shoes were slashed to tatters on that harsh terrain, but the rewards, for collectors of flora and fauna, amply repaid the harsh going.

(Clifford Gessler : *The Leaning Wind*.)

Raised Atoll : Niué Island

SOUTH PACIFIC

THE FORMATION of the raised coral islands will now be more easily understood. The lagoon, probably shallow from the first, has been filled up and the whole island raised perhaps 200 feet above the sea. The reef now forms the coast of the island. Its abrupt sides seldom offer anchorage and are remarkable for the great blow-holes, formed of old caverns still connected with the ocean. Through these holes each advancing wave sends the water in lofty columns, forming gigantic fountains which fall back in showers of foam and rainbow spray into the sea. The coast of Niué abounds with these blow-holes, very beautiful when watched from the deck as one approaches the island on a quiet day.

(Frederick J. Moss : *Through Atolls and Islands in the Great South Sea*.)

Raised Atoll : Ocean Island

PACIFIC OCEAN

THE ISLAND is roughly round in shape, save for a bay which extends for about three-quarters of a mile along the southern face, and in which is the only natural landing-place for boats or canoes. The diameter is about the same, north and south and east and west, roughly 1½ mile, and the highest point is about 280 feet over the sea-level. The coral reef which clings closely to the coast all round the island is at no place more than 150 yards broad (in some places it is far narrower), and beyond the edge of the reef the water deepens very rapidly, the land running down at an angle of 45 degrees, so that at 1,200 feet horizontal distance from the shore there is a depth of 1,200 feet of water. A couple of miles out to sea there are probably 12,000 feet. Thus the island forms the almost circular top of a very steep and very symmetrical submarine mountain. It is plain that at one period even the summit must have been submerged, for the whole framework of the island is composed of coral, which occurs as plentifully on the higher levels as on the sea-beach. Moreover, the land appears to be rising, as seems to be shown by the very curious system of terraces, of which the first is formed by the present reef ; the next occurs at the height of about 150 feet, and runs all round the island ; whilst the top is almost quite flat, and about 250 feet above sea-level. The coastline is composed for the most part of a wellnigh impenetrable belt of the most curious coral pinnacles, about 30 feet in height, roughly conical, and weathered to the most extraordinary degree of sharpness. I have seen some pinnacles in this belt almost the shape of a church spire, and so sharply pointed that it would be painful to rest the hand heavily on the top. But these pinnacles are of every imaginable shape and size and form, round more than half the circumference of the island, and form a barrier, only traversed by two native tracks winding round the bases of these conical coral rocks like the paths in a maze, and showing distinct traces of the handiwork of man. Away from these two paths I have often tried to get through this natural barrier, but I have never been successful, and the ruin of my clothes and boots bore testimony to its nature. Above this fringe of pinnacles a gentle slope leads up to the first terrace, and the pinnacles, which are almost as numerous here as in the lower belt, are packed in a deep layer of pure phosphate. It is not until this is removed by digging that the tops of the coral pinnacles appear. Further excavation, generally by blasting, for an average depth of about 30 feet, brings one down to their basis and to the coral skeleton of the island. This skeleton itself is, however, not solid, but is pierced by countless galleries and caves of unknown extent and, in places, of great depth. I have known 600 feet of fishing-line to be lowered into one cavity without touching any bottom.

From this second terrace rises the final slope to the summit of the island, which is almost flat, the surface consisting of pure phosphate over the same formation of coral pinnacle. All over the island, except in the belt nearest to the reef, the interstices between the pinnacles are filled with phosphate, and in some cases the chemical action which has created this wonderful place has turned what appear to have once been pinnacles of pure coral into pure phosphate.

(*1°S;170°E.*) (*Blackwood's Magazine*, No. MCXLI: "Ocean Island".)

Islands: Skerryguard

NORWAY

SHORTLY AFTERWARDS the fog came on again, and next morning it was blowing very hard from the eastward. This was the more disagreeable, as it is always very difficult, under the most favourable circumstances, to find one's way into any harbour along this coast, fenced off, as it is, from the ocean by a complicated outwork of lofty islands, which, in their turn, are hemmed in by nests of sunken rock, sown as thick as peas, for miles to seaward. There are no pilots until you are within the islands, and no longer want them—no lighthouses or beacons of any sort ; and all that you have to go by is the shape of the hill-tops : but as, on the clearest day, the outlines of the mountains have about as much variety as the teeth of a saw, and as on a cloudy day, which happens about seven times a week, you see nothing but the line of their dark roots, the unfortunate mariner, who goes poking about for the narrow passage which is to lead him between the islands—at the *back* of one of which a pilot is waiting for him—will, in all probability, have already placed his vessel in a position to render that functionary's further attendance a work of supererogation. At least, I know it was as much surprise as pleasure that I experienced, when—after having with many misgivings ventured to slip through an opening in the monotonous barricade of mountains, we found it was the right channel to our port. If the king of all the Goths would only stick up a lighthouse here and there along the edge of his Arctic seaboard, he would save many an honest fellow a heartache.

(Lord Dufferin : *Letters from High Latitudes.*)

Islands : Lofoten Islands

NORWAY

THE FIRST morning glance through the cabin porthole at Lofoten reveals to the amazed eye, first of all, a strange multitude of boulders in the most varied configurations ; they are completely bald, and golden brown on the milky opal sheet of water, and only in places, from their armpits, tufts of wiry grass are sprouting ; pleasant round boulders worn smooth by the breakers, rock towers carved out by the storms, collections of stones, groups of ledges, or solitary stones; here and there a small lighthouse, or single tower, here and there an erection of very long poles, perhaps for drying cod; this then is Lofoten. And then one goes up on deck to see still more of it, and one perceives that up from this embroidery of boulders a bouquet of mountains sprouts to heaven.

A bouquet of mountains: you can't express it in any other way; and here you see that the world blossomed in granite before it could flower in bird-cherry and lilac. "And God said: Let the waters under the heaven be gathered together unto one place, and let the dry land appear: and it was so. And God called the dry land Earth; and the gathering together of the waters called He the Sea; and God saw that it was good." It was in fact very good, nay, just superb; in Lofoten, however, the dry land arose not in one place, but in a considerable number of places which God called Moskenesøy, Flakstadøy, Vestvegøy, and many other names, and He endowed them with a special power; and in those dry places boulders and rocks began to flourish as nowhere else in the world; and then mountains began to spring up like trees in a wood; there is granite enough so that they could grow as if of the water—in fact, they really do grow straight up from the water: some bushy like ashes, oaks and elms, and others high and steep like spruces, birches, or poplars ; and a garden of mountains was brought forth which is called Lofoten ; and it was good. You say, bare rock ; but it gives you more the impression of something brimming over, of terrible abundance and exuberance ; vain glory, every thoroughgoing creation works with a surplus, and without substantial phantasy even mountains cannot appear. Therefore you have to go as far as Lofoten to see what can be done with each material, even if it is material as heavy as granite, gneiss, biotite gneiss, and primordial schist.

(68°-69°N; 13°-16°E.)   (Karel Čapek : *Travels in the North.*)

145

Island : Jan Mayen

ARCTIC OCEAN

UP TO THIS time we had seen nothing of the island, yet I knew we must be within a very few miles of it ; and now, to make things quite pleasant, there descended upon us a thicker fog than I should have thought the atmosphere capable of sustaining ; it seemed to hang in solid festoons from the masts and spars. To say that you could not see your hand, ceased almost to be any longer figurative; even the ice was hid—except those fragments immediately adjacent, whose ghastly brilliancy the mist itself could not quite extinguish, as they glimmered round the vessel like a circle of luminous phantoms. The perfect stillness of the sea and sky added very much to the solemnity of the scene ; almost every breath of wind had fallen, scarcely a ripple tinkled against the copper sheathing, as the solitary little schooner glided along at the rate of half a knot or so an hour, and the only sound we heard was the distant wash of waters, but whether on a great shore, or along a belt of solid ice, it was impossible to say. In such weather—as the original discoverers of Jan Mayen said under similar circumstances—' it was easier to hear land than to see it.' Thus, hour after hour passed by and brought no change. Fitz and Sigurdr—who had begun quite to disbelieve in the existence of the island—went to bed, while I remained pacing up and down the deck, anxiously questioning each quarter of the grey canopy that invested us. At last, about four in the morning, I fancied some change was going to take place ; the heavy wreaths of vapour seemed to be imperceptibly separating, and in a few minutes more the solid roof of grey suddenly split asunder, and I beheld through the gap—thousands of feet overhead, as if suspended in the crystal sky—a cone of illuminated snow.

You can imagine my delight. It was really that of an anchorite catching a glimpse of the seventh heaven. There at last was the long-sought-for mountain actually tumbling down upon our heads. Columbus could not have been more pleased when, after nights of watching, he saw the first fires of a new hemisphere dance upon the water ; nor, indeed, scarcely less disappointed at their sudden disappearance than I was, when, after having gone below to wake Sigurdr, and tell him we had seen bona fide terra firma, I found, on returning upon deck, that the roof of mist had closed again, and shut out all trace of the transient vision. However, I had got a clutch of the island, and no slight matter should make me let go my hold. In the meantime there was nothing for it but to wait patiently until the curtain lifted ; and no child ever stared more eagerly at a green drop-scene in expectation of the ' realm of dazzling splendour ' promised in the bill, than I did at the motionless grey folds that hung round us. At last the hour of liberation came : a purer light seemed gradually to penetrate the atmosphere, brown turned to grey, and grey to white, and white to transparent blue, until the lost horizon entirely reappeared, except where in one direction an impenetrable veil of haze still hung suspended from the zenith to the sea. Behind that veil I knew must lie Jan Mayen.

A few minutes more, and slowly, silently, in a manner you could take no count of, its dusky hem first deepened to a violet tinge, then, gradually lifting, displayed a long line of coast—in reality but the roots of Beerenberg—dyed of the darkest purple ; while, obedient to a common impulse, the clouds that wrapt its summit gently disengaged themselves, and left the mountain standing in all the magnificence of his 6,870 feet, girdled by a single zone of pearly vapour, from underneath whose floating folds seven enormous glaciers rolled down into the sea ! Nature seemed to have turned scene-shifter, so artfully were the phases of this glorious spectacle successively developed.

Although,—by reason of our having hit upon its side instead of its narrow end,—the outline of Mount Beerenberg appeared to us more like a sugar-loaf than a spire—broader at the base and rounder at the top than I had imagined—in size, colour, and effect it far surpassed anything I had anticipated. The glaciers were quite an unexpected element of beauty. Imagine a mighty river of as great a volume as the Thames—started down the side of a mountain—bursting over every impediment—whirled into a thousand eddies—tumbling and raging on from ledge to ledge in quivering cataracts of foam—then suddenly struck rigid by a power so instantaneous in its action that even the froth and fleeting wreaths of spray have stiffened to the immutability of sculpture. Unless you had seen it, it would be almost impossible to conceive the strangeness of the contrast between the actual tranquillity of these silent crystal rivers and the violent descending energy impressed upon their exterior. You must remember, too, all this is upon a scale of such prodigious magnitude, that when we succeeded subsequently in approaching the spot—where with a leap like that of Niagara one of these glaciers plunges down into the sea—the eye, no longer able to take in its fluvial character, was content to rest in simple astonishment at what then appeared a lucent precipice of grey-green ice, rising to the height of several hundred feet above the masts of the vessel.

(71°N; 9°W.)   (Lord Dufferin : *Letters from High Latitudes*.)

Island : Teneriffe

CANARY ISLANDS

THE ISLAND of Teneriffe has the advantage of a very equable climate. It is neither too hot, too cold nor too windy. The object of our party when working there was to study the human subject when at rest. In Teneriffe this object is particularly easy of attainment. No one on the island, so far as my experience goes, either takes or wants to take any violent exercise. In the Alps no one has any other object than exercise in some form or other, but to walk up the Peak of Teneriffe would be only less peculiar than to make the ascent to Col d'Olen on a mule.

The island of Teneriffe consists roughly of a huge crater about 8,000–9,000 feet in height. The diameter from lip to lip is eight miles. On the south side of the island the lip is incomplete. The inside of the lip is a steep, not quite precipitous, cliff, down which you must climb for a thousand or two feet, unless you enter the crater as we did by a gap in the cliffs called the Portillio. We were then inside the old crater ; our back was to the cliff, which in places rises in named summits, Guajera and Espigone for instance. Our faces were towards a level plateau of sand.

From the description I have given so far it might be supposed that a sandy plain now stretched before our eyes, and that in the distance, six or seven miles away, we saw the opposite lip of the old crater in front of us. But this is not so, for the new crater, which has been thrust up from within the old, intervened ; the majestic Peak itself rising to an altitude of 12,000 feet burst suddenly upon us as we emerged from the Portillio. All that is left of the plateau is a ring of level sand in close proximity to the almost vertical lip of the old crater, on the outside of this ring rise the cliffs to about 1,000 feet in height, on the inside the gradual ascent of the Peak. It was on this sand that our station was placed. No place at this altitude could have been more sheltered by natural barriers. It was quite unlike any place to be seen in Europe. Compared with much higher altitudes in the Alps, the comparison is a very remarkable one. The complete dryness of the atmosphere at the Cañadas accounts for the lack of the beautiful vegetation which makes the Alpine snow line so attractive. Go out of the laboratory at Col d'Olen ; everything is moist underneath your feet, the cracks in the rock are filled with saxifrages and gentians. Not so at the Cañadas ; the vegetation at low altitudes in Teneriffe is no less beautiful than in the Alps. To get to the Portillio one must ride through woods of giant heath which rise seven or eight feet into the air and burst into blossom above the head. But moisture condenses into clouds which hang over the island in a sheet at an altitude of 4,000–5,000 feet—through these clouds one penetrates. Once arrived within the old crater a new climate has been reached. Between one and the clouds there is an impassable rampart. No vestige of mist was seen either above us or around us during our sojourn in Las Cañadas, the occasional appearance of a cloud-top above the lip of the crater was the only reminder that such a thing as a cloud existed. Above the clouds all is barren.

(*28°30'N; 16°30'W.*)

(Joseph Barcroft : *The Respiratory Function of the Blood.*)

EARTHQUAKES, VOLCANOES AND HOT SPRINGS

EARTHQUAKES, VOLCANOES AND HOT SPRINGS

Earth Tremor

JAMAICA

EXETER ROCKS is a famous place. A bay of the sea, almost a perfect semicircle, guarded by the reef : shelving white sands to span the few feet from the water to the undercut turf : and then, almost at the mid point, a jutting out shelf of rocks right into deep water—fathoms deep. And a narrow fissure in the rocks, leading the water into a small pool, or miniature lagoon, right inside their bastion. There it was, safe from sharks or drowning, that the Fernandez children meant to soak themselves all day, like turtles in a crawl. The water of the bay was as smooth and immovable as basalt, yet clear as the finest gin : albeit the swell muttered a mile away on the reef. The water within the pool itself could not reasonably be smoother. No sea-breeze thought of stirring. No bird trespassed on the inert air.

For a while they had not energy to get into the water, but lay on their faces, looking down, down, down, at the sea-fans and sea-feathers, the scarlet-plumed barnacles and corals, the black and yellow schoolmistress-fish, the rainbow-fish—all that forest of ideal christmas trees which is a tropical sea-bottom. Then they stood up, giddy and seeing black, and in a trice were floating suspended in water like drowned ones, only their noses above the surface, under the shadow of a rocky ledge.

An hour or so after noon they clustered together, puffy from the warm water, in the insufficient shade of a Panama fern : ate such of the food they had brought as they had appetite for ; and drank all the water, wishing for more. Then a very odd thing happened : for even as they sat there they heard the most peculiar sound : a strange rushing sound that passed overhead like a gale of wind—but not a breath of breeze stirred, that was the odd thing : followed by a sharp hissing and hurtling, like a flight of rockets, or gigantic swans—very distant rocs, perhaps—on the wing. They all looked up : but there was nothing at all. The sky was empty and lucid. Long before they were back in the water again all was still. Except that after a while John noticed a sort

153

of tapping, as if someone were gently knocking the outside of a bath you were in. But the bath they were in had no outside, it was solid world. It was funny.

By sunset they were so weak from long immersion they could barely stand up, and as salted as bacon : but, with some common impulse, just before the sun went down they all left the rocks and went and stood by their clothes, where the ponies were tethered, under some palms. As he sank the sun grew even larger : and instead of red was now a sodden purple. Down he went, behind the western horn of the bay, which blackened till its water-line disappeared and substance and reflection seemed one sharp symmetrical pattern.

Not a breath of breeze even yet ruffled the water : yet momentarily it trembled of its own accord, shattering the reflections : then was glassy again. On that the children held their breath, waiting for it to happen.

A school of fish, terrified by some purely submarine event, thrust their heads right out of the water, squattering across the bay in an arrowy rush, dashing up sparkling ripples with the tiny heave of their shoulders : yet after each disturbance all was soon like hardest, dark, thick glass.

Once things vibrated slightly, like a chair in a concert-room : and again there was that mysterious winging, though there was nothing visible beneath the swollen iridescent stars.

Then it came. The water of the bay began to ebb away, as if someone had pulled up the plug : a foot or so of sand and coral gleamed for a moment new to the air : then back the sea rushed in miniature rollers which splashed right up to the feet of the palms. Mouthfuls of turf were torn away : and on the far side of the bay a small piece of cliff tumbled into the water : sand and twigs showered down, dew fell from the trees like diamonds: birds and beasts, their tongues at last loosed, screamed and bellowed: the ponies, though quite unalarmed, lifted up their heads and yelled.

That was all : a few moments. Then silence, with a rapid countermarch, recovered all his rebellious kingdom. Stillness again. The trees moved as little as the pillars of a ruin, each leaf laid sleekly in place. The bubbling foam subsided : the reflections of the stars came out among it as if from clouds. Silent, still, dark, placid, as if there could never have been a disturbance.

(Richard Hughes : *A High Wind in Jamaica*.)

Earthquake

THE PHILIPPINES

(after the eruption of the Taal volcano, January 30th, 1911).

NATURE in the tropics tends to excesses and forces human beings to set up a wall of apathy to protect the nervous system from constant shocks. The things that happen near the Equator are dramatic and appear with cyclonic suddenness. Earthquakes occur more frequently than typhoons and the inhabitants must become accustomed to these terrifying experiences or each time they would be overwhelmed. During a quake, when I used to look out of the window of my office on the narrow Calle Palacio, and observe the houses swaying toward one another, I would have the illusion that they were actually bumping heads. . . .

. . . Our work was interrupted by constantly recurring quakes which continued for several weeks. Colonel Rivers and I slept in the same tent and for the time being adopted the Filipino indifference. Our nervous systems became so adjusted to the shocks that we would sleep soundly at night, but kept a lantern burning in case we should be needed, or should have to make a quick exit. One night came a quake violent enough even to waken me. I returned to consciousness just in time to hear Colonel Rivers utter a startled ' Whoo-ooo-ooo ' as he sat up in bed and rubbed his eyes. A crack had dug diagonally across the ground covered by the tent, and the earth was sinking fast on his side. He made a leap toward me. I beat a hasty retreat under the side of the tent and he came tumbling after.

In the course of a day or so the quakes settled to their business with clock-like regularity. Every twelve minutes the ground shook, and the earth opened. When we amused ourselves straddling the clefts and riding the quakes we would receive an exaggerated sense of up and down motion. It was much like trying to stand with the right foot in one rowboat and the left foot in another when a light sea was running. These cracks might fall together at the next shock or remain gaping for months before they were filled with debris.

From the dressing stations we hauled the wounded to the coast on high, two-wheeled, canopied pony carts, using the board seats as stretchers. I was taking a full load on one of these carretelas down a long hill when suddenly a tremendous quake came and a crack appeared in the road directly ahead of us. The *cochero* could not pull up the pony in time. The animal fell into a crevasse, but the shafts bridged the gap, and the harness held him.

We knew we had twelve minutes in which to work. Saplings were hastily procured, the pony was pried out, and the board seats were laid across the crack. We continued to the coast unharmed. The hardening process we had gone through made this only an incident in the day's work.

The Filipinos who survived continued phlegmatically with their regular round of duties. I remember watching an old peasant ploughing a nearby field with his ancient and resigned carabao. When he reached the lower end, suddenly there came a tremendous quake, and that side of the field sank about three feet. The carabao never stopped, but kept methodically on and around until he came up against the raw embankment which marked the scission. I saw him cock an eye quizzically as though to say, ' Where did this come from ? I never had to climb anything like this before.' And then he wearily hoisted himself over the acclivity and monotonously continued on his way.

(*15°N; 121°E.*)   (Victor Heiser : *A Doctor's Odyssey*.)

Earthquake

INDONESIA : CELEBES

DURING MY stay at Rurúkan my curiosity was satisfied by experiencing a pretty sharp earthquake-shock. On the evening of June 29th, at a quarter after eight, as I was sitting reading, the house began shaking with a very gentle, but rapidly increasing motion. I sat still enjoying the novel sensation for some seconds ; but in less than half a minute it became strong enough to shake me in my chair, and to make the house visibly rock about, and creak and crack as if it would fall to pieces. Then began a cry throughout the village of " Tana goyang ! Tana goyang ! " (Earthquake ! earthquake !) Everybody rushed out of their houses—women screamed and children cried—and I thought it prudent to go out too. On getting up, I found my head giddy and my steps unsteady, and could hardly walk without falling. The shock continued about a minute, during which time I felt as if I had been turned round and round, and was almost sea-sick. Going into the house again, I found a lamp and a bottle of arrack upset. The tumbler which formed the lamp had been thrown out of the saucer in which it had stood. The shock appeared to be nearly vertical, rapid, vibratory, and jerking. It was sufficient, I have no doubt, to have thrown down brick chimneys and walls and church towers ; but as the houses here are all low, and strongly framed of timber, it is impossible for them to be much injured, except by a shock that would utterly destroy a European city. The people told me it was ten years since they had had a stronger shock than this, at which time many houses were thrown down and some people killed.

At intervals of ten minutes to half an hour, slight shocks and tremors were felt, sometimes strong enough to send us all out again. There was a strange mixture of the terrible and the ludicrous in our situation. We might at any moment have a much stronger shock, which would bring down the house over us, or—what I feared more—cause a landslip, and send us down into the deep ravine on the very edge of which the village is built ; yet I could not help laughing each time we ran out at a slight shock, and then in a few moments ran in again. The sublime and the ridiculous were here literally but a step apart. On the other hand, the most terrible and destructive of natural phenomena was in action around us—the rocks, the mountains, the solid earth were trembling and convulsed, and we were utterly impotent to guard against the danger that might at any moment overwhelm us. On the other hand was the spectacle of a number of men, women, and children running in and out of their houses, on what each time proved a very unnecessary alarm, as each shock ceased just as it became strong enough to frighten us. It seemed really very much like " playing at earthquakes," and made many of the people join me in a hearty laugh, even while reminding each other that it really might be no laughing matter.

At length the evening got very cold, and I became very sleepy, and determined to turn in ; leaving orders to my boys, who slept nearer the door, to wake me in case the house was in danger of falling. But I miscalculated my apathy, for I could not sleep much. The shocks continued at intervals of half an hour or an hour all night, just strong enough to wake me thoroughly each time and keep me on the alert ready to jump up in case of danger.

I was therefore very glad when morning came. Most of the inhabitants had not been to bed at all, and some had stayed out of doors all night.

(A. R. Wallace: *The Malay Archipelago.*)

Volcano : Vesuvius
ITALY

To Tacitus :

YOU ASK me to send you an account of my uncle's death, so that you may be able to give posterity an accurate description of it. I am much obliged to you, for I can see that the immortality of his fame is well assured, if you take in hand to write of it. For although he perished in a disaster which devastated some of the fairest regions of the land, and though he is sure of eternal remembrance like the peoples and cities that fell with him in that memorable calamity, though too he had written a large number of works of lasting value, yet the undying fame of which your writings are assured will secure for him a still further lease of life. For my own part, I think that those people are highly favoured by Providence who are capable either of performing deeds worthy of the historian's pen or of writing histories worthy of being read, but that they are peculiarly favoured who can do both. Among the latter I may class my uncle, thanks to his own writings and to yours. So I am all the more ready to fulfil your injunctions, nay, I am even prepared to beg to be allowed to undertake them.

My uncle was stationed at Misenum, where he was in active command of the fleet, with full powers. On the 23rd of August, about the seventh hour, my mother drew his attention to the fact that a cloud of unusual size and shape had made its appearance. He had taken his sun bath, followed by a cold one, and after a light meal he was lying down and reading. Yet he called for his sandals, and climbed up to a spot from which he could command a good view of the curious phenomenon. Those who were looking at the cloud from some distance could not make out from which mountain it was rising—it was afterwards discovered to have been Mount Vesuvius—but in likeness and form it more closely resembled a pine-tree than anything else, for what corresponded to the trunk was of great length and height, and

158

then spread out into a number of branches, the reason being, I imagine, that while the vapour was fresh, the cloud was borne upwards, but when the vapour became wasted, it lost its motion. or even became dissipated by its own weight, and spread out laterally. At times it looked white, and at other times dirty and spotted, according to the quantity of earth and cinders that were shot up.

To a man of my uncle's learning, the phenomenon appeared one of great importance, which deserved a closer study. He ordered a Liburnian galley to be got ready, and offered to take me with him, if I desired to accompany him, but I replied that I preferred to go on with my studies, and it so happened that he had assigned me some writing to do. He was just leaving the house when he received a written message from Rectina, the wife of Tascus, who was terrified at the peril threatening her—for her villa lay just beneath the mountain, and there were no means of escape save by shipboard—begging him to save her from her perilous position. So he changed his plans, and carried out with the greatest fortitude the ideas which had occurred to him as a student.

He had the galleys launched and went on board himself, in the hope of succouring, not only Rectina, but many others, for there were a number of people living along the shore owing to its delightful situation. He hastened, therefore, towards the place whence others were flying, and steering a direct course, kept the helm straight for the point of danger, so utterly devoid of fear that every movement of the looming portent and every change in its appearance he described and had noted down by his secretary, as soon as his eyes detected it. Already ashes were beginning to fall upon the ships, hotter and in thicker showers as they approached more nearly, with pumice-stones and black flints, charred and cracked by the heat of the flames, while their way was barred by the sudden shoaling of the sea bottom and the litter of the mountain on the shore. He hesitated for a moment whether to turn back, and then, when the helmsman warned him to do so, he exclaimed, " Fortune favours the bold ; try to reach Pomponianus." The latter was at Stabiæ, separated by the whole width of the bay, for the sea there pours in upon a gently rounded and curving shore. Although the danger was not yet close upon him, it was none the less clearly seen, and it travelled quickly as it came nearer, so Pomponianus had got his baggage together on shipboard, and had determined upon flight, and was waiting for the wind which was blowing on shore to fall. My uncle sailed in with the wind fair behind him, and embraced Pomponianus, who was in a state of fright, comforting and cheering him at the same time. Then in order to calm his friend's fears by showing how composed he was himself, he ordered the servants to carry him to the bath, and, after his ablutions, he sat down and had dinner in the best of spirits, or with that assumption of good spirits which is quite as remarkable as the reality.

In the meantime broad sheets of flame, which rose high in the air, were breaking out in a number of places on Mount Vesuvius and lighting up the sky, and the glare and brightness seemed all the more striking owing to the darkness of the night. My uncle, in order to allay the fear of his companions, kept declaring that the country people in their terror had left their fires burning, and that the conflagration they saw arose from the blazing and empty villas. Then he betook himself to rest and enjoyed a very deep sleep, for his breathing, which, owing to his bulk, was rather heavy and loud, was heard by those who were waiting at the door of his chamber. But by this time the courtyard leading to the room he occupied was so full of ashes and pumice-stones mingled together, and covered to such a depth, that if he had delayed any longer in the bedchamber there would have been no means of escape. So my uncle was aroused, and came out and joined Pomponianus and the rest who had been keeping watch. They held a consultation whether they should remain indoors or wander forth in the open ; for the buildings were beginning to shake with the repeated and intensely severe shocks of earthquake, and seemed to be rocking to and fro as though they had been torn from their foundations. Outside again there was danger to be apprehended from the pumice-stones, though these were light and nearly burnt through, and thus, after weighing the two perils, the latter course was decided upon. With my uncle it was a choice of reasons which prevailed, with the rest a choice of fears.

They placed pillows on their heads and secured them with napkins, as a precaution against the falling bodies. Elsewhere the day had dawned by this time, but there it was still night, and the darkness was blacker and thicker than any ordinary night. This, however, they relieved as best they could by a number of torches and other kinds of lights. They decided to make their way to the shore, and to see from the nearest point whether the sea would enable them to put out, but it was still running high and contrary. A sheet was spread on the ground, and on this my uncle lay, and twice he called for a draught of cold water, which he drank. Then the flames, and the smell of sulphur which gave warning of them, scattered the others in flight and roused him. Leaning on two slaves, he rose to his feet and immediately fell down again, owing, as I think, to his breathing being obstructed by the thickness of the fumes and congestion of the stomach, that organ being naturally weak and narrow, and subject to inflammation. When daylight returned—which was three days after his death—his body was found untouched, uninjured, and covered, dressed just as he had been in life. The corpse suggested a person asleep rather than a dead man.

Meanwhile my mother and I were at Misenum. But that is of no consequence for the purposes of history, nor indeed did you express a wish to be told of anything except of my uncle's death. So I will say no more, except to add that I have given you a full account both of the incidents which I myself witnessed and of those narrated to me immediately afterwards, when, as a rule, one gets the truest account of what has happened. You will pick out what you think will answer your purpose best, for to write a letter is a different thing from writing a history, and to write to a friend is not like writing to all and sundry. Farewell. *(40°50'N; 14°25'E.)*

(A letter of the Younger Pliny to Tacitus : *Translated by John B. Firth.*)

Volcano : Vesuvius

ITALY

" NOW, CHILDREN," said Mr. Ferguson, " remember, one rule I lay down today, which is not to be broken, you must not think and then act for yourselves, but in everything obey me or Mr. Vernon and the guides."

" You must quite understand this, because the ascent of a mountain like Vesuvius, more than two thousand, nearly three thousand feet high, is dangerous."

They all promised faithful obedience, and with very thick shoes, and thick sticks for the gentlemen of the party, off they all started. They met the Vernons at the railway station ; the horn was blown, for the guard uses one at starting instead of a bell, or whistle as with us, and twenty minutes brought them to the small town of Resina.

Here they all left the train, and went to a house in which the principal guide lives. He had received orders, so eight horses and ponies were in readiness, some guides, and a few ragged boys who went for their own pleasure.

Mary was not of the party, she had a cold ; besides which, being such a coward, Mr. Vernon felt it quite the best plan to leave her at home.

There were vineyards part of the way, growing on the lava, a little earth giving them sufficient nourishment, but soon they ceased ; and miles of black, desolate lava, raised in heaps like waves of the sea, were seen, and not a sound was to be heard but the tramp of the horses' feet.

After an hour's ride they reached the Hermitage, as it is called, a small inn ; here the baskets of provisions were left, and again they rode on.

The horses had sometimes to take a long step from stone to stone, and a hard matter some of the party found it to keep their seats.

Edith's merry laugh was heard above all the rest, as she looked back and saw one horse after another slowly straining up the ascent after her. At last all had to dismount and clamber up the cone of the mountain as best they could. The ladies had straps put round their waists, and were pulled up by the guides.

As for the children, they clambered up like goats, but soon turned into very black goats, from the ashes and rubbish which they had to climb over. They got on quicker than the rest, but were called to a halt by Mr. Ferguson. For more than an hour they were toiling and climbing up the cone. Every now and then the ground trembled under them, and a rumbling noise came like thunder. Edith and Harry gained the top first, but were so tired they threw themselves on the ground at once to get breath. One after another of the party appeared, and after resting a minute or two they walked to the edge of the crater. It looked like an immense basin filled with fire and ashes.

There they all stood in silence, looking down into it. The first feeling was that of dread, almost horror.

After awhile two of the guides went down into it, and taking some eggs out of their pockets, roasted them by putting them at the edge of the burning lava.

Mr. Vernon managed to cut a loaf into small strips, but then the difficulty was how to hold the hot egg. So he screwed up some paper into a shape something like egg-cups, and all the party sat down to eat their lunch.

After an eruption the crater is often more than two hundred feet deep, but now it was very full, only about thirteen feet from the top. The guides helped the party down into it; for part of the lava cools in black stripes, and though this is only a crust with fire beneath, it was strong enough to bear them, though the guides always knock it well with their sticks, as they can tell by the sound whether it is thick. There was something so fearful and wonderful in thus walking on the thin crust over molten fire, with heavy streams of red-hot lava oozing out of fiery clefts on each side, that even Edith could not enjoy it. Near the middle of the crater the lava was heaped up to a great height, forming a sort of chimney, out of this the smoke and red-hot stones and lava were pouring forth. As they came rather near it, the smell was so suffocating that it seemed best for none but the gentlemen to go up it. Harry begged hard to go too, so they went on, and actually climbed up this chimney, and looked right down into it, as well as the smoke would let them.

They were obliged to be very careful to get the opposite side to the one towards which the smoke was blown, or they would have been choked. The noise was like the hoarse puffing of some monstrous railway-engine. It occurred about half as frequently as one breathes. Mr. Ferguson remarked, " The poets fabled that one Enceladus, a horrible giant, was, for his crimes, buried under Etna, another burning mountain, and, by his writhings and bellowings, caused all that happened. You can imagine some such giant so buried under Vesuvius ; he breathes only half as quickly as we do, and at every breath he clears his throat of a quantity of lava ; coughing it up into the air, making a great noise !"

Some of the party were not sorry to leave this wonderful crater, and, when they had clambered out of it, long did they stand watching one explosion after another out of the mouth of this fiery giant.

The circumference of the crater is three miles and a half, so, of course, they did not walk round it.

The time now came to descend the mountain. Each one took hold of the hand of a guide. The side they went down was covered with ashes, and an opposite one to that they had come up. It was so very steep, that they were obliged to lean back, almost as if they were going to lie down ; their feet sank into the ashes above the ankle at every step.

But alas ! when the time came for them to mount the horses, each one of the party was so stiff and tired, that Donald wished he had never come. Slowly the horses picked their way amongst the stones.

After dismounting at Resina, Mr. Ferguson told them Herculaneum was buried underneath this village, and the next, Portici ; and cannot be excavated on that account, excepting about a quarter of a mile. The train soon arrived, and very weary and very stiff were all the party as they stepped into it.

(40°50′N; 14°25′E.)

(Aunt Louisa : *Harry Brightside, or The Young Traveller in Italy*.)

Volcano : Etna

SICILY

HERE IN Sicily it is so pleasant : the sunny Ionian sea, the changing jewel of Calabria, like a fire-opal moved in the light ; Italy and the panorama of Christmas clouds, night with the dog-star laying a long, luminous gleam across the sea, as if baying at us, Orion marching above ; how the dog-star Sirius looks at one, looks at one ! he is the hound of heaven, green, glamorous and fierce !—and then, oh, regal evening star, hung westward flaring over the jagged dark precipices of tall Sicily : then Etna, that wicked witch, resting her thick white snow under heaven, and slowly, slowly rolling her orange-coloured smoke. They called her the Pillar of Heaven, the Greeks. It seems wrong at first, for she trails up in a long, magical, flexible line from the sea's edge to her blunt cone, and does not seem tall. She seems rather low, under heaven. But as one knows her better, oh, awe and wizardry ! Remote under heaven, aloof, so near, yet never with us. The painters try to paint her, and the photographers to photograph her, in vain. Because why ? Because the near ridges, with their olives and white houses, these are with us. Because the river-bed, and Naxos under the lemon groves, Greek Naxos deep under dark-leaved, many-fruited lemon groves, Etna's skirts and skirt-bottoms, these still are our world, our own world. Even the high villages among the oaks, on Etna. But Etna herself, Etna of the snow and secret changing winds, she is beyond a crystal wall. When I look at her, low, white, witch-like under heaven, slowly rolling her orange smoke and giving sometimes a breath of rose-red flame, then I must look away from earth, into the ether, into the low empyrean. And there, in that remote region, Etna is alone. If you would see her, you must slowly take off your eyes from the world and go a naked seer to the strange chamber of the empyrean. Pedestal of Heaven! The Greeks had a sense of the magic truth of things. Thank goodness one still knows enough about them to find one's kinship at last. There are so many photographs, there are so infinitely many water-colour drawings and oil paintings which purport to render Etna. But pedestal of heaven! You must cross the invisible border. Between the foreground, which is our own, and Etna, pivot of winds in lower heaven, there is a dividing line. You must change your state of mind. A metempsychosis. It is no use thinking you can see and behold Etna and the foreground both at once. Never. One or the other. Foreground and a transcribed Etna. Or Etna, pedestal of heaven.

(*37°40'N; 15°E.*)   (D. H. Lawrence : *Sea and Sardinia.*)

Volcano : Stromboli

MEDITERRANEAN

ON ONE evening Stromboli was sighted. The volcano chanced to be active. When it first came into view it appeared as a small red dot on the horizon which could not be distinguished from the port light of a ship. In time the dot grew until a kind of fiery tail could be seen to trail down from it. The dot was the crater, and the tail was a stream of glowing lava on the mountain side. On a still nearer approach, the strange light came to look like a wondrous firefly skimming the black sea, and as it grew and grew it changed to a blazing column against the dark—just such a pillar of fire as led the night marches of the Israelites. As the island was passed lurid puffs of flame and smoke could be seen to well forth from the crater, while a cloud of red steam hung like a fiery baldachino over the cascade of red-hot lava. The mountain stood out black against the glare on the sky as if it were a peak of the nether world.

(*38°50'N; 15°10'E.*)

(Sir Frederick Treves : *The Other Side of the Lantern.*)

Volcano : Fuji

JAPAN

THE APPEARANCE of Mount Fuji is familar all over the world ; it is pictured on nearly every Japanese poster, advertisement and tourist booklet, and no play or film dealing with Japanese life is considered complete in which some aspect or other of it does not appear. It is, I should imagine, the best advertised mountain in the world. In spite of this, however, it does not give one the feeling, as do the better known of the Swiss Alps, that it has become self-conscious through being looked at too much. It is one of the very few famous " sights," like the New York skyscrapers, that really comes up to expectation. The mountain is visible from many parts of Tokyo, especially in the clear winter air, but it is seen at its best from the sea at dawn. At such times it seems to tower over everything, its perfect snow-capped cone, a purplish green in the light of early morning, seeming to be suspended in the sky. The beauty of Fuji is due to the simplicity of its outlines and the fact that it stands alone ; from wherever one views it there is little to distract the eye.

The ascent of the mountain does not call for even the most elementary skill in mountaineering. There is a path, rough it is true, right to the summit, up which it would be possible to ride a motor-cycle, while to a horseman the journey would not present the slightest difficulty. The road, however, is littered with advertisements, broken bottles, the remains of food and human excreta ; and at every stage the weary traveller is importuned by begging priests who spend the summer months in the various shrines situated on the mountain slopes. I made the pilgrimage with a party of my students, and we spent the afternoon and evening of a broiling August day toiling upwards over the gritty lava of which the mountain is composed. We slept the night at a hut about three-quarters of the way up and arrived on the

summit, in company with several thousand other people, shortly
before dawn. The view from the top was astounding : over a
maze of still, dark lakes and valleys we looked out right across
the Pacific, the line of the coast faintly visible, like a meandering
smear brushed in with purple ink. We stayed there only long
enough to see the rising sun dissipate the miracle, and then slid
down over the grit again, reaching Tokyo in the evening. I wish,
however, that I had not climbed Mount Fuji ; never again was
I able quite to capture the feeling of pristine beauty that it
undoubtedly gives until such time as one actually sets foot upon
its slopes. But then, as one of my Japanese friends was fond of
saying, Fuji is only a " seeing " mountain ; it was never meant to
be climbed. The Japanese, however, have a saying that there are
two kinds of fool : those who have never climbed Mount Fuji,
and those who have climbed it more than once.

(35°20'N; 139°E.)   (John Morris : *Traveller from Tokyo*.)

Volcano : Kilimanjaro

TANGANYIKA

THE SCENERY on the Uganda railroad, between the sea
and Nairobi, is often picturesque and interesting. I shall not,
however, dwell on its features, as these have been described times
without number. But one view there is of Mount Kilimanjaro
which with good fortune may be seen, and of it I want to speak.

The through express train from Mombassa to the lake, if it is
on time, passes near enough to the mountain to afford that view.
Just before sunrise I had been told to look out of the left hand
carriage window, at about five o'clock in the morning, and see
what I could see—and what I saw that clear morning three years
ago, I shall never forget.

All around was the dark plain illumined only by the stars, for
there was no moon. It was about a quarter-past five, when to
southward I saw a vast pink column, flattened on the top, that
rose distinctly against the dusky purple sky. Redder and redder
it grew, as the first sunbeam touched its snows, and then at its
base, the fringe of wooded mountains showed in the earliest light
of the coming dawn. Kilimanjaro is more than nineteen thousand
feet high, and that morning it seemed to have all the wonderful
sunrise glory to itself for quite a long time, while still the veldt at

its feet lay in the darkness. Just that column of pink, changing to scarlet—and nothing else to tell of the sun, not yet risen, on a far lower and more commonplace world. Great mountains are usually so surrounded by gradually rising country that they are robbed somewhat of their height. Kilimanjaro, however, rises sheer from a plain only two thousand feet above the sea—and over these levels it towers superbly. Like all African mountains it is broadly belted by forest. Above this it lifts itself in this one mighty cone, whose steep sides and flattened summit, no less than fourteen miles across, are covered with perpetual snow.

Half an hour after sunrise the rising mists of the woodlands have closely woven their swathing veils around it. The mountain has vanished, and you can scarcely persuade yourself, as you jolt over the dazzling plain, that the vision of an hour ago was more than a dream.

(*3°S; 37°20'E.*)   (W. S. Rainsford : *The Land of the Lion.*)

Volcanoes: Popocatepetl and Ixtaccihuatl

MEXICO

IT WAS a brilliant morning, and for once, under the blue sky of the distance, Popocatepetl stood aloof, a heavy giant presence under heaven, with a cape of snow. And rolling a long dark roll of smoke like a serpent.

Ixtaccihuatl, the White Woman, glittered and seemed near, but the other mountain, Popocatepetl, stood further back, and in shadow, a pure cone of atmospheric shadow, with glinting flashes of snow. There they were, the two monsters, watching gigantically and terribly over their lofty, bloody cradle of men, the Valley of Mexico. Alien, ponderous, the white-hung mountains seemed to emit a deep purring sound, too deep for the ear to hear, and yet audible on the blood, a sound of dread. There was no soaring or uplift or exaltation, as there is in the snowy mountains of Europe. Rather a ponderous white-shouldered weight, pressing terribly on the earth, and murmuring like two watchful lions.

(*19°N; 98°40'W.*)   (D. H. Lawrence : *The Plumed Serpent.*)

Volcano: Mont Pelée

MARTINIQUE

(The personal narrative of Chief Officer Ellery S. Scott, of the Quebec liner ss. *Roraima*, which was destroyed by a volcanic rain of fire in the harbour of St. Pierre on the morning of May 8th, 1902.)

WE LEFT New York on Saturday April 26th, aboard the Quebec Line steamship *Roraima*, Captain Muggah, bound for Demerara, *via* the Windward Islands. Our crew numbered forty-seven, and we had aboard twenty-one passengers, men, women, and children. It was Thursday, the 8th of May, that trouble came. When this day came in, overcast with partial clouds, we were lying at anchor off the Island of Dominica. At 1 a.m. we hove anchor and made a course south by east half-east for Martinique.

Everything went well till 4.45 a.m. I was on the bridge for the morning watch. The night was fair and the sea calm. Suddenly, without warning, we came into thick, heavy smoke and falling ashes, off the north-east end of the Island of Martinique. This disturbed me so much that I called the captain and asked what he thought of the weather. I had never seen an active eruption in the islands before, but years ago I saw Etna aflame, so I knew something about volcanoes, and of course we had every reason to suppose that the smoke and ashes were from Mount Pelée. The wind at this time was to the east of south, and the smoke from the mountain blew directly towards us.

We skirted the island, keeping about two miles off shore, but on account of the currents that were setting us in towards the land we had to steer various courses, sometimes drawing off and at others drawing in. The current was never steady. It ran terribly strong, and we took it for granted that this was due to some volcanic action going on. To a certain extent the captain and I were alarmed. It was a fine dust, a sharp, grey ash, that was falling. At 6.15 a.m. we anchored off St. Pierre.

* * * * *

Meantime our sailors, under the boatswain, were cleaning up the sand and dust, which lay fully a quarter of an inch thick over everything—just like white sand. The ship was covered with it from end to end. It had sifted into everything. When the captain and I came off the bridge our uniforms were completely covered with it. Passengers and crew were gathering up the sand and ashes to keep as mementoes. Some would put it in envelopes, others in tin tobacco-boxes, and I can remember a big negro giving me a cigar-box filled with it, which I took, little thinking what a plenty I should have of it before I made home again.

Meantime the officers were grouped forward on the deck enjoying the grand view of Pelée as huge volumes of smoke rose from it. The smoke appeared to roll right up into the heavens, and then southward and easterly winds drove it away to sea, so that where we were lying the air was comparatively clear. The sun was shining out nice and bright. Everything appeared to be pleasant and favourable except the column of black smoke.

It was a few moments past 8 a.m. As we stood talking there the third mate said to me : " I must get my camera. I have only one more plate, but this is a sight that must not be missed." With this he turned and made for his cabin. I never saw him again. Just then, all at once, there was a sublime outburst from the mountain. Whether more than one crater opened it would be hard to say, but a conflagration came right out of the mountain in one grand burst, with a noise so terrible that beside it a thunder-clap would sound like a pistol-shot alongside the roar of a twelve-inch gun. Then it came rolling down the mountain over the intervening hills—the molten slag, flame, and smoke, one immense cloud of it, luminous, awful, rolling down like fire. It took just a moment. As it came sweeping down there seemed to be an inexhaustible supply following it, an endless tornado of steam and ashes and burning gas. The instant we saw this grand outbreak coming towards us the captain rushed to the bridge, calling to me to heave up anchor. I sprang forward to the steam windlass ; the carpenter beside me was bending up forward to start the machine going when destruction struck us.

The thing was indescribable. It seemed to whirl earth and sea before it, just as the western cyclones wipe up the trees and everything in their paths ; but this was an explosive whirlwind, setting fire to everything as it went. It was only a few seconds of time, but as it rolled over the intervening miles towards the city that city was doomed. Lava, fire, ashes, smoke, everything combined, swept down on us in an instant. No railroad train could have escaped it. We could only see one side of the torrent, but more of it was pouring down the rear of the mountain, creating a tremendous back draught and increasing the fury about us still further.

Then came darkness blacker than night, and as the awful ruin struck the waters it just rolled along, setting fire to the shore and the ships. The *Roraima* rolled and careened far to port, then with a sudden jerk she went to starboard, plunging her lee rail far under water. The masts, smoke-stack, rigging, all were swept clean off and went by the board. The iron smoke-stack came off short, and the two steel masts broke off 2ft. above the deck, perfectly clean, without a jagged edge, just like a clay pipe-stem struck with a big stick. We had started to heave the anchor, but it never left the mud. There we were, stuck fast in hell. The darkness was something appalling. It enveloped everything, and was only broken by the burning clouds of consuming gas which gave bursts of light out of the darkness. The ship took fire in several places simultaneously, and men, women, and children were dead in a few seconds of time. This was a few minutes after eight o'clock.

The saloon and the after end of the ship blazed up at once. The *Roraima* was lying with a heavy list to starboard, pointing to-wards the shore. Hot ashes fell thick at first. They were soon followed by a rain of small, hot stones, ranging all the way from the size of shot to pigeons' eggs. These would drop in the water with a hissing sound ; but where they struck the ship's deck they did little damage, for the decks were protected with a thick coating of ashes from the first outburst. After the stones came a rain of hot mud, lava apparently mixed with water, of the consistency of very thin cement. Wherever it fell it formed a coating, clinging like glue, so that those who wore no caps it coated, making a complete cement mask right over their heads. For myself, when I saw the storm coming I snatched a tarpaulin cover off one of the ventilators and jammed it down over my head and neck, looking out through the opening. This saved me much, but even so my beard, face, nostrils, and eyes were so filled with the stuff that every few seconds I had to break it out of my eyes in order to see. This mud was not actually burning, but it steamed, and there was heat enough in it to dry on the head and form a crust so that it fitted like a plaster cast.

I remember that Charles Thompson, the assistant purser, a fine-looking, burly black from St. Kitts, who stood beside me, had his head so weighted down with the stuff that he seemed to feel giddy and was almost falling. When he asked me to break the casing off his head I was afraid it would scalp him when I took it off. I could feel the heat on my own head very plainly through my tarpaulin covering, and his scalp must have been badly scorched.

Everybody was not on deck at this time. Some of the passengers were dressing, some still in their bunks. In some cases they were poisoned almost instantaneously by the noxious gas. In others they were drowned by the water which swept in hot through the open port-holes of the submerged staterooms on the starboard side.

The darkness was appalling, only lit by the flames from the after-end of the ship and by the lurid glare of the conflagration on shore when some big warehouse caught fire, and the great puncheons of rum burst with a loud report and shot their blazing contents into the air. At this time I went to the lower bridge, feeling my way along, in order to find the captain. There on the bridge I almost stumbled on a crouching figure with a hideous face, burned almost beyond recognition.

" Who are you ?" I cried, for I did not know him, crouched there in the darkness.

The man looked up, his face terrible to see.

" Mr. Scott," he said, " don't you know me ?"

I said, " My God, it's the captain !"

(14°50′N; 61°10′W.)

(Chief Officer Ellery S. Scott: "The Tragedy of Martinique," *The Strand Magazine*, September, 1902.)

Volcano : Saba

LEEWARD ISLANDS

CLOSE TO St. Eustatius is the island of Saba, a place so curious that it must rank with the islands of romance and not with things of this world. It is small and round, has a diameter of two miles, and belongs to the Dutch. It is the pinnacle of a volcanic mountain of which only the peak and crater emerge from the sea. Possessing no beach, Saba is, in the words of the mariner, " bold and steep-to " all round. Its circuit indeed is that of the wall of some cyclopean fortress. As " in general a heavy surf

When the Saba ship is finished it is lowered down the side of the cliff, and has then apparently to shift for itself. The women, no doubt, wave handkerchiefs from the rim of the crater as the craft takes the sea, while the boys are told not to play with stones lest they should fall upon their fathers' heads. After all the excitement of the launch is over, one can imagine the master-builder climbing up the Ladder to his crater home, as full of pride as his shortness of breath will allow.

(*17°40'N; 63°15'W.*)

(Sir Frederick Treves : *The Cradle of the Deep.*)

The Great Geyser

ICELAND

AT LAST, after another two hours' weary jogging, we descried, straight in front, a low steep brown rugged hill, standing entirely detached from the range at the foot of which we had been riding ; and in a few minutes more, wheeling round its outer end, we found ourselves in the presence of the steaming geysers.

I do not know that I can give you a better notion of the appearance of the place than by saying that it looked as if—for about a quarter of a mile—the ground had been honeycombed by disease into numerous sores and orifices ; not a blade of grass grew on its hot, inflamed surface, which consisted of unwholesome-looking red livid clay, or crumpled shreds and shards of slough-like incrustations. Naturally enough, our first impulse on dismounting was to scamper off at once to the Great Geyser. As it lay at the furthest end of the congeries of hot springs, in order to reach it we had to run the gauntlet of all the pools of boiling water and scalding quagmires of soft clay that intervened, and consequently arrived on the spot with our ankles nicely poulticed. But the occasion justified our eagerness. A smooth siliceous basin, seventy-two feet in diameter and four feet deep, with a hole at the bottom as in a washing-basin on board a steamer, stood before us brimful of water just upon the simmer ; while up into the air above our heads rose a great column of vapour, looking as if it was going to turn into the Fisherman's Genie. The ground about the brim was composed of layers of incrusted silica, like the outside of an oyster, sloping gently down on all sides from the edge of the basin.

Having satisfied our curiosity with this cursory inspection of what we had come so far to see, hunger compelled us to look about with great anxiety for the cook ; and you may fancy our delight at seeing that functionary in the very act of dishing up dinner on a neighbouring hillock. Sent forward at an early hour, under the chaperonage of a guide, he had arrived about two hours before us, and seizing with a general's eye the key of the position, at once turned an idle babbling little Geyser into a camp-kettle, dug a bake-house in the hot soft clay, and improvising a kitchen-range at a neighbouring vent, had made himself completely master of the situation. It was about one o'clock in the morning when we sat down to dinner, and as light as day.

As the baggage-train with our tents and beds had not yet arrived, we fully appreciated our luck in being treated to so dry a night ; and having eaten everything we could lay hands on, were sat quietly down to chess, and coffee brewed in Geyser water ; when suddenly it seemed as if beneath our very feet a quantity of subterraneous cannon were going off ; the whole earth shook, and Sigurdr, starting to his feet, upset the chess-board (I was just beginning to get the best of the game), and flung off at full speed toward the great basin. By the time we reached its brim, how-ever, the noise had ceased, and all we could see was a slight movement in the centre, as if an angel had passed by and troubled the water. Irritated at this false alarm, we determined to revenge ourselves by going and tormenting the Strokr. Strokr—or *the churn*—you must know, is an unfortunate Geyser, with so little command over his temper and his stomach, that you can get a *rise* out of him whenever you like. All that is necessary is to collect a quantity of sods, and throw them down his funnel. As he has no basin to protect him from these liberties, you can approach to the very edge of the pipe, about five feet in diameter, and look down at the boiling water which is perpetually seething at the bottom. In a few minutes the dose of turf you have just administered begins to disagree with him ; he works himself into an awful passion—tormented by the qualms of incipient sick-ness, he groans and hisses, and boils up, and spits at you with malicious vehemence, until at last, with a roar of mingled pain and rage, he throws up into the air a column of water forty feet high, which carries with it all the sods that have been chucked in, and scatters them scalded and half-digested at your feet. So irritated has the poor thing's stomach become by the discipline it has undergone, that even long after all foreign matter has been thrown off, it goes on retching and sputtering, until at last nature is exhausted, when, sobbing and sighing to itself, it sinks back into the bottom of its den.

Put into the highest spirits by the success of this performance, we turned away to examine the remaining springs. I do not know, however, that any of the rest are worthy of particular attention. They all resemble in character the two I have described, the only difference being that they are infinitely smaller, and of much less power and importance. One other remarkable formation in the neighbourhood must not be passed unnoticed. Imagine a large irregular opening in the surface of the soft white clay, filled to the very brim with scalding water, perfectly still, and of as bright a blue as that of the Grotto Azzuro at Capri, through whose transparent depths you can see down into the mouth of a vast subaqueous cavern, which runs, Heaven knows how far, in a horizontal direction beneath your feet. Its walls and varied cavities really looked as if they were built of the purest lapis lazuli—and so thin seemed the crust that roofed it in, we almost fancied it might break through and tumble us all into the fearful beautiful bath.

Having by this time taken a pretty good look at the principal features of our new domain, I wrapped myself up in a cloak and went to sleep ; leaving orders that I should not be called until after the tent had arrived and our beds were ready. Sigurdr followed my example, but the Doctor went out shooting.

As our principal object in coming so far was to see an eruption of the Great Geyser, it was of course necessary we should wait upon his pleasure ; in fact, our movements entirely depended upon his. For the next two or three days, therefore, like pilgrims round some ancient shrine, we patiently kept watch ; but he scarcely deigned to vouchsafe us the slightest manifestation of his latent energies. Two or three times the cannonading we had heard immediately after our arrival recommenced—and once an eruption to the height of about ten feet occurred ; but so brief was its duration, that by the time we were on the spot, although the tent was not eighty yards distant, all was over. As after every effort of the fountain the water in the basin mysteriously ebbs back into the funnel, this performance, though unsatisfactory in itself, gave us an opportunity of approaching the mouth of the pipe and looking down into its scalded gullet. In an hour afterwards, the basin was brimful as ever.

. . . . We had now been keeping watch for three days over the Geyser, in languid expectation of the eruption which was to set us free. All the morning of the fourth day I had been playing chess with Sigurdr ; Fitzgerald was photographing, Wilson was in the act of announcing luncheon, when a cry from the guides made us start to our feet, and with one common impulse rush towards the basin. The usual subterranean thunders had already commenced. A violent agitation was disturbing the centre of the pool. Suddenly a dome of water lifted itself up to the height of eight or ten feet—then burst, and fell ; immediately after which a shining liquid column, or rather a sheaf of columns wreathed in robes of vapour, sprang into the air, and in a succession of jerking leaps, each higher than the last, flung their silver crests against the sky. For a few minutes the fountain held its own, then all at once appeared to lose its ascending energy. The unstable waters faltered—drooped—fell, " like a broken purpose," back upon themselves, and were immediately sucked down into the recesses of their pipe.

The spectacle was certainly magnificent ; but no description can give any idea of its most striking features. The enormous wealth of water, its vitality, its hidden power—the illimitable breadth of sunlit vapour, rolling out in exhaustless profusion—all combined to make one feel the stupendous energy of nature's slightest movements.

And yet I do not believe the exhibition was so fine as some that have been seen : from the first burst upwards, to the moment the last jet retreated into the pipe, was no more than a space of seven or eight minutes, and at no moment did the crown of the column reach higher than sixty or seventy feet above the surface of the basin. Now, early travellers talk of three hundred feet, which must, of course, be fabulous ; but many trustworthy persons have judged the eruptions at two hundred feet, while well-authenticated accounts—when the elevation of the jet has been actually measured—make it to have attained a height of upwards of one hundred feet.

(Lord Dufferin : *Letters from High Latitudes*.)

Geysers, Mud Volcanoes

WYOMING : YELLOWSTONE NATIONAL PARK

TWICE HAVE I written this letter from end to end. Twice have I torn it up, fearing lest those across the water should say that I had gone mad on a sudden. Now we will begin for the third time quite solemnly and soberly. I have been through the Yellowstone National Park in a buggy, in the company of an adventurous old lady from Chicago and her husband, who disapproved of scenery as being " ongodly". I fancy it scared them.

We began, as you know, with the Mammoth Hot Springs. They are only a gigantic edition of those pink and white terraces not long ago destroyed by earthquake in New Zealand. At one end of the little valley in which the hotel stands, the lime-laden springs that break from the pine-covered hillsides have formed a frozen cataract of white, lemon, and palest pink formation, through and over and in which water of the warmest bubbles and drips and trickles from pale-green lagoon to exquisitely fretted basin. The ground rings hollow as a kerosene-tin, and some day the Mammoth Hotel, guests and all, will sink into the caverns below and be turned into a stalactite. When I set foot on the first of the terraces, a tourist-trampled ramp of scabby grey stuff, I met a stream of iron-red hot water which ducked into a hole like a rabbit. Followed a gentle chuckle of laughter, and then a deep, exhausted sigh from nowhere in particular. Fifty feet above my head a jet of steam rose up and died out in the blue. It was worse than the boiling mountain at Myanoshita. The dirty white deposit gave place to lime whiter than snow ; and I found a basin which some learned hotel-keeper has christened Cleopatra's pitcher, or Mark Antony's whisky-jug, or something equally poetical. It was made of frosted silver ; it was filled with water as clear as the sky. I do not know the depth of that wonder. The eye looked down beyond grottoes and caves of beryl into an abyss that communicated directly with the central fires of earth. And the pool was in pain, so that it could not refrain from talking about it ; muttering and chattering and moaning. From the lips of the lime-ledges, forty feet under water, spurts of silver bubbles would fly up and break the peace of the crystal atop. Then the whole pool would shake and grow dim, and there were noises. I removed

myself only to find other pools all equally unhappy, rifts in the
ground, full of running, red-hot water, slippery sheets of deposit
overlaid with greenish-grey hot water, and here and there pit-
holes dry as a rifled tomb in India, dusty and waterless. Elsewhere the infernal waters had first boiled dead and then em-
balmed the pines and underwood, or the forest trees had taken
heart and smothered up a blind formation with greenery, so it
was only by scraping the earth you could tell what fires had
raged beneath.

*   *   *   *   *

By companies after tiffin we walked chattering to the uplands
of Hell. They call it the Norris Geyser Basin on Earth. It was as
though the tide of desolation had gone out, but would presently
return, across innumerable acres of dazzling white geyser formation. There were no terraces here, but all other horrors. Not
ten yards from the road a blast of steam shot up roaring every
few seconds, a mud volcano spat filth to Heaven, streams of hot
water rumbled under foot, plunged through the dead pines in
steaming cataracts and died on a waste of white where green-
grey, black-yellow and pink pools roared, shouted, bubbled, or
hissed as their wicked fancies prompted. By the look of the eye
the place should have been frozen over. By the feel of the feet it
was warm. I ventured out among the pools, carefully following
tracks, but one unwary foot began to sink, a squirt of water
followed, and having no desire to descend quick into Tophet I
returned to the shore where the mud and the sulphur and the
nameless fat ooze-vegetation of Lethe lay. But the very road
rang as though built over a gulf ; and besides, how was I to tell
when the raving blast of steam would find its vent insufficient and
blow the whole affair into Nirvana ? There was a potent stench
of stale eggs everywhere, and crystals of sulphur crumbled under
the foot, and the glare of the sun on the white stuff was blinding.

*   *   *   *   *

Imagine mighty green fields splattered with lime beds : all the
flowers of the summer growing up to the very edge of the lime.
That was the first glimpse of the geyser basins. The buggy
had pulled up close to a rough, broken, blistered cone of stuff
between ten and twenty feet high. There was trouble in that
place—moaning, splashing, gurgling, and the clank of machinery.
A spurt of boiling water jumped into the air and a wash of

180

water followed. I removed swiftly. The old lady from Chicago shrieked. " What a wicked waste ! " said her husband. I think they call it the Riverside Geyser. Its spout was torn and ragged like the mouth of a gun when a shell has burst there. It grumbled madly for a moment or two and then was still. I crept over the steaming lime—it was the burning marl on which Satan lay—and looked fearfully down its mouth. You should never look a gift geyser in the mouth. I beheld a horrible, slippery, slimy funnel with water rising and falling ten feet at a time. Then the water rose to lip-level with a rush and an infernal bubbling troubled this Devil's Bethesda before the sullen heave of the crest of a wave lapped over the edge and made me run. Mark the nature of the human soul! I had begun with awe, not to say terror. I stepped back from the flanks of the Riverside Geyser saying " Pooh ! Is that all it can do ?" Yet for aught I knew the whole thing might have blown up at a minute's notice ; she, he, or it, being an arrangement of uncertain temper.

The old lady from Chicago poked with her parasol at the pools as though they had been alive. On one particularly innocent-looking little puddle she turned her back for a moment, and there rose behind her a twenty-foot column of water and steam. Then she shrieked and protested that " she never thought it would ha' done it", and the old man chewed his tobacco steadily, and mourned for steam-power wasted. I embraced the whitened stump of a middle-sized pine that had grown all too close to a hot pool's lip, and the whole thing turned over under my hand as a tree would do in a nightmare. From right and left came the trumpet-ings of elephants at play. I stepped into a pool of old dried blood rimmed with the nodding cornflowers ; the blood changed to ink even as I trod ; and the ink and blood were washed away in a spurt of boiling sulphurous water spat out from the lee of a bank of flowers. This sounds mad, doesn't it ?

We rounded a low spur of hill, and came out upon a field of aching snowy lime, rolled in sheets, twisted into knots, riven with rents and diamonds and stars, stretching for more than half a mile in every direction. In this place of despair lay most of the big geysers who know when there is trouble in Krakatoa, who tell the pines when there is a cyclone on the Atlantic seaboard, and who—are exhibited to visitors under pretty and fanciful names. The first mound that I encountered belonged to a goblin splashing in his tub. I heard him kick, pull a shower-bath on his shoulders, gasp, crack his joints, and rub himself down with a towel ; then he let the water out of the bath, as a thoughtful man should, and it all sank down out of sight till another goblin arrived. Yet they called this place the Lioness and the Cubs. It lies not very far from the Lion, which is a sullen, roaring beast, and they say that when it is very active the other geysers presently follow suit. After the Krakatoa eruption all the geysers went mad together, spouting, spurting and bellowing till men feared that they would rip up the whole field. Mysterious sympathies exist among them, and when the Giantess speaks, they all hold their peace.

(*45°N; 111°W.*)

(Rudyard Kipling : *From Sea to Sea*, Vol. II, No. XXX.)

Hot Springs

JAPAN

THE JAPANESE mountains are of volcanic origin, and hot springs are numerous in the mountain resorts. Nothing is more enjoyable than the unique pleasure of finishing a hard day's ski-ing with a swim in an open-air pool so hot that the surrounding frozen air causes clouds of steam to rise.

(John Morris : *Traveller from Tokyo*.)

Hot Springs

NEW ZEALAND : LAKE ROTORUA

ONCE MORE in the clear country, we saw in the distance a blue, singular range of mountains, while immediately underneath us, a thousand feet down, stretched a long, greenish lake with an island in the middle of it, and a cluster of white houses six miles off standing on the shore. The lake was Rotorua ; the white houses were Ohinemotu, the end of our immediate journey. As we drew nearer to our destination both Ohinemotu and the district touching it seemed to be on fire. Columns of what appeared to be smoke were rising out of the Ti-tree bush, from the lake shore, and from the ditches by the roadside. We should have found the lake itself lukewarm if we could have dipped our hands in the water. At length we reached the foot of a steep bit of road, ascended it, and found ourselves at the door of our hotel, lodging-house, boarding-house—whatever we please to call it. There were two in the place, as at Cambridge, which of course were rivals. Stables, stores, and shops were sprinkled about miscellaneously, and all round lay a primitive Maori village, consisting of perhaps a hundred or a hundred and fifty families, descendants of the warrior tribes who within living memory had fought fierce and bloody battles on these waters, and had cooked their prisoners at these natural fireplaces. The smoke which we had seen was steam rising from boiling springs—alkaline, siliceous, sulphuretted, and violently acid—not confined, too, exactly to the same spot, but bursting out where they please through the crust of the soil. You walk one day over firm ground, where the next you find a bubbling hole, into which if you unwarily step, your foot will be of no further service to you. These springs extend for many miles ; they are in the island on the lake ; they must be under the lake itself to account for its temperature. Across the water among the trees a few miles off, a tall column of steam ascends, as if from an engine. It arises from a gorge where a sulphurous and foul-smelling liquid, black as Cocytus or Acheron, bubbles and boils and spouts its filthy mud eternally. I have no taste for horrors, and did not visit this foul place, which they call Tikiteri. A Scotchman, they say, went to look at it, gazed breathless for a moment or two, and when he found his voice exclaimed, " By God, I will never swear again." Indeed, the condition of things all about suggests the alarming nearness of the burning regions. The native settlement was at one time very large, and must have been one of the most important in New Zealand. It owed its origin doubtless to these springs, not from any superstitious reason, but for the practical uses to which the Maori apply them. They cook their cray-fish and white-fish, which they catch in the lake, in them ; they boil their cabbage, they wash their clothes in them, and they wash themselves. They own the district as a village community. The Government rents it of them. They live on their income, like ladies and gentlemen, and having no work to do, or not caring to do any, they prefer to enjoy themselves. They dig out baths, bring streams from cold springs to temper the hot, and pass half their time lounging in the tepid water. I heard a grunt as I passed one of these pools. I supposed it was a pig. Looking round, I beheld a copper-coloured face and shoulders, a white head, and a pipe sticking out of the mouth. They find existence very tolerable on these terms. Old men, women, and children paddle about all day ; young men swim in the warm corners of the lake. Now and then some small boy or girl falls into a boiling hole, and the parents are relieved of further trouble with them.

(38°10'S; 176°25'E.)   (J. A. Froude : *Oceana*.)

Hot Springs and Mud Volcanoes
INDONESIA : CELEBES

THE NEXT morning I went to see the hot-springs and mud volcanoes, for which this place is celebrated. A picturesque path among plantations and ravines, brought us to a beautiful circular basin about forty feet diameter, bordered by a calcareous ledge, so uniform and truly curved that it looked like a work of art. It was filled with clear water very near the boiling point, and emitting clouds of steam with a strong sulphureous odour. It overflows at one point and forms a little stream of hot water, which at a hundred yards' distance is still too hot to hold the hand in. A little further on, in a piece of rough wood, were two other springs not so regular in outline, but appearing to be much hotter, as they were in a continual state of active ebullition. At intervals of a few minutes a great escape of steam or gas took place, throwing up a column of water three or four feet high.

We then went to the mud-springs, which are about a mile off, and are still more curious. On a sloping tract of ground in a slight hollow is a small lake of liquid mud, in patches of blue, red, or white, and in many places boiling or bubbling most furiously. All around on the indurated clay, are small wells and craters full of boiling mud. These seem to be forming continually, a small hole appearing first, which emits jets of steam and boiling mud, which on hardening, forms a little cone with a crater in the middle. The ground for some distance is very unsafe, as it is evidently liquid at a small depth, and bends with pressure like thin ice. At one of the smaller marginal jets which I managed to approach, I held my hand to see if it was really as hot as it looked, when a little drop of mud that spurted on to my finger scalded like boiling water. A short distance off there was a flat bare surface of rock, as smooth and hot as an oven floor, which

184

was evidently an old mud-pool dried up and hardened. For hundreds of yards round where there were banks of reddish and white clay used for whitewash, it was still so hot close to the surface that the hand could hardly bear to be held in cracks a few inches deep, and from which arose a strong sulphureous vapour. I was informed that some years back a French gentleman who visited these springs ventured too near the liquid mud, when the crust gave way and he was engulfed in the horrible cauldron.

(A. R. Wallace : *The Malay Archipelago*.)

Mud Volcanoes

NEW ZEALAND

THEY HAD rounded the flank of the hill and now came in sight of the native settlement. The swift northern dusk had fallen upon the countryside with no suggestion of density. The darkening of the air seemed merely to be a change in translucence. It was very still, and as they stood listening Dikon became aware of a curious sound. It was as if a giant somewhere close at hand was blowing thick bubbles very slowly and complacently ; or as if, over the brink of the hill, a vast porridge pot had just come to boiling point. The sounds were irregular, each one mounting to its point of explosion. Plop. Plop-plop . . . plop.

They moved forward and reached a point where the scrub and grass came to an end and the path descended a steep bank to traverse a region of solidified blue mud, sinter mounds, hot pools and geysers. The sulphurous smell was very strong. The track, defined at intervals by stakes to which pieces of white rag had been tied, went forward over naked hillocks towards the hip-roofs of the native settlement.

" Shall we go farther ?" asked Dixon.

" It's a detestable place, but I think we must see this infernal brew."

" We must keep to the track, then. Shall I go first ?"

They walked on and presently, through the soles of their feet, received a strange experience. The ground beneath them was unsteady, quivering a little, telling them that, after all, there was no stability in the earth by which we symbolise stability. They moved across a skin, and the organism beneath it was restless.

" This is abominable," said Gaunt. " The whole place works secretly. It's alive."

" Look to your right," said Dikon. They had come to a hillock ; the path divided, and, where it turned to the right, was marked by red flags.

" They told me you used to be able to walk along there," Dikon explained, " but it's not safe now. Taupo-tapu is encroaching."

They followed the white flags, climbed steeply, and at last, from the top of the hillock, looked down on Taupo-tapu.

It was perhaps fifteen feet across, dun-coloured and glistening, a working ulcer in the body of the earth. Great bubbles of mud formed themselves deliberately, swelled, and broke with the sounds which they had noticed a few minutes before and which were now loud and insistent. With each eruption, unctuous rings momentarily creased the surface of the brew. It was impossible to escape the notion that Taupo-tapu had some idiotic purpose of its own.

For perhaps two minutes Gaunt looked at it in silence. " Quite obscene, isn't it ?" he said at last. " If you know anything about it, don't tell me."

" The only story I've heard," Dikon said, " is not a pretty one. I won't."

Gaunt's reply was unexpected. " I should prefer to hear it from a Maori," he said.

" You can see where the thing has eaten into the old path," Dikon pointed out. " The red flags begin again on the other side and rejoin our track just below us. Just as well. It would be an unpleasant error to mistake the paths, wouldn't it ?"

" Don't, for God's sake," said Gaunt. " It's getting dark. Let's go home."

When they turned back, Dikon found that he had to make a deliberate effort to prevent himself from hurrying, and he thought he sensed Gaunt's impatience too. The firm dry earth felt wholesome under their feet as once more they circled the hill. Behind them in the native village a drift of song rose on the cool air, intolerably plaintive and lonely.

" What's that ?"

" One of their songs," said Dikon. " Perhaps they're rehearsing for your concert. It's the genuine thing. You get the authentic music up here."

The shoulder of the hill came between them and the song. It was almost dark as they walked along the brushwood fence towards Wai-ata-tapu. Steam from the hot pools drifted in wraiths across the still night air.

(Ngaio Marsh : *Colour Scheme.*)

The Pink and White Terraces
NEW ZEALAND

AFTER a winding walk of half a mile, we came again on the river, which was rushing deep and swift through reeds and Ti-tree. A rickety canoe was waiting there, in which we crossed, climbed up a bank, and stretched before us we saw the White Terrace in all its strangeness ; a crystal staircase, glittering and stainless as if it were ice, spreading out like an open fan from a point above us on the hillside, and projecting at the bottom into a lake, where it was perhaps two hundred yards wide. The summit was concealed behind the volumes of steam rising out of the boiling fountain, from which the siliceous stream proceeded. The stairs were about twenty in number, the height of each being six or seven feet. The floors dividing them were horizontal, as if laid out with a spirit-level. They were of uneven breadth ; twenty, thirty, fifty feet, or even more ; each step down being always perpendicular, and all forming arcs of a circle of which the crater was the centre. On reaching the lake the silica flowed away into the water, where it lay in a sheet half-submerged, like ice at the beginning of a thaw. There was nothing in the fall of the ground to account for the regularity of shape. A crater has been opened through the rock a hundred and twenty feet above the lake. The water, which comes up boiling from below, is charged as heavily as it will bear with silicic acid. The silica crystallises as it is exposed to the air. The water continues to flow over the hardened surface, continually adding a fresh coating to the deposits already laid down ; and, for reasons which men of science can no doubt supply, the crystals take the form which I have described. The process is a rapid one ; a piece of newspaper left behind by a recent visitor was already stiff as the starched collar of a shirt. Tourists ambitious of immortality had pencilled their names and the date of their visit on the white surface over which the stream was running. Some of these inscriptions were six and seven years old, yet the strokes were as fresh as on the day they were made, being protected by the film of glass which was instantly drawn over them.

The thickness of the crust is, I believe, unascertained, the Maories objecting to scientific examination of their treasure. It struck me, however, that this singular cascade must have been of recent, indeed measurably recent, origin. In the middle of the terrace were the remains of a Ti-tree bush, which was standing where a small patch of soil was still uncovered. Part of this, where the silica had not reached the roots, was in leaf and alive. The rest had been similarly alive within a year or two, for it had not yet rotted, but had died as the crust rose round it. Clearly nothing could grow through the crust, and the bush was a living evidence of the rate at which it was forming. It appeared to me that this particular staircase was not perhaps a hundred years old, but that terraces like it had successively been formed all along the hillside as the crater opened now at one spot and now at another. Wherever the rock showed elsewhere through the soil it was of the same material as that which I saw growing. If the supply of silicic acid was stopped the surface would dry and crack. Ti-trees would then spring up over it. The crystal steps would crumble into less regular outlines, and in a century or two the fairy-like wonder which we were gazing at would be indistinguishable from the adjoining slopes. We walked, or rather waded, upwards to the boiling pool; it was not in this that we were to be bathed. It was about sixty feet across, and was of unknown depth. The heat was too intense to allow us to approach the edge, and we could see little, from the dense clouds of steam which lay upon it. We were more fortunate afterwards at the crater of the second terrace.

The crystallisation is ice-like, and the phenomenon, except for the alternate horizontal and vertical arrangement of the deposited silica, is like what would be seen in any Northern region when a severe frost suddenly seizes hold of a waterfall before snow has fallen and buried it.

. . . The lake into which the Terrace descended lay close below us. It was green and hot (the temperature near 100°), patched over with beds of rank reed and rush, which were forced into unnatural luxuriance. After leaving the mud-heaps we went down to the waterside, where we found our luncheon laid out in an open-air saloon, with a smooth floor of silica, and natural slabs of silica ranged round the sides as benches. Steam-fountains were playing in half-a-dozen places. The floor was hot—a mere skin between us and Cocytus. The slabs were hot, just to the point of being agreeable to sit upon. This spot was a favourite winter resort of the Maori—their palavering hall, where they had their constitutional debates, their store-room, their kitchen, and their dining-room. Here they had their innocent meals on dried fish and fruit, here also their less innocent on dried slices of their enemies. At present it seemed to be made over to visitors like ourselves. The ground was littered with broken bottles, emptied tins, and scraps of sandwich papers. We contributed our share to the general mess. . . .

. . . The Pink Terrace, the object of our voyage, opened out before us on the opposite shore. It was formed on the same lines as the other, save that it was narrower, and was flushed with pale-rose colour. Oxide of iron is said to be the cause, but there is probably something besides. The water has not, I believe, been completely analysed. . . . The youth took charge of us and led us up the shining stairs. The crystals were even more beautiful than those which we had seen, falling like clusters of rosy icicles, or hanging in festoons like creepers trailing from a rail. At the foot of each cascade the water lay in pools of ultramarine, their exquisite colour being due in part, I suppose, to the light of the sky refracted upwards from the bottom. In the deepest of these we were to bathe. The temperature was 94° or 95°. The water lay inviting in its crystal basin . . . deep enough to swim in comfortably, though not over our heads. We lay on our backs and floated for ten minutes in exquisite enjoyment, and the alkali, or the flint, or the perfect purity of the element, seemed to saturate our systems. I, for one, when I was dressed again, could have fancied myself back in the old days when I did not know that I had a body, and could run up hill as lightly as down. The bath over, we pursued our way. The marvel of the Terrace was still before us, reserved to the last like the finish in a pheasant battue. The crater at the White Terrace had been boiling ; the steam rushing out of it had filled the air with cloud ; and the scorching heat had kept us at a distance. Here the temperature was twenty degrees lower ; there was still vapour hovering over the surface, but it was lighter and more transparent, and a soft breeze now and then blew it completely aside. We could stand on the brim and gaze as through an opening in the earth into an azure infinity beyond. Down and down, and fainter and softer as they receded, the white crystals projected from the rocky walls over the abyss, till they seemed to dissolve not into darkness but into light. The hue of the water was something which I had never seen, and shall never again see on this side of eternity. Not the violet, not the hare-bell, nearest in its tint to heaven of all nature's flowers ; not turquoise, not sapphire, not the unfathomable æther itself could convey to one who had not looked on it a sense of that supernatural lovcliness. Comparison could only soil such inimitable purity. The only colour I ever saw in sky or on earth in the least resembling the aspect of this extraordinary pool was the flame of burning sulphur. Here was a bath, if mortal flesh could have borne to dive into it ! Had it been in Norway, we should have seen far down the floating Lorelei, inviting us to plunge and leave life and all belonging to it for such a home and such companionship. It was a bath for the gods and not for man. Artemis and her nymphs should have been swimming there, and we Actæons daring our fate to gaze on them.

(J. A. Froude : *Oceana.*)

MOUNTAINS AND PLATEAUS

Ben More

SCOTLAND

O transcendental mountain, that dost span,
In the orbit of thy universal girth,
Hills that arise out of the spirit of Man
Reared from the whirling axis of the Earth—
Those mighty mountains mystical, that loll
And brag in space, and pay not any toll
To bat-eyed Time—verily thou dost wear
Thy mortal nature with no mortal air,
O single in the multitudinous ranks
Of hostile chaos, flailing from thy flanks
The flood, for certain months and days, yet thou
For all thy height, and thy sheer mail of starkness,
Must in the flat sea sink, as low as now
Thy top towers high, above the top of darkness :
Thy light is set in ashes, in thy crown
Fate plants her pale flag ; wind and heat and frost,
The elemental hammers, rain thee down
To make of all thy vaunted mass a ghost,
Till the great Fang that labours at the foot
Of all the pillars of the gleaming world,
The sateless Sea, gnaw up thy hidden root,
And Fate lie dim in her own colours furled,
Then vail my soul her star-enrondured crest
Before the rush of that last water-line,
That mates thy massive dust in bridal rest
Minute with mine.

(Frederick Victor Branford :
Ben More: An Armistice Poem.)

The Himalayas

INDIA

" Who goes to the Hills goes to his mother."
They had crossed the Sewaliks and the half-tropical Doon, left Mussoorie behind them, and headed north along the narrow hill-roads. Day after day they struck deeper into the huddled mountains, and day after day Kim watched the lama return to a man's strength. Among the terraces of the Doon he had leaned on the boy's shoulder, ready to profit by wayside halts. Under the great ramp to Mussoorie he drew himself together as an old hunter faces a well-remembered bank, and where he should have sunk exhausted swung his long draperies about him, drew a deep double-lungful of the diamond air, and walked as only a hillman can. Kim, plains-bred and plains-fed, sweated and panted astonished. " This is *my* country," said the lama. " Beside Such-zen, this is flatter than a rice-field ; " and with steady, driving strokes from the loins he strode upwards. But it was on the steep down-hill marches, three thousand feet in three hours, that he went utterly away from Kim, whose back ached with holding back, and whose big-toe was nigh cut off by his grass sandal-string. Though the speckled shadow of the great deodar-forests ; through oak feathered and plumed with ferns ; birch, ilex, rhododendron, and pine, out on to the bare hillsides' slippery sunburnt grass, and back into the woodlands' coolth again, till oak gave way to bamboo and palm of the valley, he swung untiring.

Glancing back in the twilight at the huge ridges behind him and the faint, thin line of the road whereby they had come, he would lay out, with a hillman's generous breadth of vision, fresh marches for the morrow ; or, halting in the neck of some uplifted pass that gave on Spiti and Kulu, would stretch out his hands yearningly towards the high snows of the horizon. In the dawns they flared windy-red above stark blue, as Kedarnath and Badrinath—kings of that wilderness—took the first sunlight. All day long they lay like molten silver under the sun, and at evening put on their jewels again. At first they breathed temperately upon the travellers, winds good to meet when one crawled over some gigantic hog-back ; but in a few days, at a height of nine or ten thousand feet, those breezes bit ; and Kim kindly allowed a village of hillmen to acquire merit by giving him a rough blanket-coat. The lama was mildly surprised that anyone should object to the knife-edged breezes which had cut the years off his shoulders.

" These are but the lower hills, *chela*. There is no cold till we come to the true Hills."

* * * * *

They crossed a snowy pass in cold moonlight, when the lama, mildly chaffing Kim, went through up to his knees, like a Bactrian camel—the snow-bred, shag-haired sort that come into the Kashmir Serai. They dipped across beds of light snow and snow-powdered shale, where they took refuge from a gale in a camp of Tibetans hurrying down tiny sheep, each laden with a bag of borax. They came out upon grassy shoulders still snow-speckled, and through forest, to grass anew. For all their marchings, Kedarnath and Badrinath were not impressed ; and it was only after days of travel that Kim, uplifted upon some insignificant ten thousand-foot hummock, could see that a shoulder-knot or horn of the two great lords had—ever so slightly—changed outline.

At last they entered a world within a world—a valley of leagues where the high hills were fashioned of the mere rubble and refuse from off the knees of the mountains. Here one day's march carried them no farther, it seemed, than a dreamer's clogged pace bears him in a nightmare. They skirted a shoulder painfully for hours, and, behold, it was but an outlying boss in an outlying buttress of the main pile ! A rounded meadow revealed itself, when they had reached it, for a vast tableland running far into the valley. Three days later, it was a dim fold in the earth to southward.

" Surely the Gods live here," said Kim, beaten down by the silence and the appalling sweep and dispersal of the cloud-shadows after rain. " This is no place for men ! "

" Long and long ago," said the lama, as to himself, " it was asked of the Lord whether the world were everlasting. To this the Excellent One returned no answer. . . . When I was in Ceylon, a wise Seeker confirmed that from the gospel which is written in Pali. Certainly, since we know the way to Freedom, the question were unprofitable, but—look, and know illusion, *chela* ! These are the true Hills ! They are like my hills by Such-zen. Never were such hills ! "

Above them, still enormously above them, earth towered away towards the snow-line, where from east to west across hundreds of miles, ruled as with a ruler, the last of the bold birches stopped.

Above that, in scarps and blocks upheaved, the rocks strove to fight their heads above the white smother. Above these again, changeless since the world's beginning, but changing to every mood of sun and cloud, lay out the eternal snow. They could see blots and blurs on its face where storm and wandering wullie-wa got up to dance. Below them, as they stood, the forest slid away in a sheet of blue-green for mile upon mile ; below the forest was a village in its sprinkle of terraced fields and steep grazing-grounds; below the village they knew, though a thunderstorm worried and growled there for the moment, a pitch of twelve or fifteen hundred feet gave to the moist valley where the streams gather that are the mothers of young Sutluj.

(31°N; 78°E.) (Rudyard Kipling : *Kim.*)

The Himalayas

INDIA

TEMPERATURE AND season greatly influence the aspect of a country. They are the common agents of physical change. Their action in this valley presents one feature deserving of our notice : the cloud of fine dust that daily fills the sky. In the oppressive days of summer, when for weeks no rain may fall, a dense haze collects over the mountains. It hangs thick over the valleys, and, like a veil, envelops even the highest peaks. The burning cliffs radiate a fierce heat and there is scarce a movement in the breathless air. All objects are obscured as though in a dim mist. The trees are unreal ; the hills are ill-defined ; they look bleak and uninviting, as though we looked through a moist fog on to a rocky shore. From a summit we obtain no sight of a distant range, where the plains are concealed beneath a shroud of dust. The atmosphere looks polluted, foul and murky, a vision of discomfort. Sickness increases. All vitality is lost when the cloud of heat obscures the sky. This haze is due to the permeation of the atmosphere with a very fine dust carried up by ascending convection currents generated by the contact of the air with the heated rocks. That these currents rise with great force from the valleys is indicated by the ease with which the plumed seeds are swept aloft from between the cliffs into the open sky, or the way in which a rain-cloud pouring over a ridge is opposed by an ascending stream within the valley and driven upwards as though in wreaths of smoke. The mornings show a clearer sky. The dust has settled in the cool of night. But it is only a temporary lapse ; the haze again deepens with the daily heat. Nothing but rain can now purify the air.

At last the clouds collect over the hills ; first in silvery wisps increasing each evening into heavy cumuli, and backing away at night, leaving a clear sky. Finally the clouds burst ; a sense of relief is felt as the rain pours down in torrents. The sky clears and we see that the haze of dust has been swept to earth. A vast panorama is now exposed ; thousands of square miles of mountains are seen in a single view. All that was wrapped in gloom appears through a transparent sky. So clear is the prospect that every object looks magnified as though drawn miles nearer to our vision. Shadows cast by a passing cloud or by a mountain side roll across the clear valleys. Sinuous rivers sparkle in the sunlight ; tiny villages or strips of cultivated soil, hiding in some narrow glen, for the first time appear to view ; the nearer hills are tinged with blue as if reflecting the azure of the sky, and the snowy peaks climbing above the wooded slopes contend with the whiteness of the clouds.

(R. W. G. Hingston : *A Naturalist in Himalaya*.)

Adams Peak

CEYLON

IN THE middle of the hills of Ceylon, now sacred to tea, there towers a mountain so famous that the literature of two thousand years in several languages would have to be searched if all the references to it were to be assembled in one book. Hindus and Buddhists, Mahomedans and Eastern Christians alike revere the mountain as a holy place, and there is some evidence that the jungle people that came before all these did likewise. It is certain that the Peak was holy fifteen centuries ago, when the oldest Sinhalese literature that has survived was composed out of fragments and books already old and being forgotten ; and it is almost as certain that it was holy a thousand years before that, when legends of Buddha attach to it, and when it became the refuge of some of the aboriginal inhabitants of Lanka who fled before the advance of the earliest Sinhalese invaders. Whether it was holy even earlier than that, in the days when the men of those mountains used chert and crystal flakes for their tools and weapons, there is nothing directly to say ; but deposits of their artifacts lie upon so many of the lesser hills around the Peak that this too seems not unreasonable to suppose.

The Peak must be one of the vastest and most widely reverenced cathedrals of the human race ; but the shrine itself is only a little tile roof raised upon four pillars, or it may be eight, open on all four sides to every wind that blows, and untended by any human being for months at a time when the rains are at their heaviest, and the only other building there in my time was a small mud hut of one room, which I was lent by the monk in charge.

Right to the very summit of the Peak the forest grows, and from the parapet wall itself one may pick blossoms from the tops of old wild rhododendrons and read in their mottled throats the name of God written in letters that all may read who will. Looking down from this wall one can see how for miles and miles on every side each fold of the hills and every valley is clothed in an ancient forest that has never known the axe, and is justly named the Wilderness of the Peak. The profusion of its beauty alone would inspire any sensitive being with a feeling of awe, and it may have been this unparalleled loveliness that led some man, who knows how many thousands of years ago, to name it holy.

I climbed up once when no pilgrims had travelled the road for several months of very wet weather, and had to crush my way through masses of begonias and balsams, and to tread upon pink orchids as I climbed, while the roofs of the shelters below the cliffs were clouded over with a mist of yellow calceolaria.

In the stillness of the evening, when no pilgrims are there, voices come up from this old forest, out from the depths of the valleys thousands of feet below, and from the slopes, and from the ridges of lesser hills that reach up in reverence like disciples beside their master. Always there is the song of the streams which run hidden in their tunnels of trees festooned with orchids, dendrobium aureum, or macarthii ; and often one may hear the cries of animals, the strident roar of leopards, the horn-like challenge of sambhur stags, the scream of eagles, the deep tones of the great black monkeys of the hills, and, more tremendous than any, the trumpeting of elephants. For the forest is full of life, though in its extreme density it is rare to see any living animal other than the squirrels and monkeys who move among the tree-tops ; but their tracks and their voices betray the greater animals, and it was almost entirely due to their presence that we were able to explore at all.

This forest is a very wet one, and consequently very dense, and much of it is bound into an unbelievably impenetrable tangle by creeping bamboo, whose long tendrils, hard and thin as telegraph wire, form a mesh difficult for man to enter unless he can cut his way painfully yard by yard. To the elephants with their giant strength and weight it is a different matter. They live for the most part on wood pulp ground by their four huge teeth from the branches of trees, and this leads them to explore just as my different quests led me. All the time I was in the wilderness I found only one open space, high upon a col between two peaks, a fairyland of grass and flowers ; but I had no difficulty in marching in any direction I desired, for the elephant roads ran everywhere. Man's roads pursue valleys for the most part, but the high roads made by elephants slant up the flanks of hills to gain the ridge as early as they may, and then travel along high ground as far as they possibly can. They are firm and of easy gradient to walk, though, walled as they are by the yielding but unbreakable netting of the bamboo, they may be perilous to use unless precautions be taken not to come unawares upon their makers, for to avoid a charge or even a startled stampede would be difficult, as although the bulk of an elephant is vast compared with that of a man, his road generally suffices only for men to proceed in single file. We went with caution, as though on the heels of great game. Kiri Lamaya took a further precaution, and I followed him to set his mind at peace, for he avoided all reference to elephants by name, lest they should hear and resent it : " The Great Ones," he called them, or " The Old Ones," or simply " They."

One is tempted to think that wherever a man may climb so may an elephant, for their immense footprints, smaller only than that on the mountain's top, are to be found upon the highest ridges, and on the summits of peaks hard to scale. It is only the encircling wall that holds them from measuring their feet with Buddha's, and I have little doubt that elephants stood there before ever men did, for chains are not needed upon the Maskeliya side.

(6°50'N; 80°20'E.)   (John Still : *Jungle Tide*.)

The Alps

SWITZERLAND AND ITALY

NOTHING at all was wrong with that night. Beyond the queenly white shape of Mont Rose the moon rode gloriously high, burnished and flashing with frost, above sleeping Lombardy. Gowned in new snow and bejewelled with sparkles of light, the Weisshorn, the greatest great lady in Nature, looked as lovely to Bell as when the first sight of that pale supreme grace had taken his breath away in his youth. At the height where they stood the frost had silenced every trickle of water, leaving all space to be filled with subtler challenges to the ear. The air almost crackled with crispness : it was alive with the massed animation of millions of infinitesimal crystallisations. The Schalliberg Glacier, a little away to their right, had its own living whisper, the sum of the innumerable tiny creaks and fractures of its jostling molecules of ice. Up here, where the quiet of night was suffused with this audible stir of the forces fashioning the earth, it felt as if some murmurous joint voice of all existence were abroad and life itself were trying to make its high urgency felt.

(46°5'N; 7°45'E.) (C. E. Montague : *Action.*)

The Matterhorn

SWITZERLAND

WE WERE approaching Zermatt, consequently we were approaching the renowned Matterhorn. A month before this mountain had been only a name to us, but latterly we had been moving through a steadily thickening double row of pictures of it, done in oil, water, chromo, wood, steel, copper, crayon and photography, and so it had at length become a shape to us—and a very distinct, decided, and familiar one, too. We were expecting to recognize that mountain whenever or wherever we should run across it. We were not deceived. The monarch was far away when we first saw him, but there was no such thing as mistaking him. He has the rare peculiarity of standing by himself. He is peculiarly steep, too, and is also most oddly shaped. He towers into the sky like a colossal wedge, with the upper third of its blade bent a little to the left. The broad base of this monster wedge is planted upon a grand glacier-paved Alpine platform whose elevation is ten thousand feet above sea-level ; as the wedge itself is some five thousand feet high, it follows that its apex is about fifteen thousand feet above sea level. So the whole bulk of this stately piece of rock, this sky-cleaving monolith, is above the line of eternal snow. Yet while all its giant neighbours have the look of being built of solid snow, from their waists up, the Matterhorn stands black and naked and forbidding the year round, or merely powdered or streaked with white in places, for its sides are so steep that the snow cannot stay there. Its strange form, its august isolation, and its majestic unkinship with its own kind, make it, so to speak, the Napoleon of the mountain world. " Grand, gloomy, and peculiar," is a phrase which fits it as aptly as it fitted the great captain.

Think of a monument a mile high, standing on a pedestal two miles high ! This is what the Matterhorn is—a monument. Its office henceforth, for all time, will be to keep watch and ward over the secret resting-place of the young Lord Douglas, who in 1865 was precipitated from the summit over a precipice 4,000 feet high, and never seen again. No man ever had such a monument as this before. The most imposing of the world's other monuments are but atoms compared to it ; and they will perish, and their places will pass from memory, but this will remain.

A walk from St. Nicholas to Zermatt is a wonderful experience. Nature is built on a stupendous plan in that region. One marches continually between walls that are piled into the skies, with their upper heights broken into a confusion of sublime shapes that gleam white and cold against the background of blue ; and here and there one sees a big glacier displaying its grandeurs on the top of a precipice, or a graceful cascade leaping and flashing down the green declivities. There is nothing tame, or cheap, or trivial —it is all magnificent. That short valley is a picture gallery of a notable kind, for it contains no mediocrities ; from end to end the Creator has hung it with His masterpieces.

(46°N; 7°40'E.)   (Mark Twain : *A Tramp Abroad.*)

Mount Ida

CRETE

A DAY passed and the vessel came upon Crete. It was about an hour after sunrise that the ship was steaming along the coast of the island, and the view of it was delicate and wonderful. The cliffs that rose from the sea were lean and dim, but the mountains far inland were lit by the rising sun, so that every dome and pinnacle stood out in freshest outline. The whole range was covered with snow, and long shadows, falling across the great snowfields, deepened the brilliancy of the bare heights and the gloom of the ravines. Above the many peaks towered Mount Ida, a dome of white springing out of the snowdrifts and still tinted by the rising sun with the faint colour of the pink carnation. This dainty vision of Mount Ida was the most beautiful spectacle that had presented itself since the journey began.

(35°10′N; 24°50′E.)

(Sir Frederick Treves : *The Other Side of the Lantern.*)

The Rockies

COLORADO

AMONG the many places in different parts of the world which I have marked down as places of residence when I am a Methuselah is a certain house above the Cheeseman Park in Denver, Colorado. It is a pillared Georgian structure, about 6,000 feet above sea-level, affluent and comfortable looking, with a pleasant garden city all about it, and just across the road is the charming marble portico which a benevolent lady has erected as a memorial to her husband and an adornment to the Park. These are incidentals ; the main point is that almost every window in this house looks across the town and beyond it to the great sweeping line of the " Rockies," from Pike's Peak on the east to the great snow-fields and summits which melt away into the sky on the north-west. This is how mountains should be seen—at least by Methuselahs who have ceased to dream of climbing them— and, unless it be the view of the Himalayas from Mahatsu above Simla, I can think of no unbroken line from horizon to horizon which equals this one. The sunset on a November evening strikes near the middle of it, turning the whole range from pale amber to hazy blue, and then down the scale of amethyst and pink to the final velvety purple against an orange sky. Twilight is short in this region, and we watched it till darkness fell, and the night-chill sent us back to our hotel, but envy filled us for the owner of the house, who looks on this scene from his windows morning, noon and night.

You have the same scene behind you when you depart westward from Denver to the coast, and as you climb up to the Colorado plateau the mountains slip down the horizon till you see only their white edges on the rim of the green and brown upland.
(*39°45'N; 105°W.*)   (J. A. Spender : *The America of Today*.)

Witchita Mountains
OKLAHOMA

THE WITCHITA Mountains are singularly picturesque and beautiful ; composed of granite of different degrees of hardness, and of manifold colours, they rise abruptly from a level plain to a height varying from 650 to 700 feet. Many of these mountains are isolated, and bear a resemblance to truncated cones ; others, on the contrary, are grouped and joined together, though still retaining their circular form. At a distance their surface seems as if polished, but, near, they represent huge masses of rocks confusedly heaped one above the other. Nevertheless in some places the granite has preserved its primitive position. Red porphyry and pieces of felspar of the same colour are to be found there in abundance. All these rocks are interveined with greenstone and quartz, the latter being generally coloured with oxide of iron. The declivities of the mountains are frequently cut up by huge precipices, which are covered with wall-plants. The plains from the middle of which these mountains ascend, possess numerous and most magnificent specimens of chalcedony, jasper and agate. The sources that spring from the bosom of the rocks, or from the greensward, are limpid, and the water has a strong taste of alkaline.

Matted grass, at least ten or twelve feet long, clothes the soil of the valleys, which are shaded by black chestnut-trees, ash-trees, cotton-trees, oaks, Chinese lilacs, mesquites, and willows. Buffaloes, panthers, antelopes, roebucks, otters, beavers, turkeys, grouse, quail, partridges, and mocking-birds, live quietly together in those solitudes. Formerly, at the foot of the mountains, were many villages belonging to the Witchita Indians, who cultivated maize ; but since 1850 they have abandoned their villages and spread themselves over the prairies, probably on account of the incursions made by the Comanches. Yet it must have been delightful to dwell in this region, where the air is as pure and sweet as the kiss of a child, the climate deliciously mild, and the sky ever blue as an Oriental sapphire ; a gentle breeze, too, in sweeping over the calyx of flowers, continually embalms the atmosphere with their fragrance ; the cedars and Chinese lilacs exhale sweet perfumes ; and the colibri, the blue bird, and the cardinal flutter from branch to branch ; large nests are built by birds of prey on the summit of the rocks or in the hollows of dried-up quagmires ; tortoises crawl solitarily to the soft murmuring brook ; wormwood, amaranthus, and purple flowers, blocks of red granite from which ivy hangs, are visible under the verdant oaks ; whilst light flocculent clouds hover above the tops of motionless trees— charming scenes, which captivate the human soul, at the same time that they plunge it into a deep reverie. The Chactas, to whom these mountains belong, never venture there ; they fear the Comanches, and prefer cultivating in peace their ground within the plains rather than have to encounter these wandering tribes, whom they despise even more than they fear. In the neighbouring prairies are to be seen a great many cylindrical elevations, from thirty to one hundred yards in circumference, and of the same formation as the mountains. To the western extremity of the Witchitas, two of these cylinders are fluted into spirals ; they are thirty feet in height, and forty-five in circumference. One can scarcely explain by what process nature rears and moulds such huge blocks of granite.

(The Abbé Em. Domenech : *Seven Years' Residence in the Great Deserts of North America*, 1860.)

Sierra Nevada

CALIFORNIA

THE WESTERN margin of this continent is built of a succession of mountain chains folded in broad corrugations, like waves of stone upon whose seaward base beat the mild small breakers of the Pacific.

By far the grandest of all these ranges is the Sierra Nevada, a long and massive uplift lying between the arid deserts of the Great Basin and the Californian exuberance of grain-field and orchard ; its eastern slope, a defiant wall of rock plunging abruptly down to the plain ; the western, a long, grand sweep, well watered and overgrown with cool, stately forests ; its crest a line of sharp, snowy peaks springing into the sky and catching the alpenglow long after the sun has set for all the rest of America.

From latitude 35° to latitude 39°30′ the Sierra lifts a continuous chain, the profile culminating in several groups of peaks separated by deep depressed curves or sharp notches, the summits varying from eight to fifteen thousand feet ; seven to twelve thousand being the common range of passes. Near its southern extremity, in San Bernardino County, the range is cleft to the base with magnificent gateways opening through into the desert. From Walker's Pass for two hundred miles northward the sky-line is more uniformly elevated ; the passes averaging nine thousand feet high, the actual summit a chain of peaks from thirteen to over fourteen thousand feet. This serrated snow and granite outline of the Sierra Nevada, projected against the cold clear blue, is the blade of white teeth which suggested its Spanish name.

Northward still the range gradually sinks ; high peaks covered with perpetual snow are rarer and rarer. Its summit rolls on in broken forest-covered ridges, now and then overlooked by a solitary pile of metamorphic or irruptive rock. At length, in northern California, where it breaks down in a compressed medley of ridges, and open, level expanses of plain, the axis is maintained by a line of extinct volcanoes standing above the lowland in isolated positions. The most lofty of these, Mount Shasta, is a cone of lava fourteen thousand feet* high, its broad base girdled by noble forests, which give way at eight thousand feet to a cap of glaciers and snow.

For four hundred miles the Sierras are a definite ridge, broad and high, and having the form of a sea-wave. Buttresses of sombre-hued rock, jutting at intervals from a steep wall, form the abrupt eastern slopes ; irregular forests, in scattered growth, huddle together near the snow. The lower declivities are barren spurs, sinking into the sterile flats of the Great Basin.

* The U.S. Coast and Geodetic Survey, by precise levelling, has determined the altitude of Mount Shasta to be 14,162 feet above sea-level.

Long ridges of comparatively gentle outline characterize the western side, but this sloping table is scored from summit to base by a system of parallel transverse cañons, distant from one another often less than twenty-five miles. They are ordinarily two or three thousand feet deep, falling at times in sheer, smooth-fronted cliffs, again in sweeping curves like the hull of a ship, again in rugged V-shaped gorges, or with irregular, hilly flanks opening at last through gateways of low, rounded foot-hills out upon the horizontal plain of the San Joaquin and Sacramento.

Every cañon carries a river, derived from constant melting of the perpetual snow, which threads its way down the mountain,— a feeble type of those vast ice-streams and torrents that formerly discharged the summit accumulation of ice and snow while carving the cañons out from solid rock. Nowhere on the continent of America is there more positive evidence of the cutting power of rapid streams than in these very cañons. From the summits down half the distance to the plains, the cañons are also carved out in broad, round curves by glacial action. The summit gorges themselves are altogether the result of frost and ice. Here, even yet, may be studied the mode of blocking out mountain peaks ; the cracks riven by unequal contraction and expansion of the rock ; the slow leverage of ice, the storm, the avalanche.

The western descent, facing a moisture-laden, aerial current from the Pacific, condenses on its higher portions a great amount of water, which has piled upon the summits in the form of snow, and is absorbed upon the upper plateau by an exuberant growth of forest. This prevalent wind, which during most undisturbed periods blows continuously from the ocean, strikes first upon the western slope of the Coast Range, and there discharges, both as fog and rain, a very great sum of moisture ; but, being ever reinforced, it blows over their crest, and, hurrying eastward, strikes the Sierras at about four thousand feet above sea-level. Below this line the foot-hills are oppressed by an habitual dryness, which produces a rusty olive tone throughout nearly all the large conspicuous vegetation, scorches the red soil, and, during the long summer, overlays the whole region with a cloud of dust.

Dull and monotonous in color, there are, however, certain elements of picturesqueness in this lower zone. Its oak-clad hills wander out into the great plain like coast promontories, enclosing yellow, or in spring-time green, bays of prairie. The hill forms

206

are rounded, or stretch in long longitudinal ridges, broken across by the river cañons. Above this zone of red earth, softly modelled undulations, and dull, grayish groves, with a chain of mining towns, dotted ranches and vineyards, rise the swelling middle heights of the Sierras, a broad billowy plateau cut by sharp sudden cañons, and sweeping up, with its dark, superb growth of coniferous forest to the feet of the summit peaks.

Looking down from the summit, the forest is a closely woven vesture, which has fallen over the body of the range, clinging closely to its form, sinking into the deep cañons, covering the hill-tops with even velvety folds, and only lost here and there where a bold mass of rock gives it no foot-hold, or where around the margin of the mountain lakes bits of Alpine meadow lie open to the sun.

Along its upper limit the forest zone grows thin and irregular ; black shafts of alpine pines and firs clustering on sheltered slopes, or climbing in disordered processions up broken and rocky faces. Higher, the last gnarled forms are passed, and beyond stretches the rank of silent, white peaks, a region of rock and ice lifted above the limit of life.

In the north, domes and cones of volcanic formation are the summit, but for about three hundred miles in the south it is a succession of sharp granite aiguilles and crags. Prevalent among the granitic forms are singularly perfect conoidal domes, whose symmetrical figures, were it not for their immense size, would impress one as having an artificial finish.

The alpine gorges are usually wide and open, leading into amphitheatres, whose walls are either rock or drifts of never-melting snow. The sculpture of the summit is very evidently glacial. Beside the ordinary phenomena of polished rocks and moraines, the larger general forms are clearly the work of frost and ice ; and although this ice-period is only feebly represented today, yet the frequent avalanches of winter and freshly scored mountain flanks are constant suggestions of the past.

Strikingly contrasted are the two countries bordering the Sierra on either side. Along the western base is the plain of California, an elliptical basin four hundred and fifty miles long by sixty five broad ; level, fertile, well watered, half tropically warmed ; checkered with farms of grain, ranches of cattle, orchard, and vineyard, and homes of commonplace opulence, towns of bustling thrift.

Rivers flow over it, bordered by lines of oaks which seem character-less or gone to sleep, when compared with the vitality, the spring, and attitude of the same species higher up on the foot-hills. It is a region of great industrial future, within a narrow range, but quite without charms for the student of science. It has a certain impressive breadth when seen from some overlooking eminence, or when in early spring its brilliant carpet of flowers lies as a foreground over which the dark pine-land and white crest of the Sierra loom indistinctly.

From the Mexican frontier up into Oregon, a strip of actual desert lies under the east slope of the great chain, and stretches eastward sometimes as far as five hundred miles, varied by successions of bare white ground, effervescing under the hot sun with alkaline salts, plains covered by the low ashy-hued sage-plant, high, barren, rocky ranges, which are folds of metamorphic rocks, and piled-up lavas of bright red or yellow colors ; all over-arched by a sky which is at one time of a hot metallic brilliancy, and again the tenderest of evanescent purple or pearl.

(From 42°N; 121°W to 36°N; 118°W.)

(Clarence King : *Mountaineering in the Sierra Nevada.*)

The Andes

ARGENTINA : MENDOZA

THEY HAD been travelling all night across an endless plain, where there was nothing to be seen except dim cattle and way-stations with unlikely names. It was not easy to believe in the real existence of a junction called Vicuña Mackenna ; and when their informant added that this wild amalgam of an extinct Liberal statesman with a local quadruped was named after a distinguished poet, they made no further effort to conceal their incredulity.

They had been travelling all night across the featureless immensity ; they had been travelling across it, for the matter of that, all the day before, ever since the International drew out of Buenos Aires, headed for Chile. As it puffed comfortably all day long, the endless vistas of the Pampa stretched away to meet the sky ; and all through the night they had slept in perfect confidence that there was nothing in the world for them to look at. Outside their shuttered windows, where the dust of the San Luis desert had congealed, it must be paling now. But there would be nothing there to see except more cattle and more dusty little stations inartistically disposed on that interminable plain. Still, there could be no harm in looking ; and as they looked, the unexpected happened. For the plain, the endless plain, was still the same ; but as they looked it tilted suddenly towards the sky, and fifty miles away the Cordillera of the Andes took the morning sun.

II

You cannot keep your eyes away from it. It draws them irresistibly, wherever you may be. For there is nothing in the whole drama of landscape that can compare with it. I have not seen the Himalaya stand up out of India ; but no European range climbs half so suddenly towards the sky, and the steep rise of the Rocky Mountains above Colorado and the Great Plains seems almost gradual by comparison with the piled and towering obstruction of the Andes, where they lie across the level road from Buenos Aires to the Pacific.

That tall perspective on the sky is the unchanging background of Mendoza ; and its fascination interrupts your shopping in the little town, where more firearms are exposed for sale than seems altogether healthy and street-hawkers tempt the passer-by with arms wreathed in revolver-belts like vendors of braces in more peaceable localities. The local traffic-problem must be gravely increased by the suicidal tendency of visitors to step into the road with faces turned immovably towards the mountains on the sky. For the mountain-wall that bars the road to Chile draws the eye irresistibly. There may be other things to look at ; but you cannot keep your eyes away from it.

One had read often of a wall of mountains ; but the spectacle is far less common than the phrase, since our domesticated mountain-ranges are a little apt to huddle together with a faint air of apology for any inconvenience that they may cause. A wall of mountains on the sky is a rare spectacle. Moreover, the approach to other mountains is gradual, and the main range lurks discreetly out of sight, screened by a line of modest foothills that need occasion no alarm. But that is not the Andine way ; for the whole mountain-barrier is exposed to view in one stupendous panorama. Two hundred miles from end to end, the mountains climb along the sky. The green carpet of the plain ends suddenly

in a brown line of foothills, etched against the white behind them ;
next, the snow mountains stand ranged in order from the great
shoulder of Tupungato far to the south along the line of summits,
where the Andes go marching northwards to Peru ; and, behind
all, the mounting walls of the great fortress climb towards the
central keep of Aconcagua. For the Cordillera of the Andes is a
gigantic exercise in military architecture. First, a line of out-
works rising sharply from the plain ; then the brown redoubts of
the foothills climbing steadily towards the main defences ; and,
last of all, the freezing bastions on the sky that look down into
Chile. The mountains wait in line, watched by respectful villages
among the vineyards in the plain ; and as the great wall of the
Andes stands there in the sunshine, you cannot turn your eyes
away.

IV

The road across the plain wanders with diffidence towards the
Andes. For it would never do to make a frontal charge at that stupendous obstacle. Even the railway sidles almost furtively towards it,
as though it hoped to escape observation by the dark forces that
defend the lonely summits. In the plain behind, the afternoon
sun looks down pleasantly on the last level miles of Argentina, as
road and rail together creep round the shoulder of a ridge into the
silence of the Cordillera. There is no sound except the grating of
the wheels ; and when it stops, the little voice of the Mendoza
river in its gorge drops to a whisper. On the sky tall mountains
silently change places to watch the travellers go by. The light is
failing ; and there is a hint of menace in the deep shadows at their
base, where a pale strip of road winds through the gloom towards
the summits. The folded hills look down ; the little road winds
on ; the river whispers in its gorge ; a wheeling condor eyes the
gorge ; and as the light dies off the peaks that guard the road to
Chile, the dark forces wait.

(*32°50'S; 68°50'W.*)   (Philip Guedalla : *Argentine Tango.*)

Blue Mountains
NEW SOUTH WALES

IN THE middle of the day we baited our horses at a little Inn,
called the Weatherboard. The country here is elevated 2,800 feet
above the sea. About a mile & a half from this place there is

a view exceedingly well worth visiting ; following down a little valley & its tiny rill of water, an immense gulf is suddenly & without any preparation seen through the trees which border the pathway at the depth of perhaps 1,500 feet. Walking a few yards farther, one stands on the brink of a vast precipice, & below is the grand bay or gulf, for I know not what other name to give it, thickly covered with forest. The point of view is situated as it were at the head of the bay, for the line of cliff diverges away on each side, showing headland behind headland, as on a bold Sea coast. These cliffs are composed of horizontal strata of white Sandstone ; & so absolutely vertical are they that in many places a person standing on the edge & throwing a stone can see it strike the trees in the abyss below : so unbroken is the line, that it is said to be necessary to go round a distance of sixteen miles in order to reach the foot of the waterfall made by this little stream. In front and about five miles distant another line of cliff extends, thus having the appearance of completely encircling the valley ; hence the name of Bay is justified as applied to this grand amphitheatrical depression. If we imagine that a winding harbour with its deep water surrounded by bold cliffs was laid dry, & that a forest sprung up on the sandy bottom, we should then have the appearance & structure which is here exhibited. The class of view was to me quite novel & extremely magnificent.

(Charles Darwin : *The Beagle Diary*.)

Blue Mountains

NEW SOUTH WALES

18th.—VERY EARLY in the morning I walked about three miles to see Govett's Leap : a view of similar character with that near the Weatherboard, but perhaps even more stupendous. So early in the day the gulf was filled with a thin blue haze, which, although destroying the general effect of the view, added to the apparent depth at which the forest was stretched out beneath our feet. These valleys, which so long presented an insuperable barrier to the attempts of the most enterprising of the colonists to reach the interior, are most remarkable. Great armlike bays, expanding at their upper ends, often branch from the main valleys and penetrate the sandstone platform ; on the other hand, the platform

often sends promontories into the valleys, and even leaves them in great, almost insulated, masses. To descend into some of these valleys, it is necessary to go round twenty miles ; and into others, the surveyors have only lately penetrated, and the colonists have not yet been able to drive in their cattle. But the most remarkable feature in their structure is, that although several miles wide at their heads, they generally contract towards their mouths to such a degree as to become impassable. The Surveyor-General, Sir T. Mitchell, endeavoured in vain, first walking and then by crawling between the great fallen fragments of sandstone, to ascend through the gorge by which the River Grose joins the Nepean ; yet the valley of the Grose in its upper part, as I saw, forms a magnificent level basin some miles in width, and is on all sides surrounded by cliffs, the summits of which are believed to be nowhere less than 3,000 feet above the level of the sea. When cattle are driven into the valley of the Wolgan by a path (which I descended), partly natural and partly made by the owner of the land, they cannot escape ; for this valley is in every other part surrounded by perpendicular cliffs, and eight miles lower down it contracts from an average width of half a mile, to a mere chasm, impassable to man or beast. Sir T. Mitchell states that the great valley of the Cox River, with all its branches, contracts, where it unites with the Nepean, into a gorge 2,200 yards in width, and about 1,000 feet in depth. Other similar cases might have been added.
(33°10'S; 150°20'E to 34°S; 150°30'E.)

(Charles Darwin : *The Voyage of the Beagle*.)

Plateau : the Ebro Plain

SPAIN

I WISH I could put before men who have not seen that sight, the abrupt shock which the northern eye receives when it first looks from some rampart of the Pyrenees upon the new deserts of Spain.

" Deserts " is a term at once too violent and too simple. The effect of that amazement is by no means the effect which follows from a similar vision of the Sahara from the red-burnt and precipitous rocks of Atlas ; nor is it the effect which those stretches of white blinding sand give forth when, looking southward toward

Mexico and the sun, a man shades his eyes to catch a distant mark of human habitation along some rare river of Arizona from the cliff edge of a cut table-land.

Corn grows in that new Spain beneath one : many towns stand founded there ; Christian Churches are established ; a human society stands firmly, though sparsely, set in that broad waste of land. But to the Northern eye first seeing it—nay, to a Northerner well acquainted with it, but returning to the renewal of so strange a vision—it is always a renewed perplexity how corn, how men, how worship, how society (as he has known them) can have found a place there ; and that, although he knows that nowhere in Europe have the fundamental things of Europe been fought for harder and more steadfastly maintained than they have along this naked and burnt valley of the Ebro.

I will suppose the traveller to have made his way on foot from the boundaries of the Basque country, from the Peak of Anie, down through the high Pyrenean silences to those banks of Atragon where the river runs west between parallel ranges, each of which is a bastion of the main Pyrenean chain. I will suppose him to have crossed that roll of thick mud which the tumbling Aragon is in all these lower reaches, to have climbed the further range (which is called " The Mountains of Stone," or " The Mountains of the Rock "), and, coming upon its further southern slope, to see for the first time spread before him that vast extent of uniform dead-brown stretching through an air metallically clear to the tiny peaks far off on the horizon, which mark the springs of the Tagus. It is a characteristic of the stretched Spanish upland, from within sight of the Pyrenees to within sight of the Southern Sea, that it may thus be grasped in less than half a dozen views, wider than any views in Europe ; and, partly from the height of that interior land, partly from the Iberian aridity of its earth, these views are as sharp in detail, as inhuman in their lack of distant veils and blues, as might be the landscapes of a dead world.

The traveller who should so have passed the high ridge and watershed of the Pyrenees, would have come down from the snows of the Anie through forests not indeed as plentiful as those of the French side, but still dignified by many and noble trees, and alive with cascading water. While he was yet crossing the awful barriers (one standing out parallel before the next) which guard the mountains on their Spainward fall, he would continuously have perceived, though set in dry, unhospitable soil, bushes and clumps of trees ; something at times resembling his own Northern conception of pasture-land. The herbage upon which he would pitch his camp, the branches he would pick for firewood, still, though sparse and Southern, would have reminded him of home.

But when he has come over the furthest of these parallel reaches, and sees at last the whole sweep of the Ebro country spread out before him, it is no longer so. His eye detects no trees, save that belt of green which accompanies the course of the river, no glint of water. Though human habitation is present in that landscape, it mixes, as it were, with the mud and the dust of the earth from which it rose ; and, gazing at a distant clump in the plains beneath him, far off, the traveller asks himself doubt-fully whether these hummocks are but small, abrupt, insignificant hills or a nest of the houses of men—things with histories.

For the rest all that immeasurable sweep of yellow-brown bare earth fills up whatever is not sky, and is contained or framed upon its final limit by mountains as severe as its own empty surface. Those far and dreadful hills are unrelieved by crag or wood or mist ; they are a mere height, naked and unfruitful, running along wall-like and cutting off Aragon from the south and the old from the new Castille, save where the higher knot of the Moncayo stands tragic and enormous against the sky.

This experience of Spain, this first discovery of a thing so unexpected and so universally misstated by the pens of travellers and historians, is best seen in autumn sunsets, I think, when behind the mass of the distant mountains an angry sky lights up its unfruitful aspect of desolation, and, though lending it a colour it can never possess in commoner hours and seasons, in no way creates an illusion of fertility or of romance, of yield or of adven-ture, in that doomed silence.

The vision of which I speak does not, I know, convey this peculiar impression even to all of the few who may have seen it thus—and they are rare. They are rare because men do not now approach the old places of Europe in the old way. They come into a Spanish town of the north by those insufficient railways of our time. They return back home with no possession of great sights, no more memorable experience than of urban things done less natively, more awkwardly, more slowly than in England. Yet even those few, I say, who enter Spain from the north, as Spain should be entered—over the mountain roads—have not all of them received the impression of which I speak.

I have so received it, I know ; I could wish that to the Northerner it were the impression most commonly conveyed : a marvel that men should live in such a place : a wonder when the ear catches the sound of a distant bell, that ritual and a creed should have survived there—so absolute is its message of desolation.

With a more familiar acquaintance this impression does not diminish, but increases. Especially to one who shall make his way painfully on foot for three long days from the mountains to the mountains again, who shall toil over the great bare plain, who shall cross by some bridge over Ebro and look down, it may be, at a trickle of water hardly moving in the midst of a broad, stony bed, or it may be at a turbid spate roaring a furlong broad after the rains—in either case unusable and utterly unfriendly to man ; who shall hobble from little village to little village, despairing at the silence of men in that silent land and at their lack of smiles and at the something fixed which watches one from every wall ; who shall push on over the slight wheel-tracks which pass for roads—they are not roads—across the infinite, unmarked, undifferenced field ; to one who has done all these things, I say, getting the land into his senses hourly, there comes an appreciation of its wilful silence and of its unaccomplished soul. That knowledge fascinates, and bids him return. It is like watching with the sick who once were thought dead, who are, in your night of watching, upon the turn of their evil. It is like those hours of the night in which the mind of some troubled sleeper wakened can find neither repose nor variety, but only a perpetual return upon itself—yet waits for dawn. There lies behind all this, as behind a veil of dryness stretched from the hills to the hills, for those who will discover it, the intense, the rich, the unconquerable spirit of Spain.

(42°30'N; 1°W to 42°N; 2°W.)

(Hilaire Belloc : *On This and That and the Other.*)

Plateau

PERSIA

WE STOPPED to eat, that first day, by a brawling river at the foot of our first mountain-pass ; then left the plain and climbed, round dizzy precipitous corners, squeezing past waggons and camels—for there is always more traffic on a pass than elsewhere : the horses cannot drag their loads, and have to be unharnessed and reharnessed as trace-horses, and started off again, scrambling and slipping on the stony surface. We met little donkeys, coming down, stepping delicately, and camels, swaying down on their soft padded feet. Looking up, we could see the whole road of the pass zigzagging up the cliff-side, populous with animals and shouting, thrashing men. Looking back, as we climbed, we could see the immense prospect of the plain stretching away behind us. A savage, desolating country ! but one that filled me with extraordinary elation. I had never seen anything that pleased me so well as these Persian uplands, with their enormous views, clear light, and rocky grandeur. This was, in detail, in actuality, the region labelled " Persia " on the maps. Let me be aware, I said ; let me savour every mile of the way. But there were too many miles, and although I gazed, sitting in the front seat, the warm body of the dog pressed against me, the pungent smell of the sheepskin in my nostrils, it is only the general horizon that I remember, and not every unfolding of the way. This question of horizon, however, how important it is ; how it alters the shape of the mind ; how it expresses, essentially, one's ultimate sense of country ! That is what can never be told in words : the exact size, proportion, contour ; the new standard to which the mind must adjust itself.

After the top of the pass I expected to drop down again, to come down on the other side ; the experience of remaining up, once one has climbed, had not yet become familiar to me. I was not yet accustomed to motoring along a level road, in the close company of mountain tops. But these were the high levels of Asia. All day we continued, until darkness fell, and the shapes of hills became like the shapes of crouching beasts, uncertain, disquieting. This country, which all the day had been flooded with light, and which now and then had softened from its austerity into the gentler swell of hills like English downs, rounded, and

216

bathed in light like the pink light of sunset—even at mid-day—now reverted to its pristine secrecy ; the secrecy of days when no traveller passed that way, but only the nomad Kurds driving their flocks to other pastures ; the secrecy of darker days, when the armies of Alexander and Darius, making for Ecbatana, penetrated the unmapped, tumbled region, seizing a peasant to act as guide ; captain and emperor surveying from a summit the unknown distances. . . .

(*34°20′N ; 46°E.*)

(*Outside Teheran.*)

. . . . I do not think it a waste of time to absorb in idleness the austere splendour of this place ; also I am aware that its colour stains me through and through. Crudely speaking, the plain is brown, the mountains blue or white, the foothills tawny or purple ; but what are those words ? Plain and hills are capable of a hundred shades that with the changing light slip over the face of the land and melt into a subtlety no words can reproduce. The light here is a living thing, as varied as the human temperament and as hard to capture ; now lowering, now gay, now sensuous, now tender ; but whatever the mood may be, it is superimposed on a basis always grand, always austere, never sentimental. The bones and architecture of the country are there, whatever light and colour may sweep across them ; a soft thing passing over a hard thing, which is as it should be. The quality of the light suits this country of great distances. Hills a hundred miles away are clearly scored with the clefts of their valleys, so that their remoteness is unbelievable ; Demavend himself, seventy miles distant, looks as though he overhung the town, and might at any moment revive, to annihilate it, his dead volcanic fires. The shapes and promontories of the hills grow familiar : the spur which juts out into the plain near Karedj, the claret-coloured spine of Rhey, the great white backbone of the Elburz, beyond which lie the sub-tropical provinces of the Caspian. They stand with the hardness of an old country ; one does not feel that here swayed the sea, not so very long ago, geologically speaking; on the contrary, this plateau is among the ancient places of the earth, and something of that extreme antiquity has passed into its features, into the jagged profile of its rocks, worn by the weather for untold centuries until it could wear them no more—until it had reduced them to the first shape, and whittled them down to a primal design beneath which it was powerless to delve. Age has left only the bones.

Some complain that it is bleak ; surely the rich and changing light removes such a reproach. The light, and the space, and the colour that sweeps in waves, like a blush over a proud and sensitive face. Besides, those who say that it is bleak have not looked, or, looking, have not seen. It is, rather, full of life ; but that life is tiny, delicate, and shy, escaping the broader glance. Close and constant observation is necessary, for the population changes from week to week, almost from day to day ; a shower of rain will bring out a crop of miniature anemones, a day of hot sun will shrivel them ; the tortoises will wake with the warmth ; the waste land stirs. It is necessary to look towards the distance, and then into the few square yards immediately beneath the foot ; to be at one and the same time long-sighted and near-sighted.

(*36°40'N; 51°30'E.*)   (V. Sackville-West : *Passenger to Teheran.*)

Rift Valley

PALESTINE : WADI ARABAH

FROM KUNTILLA, the frontier track, rising steadily, led across a tilted plain of brown shingle which roared under the speeding car wheels. Through occasional gaps in a low range of hills the mountains of Transjordan twenty miles away were now visible in the east as a long frowning purple cliff.

The chasm of the Rift Valley between the distant mountains and ourselves gave a warning of its presence by a peculiar luminous haze. It was as if a belt of yellow light shone upwards from the depths in front, rather as things appear looking from roof-tops across an unseen lighted street at night.

The ground changed suddenly from brown flint to a blood red, and over a last ridge of volcanic rock we looked down 2,000 feet : on to the shimmering yellow sands of the bottom of the Wadi Arabah to the north, the sea beach at our feet and the bright blue water of the Gulf of Aqaba to the south, all enclosed in the one trough of the Rift.

Ages ago the whole of the land surface cracked in half north and south for several thousand miles. Here, as with a deep wound, the flat white skin of limestone was thrust upwards and back, at the edges of the open cut, by green and red volcanic matter welling from underneath on both sides like long festers, walling the central trench.

The ground below us fell away sharply in a confused mass of rock eroded into knife-edges between twisting gorges and chasms filled with impenetrable black shadow ; an inferno whence one expected smoky forms to rise. Far down at the bottom on the farther side a fringe of green palms curled round the water's edge separating the sands of the Wadi Arabah from the sea. By a trick of the light the depth looked enormous. Opposite, stretching to the right and left as far as the eye could see in the purple haze, towards the Dead Sea on the one side and towards Medina on the other, rose the 6,000-foot mountains of Transjordan and the Hedjaz, lapped over as the folds of a huge red curtain.

(29°30′N; 35°E.) (Ralph Bagnold : *Libyan Sands.*)

ROCKS AND SOIL

Rocks

SARDINIA

WONDERFUL TO go out on a frozen road, to see the grass in shadow bluish with hoar-frost, to see the grass in the yellow winter-sunrise beams melting and going cold-twinkly. Wonderful the bluish, cold air, and things standing up in cold distance. After two southern winters, with roses blooming all the time, this bleakness and this touch of frost in the ringing morning goes to my soul like an intoxication. I am so glad, on this lonely naked road, I don't know what to do with myself. I walk down in the shallow grassy ditches under the loose stone walls, I walk on the little ridge of grass, the little bank on which the wall is built, I cross the road across the frozen cow-droppings : and it is all so familiar to my *feet*, my very feet in contact, that I am wild as if I had made a discovery. And I realize that I hate limestone, to live on limestone or marble or any of those limey rocks. I hate them. They are dead rocks, they have no life—thrills for the feet. Even sandstone is much better. But granite ! Granite is my favourite. It is so live under the feet, it has a deep sparkle of its own. I like its roundnesses—and I hate the jaggy dryness of limestone, that burns in the sun, and withers. (*Sardinia*.)

(D. H. Lawrence : *Sea and Sardinia*.)

Weathering : Rocks

IN TRUTH, all stone weathering is stone disease. No stone resists the action of atmospheric agencies indefinitely : otherwise we would have no sediments, no soil, no natural sculpture. Chemical change belongs to the beauty and liveliness of stone : it is the natural carving that records Time in immediate form with the pattern and colour of surface. Only a few of these effects, therefore, are repulsive, exfoliation in particular, especially when it appears to be the result of a bacterial infection. As for durability, the building stones that have been well treated and that are washed by the rains, last long enough, even in the sulphurous air of London.

Of all weathering, that of limestone, as a rule, is the most vivid. It is limestone that combines with gases in the air, that is carved by the very breath we breathe out. It is limestone that forms new skins and poetic efflorescence : above all, limestone is sensitive to the most apparent of sculptural agencies, the rain. None the less, the exposed limestone that is well watered may escape harmful sulphate crusts ; and such calcium carbonate as is removed by water may well be deposited elsewhere on the building, not in sufficient quantities as to be grotesque or dangerous, but enough to intimate the sculptural communion between the masonry and the water piercing and renewing its stones. It is partly this weathering effect in particular that causes limestones to be the most attractive building materials. Clayey stones are not good for building, and their light is often dull ; while the weathering of sandstones is often an unrelieved crumbling away, if, as is usually the case, the cementing materials between the grains are more sensitive than the grains themselves. A slight crumbling of the cement entails the flaking of what might seem disproportionately large pieces from a rock otherwise so hard. Or else, sandstones of a hard, siliceous, cement approximate in character to the abrupt and impervious granite which may become friable before the assaults of frost and other thermal changes, or, in the sea, before the activities of the rock-boring clam ; but which seems to lack any communion with the elements that is continuous. It is not often that we see granite in the sensitive state of Cleopatra's needle, responsive after thousands of years of Egypt to the untoward atmosphere of London.

Even granite is heightened by human touch. Continual contact with hands and clothes causes nearly all stones to develop a smooth surface which is seldom observed to flake off. Examples of such surface are to be seen on those parts of ancient buildings that are accessible to the sculpture of touch. But, naturally, nowhere is this effect more palpable than in Venice, particularly on the banisters of the bridges, as we have observed.

Generally, however, natural sculpture would seem to militate against the durability of stone. The weathering of limestone may be beautiful ; but is limestone a strong and lasting building stone ? It is : at least many of the finer stones are most durable. Fine structure and porosity, like a fine body, can attain a beautiful adjustment, can withstand the worst ravages of the many disease to which all limestones are heirs. Whereas this is not true of the calcareous element in some dolomites and sandstones, the compactness of granular structure, the paucity of the cement, in the purer limestones, makes them exceedingly robust stones. Of great importance are their capillary powers to draw soluble salts and other damaging moistures on to the surface. Stones with large pores put the ingredients of their chemical crystallizations outward. The size of the pores rather than their number is the point ; and it is probably the greater size of the pores of Whitbed Portland that makes it a better building stone for outdoor use than the Basebed Portland.

The limestones and marbles of which Greek temples were built are today in fair condition, such as remain after rapine and earthquake. The vastly older Pyramids were built chiefly of Nummulitic limestone. The quantity employed was enormous. " The Great Pyramid alone contains sufficient stone for the erection of 10,000 dwelling houses, each of 8,000 cubic feet capacity and with walls one foot in thickness."*

Rain, we have said, does not, as a rule, wash the weathered limestone appreciably away ; yet it sculptures it more than other stone. One is aware of an intimacy in the *contact* between the marble fountain, for instance, and its water, which here produces a gleaming surface veined with unsuspected colours, here magnifies fossil or granular structure. It is a matter of degree (for all stone is influenced by water), the degree of intimacy in their connection ; and we have seen that the connections between limestone and water are diverse and poetic. One need know nothing about stones to distinguish a limestone fountain from one of granite. The sense of saturation they convey is different.† The granite fountain seems impervious, the water glassy : the limestone or marble fountain, on the other hand, seems to become organic beneath the water, to be sluiced, refreshed. It is not impervious, though solid and gleaming. The water is the finery of a caressing mother. There is re-enacted the strong, resistant coagulation of stone birth. A wet statue on a limestone fountain

---

* *Limestones*, by F. J. North : Murby, 1930.

† Contrast, for instance, the basin of the fountains' frontage in Kensington Gardens (Portland Stone) with the granite fountains in Trafalgar Square.

truly bathes. For purer limestones and marbles have an inner glow that disarms petrifaction of deathliness, though there is retained all the outwardness and objectivity of death.

(Adrian Stokes : *Stones of Rimini*.)

Weathering : Scree

AUSTRIA : BLUDENZ

SLOPES COVERED by ice or snow have their dangers, so have those decked with the innocent-looking dry grass which, for reasons I cannot explain, is so abhorrent to me that I will make any detour to avoid them ; all three of these can be tackled by firm feet and the help of an axe-head as grapnel or for step-cutting. Nothing is to be done, either with feet or with artificial appliances, on an even moderate incline of such Liassic shale, for it yields to pressure and slides down, and this is where a chamois has the advantage over us. A man may scramble about honest crags like a fly on a wall, as securely as any chamois though not so fast ; on precipices of the crumbling *Algäu-Schiefer* the animal leaps, and leaps again before the stuff has gathered momentum, and what shall man do ? Avoid them, until he has acquired the capacity of bouncing like a chamois ; in other words, like an indiarubber ball.

Indeed, shifting material of every kind is objectionable and fraught with peculiar horrors. Up behind Bludenz you may see a row of limestone cliffs called Elser Schröfen, whose foot is defended by a " talus " of rubble which has slowly dropped down from the heights above ; and a pretty thing it is, by the way, when you look closely at natural features like this talus, to observe with what flawless accuracy they have been constructed ; how these fragments of detritus pass in due order through all gradations of size down the slanting surface, from minute particles like sand at the top to the mighty blocks that form their base. Once, long ago, I conceived the playful project of crossing this rubble-slope from end to end, just below the cliffs. I started on its inclined plane, but had not gone far before realizing the situation. The talus reposed, as it naturally would repose if left to accumulate undisturbed ; that is, at the sharpest allowable angle against the cliffs, its upper barrier. It soon struck me as being rather a steep gradient, and not only steep but ominously alive—ready to gallop downhill on a hint from myself; the mere weight of my body could set the whole mass in movement and hurl me along in a rocky flood. While making this sweet reflection I found, with dismay, that it was already too late to turn back; the least additional pressure on one foot might start the mischief; once started, nothing would arrest that deluge; its beginning, without a doubt, was going to be my end.

I was in for a ticklish business. Rush down the slope diagonally and evoke the landslide but anticipate its arrival? Even that was courting disaster. I preferred to remain in the upper regions and there finished the long journey, with curious deliberation, on all fours, in order to distribute my weight; and then only by a miracle. It was one of those occasions on which one has ample leisure to look into the eye of death, and I now wish somebody could have taken a photograph of me—a coloured one, by preference; one would like to possess a record of the exact tint of one's complexion during half-hours of this kind. Whoso, therefore, intends to traverse the same place would be well advised to adopt my method of locomotion; the upright posture is not to be recommended. A pleasant farewell to all things! Never a button of you to be seen again; to be caught in a swirl, a deafening cataract of stones and, after snatching *en passant* a few grains of scientific comfort at the thought that your human interference had modified—if only temporarily—the angle of a talus, which is not everybody's affair, to be buried alive at the bottom under an imposing heap of debris.

(Norman Douglas : *Together*.)

Granite

GRANITE IS a symbolic substance—it, in common with marble, is the historic stone. As amongst beasts the lion ranks as king, being the representative of noble qualities and physical power,—as amongst plants the oak presents a picture of firmness and endurance, of proud contempt of storm and weather,—so granite represents all that is unconquerable and unchangeable in the kingdom of dead inorganic matter : it is, in the narrow material sense, a substance of eternal duration. Where monuments were to be erected for the most distant human races, visible pillars for the annals of history,—where Egyptian dynasties raised the colossal tombs of their kings in those pyramids which are still wondered at, on the borders of the desert, as the mightiest works of human power,—there the bold architect grasped the granite rock and thought that he had saved a scrap from the destruction that awaits everything wrought by human hands. The earlier inquirers into natural science constructed our earth's kernel of granite, and saw in it the grandfather of the whole mineral kingdom, and naïvely called it the "Urgestein," the primeval stone. And yet it only marks one punctuation in the history of the world's creation, an unimportant second in the cipher of eternity, a thing of the past, which will dissolve as it has arisen.

(H. Berlepsch: *The Alps:* Translated by the Rev. Leslie Stephen.)

Granite
NIGERIA : ABEOKUTA

THE FIRST aspect of Abeokuta was decidedly remarkable. The principal peculiarity was the fantastic breaking of the undulating plain by masses of grey granite—the rose-coloured is not easily seen—between twenty and thirty in number, sometimes rising two hundred and fifty to three hundred feet above the lower levels. White under the sun's glare, and cast in strange forms—knobs, pinnacles, walls, back-bones, scarps and logans— they towered over the patches of dark trees at their bases and the large brown villages, or rather towns, which separated them. There was a long dorsum, which nearly bisected the town from north to south, and which lay like a turtle's back between the scattered lines of habitations.

(7°N; 3°30′E.)

(Richard F. Burton : *Abeokuta and the Cameroon Mountains.*)

Granite
SOUTH INDIA

THE JOURNEY had already lasted some four hours when the sense of weariness, aggravated by the cadenced jolting of our zebus, became so intolerable that I had to slip through the little opening at the front of my sarcophagus, and sit for a while on the pole in the pose of a crouching monkey by the side of my driver. The daylight has waned considerably, and under the black clouds and overhanging palms it is almost twilight. The green tunnel of banyans extends as ever in front of us, but here and there fantastic objects are seen looming from the woods through the evening shadows. They resemble huge, shapeless animals; sometimes they are scattered and sometimes in flocks, or even piled on one another. These strange objects consist of granite blocks—blocks which have the soft roundness of elephants and the bronze colour of their skin; there is no connection between them, and they look as if they had come here separately, or as if they had been rolled or thrown here, like corpses heaped up after a massacre. Now the larger roots and branches of the trees take the shape of elephants' trunks; indeed, it looks as if nature had had some vague idea of this particular animal shape in all her creation, as if the first thought of the elephantine form had existed here from the remotest antiquity, even from the date when the first unconscious thought had fashioned matter with stone. At present it looks as if elephants or the embryos of elephants were crowded round us, and the resemblances are even more striking now that it is quite dim in the woods which lie about us. (*Between Tinnevelli and Trivandrum or Travancore, 8°30'N; 76°50'E.*)   (Pierre Loti: *India:* translated by George F. Inman.)

Basalt

MARTINIQUE : GRANDE ANSE

BUT THE more you become familiar with the face of the little town itself, the more you are impressed by the strange swarthy tone it preserves in all this splendid expanse of radiant tinting. There are only two points of visible colour in it,—the church and hospital, built of stone, which have been painted yellow : as a mass in the landscape, lying between the dead-gold of the cane-clad hills and the delicious azure of the sea, it remains almost black under the prodigious blaze of light. The foundations of volcanic rock, three or four feet high, on which the frames of the wooden dwellings rest, are black ; and the sea-wind appears to have the power of blackening all timber-work here through any coat of paint. Roofs and façades look as if they had been long exposed to coal-smoke, although probably no one in Grande Anse ever saw coal ; and the pavements of pebbles and cement are of a deep ash-colour, full of micaceous scintillation, and so hard as to feel disagreeable even to feet protected by good thick shoes. By-and-by you notice walls of black stone, bridges of black stone, and perceive that black forms an element of all the landscape about you. On the roads leading from the town you notice from time to time masses of jagged rock or great bowlders protruding through the green of the slopes, and dark as ink. These black surfaces also sparkle. The beds of all the neighbouring rivers are filled with dark grey stones; and many of these, broken by those violent floods which dash rocks together,—deluging the valleys, and strewing the soil of the bottom-lands (*fonds*) with dead serpents,—display black cores. Bare crags projecting from the green cliffs here and there are soot-coloured, and the outlying rocks of the coast offer a similar aspect. And the sand of the beach is funereally black—looks almost like powdered charcoal; and as you walk over it, sinking three or four inches every step, you are amazed by the multitude and brilliance of minute flashes in it, like a subtle silver effervescence.

Sometimes after great storms bright brown sand is flung up from the sea-depths; but the heavy black sand always reappears again to make the universal colour of the beach.

(*Grande Anse: 14°50′N; 61°10′W.*)

(Lafcadio Hearn: *Two Years in the French West Indies.*)

Limestone: " Karrenfields "

THE ALPS

THERE ARE still more barren and death-like regions in the mountains than the wastes of snow, broad extensive tracts in the untrodden wildernesses, which, bare of all vegetation, lie in rigid and everlasting resignation. These are the " Schratten " or " Karren " fields, called in the Romansch " Lapiaz." High up in the mountains, by the side of the frequented passes and the lively Alpine pasturages, at a height of from four to six thousand feet in the limestone Alps, lie bare, naked plains of stone, often extended almost at a dead level for hours, which are so furrowed, and crossed by deeply cut channels, that they look as if a swelling sea had been suddenly turned to stone, and left behind an inextricable net of crested waves. Below they are so terribly split and gnawed into by gutters, yards in depth, that it is impossible by any means, by jumping, clambering or careful balancing, to make way across them; for the remains of stone between these channels run across them like narrow dams, as sharp as the edge of a knife, and then suddenly break off, interrupted by cross-cuttings. They appear again like combs whose different teeth are broken off at all kinds of heights,—a plain which has been as it were hacked, hollowed out, sawn through, and carved by giant instruments,—a stony sea splintered and cracked, full of the strangest forms, which often resemble glacier " needles." Between them are deep funnel-shaped holes, like the craters of a volcano ; or they sink into canals which disappear underground. Then again they open into bowls, yards in breadth, and with bottoms riddled through like a sieve. In other places a certain law of erosion seems to have prevailed in this chaos, for the masses of ruin have nearly the appearance of cells in a beehive, on which account the shepherds call them significantly " Steinwaben," stone honeycombs. They are, indeed, a miniature picture of the most fearful destruction.

It is evident that this limestone has a very peculiar tendency to dissolve, which has produced the channelling. As not the least particle of earth finds a place on these decaying bones of rock, which in summer reflect an unendurable heat, and as in spring the waters which collect after heavy rains, or from the melting of the snow in the subalpine region, hasten down through the hollow gutters and cavities into the trackless bowels of the mountain, to appear again in springs at its foot, it is evident that these plains do not afford the necessary conditions for the growth even of the hardiest plants. As far as the eye can reach over the comfortless, pale, monotonous rocky levels, it looks dreary and deathlike. Where no flower blooms to open its cup of honey, there no insect hums, not a butterfly flutters, not a beetle whirrs past. Where no weed, not a blade of grass, can find nourishment in the clefts of the rock, where not even a moss can support its hardy existence, there not the smallest marmot will remain. Where all means of passage is so destroyed as in these Karrenfields there no chamois will wander. Even the birds seem to avoid these wildernesses. No mountain-crow or raven, no partridge or ptarmigan, no falcon or eagle is ever seen to alight on them. Hence the Schrattenfields may well be called the deserts of the Alps. Where, however, these Karrenfields border on the meadows, so that earth may be carried by the water into their depths, the most luxurious vegetation which grows on the Alps may be found amongst them.

(H. Berlepsch : *The Alps :* Translated by the Rev. Leslie Stephen.)

Limestone

WESTERN IRELAND

LOUGH MASK has no visible outlet, for the surplus water pours through subterranean crevices and channels under the couple of miles of land which separate it from Lough Corrib. This fact might have warned the government engineers when a good many years ago they commenced cutting a canal from lake to lake to permit of navigation from Galway to Ballinrobe. The canal was duly finished, and is there to this day, but the rock was a mere sieve, and the water when admitted at once poured through the bottom.

The chain of lakes along the western edge of the limestone is continued and concluded by Lough Corrib (*Coirib*, anciently *Loch Oirbsean*, Oirbsen's Lake), the largest of the series, twenty-seven miles long over all, extremely irregular in breadth, formed except in the north-west by solution of the limestone, and consequently very variable in depth, full of islets, reefs and deep holes. As in Lough Mask, a long narrow arm, in the north-west corner, runs far into the hills, which are formed in this place of ancient schists. The western side of the lake from Moycullen to Oughterard fringes strange country—a flat limestone tract, with stretches of bare pavement, peat bog, rough esker-ridges, limy swamps, and dense scrub mainly of Hazel, interesting for the botanist. At the southern end are large areas of very flat land, only slightly raised above water-level, and now much covered by peat—portions of the old bottom when the lake stood at a higher level. Additional evidence of this higher level is gained from the presence in these flat areas, often far from the present lake, of " mushroom-rocks "—large blocks of limestone now shaped like a toadstool. The top is umbrella-like—convex above, flat and horizontal below—and rests on a much narrower pillar of the same rock. The flat underside marks the former lake-level, above which solution of the limestone did not take place. Through the peaty flats the River Corrib, broad and slow, flows for several miles to Galway town, where it rushes down over limestone ledges to the sea. A stream of an unusual kind—the Terryland River—may be examined on the east bank of the Corrib a little above Galway. It looks like a tributary, but the water is flowing, swift and deep, *out of* the Corrib towards low limestone hills to the east. It twists for a couple of miles through flat meadow-land and then, dividing, disappears under the edge of the rising ground. I was told that at the several sink-holes the water rises and falls with the tide, but have no confirmation of this ; certainly the difference of level between them and the sea at high-water is very slight.

On the lake-shores, the limestone often displays a curious form of weathering, not easy to account for. The upper surface of a horizontal slab will be densely covered with hemispherical pits with sharp confluent edges, while on the under side of the slabs the pits will be much deeper, even two or three inches in length, cylindrical, with a curved conical apex, the narrow walls which separate them having edges so sharp that one can cut one's fingers on them. Another phenomenon that invites investigation !
(*L. Corrib: 53°30'N; 9°20'W.*)

(Robert Lloyd Praeger : *The Way that I Went.*)

Limestone Weathering

SOUTH-WEST AFRICA

TWO OR three hundred yards beyond our outspan was an open plain formed by two horizontal strata of limestone, the combined depth of which might be from five to six feet, each perforated vertically with holes big enough to admit a drawing pencil, giving to the blocks that were broken out the appearance of coarse-grained timber. The breaking or wearing away of a circle of the upper stratum a hundred yards in diameter had formed a kind of basin, and in this were two pits which Chapman, working with the men, had opened so that the cattle might drink, and a smaller one with water for our own use.
(Thomas Baines : *Explorations in South-West Africa.*)

Limestone Weathering

THE BAHAMAS : INAGUA

THE TRAIL was ill-defined and wound between thick clumps of tangled thorn trees and stunted bushes. In a few seconds after leaving the salt-pond the soil underfoot changed from shifting sand to a hard floor of smooth grey rock. Scattered helter-skelter over its surface were dozens of slabs of loose flat stone. These varied in thickness and in size from small dinner-plates to irregular sheets seven or eight feet in circumference. The rock floor seemed hollow and boomed cavernously even under the soft tread of my canvas shoes. Whenever I stepped on one of the loose slabs it rang with the resonance of a bell, the tone varying through several octaves depending on the width and thickness of the plates. The sound was clear and metallic ; the effect was startling. For half a mile round my presence could be detected by the clang of rock on rock. I felt as though I were walking on the keys of some gigantic piano or harpsichord, strangely off tone and prolonged as though an invisible player had his foot on the sustaining pedal. Once far off in the distance, a wild medley of discords came jangling through the thorn bush. The sounds came nearer, increasing in volume, until a small herd of wild donkeys burst through a glade in front of me and went clattering away again. The noise of their going sounded like a carnival of mad bell players. Some of the plates had a light tinkling sound, others gave off a deep ecclesiastical tone somewhat like the resonance of an organ in the shadowy lofts of a cathedral. By way of experimentation I tried ranging a series in a row to see if I could play a tune. With a big stick and by dint of much dashing to and fro, for some of the pieces were too large to haul conveniently, I managed to bang out the first five notes of " My Country 'Tis of Thee," but I got stuck on the " sweet land of liberty " part and could go no further. The slabs needed tuning badly and the music sounded horribly flat, but it had possibilities.

The land beneath the surface must be honey-combed with holes and caverns, for this hollow sound is common to many parts of the island. Inagua, like many of the Bahamas, can be compared to a gigantic stone sponge. In places the sea penetrates far underground. Ocean holes, clear blue ponds of salt sea water which rise and fall with the tide, frequently occur a dozen miles from the coast. They are quite different from the shallow lakes of dull green or pinkish water which abound everywhere. I found one of these holes several days later about four miles from the beach on the north side of the island. It was roughly sixty feet in diameter and was filled with the same liquid blue water that washes the reefs. The sides were crusted with red sponges, and deep down below the surface I could discern a few anemones and the white marks of barnacles. There was no bottom. Although the water was so clear that the walls were visible for a hundred feet the hole disappeared into infinity. Somewhere down in the dark a tunnel pierced its way out to the ocean. I would have given much to be able to explore its fastnesses. Did it emerge beyond the reefs along the edge of some towering submarine cliff or did it lead for thousands of feet down into the black depths of the ocean? What fantastic creatures lived in its dark passages; ghostly white anemones, possibly, for ever shut off from the light of day, giant morays similar to the one that frequented the hole near my bathing-pool. Such a trip would require a brave heart, and diving equipment of a type as yet undeveloped. It would be a weird, dangerous excursion down into the wet bowels of an island; a jaunt that might lead anywhere. The age of exploration is by no means completed.

(21°N; 73°30'W.)   (Gilbert Klingel : *Inagua*.)

Limestone Caverns

YUCATAN

THE ENTRANCE to the caves was only a few hundred yards beyond the last house at the western end of the village. It was a circular hole some thirty inches in diameter which led vertically downward through the crust of the earth under an overhanging bank. Down this a crudely fashioned, twenty-foot ladder was dropped, and we descended into a circular, domed chamber about twelve feet in diameter. From this a low-roofed passage sloped down into the bowels of the earth.

Yucatan is a great plateau of consolidated limestone-marl and is honeycombed with caves, underground rivers, lakes, passages, and tunnels. Unlike the majority of caves in the more ancient and solid rock formations of other countries, which are usually formed by cracks and crevices between huge shifting blocks of the country rock, those of Yucatan are water-worn tunnels of various dimensions, smooth and domed above, and with level, cave-earth floors. All that we have visited, and those at Kawa in particular, are arranged like the strands of a giant fish-net; the passageways, in plan, would divide the rock into square, oblong, or diamond-shaped blocks. This arrangement is often repeated at different levels, so that at the junctions of passages there are sometimes holes in the floor leading down to another whole set of caves lying below. This is repeated downwards until the water level is reached, and it probably continues far below that, for we have been told that during some exceptional droughts people have descended into two further levels that are normally filled with water. This would have brought them to sea level, below which the water table presumably never can fall.

. . . The first part of the passage was very dry. The floor was composed of dusty earth and many loose boulders. Further on came patches of bare, damp earth. . . . We talked it over and asked our portly friend, who alone had stayed behind with us, whether there were wetter parts farther down. He said there might be, but he knew nothing of the caves beyond this point, and doubted whether anybody in the party had ever been farther. We then bawled for Riqué, but got no answer. I had to leave Alma to continue the search, while I went ahead to look for him.

The place was a veritable maze of tunnels, all looking exactly alike. The only things to guide me were occasional footprints in the damp earth floor and, following these, I walked or crawled forward, bawling lustily every now and then. . . . I had gone a long way and was not only getting really worried about Riqué's disappearance, but was beginning to consider seriously my own predicament. Suddenly my blood nearly froze in its leisurely tracks. It was a momentary sensation, but in the deathly stillness among the eerie shadows deep down there in the earth it was stark terror. I like to believe that the bad air had something to do with my fright, but I fear there can be no disguising the fact that the sensation was pure reflex.

What had frozen me to the marrow was the most blood-curdling and Gargantuan growl or snort some way ahead in the depths of the shadows. I waited hardly breathing, and not knowing whether to flee or emulate the ostrich. I think I would have simply remained rooted to the spot out of pure terror, if there had not been a disturbance of quite a different nature to my left. You can have no idea how these other noises relieved the strain. They were so obviously solid and real, that I knew if this was indeed the shaggy, cave-dwelling monster, it was at least tangible.*

I flashed on the torch, and, behold, there was an extremely pale Riqué peering over a rock like some remnant of our pre-historic and troglodytic ancestry.

*The Indians of Yucatan believe that those underground caverns are inhabited by bears of gigantic size.

" Riqué," I called, " was that you ?"

" Ivan," he gasped, clutching the stone, "did you hear it too ?"

" Wasn't it you ?" I ran down the tunnel towards him.
" What in earth is it ?" I asked.

Then another frightful growl came echoing along the passage,
followed by a tumultuous splashing.

" Good heavens, Riqué, it must be a crocodile in a cenote."

" Yes, it might be," he said doubtfully, but the thought that it
might be just an ordinary very dangerous animal made us both
feel much better.

So we set out to track down the sounds. As the noises grew
louder, they certainly became more formidable and blood-
curdling. One needed no imagination whatever to conjure up a
vision of some monstrous bear wallowing in a pool. On the other
hand, I wanted to know if crocodiles really did live in underground
waters. The sounds certainly resembled some of the worst out-
cries of those reptiles.

As we went on, the air became fresher and damper, and the
whole cave came alive. Many bats flitted around us, and the
walls became crowded with insects. We turned a sharp corner
into a small gallery, and as we entered, the hideous, gurgling
growls suddenly blasted out at us almost from our feet. We
leaped around.

There was a long pause before they were repeated, but we then
found that they were issuing from a small hole leading into the
wall at floor level. This hole was only a foot high, and about two
feet broad. We could hear water splashing about within, apparently at a lower level. After some debate and soul searching, we
decided that I, being the slimmer, should squeeze in with a torch
and see if I could catch a glimpse of whatever was causing the
blood-curdling disturbance. With some trepidation, I began to
wriggle into the hole.

The tiny passage was very short, and gave into a round chamber.
I got far enough in to poke my head over the lip and look down.
Sure enough, there was water below, now agitated into small
waves that lapped against the sides. I was manœuvring the torch
further forward to have a better view when—*wham !*—something
caught me squarely across the back of the head, jabbing my
chin down on to the rock. I knew positively that my hour had
come, and I started to fight with the desperation of the doomed.

I yelled ; I clutched wildly, and then my hand got a hold on something cold and hard, which I instantly let go.

The torch had gone out, and I was waiting for the end, being now firmly jammed into the hole with my legs lashing about in the cave behind, and my head dangling over the waters. There was a splosh and a splash, and I had visions of a pair of great jaws coming up to get me. In my frenzy I slewed round and looked up.

Far, far above was a small, circular spot of light, and in the centre a small round thing that bobbed in and out. Puzzled, I looked again, for I could not make any sense out of what I was seeing. Then, slowly, it all began to dawn on me. I nearly fell into the water as a result ; in fact, I probably should have done so if I hadn't clutched the rope, though this came away with a rush.

I was in the bottom of a deep well ; the little dot above me was an unsuspecting Mayan lady drawing water ; the cold hard thing that had biffed me on the back of the head was a bucket whizzing downward to the water-level ; the frightful noises were the banging of the concave base of the bucket when it hit the water, and the blood-curdling gurgles and growls, the filling of the bucket magnified a thousand times and muffled out of recognition by the small sound-box leading into the cave. The disturbance in our breasts proved to be as nothing compared to the effect upon the lady above, when piercing and unearthly shrieks issued from her well and her rope was suddenly yanked out of her hand. She let go of everything and bolted, and we heard later that she was several hours recovering from her ordeal.

" Riqué," I yelled, " pull me back ! It's only a well, and I'm stuck and half knocked out by a bucket."

(*21°N; 89°W.*)   (Ivan Sanderson : *Living Treasure.*)

Marble

WHO WILL love the homogeneous marble sheets in the halls of Lyons' Corner Houses ? No hands will attempt to evoke from them a gradual life. For nowhere upon them is the human impress. Few hands have touched them, or an instrument held in the hand. They were sliced from their blocks by impervious machines. They have been shifted and hauled like so many girders. They are illumined in their lines beneath the light ; yet they are adamant.   (Adrian Stokes : *Stones of Rimini.*)

Conglomerate: The Nagelfluh

THIS CONGLOMERATE (allied to the so-called " pudding-stones ") consists of enormous layers, often several thousand feet thick, of deposited rolled stones, which are connected by means of a cement containing lime, and effervescing under the action of acids. It is often so firm that both stones and cement form a uniformly hard mass, and when broken, split into flat surfaces of fracture, passing equally through stones and cement. This firmness is so remarkable, that the nagelfluh of some places, that, for example, known as Degersheim and Solothurn marble, has been used by stone-masons for large fountain basins, and monumental work, and even for millstones. The size of the included stones varies exceedingly. Some are found lying close together of the size of grains of corn, so that the deposit has the appearance of a fine-grained sandstone. Others, again, are huge blocks, cubical yards in size.

All this however would not make the nagelfluh a specially interesting natural production, were it not for two circumstances which have not hitherto been satisfactorily explained. The nagelfluh consists, like all gravel, of fragments of stone of the most various shapes, spherical, oblong, or with both round and flat surfaces. According to its colour and quality it has been divided into the two chief groups of variegated and limestone nagelfluh. To the variegated nagelfluh belong those conglomerates which as their name expresses are splendid with a rich mosaic of colour. There we find fiery red spheres of porphyry close to clear granite pebbles of a soft apple-green, warm violet coloured cylinders of spilit close to deep green ovals of serpentine, yellow ochre-coloured rounded flints by flesh-coloured and veined spheroids of felspar. The limestone nagelfluh is less brilliant ; grey, blue, and blackish tones prevail in it. There are however specimens which vary from this, such as the nagelfluh at the foot of the Speer, near Wesen, on the Wallensee, which has almost the appearance of German sausage or Gotha brawn. For fragments of felspar are baked into the dark red cement (which contains iron), looking like fat bits of bacon ; and other stones containing lime may without much stretch of the imagination be taken for bits of crackling and forced meat. The curiosity-seeker may find fragments of this plaything of nature close behind the railway station at Wesen.

One circumstance still unexplained is this,— that fragments of rock are found in it (even in great numbers) which are either not found in the Alps at all, or at any rate only in the southern valleys (whose present river systems flow towards the south, such as the Rhone, Ticino, Inn), and that fragments of rock are entirely wanting which one would have expected to find in great numbers, because they occur frequently in the Alps. No other supposition is possible than to assume that the nagelfluh is derived from mountains which have been completely destroyed in some great convulsion of the earth, then swept away and rounded by friction in the primeval sea, and ultimately deposited in great masses, enveloped in a mud cement, and afterwards raised again from the depths when the Alps were elevated from the bottom of the sea.

A second still more interesting but still less explicable circumstance is that of the impressions. If we search only for a short time the bare rocks of nagelfluh (those, that is, whose binding cement is not so hard, but that the pebbles can be easily extracted), we shall find specimens of these, which have received deeply moulded impressions from their next neighbours, much as if one was to stamp any hard object into fresh kneaded bread. The two stones, however, are generally of equal hardness, and stone No. 2, which made the impression in stone No. 1, has again received on another side precisely similar crushings or indentations from stone No. 3. As we must suppose that the pebbles, before they were polished down, were hard and brittle, it is difficult to explain how they could have received such impressions from their hard neighbours.

If we assume that these pebbles were still tolerably soft when deposited, and therefore easily received impressions, a similar degree of softness must be assumed in those stones which produced the impressions. Two equally soft bodies may certainly flatten each other, but one can hardly penetrate into the substance of the other. But there occurs another phenomenon to prove that all the nagelfluh pebbles were already very hard when they were enveloped in cement,—namely, the mirror-like, striped, and shining polish, which they display in many places. Examples may be found, which, treated by the lapidary, shine in the sun like bright panes of glass. Others show sharply scratched and numerous lines which make the grained limestone appear like fibrous asbestos ; and others again where nature's wonderful laboratory has made such energetic incisions as if the stone had been carved by a diamond chisel. Most of these polished surfaces show a metallic lustre. No doubt the whole phenomenon has its origin in a gigantic lateral pressure produced by the Alps on the elevation of the masses, in consequence of which, the stones slide over each other with incalculable vehemence, and as they were heated by the friction mutually polished each other. (H. Berlepsch : *The Alps* : Translated by the Rev. Leslie Stephen.)

(*Note.*—Collet, in " Les Alpes", states that the pebbles of the variegated nagelfluh are derived from the higher tectonic elements of the Alps, viz., the nappes of the Prealps and of the Austrides. They were derived from the chain of the Alps as it grew, and then affected by a push coming from the Alps, which travelled forward and then rode over their own debris.)

The Soil

WHEN MOTHER in her young days was telling her fortune from cards she always whispered over one pile : " What am I treading on ?" Then I could not understand why she was so interested in what she was treading on. Only after very many years did it begin to dawn on me. I discovered that I was treading on the earth.

In fact, one does not care what one is treading on ; one rushes somewhere like mad, and at most one notices what beautiful clouds there are, or what a beautiful horizon it is, or how beautifully blue the hills are ; but one does not look under one's feet to note and praise the beautiful soil that is there. You must have a garden, though it be no bigger than a pocket-handkerchief ; you must have one bed at least to know what you are treading on. Then, dear friend, you will see that not even clouds are so diverse, so beautiful, and terrible as the soil under your feet. You will know the soil as sour, tough, clayey, cold, stony, and rotten ; you will recognize the mould puffy like pastry, warm, light, and good like bread, and you will say of this that it is beautiful, just as you say so of women or of clouds. You will feel a strange and sensual pleasure if your stick runs a yard deep into the puffy and crumbling soil, or if you crush a clod in your fingers to taste its airy and tepid warmth.

And if you have no appreciation for this strange beauty, let fate bestow upon you a couple of rods of clay—clay like lead, squelching and primeval clay out of which coldness oozes ; which yields under the spade like chewing-gum, which bakes in the sun and gets sour in the shade ; ill-tempered, unmalleable, greasy, and sticky like plaster of Paris, slippery like a snake, and dry like a brick, impermeable like tin, and heavy like lead. And now smash it with a pick-axe, cut it with a spade, break it with a hammer, turn it over and labour, cursing aloud and lamenting.

Then you will understand the animosity and callousness of dead and sterile matter which ever did defend itself, and still does, against becoming a soil of life ; and you will realize what a terrible fight life must have undergone, inch by inch, to take root in the soil of the earth, whether that life be called vegetation or man.

And then you will know that you must give more to the soil than you take away ; you must make it friable and fertile with lime, and temper it with warm manure, lighten it with ashes, and saturate it with air and sunshine. Then the baked clay disintegrates and crumbles as if it breathed in silence ; it breaks down under the spade with surprising readiness ; it is warm and malleable in the hand ; it is tamed. I tell you, to tame a couple of rods of soil is a great victory. Now it lies there, workable, crumbly, and humid ; you would like to take it and rub it all between your thumb and finger, to assure yourself of your victory ; you think no more of what you will sow in it. Is it not beautiful enough, this dark and airy soil ? Is it not more beautiful than a bed of pansies or carrots ? You are almost jealous of the vegetation which will take hold of this noble and humane work which is called the soil.

And from that time on you will not go over the earth unconscious of what you are treading on. You will try with your hand and stick every heap of clay, and every patch in a field, just as some other men look at stars, at people, or violets ; you will burst into enthusiasm over the black humus, fondly rub the smooth woodland leafmould, balance in your hand the compact sod and weigh the feathery peat. O Lord ! you will say, I should like to have a wagon of this ; and heavens ! a cart load of this leafmould would do me good ; and this humus here for putting on the top, and here a couple of those cow pancakes, and a little bit of that river sand, and some rings of these rotten wood stumps, and here a bit of sludge from the stream, and sweepings from the road would not be bad either, would they ? and still some phosphate and horn shavings, but this beautiful arable soil would also suit me. Great Scott ! There are soils as fat as bacon, light as feathers, crumbly like a cake, blond or black, dry or inflated with damp ; all these are diverse and noble kinds of beauty ; while all that is greasy, cloddy, wet, tough, cold, and sterile is ugly and rotten, unredeemed matter, given to man for a curse ; and it is as ugly as the coldness, callousness, and malice of human souls.

(Karel Čapek : *The Gardener's Year*.)

Frozen Subsoil of Tundra

SIBERIA

THE PERENNIALLY frozen soil begins in the southern parts of Yakutsk. In the neighbourhood of the city of Yakutsk, according to the calculations of the savants, the earth is frozen to a depth of 1,000 feet ! This ever-frozen soil exerts a great influence on the configuration of the lakes and rivers. It prevents the absorption of the water by the earth. There are no springs and no subterranean waters. This accounts also for the very great number of lakes and marshes in northern Siberia. For the same reason the rivers very rapidly swell above their normal limits, causing at times most disastrous inundations.

* * * * *

At the time of our visit to Olekminsk the temperature had risen to 66° Fahr. and, looking out over the green fields, I found it hard to realize the fact that I was walking on soil frozen to the depth of several hundreds of feet.

* * * * *

The city of Yakutsk is situated on the western bank of the Lena. It is built on a flat, alluvial, ever-frozen soil, forming a foundation as strong as any rock, which in summer-time melts only to a depth of three or four feet. Only a few houses of brick, however, are built on this eternal ice. The town, which in 1897, according to official reports, numbered 5,825 inhabitants, consists—besides the churches, the prison and a number of other official buildings— mainly of small dilapidated houses, yurtas and (in the outskirts of the town) earth-huts. In the broad streets the melted soil shakes beneath one's feet, here and there the thin dry crust which covers it breaks through under the pressure of the cart-wheels, and the horses sink knee-deep into the half-frozen sludge.

(62°N; 130°E.) (J. Stadling : *Through Siberia*.)

Frozen Subsoil of Tundra
SIBERIA

IT SEEMS strange that the plants above-named and many others should spring only from the dry sand of the dunes, but the apparent riddle is solved when we know that it is only the sand thus piled up, that becomes sufficiently warmed in the months of uninterrupted sunshine for these plants to flourish. Nowhere else throughout the tundra is this the case. Moor and bog, morass and swamp, even the lakes with water several yards in depth only form a thin summer covering over the eternal winter which reigns in the tundra, with destructive as well as with preserving power. Wherever one tries to penetrate to any depth in the soil one comes—in most cases scarcely a yard from the surface— upon ice, or at least on frozen soil, and it is said that one must dig about a hundred yards before breaking through the ice-crust of the earth. It is this crust which prevents the higher plants from vigorous growth, and allows only such to live as are content with the dry layer of soil which thaws in summer. It is only by digging that one can know the tundra for what it is : an immeasurable and unchangeable ice-vault which has endured, and will continue to endure, for hundreds of thousands of years. That it has thus endured is proved indisputably by the remains of prehistoric animals embedded in it, and thus preserved for us. In 1807 Adams dug from the ice of the tundras the giant mammoth, with whose flesh the dogs of the Yakuts sated their hunger, although it must have died many thousands of years before, for the race became extinct in the incalculably distant past. The icy tundra had faithfully preserved the carcase of this primitive elephant all through these hundreds of thousands of years.

(*Note.*—The plants mentioned include willow-herb, wild rose, forget-me-not, hellebore, chives, valerian, thyme, vetches and others, which grow on the dunes of wind-blown sand found along the banks of some of the large rivers.)

(Alfred Edmund Brehm : *From North Pole to Equator.*)

Soil Erosion
NORTH DAKOTA

ONE DAY in the spring of 1883 as a Scandinavian farmer, John Christiansen, plowed his fields in Montana's neighbour state of North Dakota, he looked up to find he was being watched —not by a stockman, but by an old and solemn Sioux Indian.

Silently the old Indian watched as the dark soil curled up and the prairie grass was turned under. Christiansen stopped, leaned against the plow handle, pushed his black Stetson back on his head, rolled a cigarette. He watched amusedly as the old Indian knelt, thrust his fingers into the plow furrow, measured its depth, fingered the sod and the buried grass.

Then the old Indian straightened up, looked at the farmer.

"Wrong side up," he said, and went away.

For a number of years that was regarded as a very amusing story indeed, betraying the ignorance of the poor Indian. Now there's a marker on Highway No. 10 in North Dakota on the spot where the words were spoken—a little reminder to the white man that his red brother was not so dumb.

(Joseph Kinsey Howard : *Montana : High, Wide, and Handsome.*)

Soil Erosion

OKLAHOMA

TO THE red country and part of the gray country of Oklahoma, the last rains came gently, and they did not cut the scarred earth. The plows crossed and recrossed the rivulet marks. The last rains lifted the corn quickly and scattered weed colonies and grass along the sides of the roads so that the gray country and the dark red country began to disappear under a green cover. In the last part of May the sky grew pale and the clouds that had hung in high puffs for so long in the spring were dissipated. The sun flared down on the growing corn day after day until a line of brown spread along the edge of each green bayonet. The clouds appeared, and went away, and in a while they did not try any more. The weeds grew darker green to protect themselves, and they did not spread any more. The surface of the earth crusted, a thin hard crust, and as the sky became pale, so the earth became pale, pink in the red country and white in the gray country.

In the water-cut gullies the earth dusted down in dry little streams. Gophers and ant lions started small avalanches. And as the sharp sun struck day after day, the leaves of the young corn became less stiff and erect ; they bent in a curve at first, and then, as the central ribs of strength grew weak, each leaf tilted downward. Then it was June, and the sun shone more

245

fiercely. The brown lines on the corn leaves widened and moved in on the central ribs. The weeds frayed and edged back toward their roots. The air was thin and the sky more pale ; and every day the earth paled.

In the roads where the teams moved, where the wheels milled the ground and the hooves of the horses beat the ground, the dirt crust broke and the dust formed. Every moving thing lifted the dust into the air : a walking man lifted a thin layer as high as his waist, and a wagon lifted the dust as high as the fence tops, and an automobile boiled a cloud behind it. The dust was long in settling back again.

When June was half gone, the big clouds moved up out of Texas and the Gulf, high heavy clouds, rain-heads. The men in the fields looked up at the clouds and sniffed at them and held wet fingers up to sense the wind. And the horses were nervous while the clouds were up. The rain-heads dropped a little spattering and hurried on to some other country. Behind them the sky was pale again and the sun flared. In the dust there were drop craters where the rain had fallen, and there were clean splashes on the corn, and that was all.

A gentle wind followed the rain clouds, driving them on northward, a wind that softly clashed the drying corn. A day went by and the wind increased, steady, unbroken by gusts. The dust from the roads fluffed up and spread out and fell on the weeds beside the fields, and fell into the fields a little way. Now the wind grew strong and hard and it worked at the rain crust in the cornfields. Little by little the sky was darkened by the mixing dust, and the wind felt over the earth, loosened the dust, and carried it away. The wind grew stronger. The rain crust broke and the dust lifted up out of the fields and drove gray plumes into the air like sluggish smoke. The corn threshed the wind and made a dry, rushing sound. The finest dust did not settle back to earth now, but disappeared into the darkening sky.

The wind grew stronger, whisked under stones, carried up straws and old leaves, and even little clods, marking its course as it sailed through the fields. The air and the sky darkened and through them the sun shone redly, and there was a raw sting in the air. During the night the wind raced faster over the land, dug cunningly among the rootlets of the corn, and the corn fought the wind with its weakened leaves until the roots were freed by the prying wind and then each stalk settled wearily sideways toward the earth and pointed the direction of the wind.

The dawn came, but no day. In the gray sky a red sun appeared, a dim red circle that gave a little light, like dusk ; and as that day advanced, the dusk slipped back toward darkness, and the wind cried and whimpered over the fallen corn.

Men and women huddled in their houses, and they tied handkerchiefs over their noses when they went out, and wore goggles to protect their eyes.

When the night came again it was black night, for the stars could not pierce the dust to get down, and the window lights could not even spread beyond their own yards. Now the dust was evenly mixed with the air, an emulsion of dust and air. Houses were shut tight, and cloth wedged around doors and windows, but the dust came in so thinly that it could not be seen in the air, and it settled like pollen on the chairs and tables, on the dishes. The people brushed it from their shoulders. Little lines of dust lay at the door sills.

In the middle of that night the wind passed on and left the land quiet. The dust-filled air muffled sound more completely than fog does. The people, lying in their beds, heard the wind stop. They awakened when the rushing wind was gone. They lay quietly and listened deep into the stillness. Then the roosters crowed, and their voices were muffled, and the people stirred restlessly in their beds and wanted the morning. They knew it would take a long time for the dust to settle out of the air. In the morning the dust hung like fog, and the sun was as red as ripe new blood. All day the dust sifted down from the sky, and the next day it sifted down. An even blanket covered the earth. It settled on the corn, piled up on the tops of the fence posts, piled up on the wires ; it settled on roofs, blanketed the weeds and trees.

The people came out from their houses and smelled the hot stinging air and covered their noses from it. And the children came out of the houses, but they did not run or shout as they would have done after a rain. Men stood by their fences and looked at the ruined corn, drying fast now, only a little green showing through the film of dust. The men were silent and they did not move often. And the women came out of the houses to stand beside their men—to feel whether this time the men would break. The women studied the men's faces secretly, for the corn

247

could go, as long as something else remained. The children stood near by, drawing figures in the dust with bare toes, and the children sent exploring senses out to see whether men and women would break. The children peeked at the faces of the men and women, and then drew careful lines in the dust with their toes. Horses came to the watering troughs and nuzzled the water to clear the surface dust. After a while the faces of the watching men lost their bemused perplexity and became hard and angry and resistant. Then the women knew that they were safe and that there was no break. Then they asked, What'll we do ? And the men replied, I don't know. But it was all right. The women knew it was all right, and the watching children knew it was all right. Women and children knew deep in themselves that no misfortune was too great to bear if their men were whole. The women went into the houses to their work, and the children began to play, but cautiously at first. As the day went forward the sun became less red. It flared down on the dust-blanketed land. The men sat in the doorways of their houses ; their hands were busy with sticks and little rocks. The men sat still—thinking—figuring. (*36°N; 98°W*.)   (John Steinbeck : *The Grapes of Wrath*.)

Soil Erosion

THE UNITED STATES

Most of the time till now we never thought :

There was always some place else a man could head for

There was always the forest ahead of us opening on—
The blue ash in the coves of the Great Smokies :
The hickories staking the loam on the slow Ohio :
The homestead oaks along the Illinois :
The cypresses on the Arkansas to tie to :
The cottonwoods following water : the wild plums :
The lodgepole pines along the hill horizon

There was always the grass ahead of us on and on
Father to father's son :
Prairie grass to buffalo grass. . . .
Bluegrass. . . . Prairie shoestring. . . .

Climbing out of the bottoms of rich rain
To the great shoulders of silence and sunlight
And on over the benches and over the draws—
The sloughgrass to the pommel on the prairies :
The bluestem to the stirrup on the plains :
Buffalo grass to the fetlock on the ranges :

The sage smelling of men : tasting of memory

We looked west from a rise and we saw forever

Most of the time till now we never thought

It's only now we get wondering

Now the land's behind us we get wondering

Now that the pines are behind us in Massachusetts
Now that the forests of Michigan lie behind us—
Behind the blackberry barrens : back of the brush piles :
Back of the dead stumps in the drifting sand :

Millions of acres of stumps to remember the past by—
To remember the Upper Peninsula hushed with pines :
To remember hemlocks singing in Wisconsin :
To remember over the water the birches remembering

Now that the forests of Michigan lie behind—

The east wind on the Lake for a generation
Smelled of the smoke out of Michigan . . . out of the pines.

Now that the rivers that ran under trees are behind us—
The prairie rivers with catfish and hickory shad :
The water silky with sun after thunder : the ducks on them :

The mountain rivers amber in their channels :

Now that the rivers are back of us : back of the mud-banks :
Back of the dead perch on the slimy sand :

The stream-beds stinking in the August sunlight :
The pools sluggish with sewage : choked with tree trunks :

Now that the grass is behind us : the measureless pasture
Greening before the last frost left the ground :
Yellow by middle summer : cured in autumn :
Tawny : color of hide : windy as water :
A mile up : big as a continent : clean with the
Whole sky going over it :

Sun's pasture. . . .

Now that the grass is back of us : back of the furrows :
Back of the dry-bone winters and the dust :
Back of the stock tanks full but not with water :
Back of the snakeweed greasewood ripgut thistle

Now that the land's behind us we get wondering

We wonder if the liberty was land and the
Land's gone : the liberty's back of us. . . .

We can't say

We don't know. . . .

Under our feet and our hands the land leaves us
The continent richer than any : heavy with earth :
Spade-head deep with leaf-mold where the trees were :
Handle deep with black land under grass :
The new continent : new in our time even :—
Whole counties cankered to rock and hard-pan :
One acre in twenty dead as haddock :
Two farmers in five tenants : the rest of them
Hoeing the company's mortgage for three rows :
Hoeing their own on the fourth till their backs break with it
The tilled land of the Mississippi Valley—

" The most spacious habitation for man in the
World anywhere "—
>
> goldenrod where the corn was :

A quarter and more of it—
>
> goldenrod where the corn was

And we're not telling them : not from our own front doors :

Not from the front stoops sagging towards the ditches :

Not from the gulleyed acres tilled for cotton :
Cut for burdock : harvested for stones

Not from the brittle orchards : barren gardens :
Dog-run houses with the broken windows :
Hen-shat houseyards where the children huddle
Barefoot in winter : tiny in too big rags :
Fed on porkfat : corn meal : cheap molasses :
Fed on famine rations out of fields
Where grass grew higher than a child could touch once

All we know for certain—we're not telling them :

The land's going out from us under the grants and the titles and
We're not telling them

>
> not from the tenant farms

Breaking our fingers with another's labor :
Turning another man's sod for him : planting his bean patch :

Restless rain against another's roof

Odourless lilacs in another's dooryard
Under our feet and our hands the land leaves us and
We're not telling them :
>
> not now :
>
> not from the

Worked out corn fields where the soil has left us
Silent and secret : coloring little streams :

Riling in yellow runnels after rainfall :
Dribbling from furrow down into furrow and down into
Fields fallow with winter and on down—
Falling away to the rivers and on down

Taking the life with it

Taking the bread with it :
                          taking a good man's pride in a
Clean field well tilled : his children
Fed from furrows his own plow has made them

All we know for sure—the land's going out from us :

Blown out by the dry wind in the wheat :
Blown clean to the arrow-heads under the centuries :
Blown to the stony clay . . .
                          and we get wondering :

We wonder if the liberty was land

We wonder if the liberty was grass
Greening ahead of us : grazed beyond horizons . . .

The dust chokes in our throats and we get wondering

We wonder whether the dream of American liberty
Wasn't the standing by the fence to tell them :

And we're not standing by the homestead fence
And telling any man where he can head for :

Not in these parts :

                    not with this wind blowing

Not with this wind blowing and no rain

                    (Archibald Macleish : *Land of the Free—U.S.A.*)

THE WORK OF RAIN AND RIVERS

THE WORK OF RAIN AND RIVERS

Water

FRANCE : SAVOY

NOW AND THEN an influential chief came up, and him, with the approval of the Line, we would load into the plane and carry off to see something of the world. The aim was to soften their pride, for, repositories of the truth, defenders of Allah, the only God, it was more in contempt than in hatred that he and his kind murdered their prisoners.

And so we would take them up for a little spin. Three of them even visited France in our planes. I happened to be present when they returned. I met them when they landed, went with them to their tents, and waited in infinite curiosity to hear their first words. They were of the same race as those who, having once been flown by me to the Senegal, had burst into tears at the sight of trees.

. . . Memories that moved them too deeply rose to stop their speech. Some weeks earlier they had been taken up into the French Alps. Here in Africa they were still dreaming of what they saw. Their guide had led them to a tremendous waterfall, a sort of braided column roaring over the rocks. He had said to them :

" Taste this."

It was sweet water. Water ! How many days were they wont to march in the desert to reach the nearest well ; and when they had arrived, how long they had to dig before there bubbled up a muddy liquid mixed with camels' urine ! Water ! At Cape Juby, at Cisneros, at Port Etienne, the Moorish children did not beg for coins. With empty tins in their hands they begged for water.

" Give me a little water, give ! "

" If you are a good lad. . . . "

Water ! A thing worth its weight in gold ! A thing the least drop of which drew from the sand the green sparkle of a blade of grass ! When rain has fallen anywhere, a great exodus animates the Sahara. The tribes ride towards that grass that will have sprung up two hundred miles away. And this water, this miserly water of which not a drop had fallen in Port Etienne in ten years, roared in the Savoie with the power of a cataclysm as if, from some burst cistern, the reserves of the world were pouring forth.

" Come, let us leave," their guide had said.

But they would not stir.

" Leave us here a little longer."

They had stood in silence. Mute, solemn, they had stood gazing at the unfolding of a ceremonial mystery. That which came roaring out of the belly of the mountain was life itself, was the life-blood of man. The flow of a single second would have re-suscitated whole caravans that, mad with thirst, had pressed on into the eternity of salt lakes and mirages. Here God was mani-festing Himself : it would not do to turn one's back on Him. God had opened the locks and was displaying His puissance. The three Moors stood motionless.

" That is all there is to see," their guide had said. " Come."

" We must wait."

" Wait for what ? "

" The end."

They were awaiting the moment when God would grow weary of His madness. They knew Him to be quick to repent, knew He was miserly.

" But that water has been running for a thousand years ! "

And this was why, at Port Etienne, they did not too strongly stress the matter of the waterfall. There were certain miracles about which it was better to be silent. Better, indeed, not to think too much about them for in that case one would cease to understand anything at all. Unless one was to doubt the existence of God. . . .

(Port Etienne: 21°N; 17°W.)

(Antoine de Saint-Exupéry: *Wind, Sand and Stars :* Translated by Lewis Galantière.)

Water

CENTRAL ASIA

IT WAS so silent, so still in those lofty solitudes, we felt as though we were visitors on some strange planet. The vast spaces of the sky gloomed upon us dusky blue from over the snowy summits of Arka-tagh. It was a world in which all things were motionless, rigid, eternally fixed, save for the twinkling of the stars, the slow and solemn procession of the clouds, the sparkling of the snow crystals. The only sound that reached the ear was the metallic, but musical, plash of the water as it struck against the icy mail of the river below. The nights were sublime ; in beauty they easily surpassed the days. A thousand pities no other living creature but ourselves was able to sleep under their fascinating protection ! And yet the river slept, for the frost seized it in his embrace and converted it into ice, and its babble gradually died away in slumber ;\ and so it slept until the sun rose the next morning and warmed it to life again, reminding it that for Nature's children there is no rest : they must ever be spending their energy without cessation in shaping and reshaping the crust of the patient earth.

(Sven Hedin : Through Asia.)

Rain and Flood

PENNSYLVANIA

ALL DURING the latter part of May 1889 a chill rain had been falling in torrents upon the Conemaugh Valley. The small city of Johnstown, walled in by precipitous Pennsylvania hills, was invaded by high water, which stood knee-deep in front of my father's house on Washington Street.

At the time, nobody seemed particularly concerned over the dam which rich Pittsburghers had maintained high up on the South Fork to provide water for their fishing streams. When the earthen dam had first been constructed there had been some apprehension. There was a ninety-foot head of water behind the embankment, and only a small spillway had been provided. But the dam had never burst and, with the passage of time, the townspeople, like those who live in the shadow of Vesuvius, grew hardened to the possibility of danger. " Some time," they thought, " that dam will give way, but it won't ever happen to us."

During the afternoon of the thirty-first the overflow from the river crept steadily higher, inch by inch, through the streets of the town. Although it had not yet reached the stable, which stood on higher ground than the house, my father became concerned for the safety of his fine pair of horses, which were tied in their stalls, and suggested that I make a dash for the stable and unfasten them. The rain was falling so hard that I was almost drenched as I ploughed my laborious way through the two feet of water.

I had loosed the horses and was about to leave the shelter of the doorway, when my ears were stunned by the most terrifying noise I had ever heard in my sixteen years of life. The dreadful roar was punctuated with a succession of tremendous crashes. I stood for a moment, bewildered and hesitant. I could see my mother and my father standing at an upper window in the house. My father, frantic with anxiety for my safety, was motioning me urgently toward the top of the building. Fortunately, I had made a passageway only a few days before to the red tin roof, so that some necessary repairs could be made. Thus, it was only a matter of seconds before I was up on the ridge.

From my perch I could see a huge wall advancing with incredible rapidity down the diagonal street. It was not recognizable as water ; it was a dark mass in which seethed houses, wagons, trees and animals. As this wall struck Washington Street broadside, my boyhood home was crushed like an eggshell before my eyes, and I saw it disappear.

I wanted to know how long it would take me to get to the other world, and in the split second before the stable was hit I looked at my watch. It was exactly four-twenty.

But, instead of being shattered, the big barn was ripped from its foundations and began to roll, like a barrel, over and over. Stumbling, crawling, and racing, I somehow managed to keep on top.

In the path of the revolving stable loomed suddenly the house of our neighbour, Mrs. Fenn. To avoid being hurled off by the inevitable collision, I leapt into the air at the precise moment of impact. But just as I miraculously landed on the roof of her house, its wall began to cave in. I plunged downward with the roof, but saved myself by clambering monkey-like up the slope, and before the house gave way completely another boiled up beside me. I caught hold of the eaves and swung dangling there, while the weight of my body drained the strength from my hands.

For years thereafter I was visited by recurring dreams, in which I lived over and over again that fearful experience of hanging with my finger-nails dug deep into the water-softened shingles, knowing that in the end I must let go.

When my grip finally relaxed, I dropped sickeningly into space. But once again I was saved. With a great thud I hit a piece of the old familiar barn roof, and I clutched with all my remaining power at the half-inch tin ridges. Lying on my belly, I bumped along on the surface of the flood, which was crushing, crumbling, and splintering everything before it. The screams of the injured were hardly to be distinguished above the awful clamour ; people were being killed all about me.

In that moment of terrible danger I saw the Italian fruit dealer Mussante, with his wife and two children, racing along on what seemed to be their old barn floor. A Saratoga trunk was open beside them, and the whole family was frantically packing a pile of possessions into it. Suddenly the whole mass of wreckage heaved up and crushed them out of existence.

I was borne headlong toward a jam where the wreckage was already piling up between a stone church and a three-story brick building. Into this hurly-burly I was catapulted. A tree would shoot out of the water ; a huge girder would come thundering down. As these trees and girders drove booming into the jam, I jumped them desperately, one after another. Then suddenly a wagon reared up over my head ; I could not leap that. But just as it plunged toward me the brick building gave way, and my raft shot out from beneath the wagon like a bullet from a gun.

In a moment more I was in comparatively open water. Although no landmark was visible, I could identify the space as the park which had been there only a short while before. I was still being swept along, but the danger had lessened. I had opportunity to observe other human beings in equally perilous situations. I saw the stoutish Mrs. Fenn astride an unstable tar barrel, which had covered her with its contents. Rolling far over to one side, then swaying back to the other, she was making a desperate but grotesque struggle to keep her head above water.

There was nothing I could do for anybody.

Dr. Lee's negro ostler, all alone and stark naked, was shivering on the roof of his master's house. In the penetrating rain his supplicating hands were raised towards the heavens. As I tore by I heard him shouting, " Lawd ha' mercy on dis pore cold nigger."

I was carried on toward the narrows below the city where the tracks of the Pennsylvania Railway crossed both valley and river on a high embankment and bridge. When the twisted, interlaced timbers ahead of me struck the stone arches, they plugged them tight, and in the powerful recoil my raft was swept back behind the hill which had saved the lower part of the town from complete destruction and left many buildings standing.

I passed close by a two-and-a-half-story brick dwelling which was still remaining on its foundations. Since my speed as I went up this second valley was about that of a train slowing for a stop, I was able to hop to the roof and join the small group of people already stranded there. Realizing then that I was, perhaps, not immediately destined for the other world, I pulled out my watch. It was not yet four-thirty; three thousand human beings had been wiped out in less than ten minutes.

For the remaining hours of daylight we derelicts huddled disconsolately on the roof. Now and then we were able to reach out a hand or a pole and haul in somebody drifting by, until finally we numbered nineteen. Though we were in a backwash, many of the houses had been seriously damaged below the water-line. Occasionally one would melt like a lump of sugar and vanish. We did not know whether our refuge had been undermined, but there was no way for us to escape to the surrounding hills which rose invitingly above the flood, so near and yet so impossible to reach. The cold rain was still driving down, and it was growing dark. We were so miserable that we decided to open the skylight and climb under cover.

There in the attic we spent the night, starting whenever we heard the whoo-oo-sh which meant that another building had sunk. Ours was straining and groaning. From moment to moment we could not tell whether it was to suffer the same fate as its neighbours. Although exhausted we could not sleep. The waiting, in its way, was almost worse than the previous turmoil, because if our shelter collapsed it would become a trap in which we would drown miserably.

Dawn brought a transcendent sense of relief. The rain had ceased at last, and the water had receded until it reached only part of the way up the first story. Between us and the safe hills a half-mile away was a mat of debris, broken here and there by patches of dirty water. Scrambling over the wreckage, wading through shallows, and rafting deeper spaces, with an inexpressible feeling of relief I finally set my feet on solid ground again.

I started down stream at once, trying to find my father and mother. Every one I met was on the same sad errand—looking for parents, children, relatives, or friends. Bodies were already being taken out of the ruins.

(40°20′N; 79°W.)   (Victor Heiser: *A Doctor's Odyssey*.)

Rain: Landslip

THE HIMALAYAS

THEN CAME such summer rains as had not been known in the Hills for many seasons. Through three good months the valley was wrapped in cloud and soaking mist—steady, unrelenting downfall, breaking off into thunder-shower after thunder-shower. Kali's Shrine stood above the clouds, for the most part, and there was a whole month in which the Bhagat never caught a glimpse of his village. It was packed away under a white floor of cloud that swayed and shifted and rolled on itself and bulged upwards, but never broke from its piers—the streaming flanks of the valley.

All that time he heard nothing but the sound of a million little waters, overhead from the trees, and underfoot along the ground, soaking through the pine-needles, dripping from the tongues of draggled fern, and spouting in newly-torn muddy channels down the slopes. Then the sun came out, and drew forth the good incense of the deodars and the rhododendrons, and that far-off, clean smell which the Hill people call "the smell of the snows." The hot sunshine lasted for a week, and then the rains gathered together for their last downpour, and the water fell in sheets that flayed off the skin of the ground and leaped back in mud. Purun Bhagat heaped his fire high that night, for he was sure his brothers would need warmth; but never a beast came to the shrine, though he called and called till he dropped asleep, wondering what had happened in the woods.

It was in the black heart of the night, the rain drumming like a thousand drums, that he was roused by a plucking at his blanket, and, stretching out, felt the little hand of a *langur*. "It is better here than in the trees," he said sleepily, loosening a fold of blanket; "take it and be warm." The monkey caught his hand and pulled hard. "Is it food, then?" said Purun Bhagat. "Wait awhile, and I will prepare some." As he kneeled to throw fuel on the fire the *langur* ran to the door of the shrine, crooned, and ran back again, plucking at the man's knee.

" What is it ? What is thy trouble, Brother ? " said Purun Bhagat, for the *langur's* eyes were full of things that he could not tell. " Unless one of thy caste be in a trap—and none set traps here—I will not go into that weather. Look, Brother, even the *barasingh* comes for shelter ! "

The deer's antlers clashed as he strode into the shrine, clashed against the grinning statue of Kali. He lowered them in Purun Bhagat's direction and stamped uneasily, hissing through his half-shut nostrils.

" Hai ! Hai ! Hai ! " said the Bhagat, snapping his fingers. " Is *this* payment for a night's lodging ? " But the deer pushed him towards the door, and as he did so Purun Bhagat heard the sound of something opening with a sigh, and saw two slabs of the floor draw away from each other, while the sticky earth below smacked its lips.

" Now I see," said Purun Bhagat. " No blame to my brothers that they did not sit by the fire tonight. The mountain is falling. And yet—why should I go ? " His eye fell on the empty begging-bowl, and his face changed. " They have given me good food daily since—since I came, and, if I am not swift, to-morrow there will not be one mouth in the valley. Indeed, I must go and warn them below. Back there, Brother ! Let me get to the fire."

The *barasingh* backed unwillingly as Purun Bhagat drove a pine torch deep into the flame, twirling it till it was well lit. " Ah ! ye came to warn me," he said, rising. " Better than that we shall do ; better than that. Out, now, and lend me thy neck, Brother, for I have but two feet."

He clutched the bristling withers of the *barasingh* with his right hand, held the torch away with his left, and stepped out of the shrine into the desperate night. There was no breath of wind, but the rain nearly drowned the flare as the great deer hurried down the slope, sliding on his haunches. As soon as they were clear of the forest more of the Bhagat's brothers joined them. He heard, though he could not see, the *langurs* pressing about him, and behind them the *uhh ! uhh !* of Sona. The rain matted his long white hair into ropes ; the water splashed beneath his bare feet, and his yellow robe clung to his frail old body, but he stepped down steadily, leaning against the *barasingh*. Down the steep, plashy path they poured all together, the Bhagat and his brothers, down and down till the deer's feet clicked and stumbled on the wall of a threshing-floor, and he snorted because he smelt Man. Now they were at the head of the one crooked village street, and the Bhagat beat with his crutch on the barred windows of the blacksmith's house, as his torch blazed up in the shelter of the eaves. " Up and out ! " cried Purun Bhagat ; and he did not know his own voice, for it was years since he had spoken aloud to a man. " The hill falls ! The hill is falling ! Up and out, oh, you within ! "

" It is our Bhagat," said the blacksmith's wife. " He stands among his beasts. Gather the little ones and give the call."

It ran from house to house, while the beasts, cramped in the narrow way, surged and huddled round the Bhagat, and Sona puffed impatiently.

The people hurried into the street—they were no more than seventy souls all told—and in the glare of the torches they saw their Bhagat holding back the terrified *barasingh*, while the monkeys plucked piteously at his skirts, and Sona sat on his haunches and roared.

" Across the valley and up the next hill ! " shouted Purun Bhagat. " Leave none behind ! We follow ! "

Then the people ran as only Hill folk can run, for they knew that in a landslip you must climb for the highest ground across the valley. They fled, splashing through the little river at the bottom, and panted up the terraced fields on the far side, while the Bhagat and his brethren followed. Up and up the opposite mountain they climbed, calling to each other by name—the roll-call of the village—and at their heels toiled the big *barasingh*, weighted by the failing strength of Purun Bhagat. At last the deer stopped in the shadow of a deep pinewood, five hundred feet up the hillside. His instinct, that had warned him of the coming slide, told him he would be safe here.

Purun Bhagat dropped fainting by his side, for the chill of the rain and that fierce climb were killing him ; but first he called to the scattered torches ahead, " Stay and count your numbers " ; then, whispering to the deer as he saw the lights gather in a cluster : " Stay with me, Brother. Stay—till—I—go ! "

There was a sigh in the air that grew to a mutter, and a mutter that grew to a roar, and a roar that passed all sense of hearing, and the hillside on which the villagers stood was hit in the darkness, and rocked to the blow. Then a note as steady, deep, and true as the deep C of the organ drowned everything for perhaps five minutes, while the very roots of the pines quivered to it. It died away, and the sound of the rain falling on miles of hard ground and grass changed to the muffled drum of water on soft earth. That told its own tale.

Never a villager—not even the priest—was bold enough to speak to the Bhagat who had saved their lives. They crouched under the pines and waited till the day. When it came they looked across the valley and saw that what had been forest, and terraced field, and track-threaded grazing-ground was one raw, red, fan-shaped smear, with a few trees flung head-down on the scarp. That red ran high up the hill of their refuge, damming back the little river, which had begun to spread into a brick-coloured lake. Of the village, of the road to the shrine, of the shrine itself, and the forest behind, there was no trace. For one mile in width and two thousand feet in sheer depth the mountain-side had come away bodily, planed clean from head to heel.

And the villagers, one by one, crept through the wood to pray before their Bhagat. They saw the *barasingh* standing over him, who fled when they came near, and they heard the *langurs* wailing in the branches, and Sona moaning up the hill; but their Bhagat was dead, sitting cross-legged, his back against a tree, his crutch under his armpit, and his face turned to the north-east.

The priest said: " Behold a miracle after a miracle, for in this very attitude must all Sunnyasis be buried ! Therefore where he now is we will build the temple to our holy man."

They built the temple before a year was ended—a little stone-and-earth shrine—and they called the hill the Bhagat's Hill, and they worship there with lights and flowers and offerings to this day.

(Rudyard Kipling : *The Second Jungle Book.*)

Water Action

ISLE OF MAN : BALAGLAS

WHEN WE were back there we turned aside to follow the brook up under groves of beech and Spanish chestnut. The rock is limestone, smooth and pale white, not rough and gritty, and without moss, stained red where the water runs and smoothly

and vertically hewed by the force of the brook into highwalled channels with deep pools. The water is so clear in the still pools it is like shadowy air and in the falls the white is not foamed and chalky, as at Stonyhurst, but like the white of ice or glass. Round holes are scooped in the rocks smooth and true like turning : they look like the hollow of a vault or bowl. I saw and sketched as well as in the rain I could one of them that was in the making : a blade of water played on it and shaping to it spun off making a bold big white bow coiling its edge over and splaying into ribs. But from the position it is not easy to see how the water could in this way have scooped all of them.
(54°10′N; 4°30′W.)

(The Notebooks and Papers of Gerald Manley Hopkins.)

Rivers

ENGLAND

ENGLISHMEN of this time—or at least of the time just past—perpetually and rightly complained that somehow or other they missed themselves. Some took refuge in a dream of a sort of a mystical England that was not there. Others reposed in the idea of an older England which may once have been ; others, more foolish, hoped to find England again in something overseas. None of these would have suffered their error had they learnt England down English waters, seeing the great memories of England reflected in the English rivers, and meeting them in the silence and the perfection of the streams. But our roads first, and then our railways, our commerce which is from ports, and which must go direct towards them, our life, which is now in vast cities independent of streams, has made us neglect these things.

Consider such a list as this : Arundel when you see it as you come up Arun on the full flood tide. Chichester as you see it on the flood tide from Chichester harbour. Durham as you see it coming down under that cliff with the Cathedral as massive as the rock. Chester as you see it, sailing up the Dee with a light north wind from the sea. Gloucester as you see it from the Severn. Or Winchester as you pull, if you can pull, or paddle which is easier, against the clear and violent thrust of the Itchin. Canterbury as you see it from above or from below, upon the easy water of the Stour ; and Lincoln as you see it from its little ditch—and I wonder how many men now journey up in any fashion from Boston ! So Norwich from the Yare. So Bramber for that matter from a place where the Adur grows narrow ; and what a sight Bramber must have been when the Castle stood whole upon the hill, physically blocking the advance into the Weald.

There is only one stream left, the Thames, which we still know, and we very rightly know it ; but we love it only for giving us one experience which we might, if we chose, repeat up and down England everywhere. There is no country in the world like this for rivers. The tide pushes up them to the very Midlands, from every sea. There is nothing of the history of England but is on a river, and as England is an island of birds, so is it more truly an island of rivers. Consider the River Eden, which is so difficult to descend; the Wiltshire Avon and the Hampshire Avon, and those little branch streams the Thame, the Cherwell and the Evenlode.

Best of all, I think, as a memory or an experience is the Ouse, which runs from Bedford to the Wash, and has upon it the astonishing monument of Ely. Here is a river which no one can descend without feeling as he descends it the change of English provinces from the Midlands to the sea. He should start at Bedford ; then he will pass through fields where tall elms give to the plains something more than could be given them by distant hills. The river runs between banks of deep grass in summer. It is contented everywhere ; and as you go you are in the middle of a thousand years. You pass villages that have not changed ; you carry your boat over weirs where there are mills, always shaded by large trees. Once in a day, at the most, you find an unchanging town : Huntingdon is such a one, or St. Ives, where I do believe the people are kinder than in any other town. Then, as you still go on, the land takes on another character. You begin to know that England is not only rich and full of fields but also was made by the sea. For you come to great flats—and that rather suddenly—where, as at sea, the sky is your contemplation. You notice the light, the colour, and the shapes of clouds. The birds that wheel and scream over these spaces seem to be sea-birds. You expect at any moment to hear beyond the dead line of the horizon the sound of surf and to see the glint of live water. Above such a waste rises, on what is called " an island," and is in truth " an island," the superb strength of Ely.

No one has seen Ely who has not seen it from the Ouse. It is a hill upon a hill, and now permanently present in the midst of loneliness. It is something made with a framework all round of accidental marsh and emptiness. Thenceafter the Ouse goes on. You get through and down the deep step of a lock, and beyond it is the salt water and busy energy that comes and goes from the sea. Very deep banks, alive with the salt and the swirl of the tide, shut in the boat for miles, and there are very high bridges uniting village to village above one, till at last the whole thing broadens, and one sees under the sunlight the roofs and the spars of King's Lynn ; and, if one has no misadventure, one ends the journey at some narrow quay at a narrow lane of that delightful port and town.

There is one English river out of at least thirty others. I wish that all were known ! That journey down the Ouse is three days' journey—but it is such a slice of time and character and history as teaches you most you need know upon this Island. Only I warn anyone attempting it, let the boat be light and let it be shallow, and be ready to sleep in it ; it is only thus that you can know an English river, and if you can draw, why it will be a greater pleasure. It is very cheap.

(Hilaire Belloc : *On Everything*.)

Chalk Streams

ENGLAND

IT WOULD be arrogant to say that the valleys of the Test and Itchen are better than any other part of the country in May and June, but I do say that no part is better than they are. The angler who is fishing in one of these rivers at this time of year, is seeing the most beautiful season at its best. This is the time of blossom and promise, everywhere there should be visible growth responding to increasing warmth, a sense of luxuriant and abundant young life all around us. All this is assured every year in the valleys of such rivers as the Test and the Itchen. There may be, and too often is, a spring drought in other counties, and on the great downs of Hampshire itself. Other rivers may shrink, and leave their banks dry, but the Hampshire chalk streams run brim full, and their valleys are full of water meadows, intersected by streams and runnels and channels and cuts of all sorts and sizes carrying over the land the bounty of water. Hence it is, that on the way to our river we have no thought of what order it will be in, or of what rain there has been lately. The river is sure to be found full and clear. North country rivers are fed by constant tributaries. Down every glen comes a burn, and after heavy rain there is a rush of surface water, which swells them all. A true chalk stream has few tributaries. The valleys on the higher ground near it have no streams; the rain falls upon the great expanse of high exposed downs, and sinks silently into the chalk, till somewhere in a large low valley it rises in constant springs, and a full river starts from them towards the sea. There is always something mysterious to me in looking at these rivers, so little affected by the weather of the moment, fed continually by secret springs, flowing with a sort of swiftness, but for the most part (except close to mills and large hatches) silently, and with water which looks too pure and clear for that of a river of common life.

(51°10′N; 1°20′W.)   (Viscount Grey of Fallodon : *Fly Fishing*.)

Rivers

FRANCE

EARLY IN this century I was set the pleasing task of wandering through famous scenes of France. So passing south from Normandy, I crossed the drinkshed that separates cider from wine, and emerged into the wide and sunny valley of the Loire. All France is blessed with noble rivers, running with full stream, calm and silent but strong. They come from the Alps, the Auvergne, the Cevennes, and a few lower ranges of hill, and on their course they are the symbols of fertility, the quiet life of industrious villagers, and the patient fishermen who expect no reward for patience but fishing. The Somme, the Seine and Marne, the Moselle, the Rhône, the Dordogne, the Garonne—all strong and serviceable, but each with a separate beauty—what scenes of laborious but pleasant life the names call up; recent scenes of death and horror too. But of all the rivers the Loire and its southern tributaries, the Cher, the Indre, and the Vienne, are to me the most obvious evidence of the beneficent nature that pervades all France.

Their deep and eddying waters pass noiselessly through a land spread out to the sun for man's satisfaction and delight. Everything that is good to eat and drink swells and sprouts and spouts there at a touch, and one can hardly imagine hunger or thirst amid such abundance. Through banks of reeds and hayfields the rivers pass, or along the slopes of tufa hills well planted with vines, and sometimes they go sliding below the ancient walls of castles and pleasure houses, built there for kings and nobles and their ladies, because this was the best place they could choose for life.

(47°20'N; 1°W.)   (Henry W. Nevinson : *In the Dark Backward.*)

River : the Rhone
FRANCE

. . . And gay from the glacier womb, boy-throated for gladness to
      shout where the snow-crags throng
Ran foaming the rivulet Rhone,
When the mountains were sprung for his passage, the ridges of
      granite were splintered ; and lovely the lake was
Under the vineyards of Vaud,
And at evening empurpling the peaks of the Chablais were painted
      on the sleep and deep shadow of its waters
When the sundown was flame on la Dole.
But the best of the course is the last broad slumber, O river of
      France to forget and go down
Slow-gliding and sultrily stagnant
Past Arles to the Gulf of the Lion and that azure and beautifu
      grave in the waves of the south
That are warmest and best . . . and an end . . .

    (Robinson Jeffers : *Roan Stallion, Tamar and other Poems :*
    "The Songs of the Dead Men to the Three Dancers".)

Rivers
SICILY

I ALWAYS wonder why such vast river-beds of pale boulders come out of the heart of the high-rearing, dramatic stone mountains, a few miles to the sea. A few miles only : and never more than a few threading water-trickles in river-beds wide enough for the Rhine. But that is how it is. The landscape is ancient, and classic—romantic, as if it had known far-off days and fiercer rivers and more verdure. Steep, craggy, wild, the land goes up to its points and precipices, a tangle of heights. But all jammed on top of one another. And in old landscapes, as in old people, the flesh wears away, and the bones become prominent. Rock sticks up fantastically. The jungle of peaks in this old Sicily. (*37°30′N; 14°E.*)   (D. H. Lawrence : *Sea and Sardinia.*)

River : the Euphrates
MESOPOTAMIA

THAT NIGHT the November rains began and turned the hard-caked surface of the desert to liquid slush into which the cars sank deep, especially the cars that were heavy with mails for the British in Baghdad. Day after day, from dawn till late evening we toiled. We hauled, we dug, we laid down stones for the wheels to bite on, but four nights and days were spent in mud before the Euphrates came in sight, and then, at the fort of Ramadi, we were held up again by the news that a torrent of rain made the track to the bridge at Felujah impassable. So there I walked along the bank of the ancient and famous river, which was sweeping down its course in streaks of blue and brown, like any other powerful river that had a source far away among mountains.

(Henry W. Nevinson : *In the Dark Backward.*)

River : the Tigris near Baghdad
MESOPOTAMIA

THE ONLY way to study attentively the country comprising Lower Mesopotamia and the famous regions north of the Persian Gulf, is to traverse it on horseback, or to go down the Tigris in a native craft, in order that, while quietly descending the stream, one would become better acquainted with the tribes on its banks, understand their mode of life, their power, their position with regard to the Turkish Government, and the nature of its commerce, and of the fines (or black-mail) which their chiefs exact from the traffic on the river between the cities of Baghdad and Bussoreh. I had, on several occasions, journeyed along the plains on the east and on the west, but had little communication with the natives, as they are principally found on the rivers, the great arteries of the country, so I resolved to engage two boats, the names of which I must record, as they will take a very prominent place in this record.

The *Hadedeyah* and *Wananah* were both large vessels, built of teak-wood, of from 80 to 100 tons burden, with long crescent-shaped stems and lofty poop, the latter comprising the only cabin for passengers ; the upper streak is ornamented by figures or letters nicely carved in relief ; the centre of the boat is always appropriated to cargo ; but their most constant employ is secured by the traffic in firewood, which they convey up the river to Baghdad. Their crew consists of about thirty Arabs, fifteen trackers, who when winds and currents were unfavourable had to track the craft along, and fifteen matchlock-men, Arabs of Bedouin descent : these never track, but assist in hoisting the sail, and act as guard in case of attack. As neither town nor bazaar existed for the whole route, and we were committing ourselves to the desert as to the open sea, we were obliged to take in provisions for twenty-five days, and in addition a stock of dates, pipes, and presents of various kinds for any marauding chief whose rapacity we should have occasion to buy off.

We started on March 12th with a fair wind, the collective crews formed themselves into a choir led by a man playing on the tambourine ; they danced along the gunwale and cargo and sang Arab songs : as some hoisted the sail, and as they fired off their guns and threw into every conceivable posture their naked arms and legs, a wilder scene could scarcely be imagined.

There was plenty of water in the river, the spring rise had well commenced. The Tigris is at its lowest point during the months of July, August, and September, at which period, in some places, it can only be navigated by light boats drawing not more than three feet of water. The navigation is carried on during these months by craft of this draught, but even then with difficulty, owing to the continually shifting channel. At the beginning of October the course and channel of the river become clearly defined and deepened, when navigation is easier ; the first rains in the hills begin to fall and affect the current, which, flowing more rapidly, increases the depth of water in the shoal places. After the middle of November the rise of the river commences. It is at this season that large boats, which draw, when laden, generally from five to six feet of water, begin their trade ; they descend the stream with light cargoes (seldom profitable) to Bussoreh, and wait there until a fleet is formed for mutual protection. In February or March they start for Baghdad, a journey of two months, or at least forty days, laden with the produce of India, Java, and China, conveyed to Bussoreh in buggaloes and Dutch vessels from Batavia. They reach Baghdad in March, April and May, when they find the river at its flood almost on a level with the surrounding country, and have often to sound for its channel through a sea formed by its inundations. (*33°N; 44°30'E.*)

(Thomas Kerr Lynch : *The Navigation of the Euphrates and Tigris.*)

River: the Nile, Ripon Falls
EGYPT

THE RIPON FALLS are somewhat disappointing. One has heard such a lot about their beauty, and the grandeur of the birth of the Nile, so what seems like a dam across the north end of the Napoleon Gulf—part of Lake Victoria Nyanza—with about an eighteen-foot drop, does not strike one as being over-exciting. It is necessary to be boated across from Jinja on the Usoga shore to the Uganda bank to obtain the finest view of these falls. The great swirl of water takes a sharp bend west on the very brink of the falls, and here one can get quite close down to the water's edge. Half a mile further on one faces the whole thing, which is some three-quarters of a mile across. The roar of the broad volume of the lake pouring through the different channels, combined with the spray and the tumbling and tossing of the waters rushing towards one, is most impressive. (*0°30'N; 33°E.*)

(Capt. F. A. Dickinson : *Lake Victoria to Khartoum.*)

River Delta
EGYPT : THE NILE

AFTER THE fifth day of my journey I no longer travelled over shifting hills, but came upon a dead level—a dead level bed of sand, quite hard, and studded with small shining pebbles.

The heat grew fierce ; there was no valley nor hollow, no hill, no mound, no shadow of hill nor of mound, by which I could mark the way I was making. Hour by hour I advanced, and saw no change—I was still the very centre of a round horizon ; hour by hour I advanced, and still there was the same, and the same, and the same—the same circle of flaming sky—the same circle of sand still glaring with light and fire. Over all the heaven above, over all the earth beneath, there was no visible power that could balk the fierce will of the sun ; " he rejoiced as a strong man to run a race ; his going forth was from the end of the heaven, and his circuit unto the ends of it : and there was nothing hid from the heat thereof." From pole to pole, and from the east to the west, he brandished his fiery sceptre as though he had usurped all heaven and earth. As he bid the soft Persian in ancient times, so now, and fiercely too, he bid me bow down and worship him ; so now in his pride he seemed to command me, and say, " Thou shalt have none other gods but me." I was all alone before him. There were these pitted together, and face to face ; the mighty sun for one—and for the other, this poor, pale, solitary self of mine that I always carry about with me.

But on the eighth day, and before I had yet turned away from Jehovah for the glittering god of the Persians, there appeared a dark line upon the edge of the forward horizon, and soon the line deepened into a delicate fringe that sparkled here and there as though it were sown with diamonds. There then before me were the gardens and the minarets of Egypt, and the mighty works of the Nile, and I (the eternal Ego that I am !)—I had lived to see, and I saw them.

When evening came I was still within the confines of the desert, and my tent was pitched as usual, but one of my Arabs stalked away rapidly towards the west without telling me the errand on which he was bent. After a while he returned : he had toiled on a graceful service ; he had travelled all the way on to the border of the living world, and brought me back for a token an ear of rice, full, fresh and green.

The next day I entered upon Egypt, and floated along (for the delight was as the delight of bathing) through green wavy fields of rice, and pastures fresh and plentiful, and dived into the cold verdure of groves and gardens, and quenched my hot eyes in shade, as though in a bed of deep waters.

(31°N; 32°E.)

(Kinglake : *Eothen.*)

River Delta : the Sundarbans

INDIA : THE GANGES

THE GREAT delta of the Ganges east of the Hughli, from Diamond Harbour as far as the Haringhata, is entirely river and jungle. Four thousand square miles of forest are intersected by six hundred or more channels which are big enough to have names on a 4-inch-to-the-mile survey map, and perhaps ten times as many channels which have escaped nomenclature, and yet are big enough for a ship's jolly-boat, though the trees

" High overarched embower."

The Forest Department have divided this huge tract into many thousands of sections, and each section when it has been depleted of its timber is left alone for forty years. These statistics are more eloquent of the stillness and tranquillity of the Sundarbans than any descriptive writing.

There is a sameness about all great rivers which makes a few days on a launch more monotonous than a month in the open sea, where strange fellowship and a clean horizon give one a spurious sense of freedom and even of conquest. But in estuaries the yellow water and the glare and the far-away fringe of trees are always the same, whether in the Menam, the La Plata, or the Hughli. Here breadth of view affects us, not illogically, with a sense of restraint, and it is good, if one has command of the wheel, to escape from the estuary which makes us feel confined through its perpetual vista of limitations and the suggestion of unexplored margins, which may or may not have a character of their own, into channels where one can recognize the vegetation on either bank.

In the Sundarbans these give place to narrower channels, which in turn are connected by creeks barely accessible in a dinghy, every one of which reveals the same feature—a low bank of mud haunted by the slothful mugger, and overrun by red and brown crabs and mud-fish always plying between one another's burrows on the same earnest business of love or hate or greed, and making assignations as resolutely and as disastrously as more evolved creatures. The banks are slotted with the feet of unseen things, tiger and cheetah, the hunter and hunted, which move in some mysterious way through the thick tangle, which is so congested that the roots have to send up shoots for air,—brittle, slimy things that crackle under the foot of the intruder.

Seeds fall all day long, and germinate at once in the mud, and spring up and choke one another, and writhe and struggle for light and room. The banks are thick with the fern-like *hental* palm, whose leaves turn golden, and the *golpatta,* that sends up great palmate fronds which are always tumbling over with their own weight, leaving a *débris* of roots broken off and sticking in the mud like inverted clubs glistening red and yellow in the attenuated sunlight, until they are lifted out of their bed of slime by the rising tide and borne through a labyrinth of fronds out into the broad stream seawards.

Could one cut a path through this teeming forest one would find there was no truce or respite in it till the jungle ends right in the sea, where the matted red roots of the *goran* and mangrove are left naked by the breakers in a ruddy tortuous tangle that is like nothing on earth but the dwarf rhododendron forests of Sikkim and Nepal.

Along the coast extend the sand-dunes, a line of smooth breast-like hummocks and soft depressions, where the tiger stretches himself and sleeps after his hunting. The barrier is grown over with the tall elephant-grass, whose white crests, always stirring with a faint breeze from the sea, dance and glimmer like a mirage. Between the dunes and the jungle lies the salt marsh, the stag's pasture-land, where the grass stretches in streaks of colour from citron green to dull brown according to the variation of the soil.

(*22°N; 89°E.*)   (Edmund Candler : *The Mantle of the East.*)

River: the Zambesi, Victoria Falls

RHODESIA

AT NOON I reached the western extremity of the great cataract. The Zambesi two miles above the falls runs E.N.E. and then takes a curve to the eastward, the direction in which it is rushing when it meets the chasm into which it leaps.

Mozi-oa-tunia is neither more nor less than a long trough, a gigantic crevasse, the sort of chasm for which was invented the word abyss,—an abyss profound and monstrous into which the Zambesi precipitates itself bodily to an extent of 1,978 yards.

The cleft in the basaltic rocks which form the northern wall of the abyss is perfectly traceable, running east and west.

Parallel thereto, another enormous wall of basalt, standing upon the same level, and 110 yards distant from it, forms the opposite side of the crevasse. The feet of these huge moles of black basalt form a channel through which the river rushes after its fall, a channel which is certainly much narrower than the upper aperture, but whose width it is impossible to measure.

In the southern wall, and about three-fifth parts along it, the rock has been riven asunder, and forms another gigantic chasm, perpendicular to the first ; which chasm, first taking a westerly curve and subsequently bending southwards and then eastwards, receives the river and conveys it in a capricious zigzag through a perfect maze of rocks.

The great northern wall of the cataract over which the water flows is in places perfectly vertical, with few or none of those breaks or irregularities that one is accustomed to see under such circumstances.

The Zambesi, encountering upon its way the crevasse to which we have alluded, rushes into it in three grand cataracts, because a couple of islands which occupy two great spaces in the northern wall divide the stream into three separate branches.

The first cataract is formed by a branch which passes to the south of the first island, an island which occupies, in the right angle assumed by the upper part of the cleft, the extreme west.

This is the smallest of the falls, but it is the most beautiful, or more correctly speaking, the only one that is really beautiful, for all else at Mozi-oa-tunia is sublimely horrible. That enormous gulf, black as is the basalt which forms it, dark and dense as is the cloud which enwraps it, would have been chosen, if known in biblical times, as an image of the infernal regions, a hell of water and darkness, more terrible perhaps than the hell of fire and light.

At times, when peering into the depths through that eternal mist, one may perceive a mass of confused shapes, like unto vast and frightful ruins. These are peaks of rocks of enormous height, on to which the water dashes and becomes at once converted into a cloud of spray, which rolls and tumbles about the peaks where it was formed, and will continue to do so as long as the water falls and the rocks are there to receive it.

Opposite Garden Island, through the medium of a rainbow, concentric to another and a fainter one, I could perceive from time to time, as the mist slightly shifted, confusedly appear a series of pinnacles, similar to the minarets and spires of some fantastic cathedral, which shot up, as it were, from out the mass of seething waters.

As the water which runs from the two first falls and from part of the third near Garden Island rushes eastward, it meets the remainder of the third fall coursing west, and the result is a frightful seething whirlpool, whence the creamy waters rush, after the mad conflict, into the narrow rocky channel before alluded to and go hissing away through the capricious zigzag chasm.

The islands of the cataract and the rocks which lie about it are all covered with the densest vegetation, but the green is dark, sad-coloured and monotonous, although a clump or two of palms, as they shoot their elegant heads above the thicket of evergreens which surround them, do their best to break the melancholy aspect of the picture.

Never-ending showers of spray descend upon all objects in the proximity of the falls, and a ceaseless thunder growls within the abyss.

(18°S; 26°E.)   (Major Serpa Pinto : *How I Crossed Africa*.)

River: the Mississippi

TWO OR three days and nights went by ; I reckon I might say they swum by, they slid along so quiet and smooth and lovely. Here is the way we put in the time. It was a monstrous big river down there—sometimes a mile and a half wide ; we run nights, and laid up and hid day-times ; soon as night was most gone, we stopped navigating and tied up—nearly always in the dead water under a tow-head;* and then cut young cotton-woods and willows and hid the raft with them. Then we set out the lines. Next we slid into the river and had a swim, so as to freshen up and cool off ; then we set down on the sandy bottom where the water was about knee-deep, and watched the daylight come. Not a sound anywheres—perfectly still—just like the whole world was asleep, only sometimes the bull-frogs a-clattering, maybe. The first thing to see, looking over the water, was a kind of dull line—that was the woods on t'other side—you couldn't make nothing else out ; then a pale place in the sky ; then more paleness, spreading around ; then the river softened up, away off, and warn't black

* " a sand-bar that has cotton-woods on it as thick as harrow-teeth."

any more, but grey ; you could see little dark spots drifting along, ever so far away—trading-scows, and such things ; and long black streaks—rafts ; sometimes you could hear a sweep screaking ; or jumbled-up voices, it was so still, and sounds come so far ; and by-and-by you could see a streak on the water which you know by the look of the streak that there's a snag there in a swift current which breaks on it and makes that streak look that way ; and you see the mist curl up off of the water, and the east reddens up, and the river, and you make out a log cabin in the edge of the woods, away on the bank on t'other side of the river, being a wood-yard, likely, and piled by them cheats so you can throw a dog through it anywheres ; then the nice breeze springs up, and comes fanning you from over there, so cool and fresh, and sweet to smell, on account of the woods and the flowers ; but sometimes not that way, because they've left dead fish laying around, gars, and such, and they do get pretty rank ; and next you've got the full day, and everything smiling in the sun, and the song-birds just going it !

A little smoke couldn't be noticed, now, so we would take some fish off of the lines and cook up a hot breakfast. And afterwards we would watch the lonesomeness of the river, and kind of lazy along, and by-and-by lazy off to sleep. Wake up, by-and-by, and look to see what done it, and maybe see a steamboat, coughing along up-stream, so far off towards the other side you couldn't tell nothing about her only whether she was stern-wheel or side-wheel ; then for about an hour there wouldn't be nothing to hear nor nothing to see—just solid lonesomeness. Next you'd see a raft sliding by, and maybe a galoot on it chopping, because they're most always doing it on a raft ; you'd see the axe flash, and come down—you don't hear nothing ; you see that axe go up again, and by the time it's above the man's head, then you hear the *k'chunk !*—it had took all that time to come over the water. So we would put in the day, lazying around, listening to the stillness. Once there was a thick fog, and the rafts and things that went by was beating tin pans so the steamboats wouldn't run over them. A scow or a raft went by so close we could hear them talking and cussing and laughing—heard them plain ; but we couldn't see no sign of them ; it made you feel crawly, it was like spirits carrying on that way in the air. Jim said he believed it was spirits ; but I says :

" No, spirits wouldn't say, ' dern the dern fog.' "

Soon as it was night, out we shoved ; when we got her out to about the middle, we let her alone, and let her float wherever the current wanted her to ; then we lit the pipes, and dangled our legs in the water and talked about all kinds of things—we was always naked, day and night, whenever the mosquitoes would let us—the new clothes Buck's folks made for me was too good to be comfortable, and besides, I didn't go much on clothes, nohow.

Sometimes we'd have that whole river to ourselves for the longest time. Yonder was the banks and the islands, across the water ; and maybe a spark—which was a candle in a cabin window —and sometimes on the water you could see a spark or two—on a raft or a scow, you know ; and maybe you could hear a fiddle or a song coming over from one of them crafts. It's lovely to live on a raft. We had the sky, up there, all speckled with stars, and we used to lay on our backs and look up at them, and discuss about whether they was made, or only just happened—Jim he allowed they was made, but I allowed they happened ; I judged it would have took too long to *make* so many. Jim said the moon could a *laid* them ; well, that looked kind of reasonable, so I didn't say nothing against it, because I've seen a frog lay most as many, so of course it could be done. We used to watch the stars that fell, too, and see them streak down. Jim allowed they'd got spoiled and was hove out of the nest.

Once or twice of a night we would see a steamboat slipping along in the dark, and now and then she would belch a whole world of sparks up out of her chimbleys, and they would rain down in the river and look awful pretty ; then she would turn a corner and her lights would wink out and her pow-wow shut off and leave the river still again ; and by-and-by her waves would get to us, a long time after she was gone, and joggle the raft a bit, and after that you wouldn't hear nothing for you couldn't tell how long, except maybe frogs or something.

After midnight the people on shore went to bed, and then for two or three hours the shores was black—no more sparks in the cabin windows. These sparks was our clock—the first one that showed again meant morning was coming, so we hunted a place to hide and tie up, right away.

(37°N; 89°10'W.)   (Mark Twain : *Huckleberry Finn*.)

River: the Mississippi

Entrance of the Mississippi—Balize

ON NOVEMBER 4th, 1827, I sailed from London, accompanied by my son and two daughters ; and after a favourable, though somewhat tedious voyage, arrived on Christmas-day at the mouth of the Mississippi.

The first indication of our approach to land was the appearance of this mighty river pouring forth its muddy mass of waters, and mingling with the deep blue of the Mexican Gulf. The shores of this river are so utterly flat, that no object upon them is perceptible at sea ; and we gazed with pleasure on the muddy ocean that met us, for it told us we had arrived, and seven weeks of sailing had wearied us ; yet it was not without a feeling like regret that we passed from the bright blue waves, whose varying aspect had so long furnished our chief amusement, into the murky stream which now received us.

Large flights of pelicans were seen standing upon the long masses of mud which rose above the surface of the waters, and a pilot came to guide us over the bar, long before any other indication of land was visible.

I never beheld a scene so utterly desolate as this entrance of the Mississippi. Had Dante seen it, he might have drawn images of another Bolgia from its horrors. One only object rears itself above the eddying waters : this is the mast of a vessel long since wrecked in attempting to cross the bar ; and it still stands, a dismal witness of the destruction that has been, and a boding prophet of that which is to come.

By degrees bulrushes of enormous growth become visible, and a few more miles of mud brought us within sight of a cluster of huts called the Balize, by far the most miserable station that I ever saw made the dwelling of man, but I was told that many families of pilots and fishermen lived there.

For several miles above its mouth, the Mississippi presents no objects more interesting than mud banks, monstrous bulrushes, and now and then a huge crocodile luxuriating in the slime. Another circumstance that gives to this dreary scene an aspect of desolation, is the incessant appearance of vast quantities of drift wood, which is ever finding its way to the different mouths of the Mississippi. Trees of enormous length, often bearing their

branches, and still oftener their uptorn roots entire, the victims
of the frequent hurricane, come floating down the stream. Sometimes several of these, entangled together, collect among their
boughs a quantity of floating rubbish, that gives the mass the
appearance of a moving island, bearing a forest, with its roots
mocking the heavens ; while the dishonoured branches lash the
tide in idle vengeance : this, as it approaches the vessel, and glides
swiftly past, looks like the fragment of a world in ruins.

As we advanced, however, we were cheered, notwithstanding
the season, by the bright tints of southern vegetation. The banks
continue invariably flat, but a succession of planters' villas, sometimes merely a residence, and sometimes surrounded by their sugar
grounds and negro huts, varied the scene. At no one point was there
an inch of what painters call a second distance ; and for the length
of one hundred and twenty miles, from the Balize to New Orleans,
and one hundred miles above the town, the land is defended from
the encroachments of the river by a high embankment called the
Levée ; without which the dwellings would speedily disappear, as
the river is evidently higher than the banks would be without it.
When we arrived, there had been constant rains and of long continuance, and this appearance was, therefore, unusually striking,
giving to " this great natural feature " the most unnatural appearance imaginable ; and making evident, not only that man had been
busy there, but that even the mightiest works of creation might be
made to bear his impress ; it recalled, literally, Swift's mock-
heroic :

> " Nature must give way to art " ;

yet she was looking so mighty, and so unsubdued all the time,
that I could not help fancying she would one day take the matter
into her own hands again ; and if so, farewell to New Orleans.
(*29°N; 89°10′W.*)

(Frances Trollope : *Domestic Manners of the Americans.*)

River Delta

LOUISIANA : THE MISSISSIPPI

IT IS a place that seems often unable to make up its mind
whether it will be earth or water, and so it compromises. The
result is that much of moist lower Louisiana belongs to neither
element. The line of demarcation is vague and changing. The

distinction between degrees of well-soaked ground is academic except to one who steps upon what looks like soil but finds that it is something else.

Here is a fringe of a continent, land in the slow making. While it is found in the south, much of the traditional south is not found in it. Few states have so great a volume of water in so many forms. And in all this water the predominant form is the bayou. *

Peculiar to its place, the bayou is the product of an over-supply of water pouring over a yielding soil, seeking and finding many courses toward a lower level. Several things in one, it serves as a means of drainage in an area that cannot have too much drainage ; an agency of balance, maintaining equilibrium among lakes, rivers, marshes, bays, and swamps, and between one bayou and another. The bayou is, too, a way of life, of access to the things of living for several hundred thousand men and women who live on or near its banks. Unlike streams for which it has been mistaken, it seldom dries up, because it does not depend for its flow upon such things as springs ; its waters derive from other near-by bodies, or from the rain, or from the highly impregnated ground itself. Those original Frenchmen were in error in that the bayou has its flow, but one that is governed by its own rules, and it takes its own time in its movement. It is not set in its ways. It may flow in two directions, depending on the forces that bear upon it. For most of a day it may move east into a lake ; with dusk may come a slow pull from the opposite direction, and it will turn to the west. Slow, serene, it has no rush and scouring passage ; its philosophy is in the old Gallic tradition of the agreeable life. It enjoys in leisure the scene through which it makes its quiet course. Under the circum-stances, mesdames et messieurs, can you suggest a better method ?

The bayou is not necessarily a small watercourse. Some of these waterways are deep and powerful, have been described as rivers ; others are narrow cuts, four or five feet of water or less. When two of them meet, the place may be so wide that from one bank it is hard to recognise a friend on the other ; in other instances a man can almost touch the reeds of both banks as he glides through—though in a frail bayou boat this is not a recom-mended practice.

*Pronounced bi'oo by most Louisianians who do not live near one ; bi'a by most of those who do.

The majority of the bayous are notable for things other than size. Prodigal in number and in combination, they make a kind of lacework out of land, curving, twisting, curling back on their own curves, branching to meet others, splitting and resplitting. No adequate list of them has ever been made. Some are streams of renown, celebrated in gallant song and gay anecdote. Others are familiar only to the three or four families who live upon them in their houseboats and who may have named them after Grand-père.

In the latter case it is mainly these few who know the secrets of their cobweb meshes of water lines. Only one who had spent years in tracing and retracing their patterns could be expected to find his way about them. In such terrain it is not difficult to lose one's way at a turn. Hemmed in by grass and sedge and palmetto, without a foot of wholly certain land within sight, terror may come quickly ; sometimes, death. Occasionally, even long-time residents are reported missing in the lower marsh reaches.

The bayou reaches are younger by millions of years than the rest of the South—than other parts of Louisiana. When most of the continent was dry land, the deep waters of the present Gulf of Mexico lapped over them. Land appeared only gradually, by infinitesimal stages, and largely as the gift of the waterways that moved southward. The central river—which the Indians called the Meche Sebe, and their successors the Mississippi— forced its way down through a deep, irregular valley. In its lowest reaches it shifted and wandered over many miles of yielding half-land, building up sets of side levees and thrusting forth tongues of land, then finding a new course of easier grade and beginning the same process again. Some of the present-day bayous are reduced successors to the master stream, flowing between abandoned levees ; others are carriers of Mississippi overflow. But the bayous follow their own rules, and though some are descendants, others cousins of Father Mississippi, many are unrelated. For hundreds of years before white men arrived, the central stream held its present lower course unchanged, and its civilization has been separate and highly distinct from that of the bayous.

The bayous build their own banks, push downward their own tendrils of land. Their ridges of earth are thick mounds or thin strips, depending on the age and course of the stream. For many miles these double lines of dikes are the only land to be found, dry strings above the wetness. On their borders, where they think themselves sufficiently protected, men place their cabins, as pioneers occupying outposts into a water-covered, water-threaded world.

From the hills of North Louisiana the land slips gradually downward to meet the Gulf. Soon all is flatness ; levels are only a foot or two above sealevel, and scattered over the surface is a mesh of interconnected bayous and shallow lakes, canals, inlets, cuts, and cut-offs. To those of other sections, the quality of the water is curious. The crystal-clear rivers of, say, the New England coast, are missing, as is the rock-bordered flow of the creeks. This liquid is thick, dark, stained. Earth-steeped, the color is frequently a heavy brown or purple, almost a black. Drop your hand a few inches below the surface, and it cannot be seen.

The bayous reach the sea along the 1,500 or so miles of the Louisiana Gulf coast, torn and irregular, changing from land to water to land with the years. Behind the sand of the shore line are the salt marshes of Louisiana ; no state has so wide a spread— their minimum extent ten to fifteen miles, greatly widening at a point in the center of the coast into swamps that reach nearly a hundred miles upward, and merging here and there into the fresh water. To the sides are the drier prairies of the state, wide and thickly grassed flatlands, once wet, now marked by small meandering streams.

(*30°N; 92°W.*)   (Harnett T. Kane : *The Bayous of Louisiana.*)

Waterfalls : Niagara Falls

WE CALLED at the town of Erie, at eight o'clock that night, and lay there an hour. Between five and six next morning, we arrived at Buffalo, where we breakfasted ; and being too near the Great Falls to wait patiently anywhere else, we set off by the train, the same morning at nine o'clock, to Niagara.

It was a miserable day ; chilly and raw ; a damp mist falling ; and the trees in that northern region quite bare and wintry. Whenever the train halted, I listened for the roar ; and was constantly straining my eyes in the direction where I knew the Falls must be, from seeing the river rolling on towards them ;

every moment expecting to behold the spray. Within a few moments of our stopping, not before, I saw two great clouds rising up slowly and majestically from the depths of the earth. That was all. At length we alighted : and then for the first time, I heard the mighty rush of water, and felt the ground tremble underneath my feet.

The bank is very steep, and was slippery with rain, and half-melted ice. I hardly know how I got down, but I was soon at the bottom, and climbing, with two English officers who were crossing and had joined me, over some broken rocks, deafened by the noise, half-blinded by the spray, and wet to the skin. We were at the foot of the American Fall. I could see an immense torrent of water tearing headlong down from some great height, but had no idea of shape, or situation, or anything but vague immensity.

When we were seated in the little ferry-boat, and were crossing the swollen river immediately before both cataracts, I began to feel what it was : but I was in a manner stunned, and unable to comprehend the vastness of the scene. It was not until I came on Table Rock, and looked—Great Heaven, on what a fall of bright green water !—that it came upon me in its full might and majesty.

Then, when I felt how near to my Creator I was standing, the first effect, and the enduring one—instant and lasting—of the tremendous spectacle, was Peace. Peace of Mind : Tranquillity : Calm Recollections of the Dead : Great Thoughts of Eternal Rest and Happiness : nothing of Gloom or Terror. Niagara was at once stamped upon my heart, an Image of Beauty : to remain there, changeless and indelible, until its pulses cease to beat, for ever.

Oh, how the strife and trouble of our daily life receded from my view, and lessened in the distance, during the ten memorable days we spent on that Enchanted Ground ! What voices spoke from out the thundering water ; what faces, fading from the earth, looked out upon me from its gleaming depths ; what Heavenly promise glistened in those angels' tears, the drops of many hues, that showered around, and twined themselves about the gorgeous arches which the changing rainbows made !

I never stirred in all that time from the Canadian side, whither I had gone at first. I never crossed the river again ; for I knew there were people on the other shore, and in such a place it is natural to shun strange company. To wander to and fro all day, and see the cataracts from all points of view ; to stand upon the edge of the Great Horse Shoe Fall, marking the hurried water gathering strength as it approached the verge, yet seeming, too, to pause before it shot into the gulf below ; to gaze from the river's level up at the torrent as it came streaming down ; to climb the neighbouring heights and watch it through the trees, and see the wreathing water in the rapids hurrying on to take its fearful plunge ; to linger in the shadow of the solemn rocks three miles below ; watching the river as, stirred by no visible cause, it heaved and eddied and awoke the echoes, being troubled yet, far down beneath the surface, by its giant leap ; to have Niagara before me, lighted by the sun and by the moon, red in the day's decline, and grey as evening slowly fell upon it ; to look upon it every day, and wake up in the night and hear its ceaseless voice : this was enough.

I think in every quiet season now, still do those waters roll and leap, and roar and tumble, all day long ; still are the rainbows spanning them, a hundred feet below. Still, when the sun is on them, do they shine and glow like molten gold. Still, when the day is gloomy, do they fall like snow, or seem to crumble away like the front of a great chalk cliff, or roll down the rock like dense white smoke. But always does the mighty stream appear to die as it comes down, and always from its unfathomable grave arises that tremendous ghost of spray and mist which is never laid : which has haunted this place with the same dread solemnity since Darkness brooded on the deep, and that first flood before the Deluge—Light —came rushing on Creation at the word of God.

(*43°N; 79°W.*) (Charles Dickens : *American Notes*.)

Waterfalls: Niagara Falls

BELOW THE Falls, the river runs between lofty rocks, crowned with unbroken forests ; this scene forms a striking contrast to the level shores above the cataract. The Niagara flows out of Lake Erie, a broad, deep river ; but for several miles its course is tranquil, and its shores perfectly level. By degrees its bed begins to sink, and the glassy smoothness is disturbed by a slight ripple. The inverted trees, that before lay so softly still upon its bosom, become twisted and tortured till they lose their form, and seem madly to mix in the tumult that destroys them.

The current becomes more rapid at every step, till rock after rock has chafed the stream to fury, making the green one white. This lasts for a mile, and then down sink the rocks at once, one hundred and fifty feet, and the enormous flood falls after them. God said, Let there be a cataract, and it was so. When the river has reached its new level, the precipice on either side shows a terrific chasm of solid rock ; some beautiful plants are clinging to its sides, and oaks, ash, and cedar, in many places, clothe their terrors with rich foliage.

* * * * *

The noise is greatly less than I expected ; one can hear with perfect distinctness everything said in an ordinary tone, when quite close to the cataract. The cause of this I imagine to be, that it does not fall immediately upon rocks, like the far noisier Potomac, but direct and unbroken, save by its own rebound. The colour of the water, before this rebound hides it in foam and mist, is of the brightest and most delicate green ; the violence of the impulse sends it far over the precipice before it falls, and the effect of the ever varying light through its transparency is, I think, the loveliest thing I ever looked upon.
(*43°N; 79°W.*)

(Frances Trollope : *Domestic Manners of the Americans.*)

Waterfalls: Niagara Falls

LET ME note, in passing, one of those things—they abound on the American Continent—which ought not to be beautiful but indubitably are. This is the illumination of the Falls of Niagara, which now takes place for two hours every evening, from the Canadian shore. It is a joint Canadian and United States effort and is described as the " greatest experiment in large-scale electric lighting in the world." Unlimited water-power makes it possible, and the guide-book explains that " the plant emits an illuminating force of 1,300 million power." It sounds like an atrocity, and if Niagara had been here, and English enterprise had suggested such a thing, the vindicators of unspoiled nature would have risen in arms and prepared petitions which I should have signed. As it is I can only attest that the result is one of amazing and dazzling beauty. The lights play on both the American and Canadian Falls, and run through a vividly changing scheme of colour : white, blue, orange, red, mauve, green. The white turns the rushing waters into a glistening marble veined with its own green ; the other colours produce shimmering rainbow effects of amazing intricacy and beauty. The whole scene is simultaneously illuminated from end to end, but with a glowing light which never fatigues the eye. I watched it for an hour or more from the Canadian shore and came away very reluctantly. (*43°N; 79°W*.)   (J. A. Spender : *The America of To-day*.)

Canyon: Grand Canyon of the Colorado

(As seen for the first time by Europeans, end of August, 1540.)

AFTER THEY had gone twenty days, they came to the banks of the river, which seemed to be more than three or four leagues across by airline. This country was elevated and full of low twisted pines, very cold, and lying open toward the north, so that, although this was the warm season, no one could live there on account of the cold. They passed three days along this canyon looking for a passage down to the river, which looked from above as if the water was a fathom's width across, although the Indians said it was half a league wide. To descend was impossible, for after these three days Captain Melgosa and one Juan Galeras and another companion, who were the most agile men, made an attempt to go down at the least difficult place, and descended until those who were above were unable to keep sight of them because of the rock overhang. They returned about four o'clock in the afternoon, not having succeeded in reaching the bottom on account of the great difficulties which they found, because what seemed to be so easy from above was not so, but instead very rough and steep. They said that they had been down about a third of the way and that the river seemed very large from the place which they reached, and that from what they saw they thought the Indians had given the width correctly. From the rim, some small pinnacles on the sides of the cliffs seemed to be about as tall as a man, but those who went down swore that when they reached these rocks they were bigger than the great tower of Seville.

(*36°N; 113°W*.)

(Translation of Castañeda's account, 1544: given by Winship, "The Coronado Expedition ", *14th Annual Report, Bureau of American Ethnology*, 1892-1893, Part I, pp. 329-613 : Washington, 1896.)

Canyon: Grand Canyon of the Colorado

I WAS told when I started on this journey that the hours spent
in traversing deserts must be submitted to for the felicities on
the far side, and on the morrow we were promised the high
privilege of seeing the Grand Canyon, which lies across the border
in New Mexico*. The Grand Canyon is indeed an extraordinary
thing, of which I wish to speak with all respect. It is undoubtedly
the greatest thing of its kind in the world. There can in all the
world be no other chasm thirteen miles broad and a mile deep
descending sheer to a river bottom from a flat plateau seven
thousand feet above the sea. This statistical aspect of it is justly
emphasised, and the English visitor who intends to visit it will do
well to bear it carefully in mind. But beautiful and impressive as it
is when the sun plays on it or the clouds roll about it, it has still the
air of a natural freak which somehow quenches a complete satisfaction. It would have done equally well for heaven or hell in one of
those old Bible pictures which fascinated and frightened the children of sixty years ago ; it would have served Gustave Doré as a
background for almost any scene in Paradiso or Inferno. It is,
in fact, like an enormous gravel pit quarried by defunct giants,
who departed in a hurry, leaving their colossal unfinished work-
ings behind them.

*Arizona.

(36°N; 113°W.)   (J. A. Spender : *The America of To-day*.)

Canyon: Grand Canyon of the Colorado

THE BERKSHIRES are homely scenery. Gigantic scenery is
more difficult to describe, but I will make an attempt. Suppose
yourself walking on a Surrey common—near Bagshot, let us say.
There are a good many pine trees about, the soil is sandy, and the
prospect rather dull. Suddenly the common stops, and you are
standing without any warning on the brink of a precipice which
is one mile deep. One mile into the tortured earth it goes, the
other side of the chasm is miles away, and the chasm is filled with
unbelievable deposits of rock which resemble sphinxes draped in
crimson shawls. That, as far as I can get it into a single sentence,
gives you my first impression of the Grand Canyon of the Colorado
River, but the Grand Canyon would need many sentences to
describe and many books. It is the most astounding natural

object I have ever seen. It frightens. There are many colours in it besides crimson—strata of black and of white, and rocks of ochre and pale lilac. And the Colorado River itself is, when one gets down to it, still more sinister, for it is muddy white and very swift, and it rages like an infuriated maggot between precipices of granite, gnawing at them and cutting the Canyon deeper. It was strange after two days amongst these marvels—I might say terror—to return to the surface of the earth, and go bowling away in a bus between little fir trees. (*36°N; 113°W.*)

(E. M. Forster : Impressions of the United States.)

Canyon: Grand Canyon of the Colorado

Grand Canyon
(*I attempt no description of this combat, knowing the unintelligibility and the repulsiveness of all attempts to communicate the Incommunicable.—CONFESSIONS OF AN ENGLISH OPIUM-EATER.*)

THE FORMULA is simple. Take the step-pyramid of Saqqara ; stain it a dozen shades of red, from brick-dust to a dingy crimson ; lay on the colour in great sweeping stripes, five hundred feet from edge to edge and a half-mile across, until it looks like a mountain that has struggled into a giant's football jersey ; summon twenty of its fellows in similar attire ; set them to watch a river racing angrily a mile below their summits ; enclose the watching hills in a gorge a dozen miles across ; and you have, if words can render it, the Grand Canyon of the Colorado River. A wise *Opium-Eater* once refrained from a description of the indescribable ; and he alone, perhaps, could render (as only opium could conceive) the ranged insanity of that demented landscape. Seen from the sheer edge of a cliff, where the hills of Arizona look nearly into Utah, it began and ended nowhere. That tormented pattern could surely not be final ; and one had a sudden uneasy feeling that earthquake had paused for an instant, that the writhing valley might resume its slow convulsions at any moment. It was a crowded valley ; for its floor rose up into odd, decapitated summits, where mad mountains groped for one another with discoloured buttresses. The eye was frankly scared—even the

modern eye, which can look steadily at mountains ; and that
disordered scene would have sent the Eighteenth Century, which
shrank from their horrid grandeur, sobbing in panic to its bedroom. It had, as one looked down at it again, a queer, unfinished
air, as of a Miltonic Chaos waiting for Creation. There was a total
lack of meaning in its distorted features ; heaped tablelands looked
down on nothing ; incredible *arêtes* led nowhere. Perhaps it was a
store-house of forgotten mountains, somehow mislaid among the
hills. Yet one had a sense that something no less Miltonic had
been at work there, carving the hollows, smoothing the steep
escarpments, and squaring the mountain-sides. Something,
perhaps, had built it in an evil mood to be a parody of Creation.
Even where the blind cliffs offered their red, striated sides with
fantastic hints of architecture, the resemblances were all pagan—
Egyptian pylons riding on Hindu temples, the towers of Babylon
crowned with pyramids, and *ziggurats* that ended in unlikely
minarets. Somewhere below the rioting red hills an unseen river
poured its rapids through a deep grey cleft ; and once its thin
and angry whisper drifted up from where the Colorado River,
sunk out of sight a mile below, raced roaring through the Canyon.
There was no other sound ; cascades of silent stone lay in the
sunlight, watching a slow dance of shadows across the red hillsides ; and thirteen miles away the forests of the farther rim
ruled on the sky a line of level green.

(*36°N; 113°W.*)　　(Philip Guedalla : *Conquistador: American
Fantasia.*)

River Terraces
BRITISH COLUMBIA : FRASER RIVER

WE NOW followed the valley of the Bonaparte until it joins
that of the Thompson, viewing with wonder the curious terraces
which strike the eye of a stranger so oddly, and give such a peculiar
character to the scenery of the Thompson and the Fraser. We
first observed them on the North Thompson, some thirty or forty
miles above Kamloops, and they are invariably present all along
the main river until its junction with the Fraser at Lytton. On
the Fraser they stretch from a little north of Alexandria to the
Cañons above Yale, a distance of above 300 miles. These terraces
—or benches, as they are called in this district—are perfectly
level, and of exactly the same height on each side of the river.

They differ from the so-called " parallel roads " of Glenroy in their enormous extent, being vast plains as compared with the mere ledges of the Scottish terraces, and are also free from the erratic boulders which mark the latter. In most places there are three tiers, each tier corresponding with a similar one on the opposite side of the valley. The lowest of the three, where the valley expands, presents a perfectly flat surface of often many miles in extent, raised some forty or fifty feet above the level of the river bank, with a sloping front, resembling the face of a railway embankment. Higher still, the second tier is generally cut out of the mountain side, seldom more than a few acres in extent, and raised sixty or seventy feet above the lower one; while, marked at an inaccessible height along the face of the bluffs which run down to the river, and probably 400 or 500 feet above it, is the third tier. These " benches " are quite uniform, and of even surface, entirely free from the great boulders so numerous in the present bed of the river, being composed of shale, sand, and gravel, the detritus of the neighbouring mountains. They are clothed with bunch-grass and wild sage, while here and there a few scattered pines relieve the yellow bareness so characteristic of the district. Similar terraces were noticed by Dr. Hector on the Athabasca, Kootanie, and Columbia Rivers, and they have been also observed on some rivers in California and Mexico ; but in none of these instances do they appear comparable in extent and regularity with those of the Thompson and Fraser. (*50°50'N; 121°W.*)

(Viscount Milton and W. B. Cheadle : *The North-West Passage by Land.*)

Rivers

VENEZUELA AND GUIANA

BLUE WATER ends at Trinidad ; there and from there onwards the sea is murky ; opaque, dingy stuff the colour of shabby stucco, thick with mud sweeping down from the great continental rivers—the Orinoco, the Essequibo, the Demerara, the Berbice, the Courantyne ; all along the coast their huge mouths gape amidst dune and mangrove, pouring out into the blue Caribbean the waters of the remote highlands. Later I was to tramp across part of the great continental divide, where the tributaries of the

Amazon and Essequibo dovetail into one another, tiny cascading brooks, confusing in an unmapped country because they always seemed to be flowing in the direction one did not expect ; I was to wade through them or scramble over them on slippery tree-trunks in the forest where they were ruby-clear, wine-coloured from the crimson timber ; I was to paddle tedious days down them when they had become deep and black ; leaving them months later, as I saw the water become blue and clear again I was to feel touched with regret, for they had become for a time part of my life. But now as we approached the mainland I only felt mildly depressed that bathing had ceased to be attractive. (*Approx. 7°N; 58°W.*)   (Evelyn Waugh : *Ninety-two Days.*)

River: the Amazon

BRAZIL

I HAD a picture of the Amazon, which I had long cherished. I was leaning today over the bulwarks of the *Capella*, watching the jungle pass. The Doctor was with me. I thought we were still on the Para River, and was waiting for our vessel to emerge from that stream, as through a narrow gate, dramatically, into the broad sunshine of the greatest river in the world, the king of rivers, the Amazon of my picture. We idly scanned the forest with binoculars, and saw some herons, and the ciganas, and once a sloth which was hanging to a tree. Para, I felt, was as distant as London. The silence, the immobility of it all, and the pour of the tropic sun, were beginning to be just a little subduing. We had come already to the wilderness. There was, I thought, a very great deal of this forest, and it never varied.

" We shall be on the Amazon soon," I said hopefully, to the Doctor.

" We have been on it for hours," he replied. And that is how I got there.

But the Amazon is not seen, any more than is the sea, at the first glance. What first the eye gathers is, naturally (for it is but an eye), nothing like commensurate with your own image of the river. The mind, by suggestive symbols, builds something portentous, a vague and tremendous idea. What I saw was only a swift and opaque yellow flood, not much broader, it seemed to me, than the Thames at Gravesend, and the monotonous green of the forest. It was all I saw for a considerable time.

I see something different now. It is not easily explained merely as a yellow river, with a verdant elevation on either hand, and over it a blue sky. It would be difficult to find, except by luck, a word which would convey the immensity of the land of the Amazons, something of the aloofness and separation of the points of its extremes, with months and months of adventure between them. What a journey it would be from Ino in Bolivia, on the Rio Madre de Dios, to Conception in Colombia, on the Rio Putumayo ! There is another *Odyssey* in a voyage like that. And think of the names of those places and rivers ! When I take a map of South America now, and hold it with the estuary of the Amazon as its base, my thoughts are like those might be of a lost ant, crawling in and over the furrows and ridges of an exposed root as he regards all he may of the trunk rising into the whole upper cosmos of a spreading oak. The Amazon then looks to me, properly symbolical, as a monstrous tree, and its tributaries, paranas, furos, and igarapes, as the great boughs, little boughs, and twigs of its ascending and spreading ramifications, so minutely permeating the continent with its numberless watercourses that the mind sees that dark region as an impenetrable density of green and secret leaves ; which, literally, when you go there, is what you will find. You enter the leaves, and vanish. You creep about the region of but one of its branches, under a roof of foliage which stays the midday shine and lets it through to you in the dusk of the interior but as points of distant starlight. Occasionally, as we did upon a day, you see something like Santarem. There is a break and a change in the journey. Moving blindly through the haze of green, there, hanging in the clear day at the end of a bough, you see a golden fruit.

(*Approx. 1°S; 51°W.*)

(H. M. Tomlinson : The Sea and the Jungle.)

Rivers: the Junction of Amazon and Rio Negro
BRAZIL

A BRISK wind from the east sprang up early in the morning of the 22nd, we then hoisted all sail, and made for the mouth of the Rio Negro. This noble stream at its junction with the Amazons seems, from its position, to be a direct continuation of the main river, whilst the Solimoens which joins at an angle and is somewhat narrower than its tributary, appears to be a branch instead of the main trunk of the vast water-system. One sees therefore at once how the early explorers came to give a separate name to this upper part of the Amazons. The Brazilians have lately taken to applying the convenient term Alto Amazonas (High or Upper Amazons) to the Solimoens, and it is probable that this will gradually prevail over the old name. The Rio Negro broadens considerably from its mouth upwards, and presents the appearance of a great lake ; its black-dyed waters having no current, and seeming to be dammed up by the impetuous flow of the yellow, turbid Solimoens, which here belches forth a continuous line of uprooted trees and patches of grass, and forms a striking contrast with its tributary. In crossing we passed the line, a little more than half-way over, where the waters of the two rivers meet and are sharply demarcated from each other. On reaching the opposite shore we found a remarkable change. All our insect pests had disappeared, as if by magic, even from the hold of the canoe : the turmoil of an agitated, swiftly flowing river, and its torn, perpendicular, earthy banks, had given place to tranquil water and a coast indented with snug little bays, fringed with sloping sandy beaches. The low shore and vivid light green endlessly-varied foliage, which prevailed on the south side of the Amazons, were exchanged for a hilly country, clothed with a sombre, rounded, and monotonous forest. Our tedious voyage now approached its termination ; a light wind carried us gently along the coast to the city of Barra, which lies about seven or eight miles within the mouth of the river. We stopped for an hour in a clean little bay, to bathe and dress, before showing ourselves again among civilised people. The bottom was visible at a depth of six feet, the white sand taking a brownish tinge from the stained but clear water. (*3°S; 60°W.*)
(Henry Walter Bates : *The Naturalist on the River Amazons.*)

Rivers: the Amazon and Rio Negro

BRAZIL

WITH A sigh of relief, Pater Anselmus looked out across the river. There were the familiar, low-hanging clouds, streaked and pearly, as if the river were reflecting itself in the sky. The other shore was so far away that it seemed only a blue-green line, parting the sunset colours of the water from the same colours above. A white flight of egrets rose from the little island midstream, a shrill family of parrots winged past in a green streak and was gone. Then, as the sun came out from behind a cloud, turning its seams a radiant silver, Pater Anselmus could hear the hissing of the mosquitoes, steady and familiar like a distant waterfall. The sun flattened out and went down ; it got dark very quickly, and there was lightning in three different places : this, too, deeply familiar and part of the sinking evening.

On the shores of those rivers which are called white ones in the Amazonas region, but which are really a muddy grey and yellow, the waters are filled with fish and the jungles with abundant animal life and the air with birds and butterflies and insects, and the nights are as insanely loud as if all the madmen of the American continent had been assembled there and set free to shrill and shriek and laugh and drum and blow whistles and moan and scream. But the Rio Negro belonged to the black waters, the clear, hungry waters through which one could see every rock on the bottom and every glittering grain of sand, but rarely a shoal of fish. Pater Anselmus thought of the old saying that on the Orinoco one talks of the insect plague, but on the Rio Negro one talks of hunger. He watched sadly how his four men pulled their bejuca ropes tighter round their hunger-bloated stomachs and strung their hammocks to the trees as though they had resigned themselves to going without food for another night and maybe another day. I'm a bad shepherd, he thought in bitter self-reproach, as he had thought a hundred times during their luckless expedition.

(*2°S; 61°W.*)   (Vicki Baum : *The Weeping Wood.*)

Rivers: the Junction of Amazon and Madeira
BRAZIL

THERE, AHEAD, was the Madeira now for us. We were then nearly a thousand miles from the sea, well within South America. But that meeting-place of the Amazon and its chief tributary was an expanse of water surprising in its immensity. As much light was reflected from the floor as at sea. The water was oceanic in amplitude. The forest boundaries were so far away that one could not realise, even when the time we had been on the river was remembered as a prolonged monotony, that this was the centre of a continent. The forest on our port side was near enough for us to see its limbs and its vines ; but to the south-west, where we were heading for Bolivia, and to the north, the way to the Guianas, and to the east, out of which we had come, and to the west, where was Peru, the land was but a low violet barrier, varying in altitude with distance, and with silver sections in it, marking the river roads. In the north-west there was a broad silver path through the wall, the way to the Rio Negro, Manaos, and the Orinoco. In the south, the near forest, being flooded, was a puzzle of islands. As we progressed they opened out as a line of green headlands. The Madeira appeared to have three widely separated mouths, with a complexity of intermediate and connective minor ditches. Indeed, the gate of the river was a region of inundated jungle. One began to understand why travellers here sometimes find themselves on the wrong river.
(*3°30'S; 58°30'W*.)

(H. M. Tomlinson : *The Sea and the Jungle*.)

River: the Upper Amazon or Solimões
BRAZIL

WHEN I awoke the next morning, we were progressing by espia along the left bank of the Solimoens. The rainy season had now set in over the region through which the great river flows ; the sand-banks and all the lower lands were already under water, and the tearing current, two or three miles in breadth, bore along a continuous line of uprooted trees and islets of floating plants. The prospect was most melancholy ; no sound was heard but the dull murmur of the waters ; the coast along which we travelled all day was encumbered every step of the way with fallen trees, some of which quivered in the currents which set around projecting points of land. Our old pest, the Motúca, began to torment us as soon as the sun gained power in the morning. White egrets were plentiful at the edge of the water, and humming-birds, in some places, were whirring about the flowers overhead. The desolate appearance of the landscape increased after sunset, when the moon rose in mist.

This upper river, the Alto-Amazonas, or Solimoens, is always spoken of by the Brazilians as a distinct stream. This is partly owing, as before remarked, to the direction it seems to take at the fork of the Rio Negro ; the inhabitants of the country, from their partial knowledge, not being able to comprehend the whole river system in one view. It has, however, many peculiarities to distinguish it from the lower course of the river. The trade-wind, or sea-breeze, which reaches, in the height of the dry season, as far as the mouth of the Rio Negro, 900 or 1,000 miles from the Atlantic, never blows on the upper river. The atmosphere is therefore more stagnant and sultry, and the winds that do prevail are of irregular direction and short duration. A great part of the land on the borders of the Lower Amazons is hilly ; there are extensive campos, or open plains, and long stretches of sandy soil clothed with thinner forests. The climate, in consequence, is comparatively dry, many months in succession during the fine season passing without rain. All this is changed on the Solimoens. A fortnight of clear sunny weather is a rarity ; the whole region through which the river and its affluents flow, after leaving the easternmost ridges of the Andes which Pöppig describes as rising like a wall from the level country, 240 miles from the Pacific, is a vast plain, about 1,000 miles in length, and 500 or 600 in breadth, covered with one uniform, lofty, impervious and humid forest. The soil is nowhere sandy, but always either a stiff clay, alluvium, or vegetable mould, which latter, in many places, is seen in water-worn sections of the river banks to be twenty or thirty feet in depth. With such a soil and climate, the luxuriance of vegetation, and the abundance and beauty of animal forms which are already so great in the region nearer the Atlantic, increase on the upper river. The fruits, both wild and cultivated, common to the two sections of the country, reach a progressively larger size in advancing westward, and some trees which blossom only once

a year at Pará and Santarem, yield flower and fruit all the year
round at Ega. The climate is healthy, although one lives here as
in a permanent vapour bath. I must not, however, give here a
lengthy description of the region, whilst we are yet on its threshold.
I resided and travelled on the Solimoens altogether for four years
and a half. The country on its borders is a magnificent wilderness
where civilized man, as yet, has scarcely obtained a footing ; the
cultivated ground from the Rio Negro to the Andes amounting to
only a few score acres. Man, indeed, in any condition, from his
small numbers, makes but an insignificant figure in these vast
solitudes. It may be mentioned that the Solimoens is 2,130 miles
in length, if we reckon from the source of what is usually considered the main stream (Lake Lauricocha, near Lima) ; but
2,500 miles by the route of the Ucayali, the most considerable
and practicable fork of the upper part of the river. It is navigable
at all seasons by large steamers, for upwards of 1,400 miles from
the mouth of the Rio Negro.
(4°S; 63°W.)
(Henry Walter Bates : *The Naturalist on the River Amazons.*)

River: the Paraguay

SOUTH AMERICA

FROM THE point where its headwaters unite until it is
merged in the Paraná, the Paraguay river runs in an alluvial
bottom as wide as the English Channel, in which its main channel
cuts a winding and capricious course. Long backwaters sweep
round islands and sandbanks, recoiling upon the main stream in
close horseshoe bends. Then comes a season of flood, when the
whole basin is submerged, and as the waters subside it is found
that unexpected cut-offs have formed new islands, while landmarks established elsewhere crumble away like a child's sand-
castle before the incoming tide. When the Paraguay goes down
in flood to the Plate, running 3 knots an hour, 20 feet deep
and 20 miles wide, man can but adapt himself to its caprices and
endeavour, as far as possible, to foresee them.

The banks of the Paraguay and lower Paraná are flooded for
about three months out of the year. The flood-method of the
river on either bank is distinct, though the net result is the same.
On the lowlying western shore the quebracho forests of the

Paraguayan and Bolivian Chaco close down to the river's brink, intersected only by grassy glades which mark overflow water-channels. Here in flood-time the river quietly spreads itself over thousands of square leagues of "llanos," in which the forest belts stand like islands ; indeed, a quebracho grove in the Chaco is always called an "isla" by the natives. The barrancas which bound the eastern banks of the river are higher, and are not in normal times subject to overflow ; but streams descending from the central water-parting of Paraguay and Matto Grosso, when impeded in their outlet by floods on the main stream, back up against the inland hill spurs in extensive lakes and swampy lagoons which cannot drain away till the Paraguay falls. Thus on either hand, in a succession of forest and pampa, morass and lake, we follow the banks of the river to its navigable limit at Corumbá, and, if seasons favour, to Cuyabá also. Such is the Paraguay :

> "Shallow, disreputable, vast,
> It sprawls across the western plains,"

to paraphrase Kipling ; an open door leading to fertile solitudes ; one of the fairest-seeming and most disappointing waterways that ever tempted man to trade on its goodwill.

(15°S; 57°W to 34°S; 59°W.)

(W. S. Barclay : "The River Paraná : an Economic Survey ",
Geographical Journal, January, 1909.)

Waterfalls : the Kaieteur Falls

BRITISH GUIANA

IT WAS after five when we reached Kaieteur. The landing was, of course, some way above the falls and leaving the boys to secure the boat and bring up the luggage, I hurried forward on foot to see them before it was dark. I had expected to be led there by the sound, but it was scarcely perceptible until one reached the brink and even there, so great was the depth, that only a low monotone rose to greet one.

The path led across a rock plateau totally unlike the surrounding country, bare except for cactuses and a few flowers, scattered with quartz, pebbles and sponge-like growths of crystal. A faint path led to the edge of the precipice and there a natural platform of rock allowed me to lie and study the extraordinary scene.

It has been described in detail by several travellers. I had arrived at the best time of day, for then, in late afternoon, the whole basin and gorge were clear of mist. The river was half full. Some visitors have toiled up to find only a single spout of water over which they were able to stand astride. A Russian artist went there to paint it and was obliged to fill in the river from photographs and his imagination. That evening the whole centre of the lip was covered, and the water gently spilled over it as though from a tilted dish. At the edge it was brown as the river behind it, rapidly turning to white and half-way down dissolving in spray so that it hung like a curtain of white drapery. It fell sheer from its seven hundred odd feet, for the cliff had been hollowed back in the centuries and the edge jutted over an immense black cavern. At the foot dense columns of spray rose to meet it so that the impression one received was that the water slowed down, hesitated, and then began to reascend, as though a cinema film had been reversed. And not only reversed, but taken in slow motion, for just as aeroplanes hurtling like bullets through the air seem from the ground to be gently floating across the sky, so the height here delayed and softened the vast fall, like the mason's at Buckfast, who, tumbling off the triforium, is said to have been caught half-way down by angels, lowered gently and set on his feet in the nave, breathless, bewildered but unhurt.

The basin below was heaped with rocks, reduced by distance to little boulders, among which the water was breaking in a high sea, wave after wave set in being by the fall, emanating outwards and smashing into spray against the banks like an incoming tide ; half a dozen or so minor cataracts were visible down the gorge before the river regained its tranquillity.

But more remarkable, perhaps, than the fall itself was the scene in which it stood. The scale was immense, so that the margin of forest shrank to a line of shrub and it was only by an effort that one could remind oneself that these were the great ramparts that had towered over us all day. The cleavage, too, was so abrupt that it appeared unnatural ; as though two sections in a composite panorama had been wrongly fitted ; above was the placid level on which we had travelled, below for miles ahead the river could be followed, shot black and silver ribbon, gently winding between bush-clad hills, and here, in the middle a sharp break where the edges, instead of coming together, lay apart, clumsily disjointed.

I lay on the overhanging ledge watching the light slowly fail, the colour deepen and disappear. The surrounding green was of density and intenseness that can neither be described nor reproduced ; a quicksand of colour, of shivering surface and unplumbed depth, which absorbed the vision, sucking it down and submerging it. When it was quite dark I found my way back to the others.

(5°N; 59°30'W.) (Evelyn Waugh : *Ninety-two Days*.)

Waterfalls: Falls of Guayrá and Iguazu

BRAZIL

SOME ACQUAINTANCE with the working plan of the Guayrá cataracts is necessary, since their area is too extended to be viewed from any single point upon the shore. The head fall has already eaten its way back 400 yards into the lake from the narrowest point of the outlet gorge. A secondary development is fast heading back along the eastern shore of the lake, where the swirl of water round the tail of Guayrá island, reinforced by the current of the Piquiry River, is responsible for the formation of the " Sete Quedas," or Seven falls, extending along this side, from the head of the main gorge to its base. The height of these secondary cascades varies from 50 feet at the upper end to 90 feet at the southern extremity of the funnel ; but in high flood these heights are reduced by fully two-thirds, since a few inches more water on the wide surface of Guayrá lake make a difference of many yards in the narrowest part of the outlet gorge. It is this portion, and not the actual falls, which affords the real spectacle. Including the upper cascades, the total fall from upper to lower river at Guayrá is 310 feet. At one point the cliffs are only 200 feet apart, the distance that a practised hand may throw a stone with ease. The whole impact of the Alto Paraná, backed by the reserve power of the great tributaries which have joined it from the Brazilian uplands, chafes and roars through this strait gateway. The volume of water in normal river is reckoned at 13,000,000 cubic feet* per minute, an estimate which may be doubled and even trebled in time of flood. The Guayrá cataract

* Niagara is reckoned at 18,000,000 cubic feet per minute.

is the mightiest, because it is the most compactly frantic water-power awaiting man's harness on earth. The current piles up in the centre with a corkscrew action, ever shifting to the side, and diving down again into mid-stream, where, momentarily imprisoned in caverns and pot-holes worn by long-vanished side falls, it returns to the surface in spuming eddies which leap 12 to 15 feet high, bursting with the noise of dull cannon to spread their outer circles to the shore, and so repeat. The whirlpool rapids of Niagara, where Captain Webb lost his life, are a quiet duck-pond by comparison.

From the smoking cataracts of Guayrá to the lone loveliness of the Iguazú falls, half concealed by the crowding forest, there lie but 125 miles ; yet so scored are the river's banks on either hand by cascade and torrent, that this stretch might well be called Waterfall-land. The Iguazú falls cover a large area, being approximately 3,300 yards in length. They may be divided into two sections, the Argentine side falls, and the upper or Brazilian head fall ; for at this point the river forms part of the northern boundary of the two republics. The head fall, whose cascades have originally emerged from a gorge 200 feet deep and only 300 feet wide, occurs on a very acute horseshoe bend. The side falls are working more slowly, their present action being chiefly confined to times of flood, and a long chain of islands overlooking the main channel shows how they are being gradually starved out of existence by the rapid advance of the head.

Nothing brings out more clearly the essential difference in character between the Paraguay and Alto Paraná rivers than their action in time of great floods. Taking a section along the 24th parallel of south latitude, we find that on May 25, 1905, the Paraguay river in front of Asuncion rose 12 feet, inundating the Chaco through its Pilcomayo tributary nearly to the base of the Andes. Following the same parallel of latitude, we find that the Alto Paraná, at a point between the Iguazú river and Guayrá, rose 157 feet in its steeply confining banks. At the mouth of the Iguazú the Paraná rose 146 feet, damming back the water pouring through the narrow outlet gorge of the falls, which accumulated behind. In consequence, during five days the wide bay eroded by the Iguazú falls filled up to its total height of 210 feet, the cascades became flush and disappeared, while the river overflowed in all directions to the Paraná through the surrounding forest, a distance of 7½ miles.

(Guayrá: 24°10'S; 54°40'W. Iguazú: 25°40'S; 54°40'W.)

(W. S. Barclay : " The River Paraná : an Economic Survey ", *Geographical Journal*, January, 1909.)

Break-up of Ice in Spring
SIBERIA : LENA

IN MARCH and April terrible storms prevail. The transition between winter and summer is so sudden that one can hardly speak of spring and autumn. In a couple of weeks the winter is transformed into summer. The snow melts with incredible rapidity, and the water, flowing into valleys, lakes and rivers, lifts the thick ice, which has been riven into small fragments by the winter cold. In the lakes the ice melts slowly, and the storms which drive it against the shore only crush it little by little. In the rivers, on the other hand, the ice is violently broken up and carried towards the sea by the powerful spring floods. At first the water is unable to carry with it the huge ice-floes, which in narrow places are heaped up in colossal masses, damming up the river until the barrier is broken, when, carried along with resistless force, it destroys everything in its way, sweeping away earth, rocks and entire groves of trees, which are mown down like grass. As we descended the Lena in the middle of June gigantic blocks of ice were still lying on the shores of the river, some twenty feet or more above its water-line.

(Approx. 65°N; 125°E.)   (J. Stadling : *Through Siberia*.)

Break-up of Ice in Spring
SIBERIA : YENISEI

THE YENESEI is said to be the third largest river in the world. In Yeneseisk the inhabitants claim that the waters of their river have flowed at least two thousand miles (through Lake Baikal) to their town. Here the river must be more than a mile wide, but at the Kureika, which is about eight hundred miles distant, it is a little more than three miles wide. From the Kureika to the limit of forest growth, where the delta may be said to begin, is generally reckoned another eight hundred miles, for which distance the river will average at least four miles in width. To this we must add a couple of hundred miles of delta and another couple of hundred miles of lagoon, each of which will average twenty miles in width, if not more.

Our winter quarters were very picturesque. The *Thames* was moored close to the north shore of the Kureika, at the entrance of a small gully, into which it was the captain's intention to take his ship as soon as the water rose high enough to admit of his doing so, and where he hoped to wait in safety the passing away of the ice. On one side of the ship was the steep bank of the river, about a hundred feet in height, covered with snow, except here and there, where it was too perpendicular for the snow to lie. . . To the left the Kureika, a mile wide, stretched away some four or five miles, until a sudden bend concealed it from view, whilst to the right the eye wandered across the snow-fields of the Yenesei, and by the help of a binocular the little village of Kureika might be discerned about four miles off on the opposite bank of the great river. The land was undulating rather than hilly, and everywhere covered with forests, the trees reaching frequently two and in some rare instances three feet in diameter.

On Tuesday, the 29th of May, we commenced our sixth week in the Arctic Circle, and a very eventful one it proved. The little wind there was was southerly, and the sun was hot, but still there was scarcely any perceptible thaw, and the river rose but very slowly.

On the following day it was the old story again—a clear sky and thaw in the sunshine, with a cold north wind and hard frost in the shade. The river rose three or four inches during the day, but it froze as fast as it rose.

On the 1st of June, a revolution took place in the ice. There had been scarcely any frost during the night. The wind was south, not very warm, but the sun was unusually hot. As we turned out of the cabin after breakfast we were just in time to see a small range of mountains suddenly form at the lower angle of juncture between the Kureika and the Yenisei. The river had risen considerably during the night, and the newly-formed strip of thin ice on each side of the centre ice was broader than it had ever been. The pressure of the current underneath caused a large field of ice, about a mile long, and a third of a mile wide, to break away. About half the mass found a passage down the strip of newly-formed thin ice, leaving open water behind it ; the other half rushed headlong on to the steep banks of the river, and, driven on irresistibly by the enormous pressure from behind, it piled itself up into a little range of mountains, fifty or sixty feet high, and picturesque in the extreme. Huge blocks of ice, six feet thick and twenty feet long, in many places stood up perpendicularly. Others were crushed up into fragments like broken glass. The real ice on the river did not appear to have been more than three feet thick, clear as glass and blue as an Italian sky. Upon the top of this was about four feet of white ice. This was as hard as a rock, and had no doubt been caused by the flooding of the snow when the water rose, and its subsequent freezing. On the top of the white ice was about eighteen inches of clear snow, which had evidently never been flooded. Everything remained *in statu quo* during the rest of the day. The river was certainly rising, but slowly.

We turned into our berths at half-past nine, having first instituted an anchor watch, in case any further movement of the ice should take place. We had but just fallen asleep when we were suddenly roused by the report that the river was rising rapidly and the ice beginning to break up. We immediately dressed and went on deck. The position of affairs was at once obvious. The melting of the snow down south was evidently going on rapidly, and the river was rising at such speed that it was beginning to flow up all its northern tributaries. A strong current was setting up the Kureika. Small floes were detaching themselves from the main mass and were running up the open water. In a short time the whole body of the Kureika ice broke up and began to move up-stream. As far as the Yenisei the tributary stream was soon a mass of pack-ice and floes marching up the river at a rate of three miles an hour. Some of these struck the ship some very ugly blows on the stern, doing considerable damage to the rudder, but open water was beyond, and we were soon out of the press of ice with, we hoped, no irretrievable damage. . . .

In a short time the river began to rise again rapidly, and with it our hopes that we might float and steam into safety, when suddenly we discovered, to our terror, that the ice on the Yenisei was breaking up, and that a dread phalanx of ice-floes and pack-ice was coming down upon us at quick march. On it came, smashed the rudder, ground against the stern of the ship, sometimes squeezing her against the shore so that she pitched and rolled as if she were in a heavy sea, and sometimes surrounding her with small floes which seemed to try to lift her bodily out of the water. Once or twice an ice-floe began to climb up the ship's side like a snake. . . . We were carried along in this way for about a mile, until we were finally jammed into a slight bay, wedged between blocks of pack-ice. Soon afterwards the river fell some five or six feet, the stream slackened, the ice stood still, and the ship and the pack-ice were aground.

The ice remained quiet till about midnight, when an enormous pressure from above came on somewhat suddenly. The water in the Kureika once more rose rapidly. The immense field of pack-ice began to move up-stream at the rate of five or six knots an hour. The marvel was, where all the ice that had gone up the Kureika could possibly be stowed. I calculated that at least 50,000 acres of ice had passed the ship.

Late on the night of Monday, the 4th of June, the ice on the Kureika almost entirely cleared away. Steam was got up, and by the help of ropes ashore the *Thames* was steered into the little creek below the house, where it had been the original intention of the captain to have waited in safety the passing away of the ice. The season had been so severe that the snow, which ought to have melted and swollen the river before the breaking-up of the ice, still remained upon the land. The consequence was that, when the great revolution commenced, the entrance to the creek was high and dry. The *Thames* entered the creek at two o'clock in the morning ; by noon (June 5th) the water had sunk five or six feet, and the vessel lay on her side, with her bow at least three feet aground. These sudden falls in the level of the water were, no doubt, caused by the breaking-up of the ice lower down the river, which dammed it up until the accumulated pressure from behind became irresistible. Some idea of what this pressure must have been may be realised by the fact that a part of the river a thousand miles long, beginning with a width of two miles, and ending with a width of six miles, covered over with three feet of ice, upon which was lying six feet of snow, was broken up at the rate of a hundred miles a day. Many obstacles could cause a temporary stoppage in the break-up of the ice—a sudden bend in the river, a group of islands, or a narrower place where the ice might jam. But the pressure from behind was an ever-increasing one. Although the river frequently fell for a few hours, it was constantly rising on the whole, and in ten days the rise where we were stationed was seventy feet. Such a display of irresistible power dwarfs Niagara into comparative insignificance. On several occasions we stood on the banks of the river for hours, transfixed with astonishment, staring aghast at icebergs, twenty to thirty feet high, driven down the river at a speed of from ten to twenty miles an hour.

The battle of the Yenisei raged for about a fortnight, during which the Kureika alternately rose and fell. Thousands of acres of ice were marched up-stream for some hours, then the tide turned and they were marched back again. This great annual battle between summer and winter is the chief event of the year in these regions, like the rising of the Nile in Egypt. Summer, in league with the sun, fights winter and the north wind, and is hopelessly beaten until she forms an alliance with the south wind, before whose blast the forces of winter vanish into thin water and retreat to the Pole. . . .

At last, after their fourteen days' battle, the final march-past of the beaten winter forces took place, and for seven days more the ragtag-and-bobtail of the great Arctic army came straggling down the Kureika—worn and weather-beaten little icebergs, dirty ice-floes that looked like floating mud-banks and, straggling pack-ice in the last stages of consumption. Winter was finally vanquished for the year, and the fragments of his beaten army were compelled to retreat to the triumphant music of thousands of song-birds, and amidst the waving of green leaves and the illumination of gay flowers of every hue.

(*Arctic Circle: 87°E.*)   (Henry Seebohm : *Birds of Siberia.*)

River: Lena

SIBERIA

ON THE 1st of June, we started on our way down the gigantic Lena on the small steamer *Synok*. In sailing down the river you get the impression that you are passing through a mountainous country. On each side a continuous mountain-wall towers up to the height of 1,000 feet above the water, in some places approaching the river, forming picturesque " gates " or " pillars ", at others diverging from it, and enclosing large river-basins with numerous islands. But if you ascend any of these apparent mountains, you will find that they resolve themselves into a plateau of undulating forest-clad country, through which the giant river has cut its way. Only in two places has the Lena carved a path for itself through mountain-chains—at Scherebinsk, about 1,050 miles south of Yakutsk (near the border between Irkutsk and Yakutsk), and at the most northern part of its course, where it has eroded its deep channel through the Kara Ulak mountains, which form the most northern outskirts of the Verkhoyansk chain.

Between Katschúga and Kirensk the plateau-land through which the Lena has carved its deep and tortuous channel consists mainly of horizontal layers of red sandstone and slate-marl. At Kirensk the layers of upper-silurian sandstone begin to appear, generally feebly folded. Below the river Aldan, more than 60 miles north of the city of Yakutsk, the course of the Lena lies through a flat country, built up from mesozoic rocks, while towards the mouth of the river carboniferous, brachiopod and coralliferous layers appear.

It is impossible to convey by words and figures any idea of the gigantic proportions of this superb river. Every second it empties into the ocean 10,000 tons of water, which, through its myriad tributaries, it receives from an area of one million square miles, or about five times the size of Great Britain and Ireland. The greatest part of the area drained by the river lies east of it, the water-parting between the Yenisei and the Lena running so far east that it nearly touches the shores of the latter at Kirensk, where the Lower Tunguskaya takes its rise only some ten miles east of the Lena. The principal tributaries of the Lena on its eastern side, counting from the south, are the following: the Vitim, about 1,100 miles in length, of which 300 are navigable; the Olekma, more than 1,100 miles in length, navigable about 560 miles; and the Aldan, 1,360 miles in length, and navigable for over 900 miles; the Aldan having in its turn two large tributaries, the Amga and Maya. The latter, which is of great importance as the transport-route of goods from the Pacific Ocean to Yakutsk, is navigable for nearly 400 miles. From the south-west the Lena receives only one large tributary, the Vilui, which is about 1,350 miles in length and navigable for about 750 of them.

The course of the Lena is very tortuous, thus making its absolute length so great. In its upper part the current is rapid, as also is the case near the delta ; otherwise it runs very slowly. At its source it is about 2,855 feet above the level of the sea, at Ust-Kutsk 921 feet, at Kirensk 820 feet, and at Yakutsk only 213 feet. On the upper Lena navigation commences in the first part of May and closes in the middle of October ; at the delta the breaking up of the ice takes place at the end of June, and it freezes at the beginning of October or even sooner. The breaking up of the ice on this gigantic body of water is one of nature's most stupendous phenomena, and often causes very great devastation.

*   *   *   *   *

(North of Vitim)

The wild beauty and overpowering majesty of the great Lena here reigns supreme. On the rivers and in the forests of Europe your individuality finds, so to speak, a support in the constant change of scenery ; but here it is suppressed by the monotonous, endless wilderness, and the solemn grandeur of the vast river. You steam on day after day, night after night, for hundreds of miles in the same direction, ever farther and farther away from civilisation, and nearer and nearer to the eternal domain of the polar ice. In this vast wilderness the " Mother Lena " with its ever-growing proportions and mightiness, forms the *pièce de résistance*. In its serene depth all is mirrored. Here a cyclopean wall of immense blocks of sandstone has been reared by primeval forces ; there a colossal mass of rock overhangs the water, into which it would fall were it not sustained by a row of strange and gigantic pillars of the same material. Here beneath a huge perpendicular cliff a whirlpool is ever moving in its eternal circle ; while yonder are seen cathedrals with innumerable spires and pinnacles, or ruins of fairy castles of greyish and white limestone. Columns of magnificent larch-trees and Siberian pines stand in the ravines and valleys like an army ready to attack the fortresses which are threatening above their heads, while higher up stand scattered individuals of Siberian pine, as if trying to fight their way alone and unaided towards the fort. Then the scene is changed, and a view slowly opens out of cliffs of beautifully regular layers of slate and green porphyry, producing an impression alike fantastic and unreal. Now and then the mouth of some great cave yawns before you, or hot sulphur-springs are seen welling forth at the foot of the mountain, filling the air with pungent odour. And ever and again the " shore-mountains " are cut through by nameless rivers coming from the unknown depths of the taiga, where the foot of civilised man has never trod. . . .

Having received its great tributary, the Olekma, the Lena increases to the width of about two miles, and widens more and more, until, at the city of Yakutsk, the distance between the hills which form its valley is not much under twenty miles. . . .

Having received its great tributaries, the Aldan and the Vilui, the Lena gives the impression of an interminable broad inland lake with many islands rather than a river. Often the surface of its waters fades into the horizon, and the distance between its shores widens to as much as fifteen miles or more. In stormy weather, the motion of the vessel and, maybe, the sea-sickness which accompanies it, contribute to create the illusion that you are on the open sea rather than on fresh water.

Having passed the mouth of the Vilui, one gets the first sight of the snow-clad Verkhoyansk mountains far away to the east, the outskirts of which, cut through by the Lena, form the *Utesi* or " strand mountains." The country is utterly wild and desolate. The trees become smaller, the woods thinner. North of the Vilui the pine is no more seen. Near the polar-circle the spruce ceases, and yet a little farther north the beech, until finally only the hardy Siberian larch remains and continues all the way to within a few miles of the Lena delta.

On the shores of the river were heaped masses of driftwood, and here and there, even though we were at the end of June, lay colossal blocks of ice. In the steep cliffs rising from the shore and composed of yellow and whitish sandstone, are seen layers of coal of varying thickness. Immediately north of Schigansk they have a thickness of as much as eight or nine feet. . . .

From Bulkur, where I stayed for some time, I made several excursions in different directions, as far as it was possible to do so amid the terrible storms of rain and snow which rage almost all the summer in these regions. As mentioned above, the Lena has here worked its way through the Kara Ulak mountains. On the western side of the river, where Bulkur is situated, the ancient beaches of the gigantic river form terraces for a distance of about ten miles or more inland, and through these old river-banks the tributaries of the Lena, like the river Bulkur, have cut their way. One day, following the latter river some six miles to the west, I left its valley and ascended to the highest of these terraces or ancient beaches. Here, ten miles from the Lena, and about 600 feet above its present level, in a layer of soil composed of turf and mud mixed with sand, resting on a foundation of solid ice as clean and blue as steel and of unknown depth, I found large quantities of drift-wood, evidently brought down by the river at the remote period when it had its course here. The length of this period may be imagined from the gigantic work performed by the river since that time : wearing down the Kara Ulak mountains, about 1,000 feet in height, little by little, and thus moving its course eastwards some ten miles or more.

Later I found this *boskaya*, or " rock-ice," as the natives call it, on the tundra west of Olenek, with a layer of earth above, in which the natives had found both drift-wood and remnants of the mammoth. This, as well as similar discoveries made on the New Siberian Islands, prove that this " rock-ice," and the drift-wood in the earth resting on it, belong to the period of the mammoth, or even previous to it.

(Approx. from 58°N; 108°E to 74°N; 127°E.)

(J. Stadling : *Through Siberia.*)

ICE

ICE

Inland Ice

NORWAY : SVARTIS

THAT NIGHT, I don't know : perhaps I only dreamt that I got up several times and looked out through that round port-hole in the cabin, and that I could see a landscape on the moon. They were not real mountains, and rocks that projected above the mother-of-pearl sea ; they were some kind of strange and dreadful forms ; most likely it was only a dream.

Most probably I slept, and in the meantime we crossed the Arctic Circle bellowing gloriously ; I heard *Håkon* bellowing but I didn't get up ; I thought that it was nothing, that we were only sinking, or calling for help, or something. And in the morning we were already right past the Arctic Circle ; it couldn't be helped ; we were merely in the Polar regions, without having suitably celebrated this event. All life long we hustle and bustle in the temperate zones like a bird in a cage, and then we are asleep the moment that we cross the line.

If the truth must be told, the first look at the Polar regions is a severe disappointment. These then are the Polar regions ? It's not playing fair ; for we haven't seen such a green and pleasant land since Molde : little square fields below, human habitations thickly scattered everywhere ; above that, mounds and cupolas with billowy leafy growth, and above that——

" Styrman, what is that intensely blue thing over there, hanging from the mountains ? "

The good-natured Polar bear from Tromsø who does duty as helmsman with us says : " Ja, that's Svartisen."

Ah, so that's Svartisen ; and, after all, what is that Svartisen ? It looks nearly like a glacier, but it's so incredibly blue ; and a glacier perhaps couldn't reach so far down, right among those green groves——

On drawing nearer it really is a birch grove with nothing but brown and white mushrooms, crowberry with black fruit, and creeping juniper, and dryas, spotted orchis, and golden groundsel growing there ; and then there is a bare moraine of brown detritus, and then the real glacier reaching down almost to the sea : a huge tongue of glassy ice, sticking out from the firn fields above, between the mountain peaks, about twenty yards thick, nothing but icy boulders, chasms and ledges ; and all as blue as smalt, like sulphate of copper, or ultramarine ; and if you want to know the reason why it's called the Black Ice, it is because it is so blue that your eyes smart ; lower down there is an azure lake between the turquoise ice floes——

" Don't go so near," cries an anxious conjugal voice, " in case it falls down on you ! "

The sun grows warmer, fissures rumble in the glacier ; right at the foot of the blue ice a pink campion is flowering sweetly. I tell you the world is terribly disconcerting ; one day when I recall everything that I have seen, I shan't believe that it was true. Only we are lucky to have seen it now ; they say that the glacier is always getting smaller, perhaps in twenty thousand years it will be gone, said the styrman ; but let us hope that another Ice Age will arrive before then. Up above, that glacier, they say, covers two hundred square miles ; well then, I must touch it with my finger—two hundred square miles, that now is something worth while.

Only from a distance can you see how vast it is : the towering mountains, and behind them that white and blue expanse, that is Svartisen ; and that crest there, that also is Svartisen, and that one there, that gleams so brightly, that is still more of Svartisen. You come to green islands, Grønøy they are called ; grass up to your waist, a luscious and lovely park of willows, alders and aspens, weasels are basking on the boulders ; just a typical polar landscape. Above the dear little islands, woolly like green rams, the bluish ridge of the mountains, and behind that a gleaming metallic band : that is Svartisen all the time.

(67°N; 14°E.)   (Karel Čapek : *Travels in the North*.)

Glaciers

FRANCE : SAVOY

*An account of the Glacieres or Ice Alps in Savoy, in two letters,
one from an English gentleman to his friend at Geneva ; the other
from Peter Martel, Engineer, to the said English gentleman.*
Sir,—

According to your desire I send you an account of our journey
to the *glacieres*. I shall give it to you in the plainest manner,
without endeavouring to embellish it by any florid descriptions,
although the beauty and variety of the situations and prospects
that we observed in this unfrequented part of the world, would
well deserve to be described by one, who, like you, join to so great
a skill in painting so lively and poetical an imagination ; but these
not being my talents, I will, as I said before, confine myself to
the giving you a faithful relation of the incidents of our journey,
and acquainting you with the observations we made. I shall add
a few hints, which may be useful to such as shall hereafter have
the same curiosity as we had, and who may perhaps have ad-
vantages and conveniences which we had not, to make more
accurate observations. It is really pity that so great a curiosity,
and which lies so near you, should be so little known ; for though
Scheuchzer, in his *Iter Alpinum*, describes the *glacieres* that are in
the canton of *Berne*, yet they seem to me by his description to
be very different from those of Savoy.

. . . We set out from *Geneva* the 19th of *June*, N.S. We were
eight in company, besides five servants, all of us well arm'd, and
our baggage-horses attending us, so that we had very much the
air of a caravan. The first day we went no further than *Bonneville*, a town about four leagues distant from *Geneva*, according to
the way of reckoning there ; these four leagues took us more than
six hours riding. This place is situated at the foot of the *Maule*,
and close by the river *Arve;* 'tis surrounded with beautiful
meadows and high mountains, covered with trees, which form all
together a very delightful situation. There is a very good stone
bridge near the town, but it had suffered in the late inundation
of the *Arve*, which had carried away part of it. Our inn was a
tolerable one for Savoy as to every thing but beds.

The next day being the 20th, we set out very early in the
morning, and passed the *Arve ;* our road lay between that river

and the mountains; all along it we were entertained with an agreeable variety of fine landskips. They reckon two leagues from *Bonneville* to *Cluse*, but we were three hours and a half in going it.

. . . After about three hours' riding from *Cluse*, we came to Saint *Martin's* bridge, right against *Salanches*, which is on the other side of the *Arve*. We did not care to go out of our way into the town ; but chose rather to encamp in a fine meadow near the bridge, in order to refresh ourselves.

. . . From thence we set out again on our journey, and after four hours riding through very bad ways, being obliged to cross some very dangerous torrents, we arrived at a little village called *Servoz*. Our horses suffered here very much, being tied to pickets all night in the open air for want of stabling ; besides there was neither oats, nor any other forrage, but grass fresh cut; as for ourselves, as we had brought all necessaries along with us, we were well enough off, except as to beds, and that want was supplied by clean straw in a barn.

From thence we set forward at break of day, and passed the *Arve* once more over a very bad wooden bridge, and after having clim'd over a steep mountain, where we had no small difficulty with our horses, their shoes coming off continually, and they often running the risque of tumbling into the *Arve*, which run at the bottom of the rock, we came into a pleasant valley, where we pass'd the *Arve* a fourth time over a stone bridge, and then first had a view of the *glacieres*. We continued our journey on to *Chamouny*, which is a village upon the north-side of the *Arve*, in a valley, where there is a priory belonging to the Chapter of *Salanches ;* here we encamp'd, and while our dinner was preparing, we inquired of the people of the place about the *glacieres*. They shewed us first the ends of them which reach into the valley, and were to be seen from the village ; these appear'd only like white rocks, or rather like immense icicles, made by water running down the mountain. This did not satisfy our curiosity, and we thought we were come too far to be contented with so small a matter ; we therefore strictly inquired of the peasants whether we could not by going up the mountain discover something more worth our notice. They told us we might, but the greatest part of them represented the thing as very difficult and laborious ; they told us no-body ever went there but those whose business it was to search for crystal, or to shoot *bouquetins* and *chamois*, and that all the

318

travellers, who had been to the *glacieres* hitherto, had been satisfied with what we had already seen.

The prior of the place was a good old man, who showed us many civilities, and endeavoured also to dissuade us ; there were others who represented the thing as mighty easy ; but we perceived plainly, that they expected, that after we had bargain'd with them to be our guides, we should soon tire and that they should earn their money with but little trouble. However our curiosity got the better of these discouragements, and relying on our strength and resolution, we determined to attempt climbing the mountain. We took with us several peasants, some to be our guides, and others to carry wine and provisions. These people were so much persuaded that we should never be able to go through with our task, that they took with them candles and instruments to strike fire, in case we should be overcome with fatigue, and be obliged to spend the night on the mountain. In order to prevent those among us who were most in wind, from fatiguing the rest, by pushing on too fast, we made the following rules : that no one should go out of his rank ; that he who led should go a slow and even pace ; that who ever found himself fatigued, or out of breath, might call for a halt ; and lastly, that when ever we found a spring we should drink some of our wine, mixed with water, and fill up the bottles we had emptied, with water, to serve us at other halts where we should find none. These precautions were so useful to us, that, perhaps, had we not observed them, the peasants would not have been deceived in their conjectures.

We set out about noon, the 22nd of *June,* and crossed the *Arve* over a wooden bridge. Most maps place the *glacieres* on the same side with *Chamoigny* but this is a mistake. We were quickly at the foot of the mountain, and began to ascend by a very steep path through a wood of fir and larche trees. We made many halts to refresh ourselves, and take breath, but we kept on at a good rate. After we had passed the wood, we came to a kind of meadow, full of large stones, and pieces of rock, that were broke off, and fallen down from the mountain ; the ascent was so steep that we were obliged sometimes to cling to them with our hands, and make use of sticks, with sharp irons at the end, to support ourselves. Our road lay slant ways, and we had several places to cross where the *avalanches* of snow were fallen, and had made terrible havock ; there was nothing to be seen but trees torn up by the roots, and large stones, which seemed to lie without any support ; every step we set, the ground gave way, the snow which was mixed with it made us slip, and had it not been for our staffs, and our hands, we must many times have gone down the precipice. We had an uninterrupted view quite to the bottom of the mountain, and the steepness of the descent, join'd to the height where we were, made a view terrible enough to make most people's heads turn. In short, after climbing with great labour for four hours and three quarters, we got to the top of the mountain ; from whence we had the pleasure of beholding objects of an extraordinary nature. We were on the top of a mountain, which, as well as we could judge, was least twice as high as Mount *Saleve*, from thence we had a full view of the *glacieres*. I own to you that I am extremely at a loss how to give the right idea of it ; as I know no one thing which I have ever seen that has the least resemblance to it.

The description which travellers give of the seas of *Greenland* seems to come the nearest to it. You must imagine your lake put in agitation by a strong wind, and frozen all at once, perhaps even that would not produce the same appearance.

The *glacieres* consist of three large valleys, that form a kind of Y, the tail reaches into the *Val d'Aoste*, and the two horns into the valley of *Chamoigny*, the place where we ascended was between them, from whence we saw plainly the valley, which forms one of these horns.

I had unluckily left at *Chamoigny* a pocket compass, which I had carried with me, so that I could not well tell the bearings as to its situation ; but I believe it to be pretty nearly from north to south. These valleys, although at the top of a high mountain, are surrounded by other mountains ; the tops of which being naked and craggy rocks, shoot up immensely high ; something resembling old *gothic* buildings or ruines, nothing grows upon them, they are all the year round covered with snow ; and our guides assured us, that neither the *chamois*, nor any birds, ever went so high as the top of them.

Those who search after crystal, go in the month of *August* to the foot of these rocks, and strike against them with pick-axes ; if they hear them resound as if they were hollow, they work there, and opening the rock, they find caverns full of crystalisations. We should have been very glad to have gone there, but the season was not enough advanced, the snow not being yet sufficiently melted. As far as our eyesight could reach, we saw nothing but this valley ; the height of the rocks, which surrounded it, made it impossible for the eye to judge exactly how wide it was ; but I imagine it must be near three quarters of a league. Our curiosity did not stop there, we were resolved to go down upon the ice ; we had about four hundred yards to go down, the descent was excessively steep, and all of a dry crumbling earth, mixt with gravel, and little loose stones, which afforded us no firm footing, so that we went down partly falling, and partly sliding on our hands and knees. At length we got upon the ice, where our difficulty ceased, for that was extremely rough and afforded us good footing ; we found in it an infinite number of cracks, some we could step over, others were several feet wide. These cracks were so deep, that we could not even see to the bottom ; those who go in search of crystal are often lost in them, but their bodies are generally found again after some days, perfectly well preserved. Our guides assured us, that these cracks change continually, and that the whole *glaciere* has a kind of motion. In going up the mountain we often heard something like a clap of thunder, which, as we were informed by our guides, was caused by fresh cracks then making ; but as there were none made while we were upon the ice, we could not determine whether it was that, or *avalanches* of snow, or perhaps rocks falling ; though since travellers observe, that in *Greenland* the ice cracks with a noise resembling thunder, it might very well be what our guides told us. As in all countries of ignorance people are extremely superstitious, they told us many strange stories of witches, &c., who came to play their pranks upon the *glacieres*, and dance to the sound of instruments. We should have been surprised if we had not been entertained in these parts, with some such idle legends. The *bouquetins* go in herds often to the number of fifteen or sixteen upon the ice, we saw none of them ; there were some *chamois* which we shot at, but at too great a distance to do any execution.

There is water continually issuing out of the *glacieres*, which the people look on as so very wholesome, that they say it may be drank of in any quantities without danger, even when one is hot with exercise.

The sun shone very hot, and the reverberation of the ice, and circumjacent rocks, caused a great deal of thaw'd water to lie in all the cavities of the ice ; but I fancy it freezes here constantly as soon as night comes on.

Our guides assured us that in the time of their fathers, the *glaciere* was but small, and that there was even a passage thro' these valleys, by which they could get into the *Val d' Aoste* in six hours : but that the *glaciere* was so much increased, that the passage was then quite stopped up, and that it went on increasing every year.

We found on the edge of the *glaciere* several pieces of ice, which we took at first for rocks, being as big as a house ; these were pieces quite separate from the *glaciere*. It is difficult to conceive how they came to be formed there.

Having remained about half an hour upon the *glaciere*, and having drank there in ceremony Admiral *Vernon's* health, and success to the *British* arms, we climb'd to the summit, from whence we came, with incredible difficulty, the earth giving way at every step we set. From thence, after having rested ourselves a few minutes, we began to descend, and arrived at *Chamouny* just about sun-set, to the great astonishment of all the people of the place, and even of our guides, who owned to us they thought we should not have gone through with our undertaking. (45°55'N; 6°53'E.)

(Quoted in G. R. de Beer : *Early Travellers in the Alps*.)

Alpine Glaciers

SO THEY trudged on round the bluff, and then in front of them saw what is always, always wonderful, one of those shallow upper valleys, naked, where the first waters are rocked. A flat, shallow, utterly desolate valley, wide as a wide bowl under the sky, with rock slopes and grey stone-slides and precipices all around, and the zig-zag of snow-stripes and ice-roots descending, and then rivers, streams and rivers rushing from many points downwards, down out of the ice-roots and the snow-dagger-points, waters rushing in newly-liberated frenzy downwards, down in waterfalls and cascades and threads, down into the wide, shallow bed of the valley, strewn with rocks and stones innumerable, and not a tree, not a visible bush.

Only, of course, two hotels or restaurant places. But these no more than low, sprawling, peasant-looking places lost among the stones, with stones on their roofs so that they seemed just a part of the valley bed. There was the valley, dotted with rock and rolled-down stone, and these two house-places, and woven with innumerable new waters, and one hoarse stone-tracked river in the desert, and the thin road-track winding along the desolate flat, past first one house, then the other, over one stream, then another, on to the far rock-face above which the glacier seemed to loll like some awful great tongue put out.

*   *   *   *   *

The rain had ceased. There was a wisp of sunshine from a grey sky. Alexander left the knapsack, and the two went out into the air. Before them lay the last level of the up-climb, the Lammer-boden. It was a rather gruesome hollow between the peaks, a last shallow valley about a mile long. At the end the enormous static stream of the glacier poured in from the blunt mountain-top of ice. The ice was dull, sullen-coloured, melted on the surface by the very hot summer : and so it seemed a huge, arrested, sodden flood, ending in a wave-wall of stone-speckled ice upon the valley bed of rocky débris. A gruesome descent of stone and blocks of rock, the little valley bed, with the river raving through. On the left rose the grey rock, but the glacier was there, sending down great paws of ice. It was like some great deep-furred ice-bear lying spread upon the top heights, and reaching down terrible paws of ice into the valley : like some immense sky-bear fishing in the earth's solid hollows from above. Some of the immense, furrowed paws of ice held down between the rocks were vivid blue in colour, but of a frightening, poisonous blue, like crystal copper-sulphate. Most of the ice was a sullen, semi-translucent greeny grey.

The two set off to walk through the massy, desolate stone-bed, under rocks and over waters, to the main glacier. The flowers were even more beautiful on this last reach. Particularly the dark hare-bells were large and almost black and ice-metallic : one could imagine they gave a dull ice-chink. And the grass of Parnassus stood erect, white-veined big cups held terribly naked and open to their ice-air.

From behind the great blunt summit of ice that blocked the distance at the end of the valley, a pale-grey, woolly mist or cloud was fusing up, exhaling huge, like some grey-dead aura into the sky, and covering the top of the glacier. All the way along the valley people were threading, strangely insignificant, among the grey dishevel of stone and rock, like insects.

As they came near they saw the wall of ice : the glacier end, thick crusted and speckled with stone and dirt débris. From underneath, secret in stones, water rushed out. When they came quite near, they saw the great monster was sweating all over, trickles and rivulets of sweat running down his sides of pure, slush-translucent ice. There it was, the glacier, ending abruptly in the wall of ice under which they stood. Near to, the ice was pure, but water-logged, all the surface rather rotten from the hot summer. It was sullenly translucent, and of a watery, darkish bluey-green colour. But near the earth it became again bright coloured, gleams of green like jade, gleams of blue like thin, pale sapphire, in little caverns above the wet stones where the walls trickled for ever. (D. H. Lawrence : *The Spirit of Place*.)

Glacier: The Rhone

SWITZERLAND

July 20 (1868). Fine.

WALKED DOWN to the Rhone Glacier. It has three stages— first, a smoothly-moulded bed in a pan or theatre of thorny peaks, swells of ice rising through the snow sheet—and the snow itself tossing and fretting into the sides of the rock walls in spray-like points : this is the first stage of the glaciers generally ; it is like bright-plucked water swaying in a pail—; second, after a slope nearly covered with landslips of moraine, was a ruck of horned waves steep and narrow in the gut : now in the upper Grindelwald Glacier between the bed or highest stage was a descending limb which was like the rude and knotty bossings of a strombus shell—; third the foot, a broad limb opening out and reaching the plain, shaped like the fan-fin of a dolphin or a great bivalve shell turned on its face, the flutings in either case being suggested by the crevasses and the ribs by the risings between them, these being swerved and inscaped strictly to the motion of the mass. Or you may compare the three stages to the heel, instep, and ball or toes of a foot.—The second stage looked at from nearer appeared like a box of plaster of Paris or starch or tooth-powder, a little moist, tilted up and then struck and jarred so that the powder broke and tumbled in shapes and rifts.

We went into the grotto and also the vault from which the Rhone flows. It looked like a blue tent and as you went further in changed to lilac. As you come out the daylight glazes the groins with gleaming rosecolour. The ice inside has a branchy wire texture. The man shewed us the odd way in which a little piece of ice will stick against the walls—as if drawn by a magnet.

I had a trudge over the glacier and a tumble over the side moraine, which was one landslip of limestone. It was neighboured however by not sweet smells and many flowers—small crimson pinks, the brown tulip-like flower we have seen so often, another which we first saw yesterday like Solomon's seal but rather coarser with a spike of greenish veiny-leaved blossom, etc. (*46°35'N; 8°20' W.*)

(*The Notebooks and Papers of Gerard Manley Hopkins.*)

Glaciers

FRANCE : SAVOY

THE DERIVATION of the German name for glacier, *gletscher*, is suggested as coming not from their icy material, but their perpetual motion, from *glitschen* to glide ; more probably, however, from the idea of gliding upon their surface. These glaciers come down from the air, down out of heaven, a perpetual frozen motion ever changing and gliding, from the first fall of snow in the atmosphere through the state of consolidated grinding blocks of ice, and then into musical streams that water the valleys. First it is a powdery, feathery snow, then granulated like hail, and denominated *firn*, forming vast beds and sheets around the highest mountain summits, then frozen into masses, by which time it has travelled down to within seven thousand feet of the level of the sea, where commences the great ice-ocean that fills the uninhabitable Alpine valleys, unceasingly freezing, melting, and moving down. It has been estimated by Saussure and others that these seas of ice, at their greatest thickness, are six or eight hundred feet deep. They are traversed by deep fissures, and as they approach the great precipices, over which they plunge like a cataract into the vales, they are split in all directions, and heaved up into the waves, reefs, peaks, pinnacles, and minarets. Underneath they are traversed by as many galleries and caverns, through which run the rills and torrents constantly gathering from the melting masses above.

These innumerable streams, gathering in one as they approach the termination of the glacier, rush out from beneath it, under a great vault of ice, and thus are born into the breathing world, full-grown roaring rivers, from night, frost, and chaos.

A peasant has been known to have fallen into an ice-gulf in one of these seas, near one of the flowing sub-glacial torrents, and, following the course of the stream to the foot of the glacier, he came out alive ! The German naturalist, Hugi, set out to explore the recesses of one of the glaciers through the bed of a former torrent, and wandered on in its ice caverns the distance of a mile. " The ice was everywhere eaten away into dome-shaped hollows, varying from two to twelve feet in height, so that the whole mass of the glacier rested at intervals on pillars, or feet of ice, irregular in size and shape, which had been left standing. As soon as any of these props gave way, a portion of the glacier would of course fall in and move on. A dim twilight, scantily transmitted through the mass of ice above, prevailed in these caverns of ice, not sufficient to allow one to read, except close to the fissures, which directly admitted the daylight. The intense blue of the mass of the ice contrasted remarkably with the pure white of the icy stalactites or pendants descending from the roof. The water streamed down upon him from all sides, so that after wandering about for two hours, at times bending and creeping, to get along under the low vault, he returned to the open air, quite drenched and half frozen."
(George B. Cheever : *Wanderings of a Pilgrim in the Shadow of Mont Blanc.*)

Snow

THE ANDES : NIEVES PENITENTES

WE HAD a fine view of a mass of Mountains called Tupungato, the whole clothed with unbroken snow ; from one peak my Arriero said he had once seen smoke proceeding ; I thought I could distinguish the form of a large crater. In the maps Tupungato flourishes as a single mountain ; this Chileno method of giving one name to a group of mountains is a fruitful source of error. In this region of snow there was a blue patch ; no doubt a glacier. A phenomenon which is not thought to occur in these mountains.

Again we had a heavy and long climb similar to that up the Puqueres range. On each hand were bold conical hills of red granite. We had to pass over still broader pieces of perpetual snow ; this by the action of the thaw had assumed the form of numberless pinnacles, which as they were close together & high, rendered it difficult for the Cargo Mules to pass. A frozen horse was exposed, sticking to one of these points as to a pedestal, with its hind legs straight up in the air ; the animal must have fallen into a hole head downmost & thus have died.
(33°20'S; 70°W.) (Charles Darwin : *The Beagle Diary*.)

Glacier Ice
SWITZERLAND : WEISSHORN

BY ONE o'clock he had reached the tail end—some would call it the snout—of the big Weisshorn Glacier, eaten his rations and set a first foot on the rough convex swell of honey-combed ice with water flushing out its millions of cells ; for the sun was on it. He pawed the stuff tenderly with his axe. Perdition catch his soul but he did love it—strong as iron, carvable as cheese : what genius could have conceived so delicious a union of opposites if, by some disaster, no glaciers had been made ?
(46°5'N; 7°40'E.) (C. E. Montague : *Action*.)

Ice Erosion
NORWAY

—and then Krøderen suddenly appears, lake Krøderen amidst the granite cupolas upon which sits the curly wig of leafy woods ; they are such massive, rounded mountains, turned out with the mastery of the lathe. Here all you can do is to look at the world with an eye for geology ; for instance these granite cupolas below Norefjell prove that at its creation the world was not thrown up as if from some kind of hot porridge but fashioned with great care, turned and ground, etched and polished, until finally some glacier ran its fond and expert finger over the mountains above Krøderen, and felt satisfied with its contours ; yes, it is good ; can anyone show me another glacier as clever !

* * * * *

Well then, onward, and mind the icebergs ; they used to be all over the place here, that was only a couple of hundred thousand years ago; and everywhere they have left the prints of their mighty fingers. You can find out here, by watching, their method of work : an iceberg like that files the highest mountains into sharp spikes and steeples, while it slices the smaller ones off smooth, or it planes them into sharp crests. And where it gets to work with a real massif, it pulls its sleeves up, and then it crushes, grinds, scrapes, and files, until it has ground out a deep hollow between the mountain peaks ; the sawdust it throws up and rolls out like a moraine, the hollow it makes into a small lake, and from it suspends a waterfall, and that's all. In fact it's quite simple, and all the same throughout, but you never can sufficiently appreciate how beautifully and vigorously it is done.

(60°N; 10°E.)   (Karel Čapek : *Travels in the North.*)

Laurentian Shield

LABRADOR

IT IS a wonderful place, this roof of the Labrador. Ridge on ridge, some of considerable height, roll away seemingly to the world's end. In the valleys and cups of the hills lie thousands of nameless lakes. The winds, during the greater part of the year, rage over it. It is sheer desolation, abysmal and chaotic. Of dominant notes there are but two, the ivory-coloured reindeer moss and the dark Laurentian stone. On the flanks and on the peaks of the mountains, in the beds of the brooks, on the shore of the lakes all over this huge tableland, are strewn the grey Laurentian boulders in their infinite millions—gigantic and glacier-born seeds sown in the dawning of the world. When the sun shines, to quote Saltatha, the Yellowknife Indian, " the lakes are sometimes misty, and sometimes blue, and the loons cry very often ". Then it is a land of stern and imposing beauty, perhaps unlike any other on earth, where sky and clouds are mirrored in the shallow lakes, and the lazy, monster fish rise among the ripples in the red and gold of evening. But when the clouds ride it, and the wind and rain, sleet and snow rave over it, as they do nearly all the year round, a desolation more appalling cannot be conceived. There is no shelter for him who travels it ; hardly one of the glacier-driven stones is more than four feet high ; every lake is driven into wrath and thunders on its shores ; the loon may cry out there in the storm, but no human ear could hear him. Lucky

the man if he can find a rock beneath which to creep, and in that
cold refuge shiver as he peers out and watches the elemental
Spirit of the Tempest rejoicing in what seems to be the very
heart of his kingdom.
(*55°N; 65°W.*)

(H. Hesketh Prichard : *Through Trackless Labrador.*)

Glacial Lakes

SOUTH SWEDEN

THE ROUTE from Stockholm to Oslo consists chiefly of lakes ;
counting only from Laxå, there you have lakes Toften and Testen,
then immense, flat Vänern, then Värmeln (this already is Värm-
land, the land of Gösta Berling), and Glafsfjorden, Nysorkensjön,
and Bysjön. Strange : such a lake like Vänern, that is too big,
has in it something fundamentally unromantic, and I should
almost say modern ; it must be those dimensions. A romantic
lake must be small ; the smaller the more antique it looks, lonelier,
more fairylike, or how should I express it. Of course, a watersprite
in Vänern would have to be called a *general manager*, or an under-
secretary of state ; such a big concern it is, that Vänern. But there
are also smooth lakes, like mirrors of heaven, and bottomless
little lakes in the depths of the woods, and long, narrow river
lakes, yes, and rivers, or *älvar*, slow, cutting into dark woods, and
languidly, with a kind of eternity, bearing the trunks of felled
trees ; and the woods observe how on the river slowly, endlessly,
irresistibly, the woods are flowing away.

(*About 59°N; 13°E.*)   (Karel Čapek : *Travels in the North.*)

Erratic Blocks

THE ALPS AND JURA

YES ! MANY towns of the Alpine land stand upon ruins ; on
walls of blocks and rock fragments, which have come from the
central chains of the mountains. Certainly this base of ruins does
not lie everywhere open to the day. The workman who is laying
the foundations of a new house, or the miner who is digging for
a new well, comes across it at the bottom of the highest layer of
soil. But not merely covered up in the earth, but in the open air,
on the meadows and forests of the hill-country, even high up on

the outliers of the Alps and on the Jura, blocks of stone are to be found which, from the nature of their material, must have had their home far off in the central Alps, twenty-eight geographical miles away. They have been called " foundlings " or wandering blocks. They show partly rounded surfaces, like rolled stones from river-beds ; partly fresh, sharp-angled lines of fracture, as if they had just been severed from their parent rocks. They are of all sizes, from that of a skittle-ball up to bodies of such cubical contents that from the substance of a single one lying in a field at Höngg, near Zurich, called the " red ackerstein " (field stone), a solid, respectable two-storied house was built, which bears the following inscription :—

> " From out a great red ' acre-stone '
> To many little pieces blown
> By hand of man and powder's blast,
> Was made this house so firm and fast.
> God in His mercy keep it sound ;
> Let no ill-luck its walls confound."

It once belonged to the Count Benzel-Sternau. But the block of which the house was built came from the recesses of the mountains of Glarus, perhaps from the Freiberg, or out of the Sernfthal.

Science has had little trouble in answering the question " Whence ? " From the structure, colour, and mineral composition of the granite, gneiss, mica, verrucano, and slate erratics, and from the position of their site in regard to the valley systems of the Alps, it could easily be deciphered from which of the central masses they had come. But the " How ? " of the transport caused many disputes among the investigators of the last fifty years. . . . At last, when the theory of the nature and motion of glaciers, first treated of by the Valaisan engineer Venetz, and worked out by Forbes and Agassiz, cleared up a number of the strangest phenomena of the Alps, the conclusion was varied at, *that the erratic blocks have been carried to their present position by former enormously great glaciers, which must have reached right into the Swiss " middle-land."* As will be shown further on, the glaciers move slowly from the heights to the valley, bearing on their backs the stones which have crumbled from the rocks on their banks, down to the place where they melt away in the warmer temperature and deposit their burden. These walls of stone which are heaped about the end of a glacier are named frontal moraines.

The existence of such mounds heaped up in the shape of horse-shoes in the Swiss middle-land, *e.g.* at Berne, Sursee, Bremgarten, Zürich, Rapperschwyl, &c., gave the first proof of the transport of the erratic blocks. In Zürich the promenade hill, the heights on which the cathedral, the church of Neumünster, the Lindenhof, &c., stand, are remains of such extinct frontal moraines. A second proof was drawn from the fact that the erratics, even when formed of the hardest rock, present scratched lines and furrows exactly similar to those of rocks scored by existing glaciers. By means of the vast pressure of the superincumbent ice, the small, intensely hard and sharp crystals of quartz carve lines in the rock, which seem to have been cut by a glazier's diamond. The rolled blocks which have been carried down by the wild Alpine torrents do not present these scratches. Thus the erratic blocks carried as it were Nature's handwriting like the passport of their previous wanderings, with the *visa* of every valley through which they have passed.

The third and most important argument for the transport of these erratics by extinct glaciers is to be found in the " Rund-höckern " (*roches moutonnées*). In most Alpine valleys whose walls are formed of weather-beaten granitic rocks, are to be seen in certain places (often 1,000 feet above the present level of the valley) rounded surfaces regularly striped and smoothed, which have often received so fine a polish as to glitter like mirrors in the sun. On the descent from the Todtensee to the Grimsel hospice, and thence to the Höllenplatte, on the field of ruins by the St. Gotthard hospice, and in hundreds of other Swiss places, one may see and feel such " roches moutonnées," and, where they are not overgrown by the sulphur-coloured lichen (*Lecidea geographica*), may wonder at their polish. The same phenomenon also appears close to the glaciers, by those, for example, of the Görner, Viesch, Aletsch, Findelen, and Zinal valleys : we can follow it from the glacier bank under the ice till far down the valley walls ; we can follow it in horizontal lines for hours down the valley, uninterrupted by the change in the stratification or the nature of the rocks. Such proofs increase the probability to a certainty that these valleys, now partly overgrown with ancient forests, were once the beds of gigantic glaciers. There is finally one proof in the regularity of the deposition of these erratics, which fully supports and completes the others. By " regularity " is to be understood not the uniformity of deposition already mentioned along lines of equal elevation upon the lower outlying hills of the Alps, but the regular grouping of the blocks according to colour and material of the stone. For example, on the two sides of a broad valley which again branches out into various side-valleys amongst the higher mountains, the masses of granite, diorite, gneiss, or limestone are not to be found scattered up and down amongst each other, of all colours, green, red, white, and brown, of coarse and fine grain, fibrous and laminated : they will be in separate groups. Let us make this a little clearer. Let us think of the glacier as a main stream, arising from the confluence of many mountain rivers, each of which again receives its due supply of water from various sources. Suppose again that each of these sources brings down fragments from its rocky shores. They would probably mix up the stones which they brought down, as the water is mixed up in its course. But the glaciers as solid bodies of ice (if we keep to the image of a river system) do not mix, when they come together in the broad valleys, like the flowing moving water, but continue their journey side by side, even though apparently united. Thus the long lines of ruins (moraines) resting upon them show far off, of how many side glaciers the main glacier is composed. Thus too the stones from different valleys remain separate, and thus the former gigantic glaciers deposited their blocks only on that side of the valley which corresponds to the lateral valleys lying further up in the mountains.

(H. Berlepsch: *The Alps:* Translated by the Rev. Leslie Stephen.)

Glacial Outwash Plain or Sandur

ICELAND

THIS WAS the first time I was to see one of Iceland's famous *sandurs*, a formation of which I had preserved a most vivid recollection as something very remarkable ever since my first term at university, when Professor Gerhard De Geer mentioned them as a present-day equivalent of the regimental training grounds of Sweden in their original state. They are of exactly the same nature as the enormous sand plains of North Germany, particularly those in Prussia.

Breidamerkur Jökull loomed in front of us with its mass of ice, domed like a shield, and behind it Öraefa Jökull, now so close that its various arms could be seen clearly with their enormous falls, a thousand metres high and more.

The first impression of Breidamerkursandur is that of a desert, not a picture-postcard desert with yellow sand in wavy dunes, but an almost smooth plain of dark, blackish gravel which from the end-moraines of the glaciers, high as the ramparts of a fort, sloped gently down towards the sea. It was impossible to see the end of it, for the *sandur* measures 35 kilometres in length.

Before we rode out on to this plain we had to pass through vast fields of coarse gravel and enormous boulders which the ice-rivers had unloaded not so very long ago. As late as the year 1870 the wealthy farm of Fell had stood there, but when the glaciers began to advance the rivers tore away every year more and more of its lands, until one night they overwhelmed the buildings themselves. Now there was not a trace left of that which had been, and hundreds of years will pass before these fields will once again be pastures. Fell was the first of a terrifyingly long row of farms which had been laid waste and then erased by the glaciers from the regions towards which we were riding.

The water from the ice for ever changes its course ; where one year there may be a river, the next year will be dry ground ; where no water has flowed within the memory of man, a torrent, brown and muddy, will suddenly rush forth. The swiftest rivers change their course almost daily, on account of the huge quantities of gravel which they carry with them ; as soon as the river slows down a little on reaching more level ground, the gravel becomes deposited, blocking up the bed and forcing the river to the side.

The history of the sandy plains is the history of the glacier whose water has created them. All the earth and stones it carries within its ice and on its back, or squeezes out from underneath it, sooner or later reaches the *sandur* with the water which flows from the glacier all the year round, but naturally chiefly in the summer, when melting is greatest. If the glacier suddenly increases in size and advances, the whole drainage system formed during a period when the margin of the glacier was standing still or receding, is upset and changed. Thus in the course of decades and centuries the same thing happens on a large scale which takes place yearly and daily on a small scale. Nothing endures either out here on

the *sandur* or anywhere the ablation waters of Vatna Jökull
stream forth. " Vatna Jökull " means " the glacier which gives
water " ; it could not have received a more apt or descriptive
name. The size and strength of the rivers makes it impossible for
man to tame and constrain them. Everything which lies within
their reach belongs to the kingdom of Vatna Jökull, where man
is a slave and the whole inhabited part of the country is at the
mercy of the glacier.

No one previously had understood this better than we did, no
one had known the values which determine these fluctuating
masses of water until we dug our pits up there on the glacier and
went from stake to stake to measure the rate of ablation. The
factors had never been accurately measured, which decide the
movements of Vatna Jökull, its omnipotent advances, its shrinking
recessions or periods of equilibrium when its front remains stationary. For the first time material had been collected on which
could be founded an exact knowledge of the size of the forces which
give the glacier its life. No doubt geologists previously always supposed them to be considerable, but it was left to us to discover
how enormous they really are. Catastrophes when the forces of
nature break loose in all their untamed fury are common in
Iceland, particularly, perhaps, round Vatna Jökull and its neighbourhood, but then the massing of snow in the winter and the
summer melting which are here repeated every year in the normal
course of nature, reach dimensions of hitherto unsuspected mag
nitude. On Vatna Jökull and in its neighbourhood the air-masses
from the Atlantic meet the cold from the high plateaus, with the
result that snow, ice and water are precipitated to such an extent
and in such mutual alternation that few places on earth can have
anything approaching it.

A couple of hours' riding brought us to Jökulsá, whose flow of
water is greater than that of any other river on Iceland, although
it is barely one kilometre long. Its short length is due to the
fact that Breidamerkur Jökull, the glacier out of which it flows,
here reaches almost down to the sea. Only a couple of years ago
the distance between sea and glacier was still less, but the river
is quick to build its *sandur* farther and farther out in spite of
currents and breakers. The river divides into two arms, each as
broad as the Indals River. It is possible to row across the first
and lesser arm, though one has to be careful of the ice-blocks

which come sailing down on the rapid current ; so far as the other arm is concerned, it is necessary to climb the glacier as far as its source and walk round it, " á undirvarpi ", as it is called in Icelandic.

This we did, and when we reached the head of the river I saw the enormous volume of water pouring out of the glacier, not through a hole, as most rivers do, but literally welling up from underneath it ; it looked like a witch's cauldron filled with greyish-brown brew, cold as the ice itself, yet boiling, bubbling, frothing. . . ! What enormous quantities of mud and gravel here saw the light of day again after their long journey underneath the glacier ! With what intensity the mighty torrents were working and how much efficiency they displayed ! Is everything here in Iceland just a concentrated fury of energy like those restless volcanoes which even now are waiting to break out ? It was as if the whole glacier might at any moment rise up in a world-shaking explosion from the tensions which must exist inside it.

On the shores of the glacier-river lay cockle-shells thrown up by the waters ; they too had been brought down from the bed of the glacier where they had lived during a warmer period when there was sea where now is ice. They bore witness to the same mild period and the same change in climate as the logs of birch had done outside Hoffells Jökull which we found on our first day in front of the Vatna Glacier.

Up on the ice the water gushed in brooks and rivers which wound their way through corkscrew canals, dived into deep holes in order to rush out a little farther down, or were only perceptible as a hollow roar rising from the bottom of a crevasse. The ice was hollowed out into the strangest tunnels and caves and from its surface, torn as though by an earthquake, black pyramids and towers jutted whose cloak of gravel had saved them from being consumed as rapidly as the naked ice. They were three or four metres high ; exactly so much ice had melted since the winter when the whole surface of the glacier margin was level with the tops of these peaks.

We slipped with our luggage on the bare ice, jumped across streams and crevasses, balanced perilously across ice-bridges, fell and covered ourselves with clay where there was clay on the slippery blue ice, tried to crawl up the last banks on all fours, and finally reached the edge again, landing with a rush of loose gravel near the fresh ponies, which were standing waiting for us under the indifferent supervision of Einar from Kvísker.

Some years ago when the postman rode across the ice here, it suddenly gave way beneath him and horse and man disappeared. Next summer they were both found again, dead of course, but neither crushed nor otherwise marked. The mail-bag was so well preserved that the registered letters could be distributed to their addresses. It is said in Iceland that Vatna Jökull always gives back what it has taken. I was told this already in Reykjavik when we were about to start off for the glacier ; it was probably meant as a consolation in regard to our relatives.

I now began to be gently conscious of the fact that I had been riding for about five or six hours, but I can hardly imagine how sore one must be not to be able to forget the discomfort and everything else unessential, when fording the big rivers. Breidá and Fjallsá emerge from the ice at the foot of Öraefa Jökull and flow across the *sandur*, forming such a wide and complicated delta that from a distance the whole district looks like a continuous sheet of water, half a mile across, a bay of the sea washing the foot of the great volcano with its glaciers. Even the postman who passes through regularly has to ride here with a guide from Kvísker, for the network of streams alters its courses so frequently that only a person who inspects every day the changes in the water-beds and fords can pilot himself across safely.

One follows the guide and his horse blindly across the river, whether one is a beginner like myself or an old and experienced rider like Jøn Eythorsson. I merely had to cling on to my saddle and take care not to become dizzy from seeing the swirling water which draws one's eyes along with it so that the shore appears to be shooting off in an opposite direction to the current and the horse seems to be walking backwards. However, I had to look sometimes at the river and sometimes at the shore, but—possibly because it was my first experience of this kind of thing—I did certainly find that it was asking rather much to expect me to keep my eyes fixed on a little sandbank in the distance while the water rose and rose, first covering the legs of the horse, then reaching higher over its belly and sides, until finally it broke like a torrent against its shoulders. Where the water was deepest and the current most violent the horse had to strain forward, ploughing along heavily as it placed its hoofs with unerring assurance between the loose stones on the bottom which, in spite of the roar from the water, could be heard rolling and bumping against each other. The whole passage is not rendered more easy by the fact that the water is icy cold, measuring zero degrees to all intents and purposes, and so thick with mud that one can hardly see more than a centimetre deep.

With the first arm of Breidá the worst is now over, the horse gives a jerk and climbs up the opposite bank, which, however, is merely the edge of a bank or island in the network of streams. We go on immediately through the next arm. Sometimes the bank towards which we are steering appears to be quite close, sometimes it glides away so that it seems as if we shall never reach it. So we continue for a full three-quarters of an hour. The horses appear completely unconcerned, they do not even trouble to shake off the water when they get up on land but simply follow with the same immovable placidity as before close behind the leading horse as this one steps down into the next ford.

. . . We rode out on to a part of the *sandur* where the rivers had left behind them only gravel and stones ; an hour's journeying brought us to the first big glacier, Fall Jökull. Here it was not only history, tradition and legends which told the tragic story of the eruption of the volcano—the landscape itself spoke only too plainly.

When two hundred years ago the latent forces of Öraefa Jökull broke out, when the fire flamed up, the gases exploded, the earth shook and the lava seethed and welled out over the rim of the crater, then the ice was melted from underneath. The glacier suddenly slid with enormous floods of water down over the lowlands and washed away whatever blocked its path. Everything perished. That which was not crushed by the ice was drowned in the floods, that which was not consumed by fire was buried beneath the ash and the pumice.

Such was the story told by the chaos of hills and ridges, gravel and boulders and empty water-beds before which we now stood. Together they constituted what in scientific language is called a "dead-ice" landscape such as was formed in Lapland and the northern parts of Finland when the last remnants of the inland glaciers died. However, so far as I know, none of these has been formed as this one was, where a whole glacier was suddenly loosened and hurled down on to the plain below, subsequently melting away slowly under the masses of loose material beneath which it became buried.

(64°N; 17°W.)

(Hans Wilhelmsson Ahlmann : *Land of Ice and Fire:* Translated by Klares and Herbert Lewis.)

Glacial Valley Steps

THE PYRENEES

ALL THE high valleys of mountains go in steps, but those of the Pyrenees in a manner more regular even than those of the Sierra Nevada out in California, which the Pyrenees so greatly resemble. For the steps here are nearly always three in number between the plain and the main chain, and each is entered by a regular gate of rock. So it is in the valley of the Ariège, and so it is in that of the Aston, and so it is in every other valley until you get to the far end where live the cleanly but incomprehensible Basques. Each of these steps is perfectly level, somewhat oval in shape, a mile or two or sometimes five miles long, but not often a mile broad. Through each will run the river of the valley, and upon each side of it there will be rich pastures, and a high plain of this sort is called a *jasse*, the same as in California is called a " flat " : as " Dutch Flat," " Poverty Flat," and other famous flats.

First, then, will come a great gorge through which one marches up from the plain, and then at the head of it very often a waterfall of some kind, along the side of which one forces one's way up painfully through a narrow chasm of rock and finds above one the great green level of the first jasse with the mountains standing solemnly around it. And then when one has marched all along this level one will come to another gorge and another chasm, and when one has climbed over the barrier of rock and risen up another two thousand feet or so, one comes to a second jasse, smaller as a rule than the lower one ; but so high are the mountains that all this climbing into the heart of them does not seem to have reduced their height at all. And then one marches along this second jasse and one comes to yet another gorge and climbs up just as one did the two others, through a chasm where there will be a little waterfall or a large one, and one finds at the top the smallest and most lonely of the jasses. This often has a lake in it. The mountains round it will usually be cliffs, forming sometimes a perfect ring, and so called cirques, or, by the Spaniards, cooking-pots ; and as one stands on the level floor of one such last highest jasse and looks up at the summit of the cliffs, one knows that one is looking at the ridge of the main chain. Then it is one's business, if one desires to conquer the high Pyrenees, to find a sloping place up the cliffs to reach their summits and to go down into the further Spanish valleys. This is the order of the Pyrenean dale, and this was the order of that of the Aston.

(Hilaire Belloc : *The Wing of Dalua*.)

Fjords

NORWAY

THERE ARE few places in the world so strange and still as the furthest end of the deep pocket which is called a fjord. Usually it is quite narrow, and shut in between perpendicular rocks ; it is equally the end of the world as well as the last projection of the land into the limitless sea ; it is the last projection of navigable sea in the midst of a vast, uncouth and generally desolate land. Yet on a ledge of rock under the waterfall a turbine gets a hold, a row of little houses is constructed, and that's all ; the rest is bare, perpendicular rock drapery, majestically folded and mirrored in green water. Out towards the sea a fjord makes a strip of shore ; and already there is a little field, a hut, and a peasant village widely scattered ; there is an aroma of peace, hay and cod, for here the soil is manured with the bones of cod fish.

*   *   *   *   *

And now, let us say, we are again on the lee side of an island ; only choppy waves strike the side of the boat with unpleasant thuds ; across the *sund* there is the glitter of a silvery line ; quite unprepared we sail along a long lake that is tenderly and sweetly rippled ; through its thousands of tiny, scintillating facets, blue and golden rocks, with white snows above, make their image. The *sund* narrows, it is already only just a little path between the rocks ; here the water subsides into absolute unreality, deeply green, as smooth as oil, and silent like a dream ; you must not even breathe so as not to disturb and shatter in it that terrible and unblemished picture of the mountains ; only behind the boat, in the undulating water from the keel, is the trail of a superb peacock's tail. The mountains move apart, and a vast bright sheet is filled with the sky, crinkled like silk the better to shine, glistening and nacreous, and soft like oil ; in lithesome, gliding flashes the gold and amethyst chains of the mountains are mirrored in it ! God, what am I to do with it ! But that is still not the right thing ; a sund is only a sund ; on the other hand, a fjord is, how shall I say it ; in short, it is no longer of this world, and it is impossible to draw it, describe it, or play it on a violin ; dear me, I give it up ; as if I could report on something that is not of this world ! Briefly, it is all rock, and below is the smooth water in which everything is reflected ; and that's it. And on those rocks eternal snow is lying, and waterfalls hang down like veils ; that water is transparent, and green like emerald or something, and as quiet as death, or like infinity, and terrible like the Milky Way ; and these mountains are quite unreal, because they do not stand upon any shore, but on a mere bottomless mirage ; haven't I told you that it is all an illusion ! And sometimes, when in the genuine world the evening hour draws near, such a fine and straight veil of mist rises from that water, and above it peaks and chains of mountains raise themselves, of cosmic nebulous breath ; and so you see, didn't I tell you that it is another world ? And this is not the *Hâkon Adalstein*, but a phantom boat which glides without sound on the silent expanse ; and it is the zero hour, which on the human planet they call midnight, but in this world there is no night, or time. And I saw midnight rainbows hanging from one shore to the other ; a mild and golden sunset mirrored in the sea before a frosty morning dawn ; I saw evening and morning glows dissolve in the tremulous radiance of the waters, the silver comb of the sun teased the sparkling sheet of the ocean ; then the shiny paths of the tritons began to sparkle fearsomely on the sea, and it was day. Goodnight, goodnight, for it is already day, the first hour ; the mountains have screened themselves with a luminous veil, to the North the open sund is glistening white, the sea gurgles coldly, and the last shivering passenger on board begins to read another book.

(Karel Čapek : *Travels in the North*.)

DESERTS

DESERTS

The Desert by Day

SYRIA

AS LONG as you are journeying in the interior of the Desert
you have no particular point to make for as your resting-place.
The endless sands yield nothing but small stunted shrubs ; even
these fail after the first two or three days, and from that time
you pass over broad plains—you pass over newly-reared hills—
you pass through valleys dug out by the last week's storm—and
the hills and the valleys are sand, sand, sand, still sand, and only
sand, and sand, and sand again. The earth is so samely that
your eyes turn towards heaven—towards heaven, I mean, in sense
of sky. You look to the sun, for he is your task-master, and by
him you know the measure of the work that you have done, and
the measure of the work that remains for you to do. He comes
when you strike your tent in the early morning, and then, for the
first hour of the day, as you move forward on your camel, he
stands at your near side, and makes you know that the whole
day's toil is before you ; then for a while, and a long while, you
see him no more, for you are veiled and shrouded, and dare not
look upon the greatness of his glory, but you know where he
strides overhead by the touch of his flaming sword. No words
are spoken, but your Arabs moan, your camels sigh, your skin
glows, your shoulders ache, and for sights you see the pattern and
the web of the silk that veils your eyes, and the glare of the outer
light. Time labours on—your skin glows, your shoulders ache,
your Arabs moan, your camels sigh, and you see the same pattern
in the silk, and the same glare of light beyond ; but conquering
time marches on, and by-and-by the descending sun has com-
passed the heaven, and now softly touches your right arm, and
throws your lank shadow over the sand right along on the way
for Persia. Then again you look upon his face, and the redness of
flames has become the redness of roses ; the fair, wavy cloud that
fled in the morning now comes to his sight once more—comes
blushing, yet still comes on—comes burning with blushes, yet
comes and clings to his side. (Kinglake : *Eothen*.)

The Desert by Night

HE WHO would describe a night in the desert should be, by the grace of God, a poet. For how can its beauty be described, even by one who has watched, revelled, and dreamed through it all ? After the heat of the day it comes as the gentle, compensating, reconciling bestower of unspeakable comfort and inspiration, bringing peace and joy, for which a man longs as for his beloved who atones to him for his long waiting. " Leïla ", the starry night of the desert, Leïla is with justice the Arab's image of all that is fair and joyous. Leïla he calls his daughter ; with the words, " my starry night ", he embraces his beloved ; " Leïla, O Leïla ! " is the musical refrain of his songs. And what a night it is, which here in the desert, after all the burden and discomfort of the day, soothes every sense and feeling ! In undreamt-of purity and brightness the stars shine forth from the dark dome of heaven : the light of the nearest is strong enough to cast slight shadows on the pale ground. With full chest one breathes the pure, fresh, cooling, and invigorating air ; with delight one gazes from star to star, and as their light seems to come nearer and nearer, the soul breaks through the fetters which bind it to the dust and holds converse with other worlds. Not a sound, not a rustle, not even the chirping of a grasshopper interrupts the current of thought and feeling. The majesty, the sublimity of the desert is now for the first time appreciated ; its unutterable peace steals into the traveller's heart.

(Alfred Edmund Brehm : *From North Pole to Equator*.)

Desert: The Southern Sahara

AFTER THE thorn-bush and the solid grassy dunes, the sand begins and does not leave off till it reaches the Libyan coast, the buttresses of the Atlas Mountains, and the Moroccan seaboard, on the Atlantic Ocean. Sometimes it sinks into the bed of a dead river, on the borders of which traces of forsaken cities remain ; sometimes it comes up against mountain masses, like enormous islands, or steep cliffs, but it goes through and over them and continues on its way till finally it is brought to a stop by the shores of the French sea. These vast spaces, which seem boundless to the caravaneer, the motorist, and the airman, form the northern part of Chad. They cover an area nearly as big as France. It takes at least eight days to go by lorry from Fort-Lamy to Faya (Largeau). The Bahr el Ghazal (French), about which there used to be doubt whether it had its source from the Chad or was itself the source of the lake, has solved the problem simply by no longer having any water at all. The Low Countries of Chad (around Faya, the chief town of Borkou-Ennedi-Tibesti) are nothing like the European Low Countries with their white sails everywhere. They resemble a sandy Holland traversed by camels.

Once upon a time—whether yesterday, or under Napoleon, Cæsar, or Sesostris, nobody knows—there were lakes and forests in these desert regions. Here Hannibal came for his supply of elephants with which to conquer Rome ; on the faces of certain rocks drawings of giraffe-hunters can be seen, carved with burins or a harder piece of stone ; in some parts neolithic sites have been discovered, with axes, razors, and other objects in carved stone ; sometimes, beneath an ancient village, still more ancient foundations are exposed by chance in the sand, when a new post is being built, where the baked bricks, the cement, the general design of the walls, and the plan of the city suggests a Roman origin, and which the verbal tradition of the country always attributes to what are called the " Nazarenes," that is to say the whites.

One may attempt to name a date for these works by noting the time when the frontiers were fixed by Islam, which forbade drawings, or by Septimus Severus, who first introduced camels. But it requires the minutest research to discover whether these monumental graffiti on the rocks of Ennedi were inscribed by the great-grandfathers of the present-day population or by men of the first, or quaternary, period, and whether Galaka is 800 years old or is not rather the town that Pliny mentions in the triumph of Balbus by the prophetic name of " Debris ".

The rivers here have disappeared in the sand just as the empires on their banks have passed away into the silence of history.

There remains a population of about 30,000 people, who drive their camels from well to well ; some of them keep oxen, and all of them have sheep or goats. The Teddas, Toubbous, Arnas, Gouroas, Kokordas, Gaëdas, Mourdias, Bidéyats, and Makazas, nomads and semi-nomads mostly of unknown origin, form a density of no more than 0·05 per square kilometre.

The desert, however, provides food enough to live on, so long as the rain falls or water can be obtained from the springs. There is very little rain. In some places there are posts that have had as much as two years of complete drought. But in the neighbourhood of the mountains, which are of volcanic origin, water often rises from the depths of the earth in the form of springs or lakes.

Occasionally a watercourse will suddenly relieve the monotony of a barren stony plateau. In the valleys, among the reeds where the water is hidden between banks of natron, spread clusters of green palms and the hairy trunks of date-trees. These palm-groves are sometimes dense, sometimes sparsely grown ; sometimes they will cling in a mass to a steep slope ; or again they will spread themselves sumptuously beside the broad rings of water. In the date season the whole population makes for these groves and gathers enough provisions for a year ; dates form almost the entire diet of the Teddas.

There are thirty thousand palms around Zougra, Odowéno, Harmanchibé, Dodoua, Kisa, Teski, Yougour, and Sobotéguei ; six thousand at Zoui ; seven thousand spread about the centre of Tibesti in various oases ; as many in the north ; and a fringe to the east at Yedri, Toudoufou, Bonwha, Ofoudoni, and Abo.

The names of the dates are as delightful as the names of the oases or as their taste is to a dried-up palate : " Egnéchi ", yellow and sweet ; " Merno ", red and sugary ; " Fiassou ", oblong ones from Bardaigne ; " Boroguo ", dark red ; and " Foufi ", whitish ; all grown in Tibesti.

They are eaten sometimes fresh, as they are picked, sometimes dried, hardened and compressed in goat-skins, sometimes crushed in butter or milk, and sometimes ground and made into cakes with millet flour.

The core of the young palm is minced and boiled to take away the sharp taste of the juice, and is afterwards dried, ground, and eaten with milk. A notch is made in the trunk, and the sap is extracted, fermented, and made into a wine highly relished by the natives.

A palm-tree is sold, exchanged, mortgaged, given away, or bequeathed in a legacy, just like a piece of property. Eight palms are worth one camel ; eight pieces of white material are worth one palm.

Beneath the shade of the palm-groves, among the meanderings of the *enneris*, there is a certain amount of arable land. Here there are a number of small fields crowded together, usually known as gardens, where wheat is grown ; the ears have scarcely time to become golden before they are gathered by the natives, who are in a hurry to reap their harvest. Here rye and barley ripen, as well as maize, and fine-grained millet ; and occasionally tobacco. A narrow ditch runs round each plot, supplying the precious water, and here and there rise the long poles of the wells.

. . . In 1934, when the survey of the boundaries was begun in the direction of the Libyan frontier, a plateau was discovered, surrounded on one side by steep crags and on the other by more accessible slopes, and identified by the name of Ennedi.

The sides of this plateau are of an almost identical height, about four or five hundred feet. The appearance of the forbidding rocks varies according to the wind to which they are exposed. The side facing the prevailing wind is eaten away, crumbling, dilapidated, and covered with sand. The others are solid and sharp, bleak and lonely, without a trace of sand, and present an unscalable wall ; above, their vertical peaks form a frieze to the flat plateau, which is supported below by masses of fallen rocks.

. . . Ennedi is a triangular plateau or group of plateaux. The base of the triangle measures about 190 miles, and is between longitudes 16° and 18°. The other sides are about 250 miles long. Its altitude is 4,000 to 4,500 feet.

These dimensions are exceeded by the solid mass of Tibesti. This pile of sandstone stretches northward in two ridges uniting in the region of Koussi, where they are amplified by this volcano and culminate in a peak of nearly 13,000 feet.

Before this peak is reached, however, one of the highest in Africa, a bleak barren plain has to be crossed, covered with volcanic fragments that crackle under the feet, after which rises a sort of enormous lip forming the edge of the crater.

The sharp and angular contours are perfectly clear-cut. The rocks, now smooth, now shelving, appear to be steeper than they actually are owing to the extreme limpidity of the air, which distorts the perspective : distances seem shorter, the reliefs are exaggerated. At the bottom of the abyss, 1,000 feet below, stretches a carpet of natron, like a snow-lake. No living creature is to be seen. One wonders how many millions of tons of carbonate of soda are contained in this reservoir. The thick slabs and enormous crystals are jammed together in a colossal pile inside the crater for an unimagined depth. After ceasing to be active, the volcano of Koussi acquired a lake. The lake then dried up, leaving a vast bowl of natron. This was perhaps hundreds of centuries, millions of years ago.

After climbing a little towards the northerly heights, one is surprised to come across an unexpected valley, bristling with jagged rocks, quite narrow, and of a most forbidding aspect. Here there is a strange village of troglodytes, so completely hidden among the crags that one fails to see it till one is nearly upon it. Three doors open on to a courtyard thick with goats' dung ; all around small niches have been carved in the rock, the entrances to which are barred by shutters of dry stone.

A stiff climb up a rocky stairway leads to the pass of Tiribor, through which go the roads to Misky to the north-west and to Tozeur and Goumeur towards the north-east.

In front of us the mountain slopes down in sharp gradients to the north ; the heights of Tibesti rear their jagged outlines against the sky till they are lost to view. On our left the walls of the crater fade into the rocky mass ; to our right rise numerous pointed peaks.

At the very top there is a small platform cluttered with rocks and covered with red and mauve flowers, where the view extends over an immense area of rugged crests, isolated rocks, dark gorges, and open escarpments. Every mountain range is tinted with purest rose, rich in the foreground, shaded with violet as it recedes farther into the distance. The heights of Tibesti shelve down eastwards in gigantic steps. Westward, the mountains close round a seemingly endless plain, a sombre desert of stone whose dark shadows enhance the purple magnificence of the loftier ridges. A sky of deepest blue enfolds the summits. Faya, or Largeau, as it is called officially, is the chief town of the Department of Borkou-Ennedi-Tibesti.

(*Between about 20°N; 15°E. and 17°N; 22°E.*)
(Pierre Olivier Lapie : *My Travels Through Chad:* Translated by Leslie Bull.)

Deserts: The Northern Sahara and the Schotts

IT WAS on our second day out that we came to a deep and far-reaching depression in the desert's surface. The stony ground broke away suddenly in a long irregular slant, and descended steeply to the bottom of the valley. Standing on the summit we had a view across to the low cliffs a few miles off on the opposite side. Eastward the flats, widening as they went, stretched to the horizon. That part which we were about to cross was but a narrow tongue ; the last creek or bay, evidently, of this vast trough.

But the peculiarity of the view, and what arrests one in some astonishment, is that all the floor of the hollow is loosely paved with what at this distance seem like broken fragments of ice. The scales and pieces, twinkling and flashing in the sunlight and stretching away for miles into the distance, look exactly like the photographs and sketches one has seen of ice-floes in the northern seas.

This depression of which we stand on the verge is one of the most noteworthy features in the Sahara. From here eastward there stretches a chain of these salt lakes for over two hundred miles to the east coast of Tunisia. The Shott Melrir is the westernmost of the line. It is followed by the Shott Rharsa, the much larger Shott Jerid, and the Shott al-Fejij, which reaches to within about twenty miles of Gabes on the Tunisian coast. These lakes, which once formed a deep bay of the sea, are still considerably below sea-level, from which they are cut off by the sandbanks of the east coast. It has been shown that before the present total sterilisation of the Sahara, a large river system, both from north and south, drained into this now extinct sea. It received the torrents from the Atlas range, and it received, what was far more important, the large rivers which drained the mountains and plains of Central Africa.

As the desert spread, and gradually encroached upon, and finally blotted out, the verdure of the country, these mighty streams dried up, or sank such waters as they collected from the mountain rainfall below the sandy floor of the desert. Unfed by tributary rivers, the arm of sea gradually contracted and silted up. The sandbanks grew and extended across its mouth until they joined, and, forming a continuous chain, cut it off from the sea altogether, and then under the fierce African sun its waters rapidly evaporated. In winter, when the streams come down from the northern mountains, a few reach as far as these lakes, which then turn into salt marshes dangerous to cross. With summer the streams fail, the water dries up, and a glittering field of white and scaly salt is all that remains.

Any one who knows the Arab love of metaphor will expect to hear that a sight so extraordinary as this dazzling view in mid-desert will have been made a target of by their metaphorical marksmen. Quite a number of pretty phrases have become embroidered round it. It is like a bowl of glittering soapsuds, like a cake of camphor, like a sea of opal, like a cake of florescent crystal, like a pail of molten lead and gold ; and in the evening, when the peaks of the Aurés fade away, purple and blood-coloured in the short twilight, it is like a leaf of blanched silver.

What in remote antiquity was the aspect of this northern depression it is impossible to divine. But the existence of these great rivers is proof of the fertility of the regions through which they passed. And of the existence of the rivers there is no question. In the midst of this deadness and sterility one can still read, in the wide beds and chiselled rocks, the evidence of the force and volume of water that once poured through this waste. Still the upper Irgharghar, rising in the Ahaggar range in mid-desert, sometimes after heavy rains will carry a current as far as Amguid. The lower river carries no water at any time in the year, though its course is traceable in places by the rounded fragments of rock of its bed. Yet explorers have narrated that the old channels of the great Saharan rivers, like the Mia and the Irgharghar, sometimes after a rare, torrential downpour develop in an instant a majestic flood that rolls proudly in mid-desert with the strength of old days for a few hours and a few miles, and is then sucked down into the porous soil.

The Ahaggar range girdles the basin on the south, while the Tademait Plateau bounds it on the south-west. In these two mountain-formations the two main streams of the basin had their source. They united near Tugurt and flowed thence to the sea. Curiously enough, it is the ends and feeble tributaries of these extinct Niles that still survive, while the main rivers they fed have long disappeared. The smaller streams, raised above the reach of the encroaching sand, still gather the occasional rains that fall upon the uplands ; but betwixt those mountains and the site of the old sea stretches an ocean of tumbled sand-dunes, their rounded monotonous summits, unrelieved by a speck of green, not unlike the petrified billows of some ocean solitude. They have wiped out and buried the old rivers, whose course is now fitfully traceable where the surface is hard, or by the wells that have been sunk to tap the water beneath, or the moisture that rises in the depressions between the dunes and gives life to a grove of date-palms and an Arab village.

(34°30′N; 6°E.) (L. March Phillipps : *In the Desert.*)

Desert

LIBYA

ON THE second day we reached the main body of the serried sand-dunes which run in parallel lines southwards from Siwa towards the Sudan border. They stretched right across our path, and, mounting to the top of a dune some hundred feet high, we looked over a truly awe-inspiring waste of billowed sand. To get some idea of its appearance one has to envisage the Bay of Biscay or the sea off the Cape of Good Hope in a gale of wind and imagine it suddenly immobilized and turned a pale putty-coloured yellow with the shadows under the wave-crests picked out in purples and mauves. In a way it was grandly beautiful, but it was also extremely forbidding, and the fact that the waves of sand where they faded into the haze of the horizon appeared to be steeper and more colossal than those close at hand made our prospects of finding our way through seem small indeed.

(29°N; 25°E.) (C. S. Jarvis : *Three Deserts.*)

Desert: Seif Dunes

THE SAND-SEA OF THE LIBYAN SAHARA

THEN THE scenery changed again. We emerged once more on to open unbroken ground of hard grey rock spotted with pools of good firm sand. Ahead not far away, along the whole of the western horizon, lit up by an early morning sun, lay the golden wall of the dunes. Through field-glasses their regular rows of summits could be seen. There was nothing else. The earth was dead flat, and on nearer approach to the dunes they seemed in contrast to rise up in front as mountain ranges. By noon the outermost rampart of sand was reached, a straight line of summits running across our path. Regularly spaced crests towered up as if a giant wave were about to break.

Leaving the cars on hard ground at the foot we climbed the highest crest. The surface rose easily at first at an angle of not more than one in three, but steepened suddenly after the first hundred feet to the maximum angle, that at which sand begins to collapse if disturbed. Rivers of sand started to descend with each new step, carrying one's feet downwards almost as fast as they were raised. The aneroid showed the range of dunes to be well over three hundred feet in height.

From the top the view was distinctly encouraging. The range was a single knife-edge ridge fifteen or twenty miles long but with a definite southern end. Farther west lay more flat rocky ground for several miles, then another parallel range of sand also limited in length, dwindling southwards to a pointed snout ; beyond that lay another and another overlapping each other. It looked as if by winding up and down we might be able to work round these dunes, keeping on hard ground all the time. But it was difficult to tell ; everything was on such a big scale, and the dunes, casting no shadow, seemed unreal, merging sometimes with the sky and sometimes with the ground.

Ten miles farther south the cars rounded our dune range without difficulty through a gap between it and another over-lapping one. But things looked different down on the level ground; in the general dazzle little could be distinguished of what we had seen from up above. Soon another bank of yellow loomed up ahead continuous, smooth and featureless, an uncertain distance away. Should we attempt to cross it ? There was no alternative unless we gave up altogether, and we were already through the outer rampart which others had looked at and deemed un-crossable.

I increased speed to forty miles an hour, feeling like a small boy on a horse about to take his first big fence. I saw Burridge holding on to the side of the lorry grimly. Suddenly the light doubled in strength as if more suns had been switched on. A huge glaring wall of yellow shot up high into the sky a yard in front of us. The lorry tipped violently backwards—and we rose as in a lift, smoothly without vibration. We floated up and up on a yellow cloud. All the accustomed car movements had ceased ; only the speedometer told us we were still moving fast. It was incredible. Instead of sticking deep in loose sand at the bottom as instinct and experience both foretold, we were now near the top a hundred feet above the ground. Then the skyline receded disclosing a smooth blank surface of some sort, nearly level. The glare was intense ; one could distinguish nothing, but from the slow rolling movements of the lorry we must be going over a series of gentle undulations.

I cut off the engine and let the car come to rest gently to wait for the others. The sand was covered with little ripples that had flown by too fast to be seen while the car was on the move. Our wheel tracks behind were barely half an inch deep ; they trailed out behind quite cleanly like a pair of railway lines. Yet the sand was quite soft ; I ran my fingers through it easily, and there was no surface crust to support the wheels. It was just the special way the grains were packed.

I remembered then for the first time a chance remark of Clayton's while describing his boundary commission trip two years previously, about running along the tops of some dunes instead of between them because it was easier. Not understanding what he meant and thinking I had heard him wrong I had dismissed it without a thought.

This was like no dune we had seen before. It wasn't a dune at all. It had no steep collapsing breakers along its top, and was almost flat. We drove for over a half mile across it before dropping over its westward decline on to solid ground once more. To the north and south this streak or whaleback of sand ran on quite straight as far as we could see, but some miles away the ordinary steep-sided crested dunes were growing on the broad top of it like a line of parasitic fungi upon a fallen tree-trunk.

Another strip of solid ground, this time only two miles wide, separated this sand from its neighbour farther west. The latter looked quite different, breaker-like as the first one we had met, an uncrossable chain of loose collapsing crests with no gap for many miles, till at length after running southwards along its foot the crests were found to shrink in size and to disappear for a space, disclosing the real bulk behind, another great whaleback similar to the one we had crossed.

We penetrated another fifteen miles into the dunes that day, working north or south along the ranges until a gap in the crests was found, and crossed six ranges before camping for the night on the top of a particularly large whaleback. Every range was of the same dual character for the greater part of its length : a low whaleback up to a mile wide of coarse firm sand, with a chain of crests of fine mobile grains lying on the top along the brink of the eastern side. Sometimes if the crested chain was very big it occupied most of the top, sometimes it was absent altogether, in which case the eastern slope of the whaleback was very firm and easily climbed.

Anywhere in the neighbourhood of the crests, though, the sand was soft and yielding. We got stuck many times even after learning to avoid the obviously dangerous spots ; for there were other places, pools of " liquid " sand, in appearance just like the rest of the surface, but so soft one could plunge a six-foot rod vertically into them without effort.

(Ralph A. Bagnold : *Libyan Sands*.)

Desert: The Erg

THE OUED SOUF, lying eastward of Tuggurt, forms a portion of the Grand Erg, the region of pure sand-dunes. The decomposition of the desert's structure—of rock and cliff and plateau—is here completely carried out. The last pebble has been resolved into the grains that composed it. The whole landscape is a testimony to the successful perseverance of the sand, and bears witness to its victory.

Hour after hour, and day after day for several days, the curved slopes of sand lay round us as pure as drifts of snow just fallen. Not a blade of green marked their surface. The whiteness of the sand was dazzling, and its absolute monotony and sameness, combined with the deep, equally unvarying blue of the sky, produced an effect of eccentricity not far removed from the grotesque.

The dunes succeeded each other in an endless array of hillocks, rarely divided, in my recollection, by any appreciable flat. The caravan proceeds by winding in and out between their bases. Let the reader picture a field sprinkled, as thickly as they can be set together, with molehills. Let him, if he can, by an effort of the imagination, turn those molehills pure white, and see with his mind's eye a string of black insects making a corkscrew progress by winding in and out between them, and he will have a bird's-eye view of our caravan among the dunes.

As we entered into these white defiles an unutterable deadness, emptiness, and mortal stillness seemed to close about us. The unreality of the landscape was added to by the loss of all sense of proportion. The scenery is mountainous on a diminutive scale.

It suggests an endless array of chains of hills and mountain summits, the similarity of which in shape to formations of real ranges gives the idea of considerable size. Crest beyond crest and ridge beyond ridge, they stretch away into the distance. It is impossible to judge their dimensions or the width of the valleys that separate them. Nothing exists that can supply a standard of measurement ; no tree, or house, or rock, or other object gives scale to the picture. No atmospheric effect softens the further outlines and suggests their distance. In this pure air you see all things, as it were, in a vacuum, and the distant ranges are as clear and white as the nearer ones.

Under these circumstances the instinct of a European is enormously to exaggerate the size and distance apart of the hills. The peak you see some way off, lifting its head above its fellows, will seem a Mont Blanc, to be measured in thousands of feet. The last range you can distinguish on the horizon will seem a day's journey off. In five minutes you are passing under Mont Blanc, which turns out to be a hillock of two or three hundred feet high, and in another five are crossing the range where you thought to camp for the night.

In spite of constant correction I never could get the hang of this scenery. Again and again I rubbed the illusion of great size and great space out of my eyes, but it always returned. Our caravan itself was the only object that could give a standard, and this it sometimes did with very startling effect. Repeatedly, after riding forward, H—— and I would sit on some blond summit and watch the vast tumbled expanse that lay around us until we had all unconsciously received the impression of its vastness. Then through a gap far away would come a terrifying spectacle— gigantic beasts, half as big as the hills themselves, with curved, outstretched necks, and huge men lolling on their backs. They came bearing down upon us with leisurely gait, that somehow left hills and valleys behind in a few steps. For a moment one was aware of a struggle between scenery and camels as to the correct size of scale. Then as the realisation of Ahmeda's cooking-pots asserted itself the scenery would give in and collapse pitifully to its real dimensions.

(*33°N; 7°30′E.*) (L. March Phillipps : *In the Desert.*)

Desert: Barchan Dunes

THE OASIS (Bir Natrun) lies in a typical Libyan desert depression, with cliffs rising above it to the north-east and east. The prevailing wind which in this latitude blows from the north-east has worn the cliff away, stringing out the debris as a field of sand dunes along gently rising ground for sixty miles to leeward.

These dunes, however, in fact all the dunes in the south-eastern portion of the Libyan Desert, are of quite a different type from the long continuous ridges, or " swords " (Seif) as the Arabs call them, which cover such huge areas in the north and west. The shape of this second type of dune, the Barchan or Crescent Dune, is distinctive. It may be described as a circular dome of sand, from the leeward side of which a big bite has been taken, leaving a steep slope of loose flowing grains in the form of a hollow semi-circle. The Barchan advances down-wind as a crescent with its two horns, each tapering to a point of sand on the ground, reaching out in front of it. The horns of a single Barchan may be as far apart as 400 yards, its maximum height may be 70 to 100 feet, and its weight something up to half a million tons.

Individual dunes of this type can exist by themselves many miles from their nearest neighbours and in country otherwise quite free from scattered sand grains ; but it is usual for them to grow in colonies reaching down-wind in a broad belt, separated by shorter and shorter distances from one another as one goes towards the source of the sand, that is, toward the windward end of the colony. Here the individuals are packed so close together that they run into one another, but in all cases the characteristic crescent bite is preserved.

The Barchan consists of two simple surfaces, the dome and the concave surface of loose collapsing sand round the bite. The dune keeps its simple geometrical shape intact with extraordinary persistence even while it is on the move, and while it is passing over such large obstacles as rocks, small hillocks, and villages.

Some innate tendency, some unknown effect of the interaction of wind and sand, keeps the ends of the two widely separated horns exactly level with each other. One can imagine some consciousness sitting on the domed top like a charioteer, checking each of them in turn in their blind advance, with a pair of invisible reins. Perhaps the fundamental difference between these

Barchans and the longitudinal Seif dunes described previously in this book can be pictured by imagining the above checking tendency to be abolished, the reins broken, so that one of the two heads bolts ahead, leaving the other behind to shrink and disappear. The inside face of the crescent, which has up to now been dragged forward evenly between the heads, is now left behind waving sinuously in the wind, forming the long single crest of a Seif dune.

I think the desert dunes, specially the Barchans, must be accounted definite organisms, existing by themselves and owing nothing to the surrounding land for their shape, which seems to be as inherent in them as is that of an organism of the life to which we are accustomed. I do not mean " live " in the animistic sense in which I have spoken of them before, the sense in which a traveller or climber endows obstacles and mountains with hostility or friendliness, but in the much more real sense that these dunes appear to ape most of the attributes we think essential for a definition of life.

For as long as they are fed with a supply of grains, and as long as a motive power is available from the wind—just as the true life requires food and motive power from the sun's rays to keep it alive—the dunes can move from place to place, can grow in size, can maintain their own particular shape and repair any damage done to them, and lastly, in the case of the Barchan dunes, there is some evidence that they are capable of a sort of reproduction whereby baby dunes are formed in the open a hundred yards or so down-wind of the horn of a fully-grown parent. (Ralph A. Bagnold : *Libyan Sands*.)

Mirage

SYRIAN DESERT BETWEEN HOMS AND BAGHDAD

AS I drove through the Syrian desert from Tripoli through Homs on my way to Baghdad I had to pass through the rows of orange columns and arcades which mark the site of Palmyra, the city of the noble-hearted queen Zenobia, who dared to stand against the power of Rome nearly seventeen centuries ago. Her city, among the beautiful relics of which a few Arab huts and a wretched khan now seek shelter from the sun, has been superb in splendour, and amid the sandstone cliffs and desert spaces one came upon it as a miracle. But where, I wondered, was water for so magnificent a place? One small well for the villagers was evident in the middle of an open square, but that was all. I drove on, regretfully leaving so strange a memorial of an almost forgotten age and woman, but as I entered upon the flat desert that extends almost to the Euphrates, I looked south and there lay a vast sheet of brilliant water, the edge not more than a mile or two away, and here and there it was fringed with palm trees and bushes, wavering in the steamy heat.

" Plenty of water there for all the queens of the world to drink and wash in," I thought, and asked the driver to turn aside so that I might swim out into the lake and be cool.

" It is a mirage," he objected.

" Why is it there ? " I asked, unable to believe him.

" By God's will," he answered ; " it is always there."
(*34°30'N; 38°15'E.*)

(Henry W. Nevinson : *In the Dark Backward.*)

Mirage

LIBYAN DESERT SOUTH-WEST OF KHARGA OASIS

AFTER LEAVING camp next day there was nothing at all to be seen, except at intervals a range of unknown hills far away to the west. The rock outcrops dwindled to mere patches of loose flake and then ceased altogether. Only a boundless sand-sheet remained, whose tiny ripples glided by without any perceptible vibration of the car. As the surface warmed up, a mirage, hovering in the distance, approached to within half a mile, to surround us on every side like a vast sheet of steaming water. We were flies crawling across the upper surface of an almost submerged ball revolving slowly in a round pool. During all the midday hours there was no land in sight, not even a horizon, for the mirage curled up into the sky—nothing but the sun and the blue disc above, and the sandy disc below, the two separated by a close wall of dazzling shimmer. We would stop to wait for the other cars humming invisibly behind. Presently a sea-beast would break through the surface of the mirage, elongate quickly to a factory chimney, and as quickly shrink to a motor-car as it reached the shore of reality.

(*24°N; 29°E.*) (Ralph A. Bagnold : *Libyan Sands.*)

358

Oases

TUNIS

THERE ARE in the desert of southern Tunisia three great oases : Gabes by the sea, a little north of that island of Djerba which is, traditionally, the classical Island of the Lotus Eaters ; Tozeur, to the west of it, some seventy miles inland ; and Nefta, fifteen miles west of Tozeur, the starting-point of the caravans which trade between southern Tunisia and the great oases of the Algerian Sahara, Biskra and Touggourt. These oases are all of much the same size, each consisting of some six or seven thousand acres of cultivated ground, and are all three remarkable for their numerous and copious springs. In the middle of the desert, suddenly, a hundred fountains come welling out of the sand ; rivers run, a network of little canals is dug. An innumerable forest of date-palms springs up—a forest whose undergrowth is corn and roses, vines and apricot trees, olives and pomegranates, pepper trees, castor-oil trees, banana trees, every precious plant of the temperate and the sub-tropical zones. No rain falls on these little Edens—except on the days of my arrival—but the springs, fed from who knows what distant source, flow inexhaustibly and have flowed at least since Roman times. Islanded among the sands, their green luxuriance is a standing miracle. That it should have been in a desert, with here and there such islands of palm trees, that Judaism and Mohammedanism took their rise is a thing which, since I have seen an oasis, astonishes me. The religion which, in such a country, would naturally suggest itself to me would be no abstract monotheism, but the adoration of life, of the forces of green and growing nature. In an oasis, it seems to me, the worship of Pan and of the Great Mother should be celebrated with an almost desperate earnestness. The nymphs of water and of trees ought surely, here, to receive a passionate gratitude. In the desert, I should infallibly have invented the Greek mythology. The Jews and the Arabs discovered Jahweh and Allah. I find it strange.

A fertile oasis possesses a characteristic colour scheme of its own, which is entirely unlike that of any landscape in Italy or the north. The fundamental note is struck by the palms. Their foliage, except where the stiff shiny leaves metallically reflect the light, is a rich blue-green. Beneath them, one walks in a luminous aquarium shadow, broken by innumerable vivid shafts of sunlight that scatter gold over the ground or, touching the trunks of the palm trees, make them shine a pale ashy pink through the sub-aqueous shadow. There is pink, too, in the glaring whiteness of the sand beyond the fringes of the oasis. Under the palms, beside the brown or jade-coloured water, glows the bright emerald green of corn or the deciduous trees of the north, with here and there the huge yellowish leaves of a banana tree, the smoky grey of olives, or the bare bone-white and writhing form of a fig tree.

As the sun gradually sinks, the aquarium shadow beneath the palm trees grows bluer, denser ; you imagine yourself descending through layer after darkening layer of water. Only the pale skeletons of the fig-trees stand out distinctly ; the waters gleam like eyes in the dark ground ; the ghost of a little marabout or chapel shows its domed silhouette, white and strangely definite in the growing darkness, through a gap in the trees. But looking up from the depths of this submarine twilight, one sees the bright pale sky of evening, and against it, still touched by the level, rosily-golden light, gleaming as though transmuted into sheets of precious metal, the highest leaves of the palm trees.

A little wind springs up ; the palm leaves rattle together ; it is suddenly cold. " *En avant*," we call. Our little guides quicken their pace. We follow them through the darkening mazes of the palm forest, out into the open. The village lies high on the desert plateau above the oasis, desert-coloured, like an arid outcrop of the tawny rock. We mount to its nearest gate. Through passage-ways between blank walls, under long dark tunnels the children lead us—an obscure and tortuous way which we never succeeded in thoroughly mastering—back to the square market-place at the centre of the town. The windows of the inn glimmer invitingly. We enter. Within the hotel it is provincial France.

(*34°N; 8°30'E.*)   (Aldous Huxley : *The Olive Tree.*)

Oasis

SAHARA SOUTH OF THE SCHOTTS

WHAT ONE has to remember is that the constant war which the desert wages against any form of settlement and fixed abode is the dominating fact of desert life. Every inch of cultivated ground, and they are few and far between, has to be daily defended against the enemy. Sand penetrates like water, and just as the sailor has to be constantly at work caulking and overhauling every part of his vessel to keep it seaworthy and watertight, so the Arab in the desert has to guard and repair his oasis to keep it sandtight.

It is no easy task. The sand is constantly on the move. When the wind rises, the dunes, as the Arabs say, " walk." The word is very expressive of what takes place, for the rustling of the sand as it pours along the ground, and the rapid change in the shape of the drifts, give a strong impression of actual motion in the whole landscape. To prevent the obliteration of their gardens the Arabs plant rows of palm-leaves round the brims of the hollows, and along all the crests of the neighbouring dunes. It looks a childish expedient, but it is not without its effect. The sand is first set in motion along the sides of the dunes, and pours and rushes up the slope (each grain rounded to a marble in the process), and it is not till it reaches the crest of the ridge that it rises like smoke into the air. At this point the palm-leaf borders intercept it and lay it to rest. When, indeed, the dunes walk in good earnest, nothing can arrest them. The sand rises at every point under the lashing wind, turns the sky a uniform, swarthy red, and blots out the view at the distance of a hundred yards. The spectacle of a landscape of dunes in rapid motion all around you, their crests melting and smoking in the wind, is one of the most curious, but to the husbandman or the traveller the most menacing that the desert has to offer.

(33°N; 7°30'E.) (L. March Phillipps : *In the Desert.*)

Desert: The Gobi, just East of Ansi-Chow
MONGOLIA

THIRTY-FIVE MILES further on is Pulungki, a city that must once have held at least fifty thousand inhabitants, but which is now nothing but scattered ruins, a few poor inns, and an encircling wall of immense area. During the next few nights we counted ten more deserted towns and villages, and no words can adequately convey the extraordinary sensations evoked by crossing in the moonlight, or in the uncertain pallor of dawn, these abodes of the past, whose deserted streets are sometimes still clearly defined, and where abandoned houses, with yawning doorways, stand tenantless on

either side. From dateless ages the Gobi Desert has approached with stealthy steps ; moving, like some sluggish organism, till with soft, hungry lips it has seized its prey and absorbed it ; and then, replete and satisfied, has lain down triumphant. The surrounding scene is of an unspeakably desolate character, reminding one of a landscape on the moon, only that instead of extinct craters, here are dead and forgotten cities, towns, and villages.
(41°N; 97°E.)
(Mildred Cable and Francesca French : *Through Jade Gate and Central Asia.*)

Desert Hollows

MONGOLIA : THE GOBI

ON THE night of April 23, 1922, we camped near the telegraph station of P'ang Kiang, on the floor of the first large, clearly defined desert hollow which we had crossed in our journey. Subsequently we were to see hundreds of such hollows, some larger and many smaller than the one at P'ang Kiang. They are all formed in the same way, and are of later origin than the Gobi erosion plane in which they are cut. We gave the name " P'ang Kiang " to the stage of erosion which they represent.

The desert hollows could not possibly be excavated without the work of wind ; no other agency could lift material out of an enclosed lowland. Almost every day while we were camped in such a hollow, we saw the "whirling pillars " of dust racing across its dry floor. During violent windstorms the air was dark with flying dust and sand and the sun was dim and red. Dust veils hung in the air for several days after the biggest windstorms. Much of the stirred-up sand and dust settles upon the surrounding country, but no doubt some of the finer material is exported to great distances, even beyond the rim of the Gobi.

The sides of the hollow are dissected by rainwash and by rills from the upland. During epochs of active erosion, the sloping bluffs are fretted into typical badlands, and the loose sediment is washed down to the floor of the hollow. As soon as the thin flat apron of sediment is dry, it is exposed to the tireless winds, which carry much of it out of the hollow. The retreat of the bluffs and the lateral enlargement of the hollow is thus mainly the work of running water. Because most of the streams that run into the hollow are temporary rills that flow only while the rain falls, vigorous cutting will not be done, except on the steep slopes. Gullies are rarely seen on the floor of the hollow, and still more rarely on the upland. The gullies along the bluffs are very short, heading a little way behind the edge of the scarp and dying out a short distance beyond its foot. There is thus a narrow zone of active stream-dissection along the scarp—a zone which retreats with the scarp as the latter is cut back.

Undrained hollows were found in granite regions also. They are most common in coarse-grained granites, and seem to coincide, in part at least, with the pattern of stream courses. There is surprisingly little waste in the hollows—only a thin cover of arkosic sand and, locally, a rubble of disintegrating granite blocks. The coarse granite tends to break up under the action of frost and changes of temperature. It weathers chemically also, for the rock bears rusty stains, and the feldspars are somewhat kaolinized. As the rock disintegrates into grains which the wind can carry, these grains are removed, and the hollow deepens until it approaches the depth at which ground-water lies. The sides of the growing hollow are carved by short evanescent streams, just as in the sediment-basins. During dry seasons or cycles, the wind will continue to blow away the finer dust and to deepen the excavation. Should the ground water level rise during a season or cycle of heavier rainfall, a pond will form in the bottom of the hollow, and the exportation of material will be checked, although rills which course down the sides of the bowl may continue to enlarge it laterally.

(Charles P. Berkey and Frederick K. Morris : *The Geology of Mongolia*.)

Desert Pediment

MONGOLIA

IN AUGUST, 1922, we were camped at the foot of Artsa Bogdo, on the rock shelf which stands forty feet above the streams issuing from the mountain, and has a slope of eight degrees. During a rainstorm which lasted for about two hours, the water swept in a sheet under our tents, though after the heaviest squall it settled into shallow runways. The rock surface of the erosion plane is marked by an infinite network of shallow rill courses, and is thinly and unevenly strewn with small chips of native rock, which no doubt are carried by vigorous little streams such as we saw form and fade during the storm. They are the tools with which the running water abrades the bedrock, which is so deeply weathered and disintegrated that we found it impossible to secure fresh samples, except in the walls of the deeper gullies ; for mechanical and chemical weatherings are especially active along the mountain foot, where rocks are alternately saturated and dried at frequent intervals, and where the surface run-off and the underground escape of water are slower than in the steep mountains. The wind does not contribute to the carving of the erosion surface, except in a very minor degree ; the chief role must be ascribed to the myriad short-lived streamlets acting upon the weathered rock of the piedmont. These transient rills run together into little drainage systems, which are not wholly integrated, but may either fall into some larger channel, or may die out leaving a thin, flat cover of angular fragments over the slope.

(Charles B. Berkey and Frederick K. Morris : *The Geology of Mongolia*.)

Salt Steppes

EVEN WHEN we traverse the monotonous valleys many miles in breadth, or the almost unbroken plains, whose far horizon is but an undulating line, when we see one almost identical picture to north, south, east, and west, when the apparent infinitude raises a feeling of loneliness and abandonment, even then we must allow that the steppes have more to show than our heaths, for the vegetation is much richer, more brilliant, and more changeful. Indeed, it is only here and there, where the salt-steppes broaden out around a lake, that the landscape seems dreary and desolate. In such places none of the steppe plants flourish, and their place is taken by a small, scrubby saltwort, not unlike stunted heather, only here and there attaining the size of low bushes. The salt lies as a more or less thick layer on the ground, filling the hollows between the bushes so that they look like pools covered with ice. Salt covers the whole land, keeping the mud beneath permanently moist, adhering firmly to the ground, and hardly separable from it. Great balls of salt and mud are raised by the traveller's feet and the horses' hoofs at every step, just as if the ground were

364

covered with slushy snow. The waggon makes a deep track in
the tough substratum, and the trundling wheels sometimes leave
marks on the salt like those left on snow in time of hard frost.
Such regions are in truth indescribably dismal and depressing,
but elsewhere it is not so.

(Alfred Edmund Brehm : *From North Pole to Equator*.)

Loess

NORTH CHINA

THE SUPREME hold of the yellow earth upon the people and
their lives is due to its unique topographical role. Where the
yellow earth prevails, it rules over the land and the waters, and
even over the air, which is filled with its fine dust with every
storm that blows.

Huang T'u, the yellow earth, is the name given by the Chinese
to the dust-fine soil which rules over Northern China. Western
science has taught us to call it loess, because in the Rhineland a
similar soil has been thus named.

The most striking thing about the Northern Chinese loess formation is its particularly fantastic topography. Broadly speaking,
the loess deposits form a cover which fills up the valleys and above
which the mountain ridges rise in much the same way as our own
mountains stick up in winter out of the cover of snow. Indeed,
this comparison with a snow-covered landscape is in reality very
significant, for according to Richthofen's now generally accepted
theory of the formation of the loess it is, like snow, an Eolian
sediment, i.e. it has been transported by the wind and laid to rest
where the velocity of the wind is least and where the configuration
of the ground offers shelter and protection.

But we now come to a description of the process, later than the
formation of the loess deposits, which has imparted to the modern
landscape its picturesque, puzzling, and to the inexperienced
traveller, positively bewildering character. The once unbroken
cover of loess has been disintegrated and intersected by rain-
water, so that an excursion in the loess region becomes a wonderful
experience, in which the wanderer often stops short with surprise
and even trembling before perpendicular drops of 30 metres or
more. Or he may meet thin, fantastic pillars of the yellow earth,
or he will glimpse bits of landscape through natural tunnels or

arches which remain standing for some time while the washing away of the loess proceeds. The loess ravines are gulleys with almost perpendicular walls and are so narrow that not infrequently the depth is greater than the breadth. If we follow such a gulley to its innermost part we shall find to our surprise in most cases that it has its full depth from the beginning. It will soon become clear to the acute observer that these ravines were not formed by water running on the surface. During the great summer rains, it is true, the water rushes in cascades from the fields down into the depths, but the essential process of erosion is of quite a different kind.

In order to understand the manner of formation of the loess ravines we must examine the yellow earth a little more closely. The typical Huang T'u is a greyish yellow dust which does not as a rule show any stratification, but shows, on the other hand, a remarkable capacity for adhering to perpendicular cliffs. This fine, porous earth easily lets through the water which falls upon its surface. Consequently only a part of the summer rains drain off its surface. For a large part of the rainfall it acts like a sponge, or, perhaps better, like a gigantic filter, through which the water sinks to the bedrock of the loess deposits, consisting of gravel, Tertiary clay or solid rock. The lower part of the loess soil in this way often becomes saturated with water and assumes a consistency like that of a thin porridge or gruel. This bottom layer then slowly begins to move and slides down any slope, and in proportion as the saturated bottom slides away towards the open valley, the superimposed, relatively dry mass of loess sinks down perpendicularly. This vertical movement may be studied everywhere in the ravines, in which one sees large and small blocks of the old vegetation-covered surface in all sorts of more or less inclined positions half-way or more down to the bottom of the ravine. Only when we have clearly understood this curious process of erosion, which occurs, not on the surface, but, on the contrary, by the flow of the basic portion of the loess, shall we be able to understand the remarkable and extremely fantastic topography of the loess landscape ; the narrow ravines with their perpendicular walls and uniform depth right to their source, the detached islands and castle-like pillars, and, not least, the frail vaults and arches.

. . . That large parts of Northern China were an undrained grass steppe during the period of loess formation I can prove directly by my investigations on the Yellow River. I have had occasion to navigate or otherwise follow this mighty and peculiar river for long stretches, from its emergence from the Tibetan highlands right down to the point at the Peking-Hankow railway bridge where it flows into the great Northern Chinese alluvial plain. Almost everywhere along this stretch of 2,000 km. the river is surrounded by loess formations, which in many places form high, almost perpendicular banks. From the two banks of the river these face each other in such a manner that there cannot be the least doubt that at one time the loess deposit constituted one great whole in the form of a gently undulating grass steppe, even where the mighty river now rolls along with its yellow waters of muddy loess soil.

Therefore the Yellow River and its tributaries did not flow at the time when the loess was deposited. Over Northern China there extended an undulating grass land, a landscape probably similar to that of the steppes of Southern Mongolia today.

The vision of the great steppes of Northern China during the loess period became real to me one day in 1923 when on the march to Kansu. Just in the district from which Fig. 51 is drawn I stood on the edge of the loess deposits and looked down on the mighty river. I then saw how the river had cut its way down by erosion, not only through the loess cover and its foundation of gravel and conglomerate, but also through a good piece of the ancient red sandstone which is the bedrock of this district. It was a picture of a tremendous process of erosion, later than the loess formation, which I saw revealed here in the perpendicular banks.

Then I walked back about 10 yards on to the loess plateau. The river had suddenly vanished, the two opposite precipices merged into each other and the picture of the ancient unbroken loess plateau stood clearly before me.

(*About 36°N; 110°E.*)

(J. Gunnar Andersson : *Children of the Yellow Earth.*)

Stony Desert

AUSTRALIA : LOPPERRAMANNA, EAST OF LAKE EYRE

THE KNOLL of Desert Sandstone at Nungunpurananni clearly showed the origin of the " Stony Deserts," an origin that has been much disputed. This problem naturally excited the interest of the early travellers ; for these wide wastes of stones are most impressive in their awful desolation and barrenness. The pebbles are sometimes so closely packed that a cart leaves no wheel-ruts ; and, as the South Australian police know to their cost, aboriginal fugitives can cross the country without leaving the slightest trace of their footprints. I was told of one South Australian police officer who gained the affection of the aborigines by keeping them well supplied with dogs. His motive, however, was not generosity. He was thus enabled to track the aborigines across the Stony Deserts, as the clumsy dogs disturbed the stones, or put their feet between them and left footprints on the soft clay.

The stones on these plains are angular, and are said in places to fit together with the accuracy of a mosaic ; and when the pebbles are thus closely packed, patches of the Stony Desert appear like a tesselated pavement.

Sturt was the first man who gave any detailed description of the Stony Desert, and he explained it as due to the action of a former sea. He regarded " the sandy desert as once undoubtedly a sea-bed," and saw in each belt of stony desert " the focus of a mighty current " sweeping across an old sea floor. The pebbles of the stony plains, however, show no signs of water action. Sturt's view is an illustration of the habit so prevalent in the middle of the last century of regarding water as the universal geological agent.

The Stony Desert, in fact, is due to the absence of water. The country where it occurs was once covered by a sheet of the rock known as Desert Sandstone, in which there are abundant pebbles of quartz, sandstone, and other hard materials. The Desert Sandstone has slowly decayed under the action of the weather ; the loose sand has been blown away by the wind, and the hard fragments remain scattered over the ground. The Desert Sandstone once spread in a continuous sheet all across the Lake Eyre plains ; and wherever the waste from the Desert Sandstone has not been covered by later deposits, it litters the ground as the barren Stony Desert.

(28°30′S; 138°40′E.)

(J. W. Gregory : *The Dead Heart of Australia*.)

Desert: Simpson Desert

AUSTRALIA

BIRDSVILLE LIES only a few miles inside the Queensland border, so I made a motor trip to Pandi Pandi Station, twelve miles away down the Diamantina, in South Australia. This afforded a good opportunity of studying the sand-ridges and their formation and movement. It was clear in this district that the long, straight sand-ridges move in the direction of their length. They were seen encroaching on the river flats, which are normally kept clear of sand by the floods, from the southern side of the river, and to be clearing away on the northern side of the river, leaving tufts of cane-grass, once growing on the ridges, standing on long columns of sand, held together by the roots of the plants, and to be seen only at the south-eastern ends of the ridges. The sand is moving to the north-west. This fact is well recognized by the pastoralists; those in South Australia, in that corner of the State, often say that if they can wait long enough all the sand in South Australia will pass off into Queensland.

On most stations, the cook-house and dining-room are a separate building from the living quarters, and at Pandi this was so. But a long, narrow sand-dune had crept up from the south and thrust itself like a snake between the two buildings, so that to get to meals one had to climb this dune. They had laid a track over it of wire-netting to make the going easier.

*   *   *   *   *

Three flights were made over the Simpson Desert; the first diagonally through the centre from Birdsville to Alice Springs, the second across the northern end to Lake Caroline and the Hay, and the third down the complete length of the area towards its western side.

The first ninety miles of the first flight, from Birdsville to the Queensland border, was in the south-western corner of Queensland, over country all held under pastoral lease. The country there is all the same, sand-ridges fifty feet high running N. 30° W., with clay flats between them. These sand-ridges are all precipitous on the north-eastern side, gently sloping on the south-western, rise to heights of up to a hundred feet, and average about a quarter of a mile apart. The strips between them are stony gibber flats, with occasional clay-pans, and very few lines of drainage. The commonest vegetation is the cane-grass bush, which favours the sand-hills. Spinifex is at first rare, but gidgee, mulga, and other acacias are scattered about the clay-pans and watercourses; eucalypts are absent, except for the lines of box-gum along all the major watercourses. The course of the Mulligan is very well defined, running parallel to the sand-ridges, a white strip of sand between two dark lines of box-gum ; the Hay was not recognizable on this course ; it may have been represented by a series of clay-pans, but there was no defined channel ; that must have lain to the north of us.

After the Northern Territory border was crossed, the country became worse, and at thirty-five miles into the Territory, there were no longer any loam flats or clay-pans between the sand-ridges, but only drift sand. These conditions prevailed for the next hundred miles, which were nothing but a dreary waste of sand-ridges, spinifex, and gidgee. The spinifex increased greatly after the border was crossed ; it was easily recognized from the air by its hollow rings, outward-growing masses from which the central portion has decayed away.

In the better country the ground between the sand-ridges is grey, denoting clay and loam, but here it was pink, with sand between the red sand-ridges. The ridges themselves became more continuous, straight, and strictly parallel ; each ridge could be traced for the full range of vision, some fifty miles. Occasionally two would converge and continue as one, the single stem of the Y thus formed always being to the north-west. From the air the earth appeared as a flat, pink disc, ribbed in a giant grid from horizon to horizon by the red sand-ridges, and streaked by the darker lines between the sand-ridges where the acacias and spinifex grew closer. There were no watercourses or clay-pans. The precipitation, such as it is, sinks straight into the sand, where it is absorbed by the roots of the hardy plants whose scant foliage braves the scorching air above.

The miles flitted by. Every now and again we swooped down to within a hundred feet of the ground, and felt its hot breath, escaping gladly again to the cooler upper air. From a very low altitude the country looked less desolate, less uniform ; the acacias offered some shade, the strips between the sand-ridges looked less uninviting, and the skyline was broken by the high ridges.

At 280 miles from Birdsville, and ninety miles from Alice Springs, the first range was crossed, a long narrow ridge, extending far to the westward. The sand-ridges are bounded on that side of the desert by this range ; they could be seen literally lapping up against the dark rock. The Todd flows past the eastern end of the range. (*25°50'S; 139°20'E to 23°30'S; 133°50'E.*)

(C. T. Madigan : *Central Australia.*)

North American Deserts
NEVADA, NEW MEXICO, ARIZONA

THE TRAIN passes on into the Nevada desert, which to the English eye is a real novelty in landscape and a thing of rare beauty. Right and left are vast rolling expanses of sage-brush, grey brown and spring-green on the sandy soil, and closing the horizon on either side jagged, deep-blue mountains, with flashes of vermilion on their flanks. The scene changes incessantly as the sun rises and sinks, and new mountains come into view and are swept with waves of colour. It is not wholly desert ; cattle, goats and even horses find a living on the sage-brush ; and there are immense ranches where now and again one may see the steers being rounded up and get exciting glimpses of real cowboys doing their own business in the wild. Darkness comes on a winter evening long before you are tired of this desert.

* * * * *

The deserts . . . are sheer natural loveliness. All through New Mexico and Arizona one looks out on the sea of sage-brush, with beautifully sculptured mountains in a haze of pale blue rising out of it like Greek islands from the Ægean. The air on these high plateaux is amazingly exhilarating, and one feels a sense of well-being in merely passing through them.

(J. A. Spender : *The America of To-day.*)

North American Desert
ARIZONA

THESE ARIZONA deserts are not barren and desolate wastes, but literally teeming with plant and tree life. The plain looks exactly like a nursery devoted to but one or two shrub species. According to the water supply, the creosote bushes or the mes-quites will be two feet high—all of them—or three feet, or six feet, as the case may be. On different areas the standard of height varies, but on any given plain, as far around you as you can see, the height is remarkably uniform, and the spacing of the clumps is very regular.

Try as you will to get rid of it, the nursery idea sticks in your mind ; and the more you see of these deserts, the more fixed does it become. One plain will be found devoted to the mesquite, another to the creosote bush, another to choya cacti, and others, but of smaller area, to the tall and rank galleta grass, with a mixture of other things. And many times, also, will your overland progress lead you to a five or ten-acre tract of desert botanical garden, whereon you will find that Nature has joyously thrown together a fine sample lot of all the species that have been used in planting operations for twenty miles around.

(William T. Hornaday : *Camp Fires on Desert and Lava.*)

Full descriptions of the plants here mentioned are given in the book.

North American Desert: the Colorado
To the Colorado Desert

Thou brown, bare-breasted, voiceless mystery,
Hot sphynx of nature, cactus-crowned, what hast thou done?
Unclothed and mute as when the groans of chaos turned
Thy naked burning bosom to the sun.
The mountain silences have speech, the rivers sing,
Thou answerest never unto anything.
Pink throated lizards pant in thy slim shade ;
The hornèd toad runs rustling in the heat ;
The shadowy gray coyote, born afraid,
Steals to some brackish spring, and leaps and prowls
Away, and howls and howls and howls and howls,
Until the solitude is shaken with added loneliness.
The sharp mescal shoots up a giant stalk,
Its centuries of yearning to the sunburnt skies,
And drops rare honey from the lips
Of yellow waxen flowers, and dies.
Some lengthwise sun-dried shapes with feet and hands,
And thirsty mouths pressed on the sweltering sands,
Make here and there a gruesome graveless spot
Where someone drank the scorching hotness and is not.
God must have made thee in His anger, and forgot.

(Madge Morris Wagner : *The Lure of the Desert.*)

North American Desert:
the Colorado Desert and the Salton Sink

IT WAS in early May, 1866. My companion, Mr. James T. Gardner, and I got into the saddle on the bank of the Colorado River, and headed westward over the road from La Paz to San Bernardino. My mount was a tough, magnanimous sort of mule, who at all times did his very best ; that of my friend, an animal still hardier, but altogether wanting in moral attributes. He developed a singular antipathy for my mule, and utterly refused to march within a quarter of a mile of me ; so that over a wearying route of three hundred miles we were obliged to travel just beyond the reach of a shout. Hour after hour, plodding along at a dog-trot, we pursued our solitary way without the spice of companionship, and altogether deprived of the melodramatic satisfaction of loneliness.

Far ahead of us a white line traced across the barren plain marked our road. It seemed to lead to nowhere, except onward over more and more arid reaches of desert. Rolling hills of crude color and low gloomy contour rose above the general level. Here and there the eye was arrested by a towering crag, or an elevated, rocky mountain group, whose naked sides sank down into the desert, unrelieved by the shade of a solitary tree. The whole aspect of nature was dull in color, and gloomy with an all-pervading silence of death. Although the summer had not fairly opened, a torrid sun beat down with cruel severity, blinding the eye with its brilliance, and inducing a painful, slow fever. The very plants, scorched to a crisp, were ready, at the first blast of a sirocco, to be whirled away and ground to dust. Certain bare zones lay swept clean of the last dry stems across our path, marking the track of whirlwinds. Water was only found at intervals of sixty or seventy miles, and, when reached, was more of an aggravation than a pleasure,—bitter, turbid, and scarce ; we rode for it all day, and berated it all night, only to leave it at sunrise with a secret fear that we might fare worse next time.

About noon on the third day of our march, having reached the borders of the Cabezon Valley, we emerged from a rough, rocky gateway in the mountains, and I paused while my companion made up his quarter of a mile, that we might hold council and determine our course, for the water question was becoming serious;

springs which looked cool and seductive on our maps proving to be dried up and obsolete upon the ground.

Gardner reached me in a few minutes, and we dismounted to rest the tired mules, and to scan the landscape before us. We were on the margin of a great basin* whose gently shelving rim sank from our feet to a perfectly level plain, which stretched southward as far as the eye could reach, bounded by a dim, level horizon, like the sea, but walled in to the west, at a distance of about forty miles, by the high frowning wall of the Sierras. This plain was a level floor, as white as marble, and into it the rocky spurs from our own mountain range descended, like promontories into the sea. Wide, deeply indented white bays wound in and out among the foot-hills, and, traced upon the barren slopes of this rocky coast, was marked, at a considerable elevation above the plain, the shore-line of an ancient sea,—a white stain defining its former margin as clearly as if the water had but just receded. On the dim, distant base of the Sierras the same primeval beach could be seen. This water-mark, the level white valley, and the utter absence upon its surface of any vegetation, gave a strange and weird aspect to the country, as if a vast tide had but just ebbed, and the brilliant scorching sun had hurriedly dried up its last traces of moisture.

In the indistinct glare of the southern horizon, it needed but slight aid from the imagination to see a lifting and tumbling of billows, as if the old tide were coming ; but they were only shudderings of heat. As we sat there surveying this unusual scene, the white expanse became suddenly transformed into a placid blue sea, along whose rippling shores were the white blocks of roofs, groups of spire-crowned villages, and cool stretches of green grove. A soft, vapory atmosphere hung over this sea ; shadows, purple and blue, floated slowly across it, producing the most enchanting effect of light and color. The dreamy richness of the tropics, the serene sapphire sky of the desert, and the cool, purple distance of mountains, were grouped as by miracle. It was as if Nature were about to repay us an hundred-fold for the lie she had given the topographers and their maps.

In a moment the illusion vanished. It was gone, leaving the white desert unrelieved by a shadow ; a blaze of white light falling full on the plain ; the sun-struck air reeling in whirlwind columns,

* The Salton Sink.

white with the dust of the desert, up, up, and vanishing into the sky. Waves of heat rolled like billows across the valley, the old shores became indistinct, the whole lowland unreal. Shades of misty blue crossed over it and disappeared. Lakes with ragged shores gleamed out, reflecting the sky, and in a moment disappeared.

The bewildering effect of this natural magic, and perhaps the feverish thirst, produced the impression of a dream, which might have taken fatal possession of us, but for the importunate braying of Gardner's mule, whose piteous discords (for he made three noises at once) banished all hallucination, and brought us gently back from the mysterious spectacle to the practical question of water. We had but one canteen of that precious elixir left ; the elixir in this case being composed of one part pure water, one part sand, one part alum, one part saleratus, with liberal traces of Colorado mud, representing a very disgusting taste, and very great range of geological formations.

To search for the mountain springs laid down upon our maps was probably to find them dry, and afforded us little more induce- ment than to chase the mirages. The only well-known water was at an oasis somewhere on the margin of the Cabezon, and should, if the information was correct, have been in sight from our resting-place.

We eagerly scanned the distance, but were unable, among the phantom lakes and the ever-changing illusions of the desert, to fix upon any probable point. Indian trails led out in all directions, and our only clew to the right path was far in the northwest, where, looming against the sky, stood two conspicuous mountain piles lifted above the general wall of the Sierra, their bases rooted in the desert, and their precipitous fronts rising boldly on each side of an open gateway. The two summits, high above the magical stratum of desert air, were sharply defined and singularly distinct in all the details of rock-form and snow-field. From their position we knew them to be walls of the San Gorgonio Pass, and through this gateway lay our road.

After brief deliberation we chose what seemed to be the most beaten road leading in that direction, and I mounted my mule and started, leaving my friend patiently seated in his saddle waiting for the *afflatus* of his mule to take effect. Thus we rode down into the desert, and hour after hour travelled silently on, straining our eyes forward to a spot of green which we hoped might mark our oasis.

So incredulous had I become, that I prided myself upon having penetrated the flimsy disguise of an unusually deceptive mirage, and philosophized, to a considerable extent, upon the superiority of my reason over the instinct of the mule, whose quickened pace and nervous manner showed him to be, as I thought, a dupe.

Whenever there comes to be a clearly defined mental issue between man and mule, the stubbornness of the latter is the expression of an adamantine moral resolve, founded in eternal right. The man is invariably wrong. Thus on this occasion, as at a thousand other times, I was obliged to own up worsted, and I drummed for a while with Spanish spurs upon the ribs of my conqueror ; that being my habitual mode of covering my retreat.

It *was* the oasis, and not the mirage. John lifted up his voice, now many days hushed, and gave out spasmodic gusts of baritone, which were as dry and harsh as if he had drunk mirages only.

The heart of Gardner's mule relented. Of his own accord he galloped up to my side, and, for the first time together, we rode forward to the margin of the oasis. Under the palms we hastily threw off our saddles and allowed the parched brutes to drink their fill. We lay down in the grass, drank, bathed our faces, and played in the water like children. We picketed our mules knee-deep in the freshest of grass, and, unpacking our saddle-bags, sent up a smoke to heaven, and achieved that most precious solace of the desert traveller, a pot of tea.

By and by we plunged into the pool, which was perhaps thirty feet long, and deep enough to give us a pleasant swim. The water being almost blood-warm, we absorbed it in every pore, dilated like sponges, and came out refreshed.

With its isolation, its strange warm fountain, its charming vegetation varied with grasses, trailing water-plants, bright parterres in which were minute flowers of turquoise blue, pale gold, mauve, and rose, and its two graceful palms, this oasis evoked a strange sentiment. I have never felt such a sense of absolute and remote seclusion ; the hot, trackless plain and distant groups of mountains shut it away from all the world. Its humid and fragrant air hung over us in delicious contrast with the oven-breath through which we had ridden. Weary little birds alighted, panting, and drank and drank again, without showing the least fear of us. Wild doves fluttering down bathed in the pool and fed about among our mules.

After straining over one hundred and fifty miles of silent desert, hearing no sound but the shoes of our mules grating upon hot sand, after the white glare, and that fever-thirst which comes from drinking alkali-water, it was a deep pleasure to lie under the palms and look up at their slow-moving green fans, and hear in those shaded recesses the mild, sweet twittering of our traveller-friends, the birds, who stayed, like ourselves, overcome with the languor of perfect repose.

(33°40′N; 116°W to 34°N; 117°W.)

(Clarence King : *Mountaineering in the Sierra Nevada.*)

N.B. The San Gorgonio Pass lies between the San Bernardino and the San Tacinto Mountains about 100 miles east of Los Angeles.

Desert Mountains

ARIZONA

FOR A hundred miles west of Tucson the stage setting is grand and peculiar. The desert is a plain that seems to be absolutely level, but it is so thickly studded with mountain ranges that every " valley," as they are oddly called, is a great natural amphitheatre, surrounded by rugged mountains. It is a rare thing for the vision to sweep across the green sea of desert verdure straight to a far-distant horizon on the level without encountering a saw-toothed range of bare grey granite. I noted this immediately, and throughout our wanderings in Arizona the clear gaps leading to the level horizon were few, indeed, and very narrow.

In about three days' overland travel one is reasonably certain to pass through, or else quite near, at least two or three independent ranges of mountains. By the end of so much travel you have honestly acquired the impression that of all mountains in the world these are the most abrupt risers, and from the levelest plains. Often there are no foothills, no premonitory symptoms of any kind. With one foot on the level desert, you plant the other on the steep side of a mountain that towers aloft in one long steep climb from base to summit ; and you must climb for all you are worth in order to rise in the world.

These mountains seem like afterthoughts, modelled in the shop long after the general plans were finished, and set up cold. They constantly reminded me of the artificial peaks of stone, or concrete, or furnace slag that have been built in several of the level zoological gardens of Europe for wild goats, ibexes and sheep to climb upon.

(*Tucson: 32°15'N; 111°W.*)

(William T. Hornaday : *Camp Fires on Desert and Lava.*)

Llano Estacado

TEXAS

THE COMANCHES call the southern arm of the Red River Ki-chi-è-qui-ho-no, that is to say, river of the town of the dogs of the prairies. This name has doubtless been given to it on account of the quantity of those little quadrupeds (*Spermophilus ludovicianus*) that inhabit these solitudes in far greater numbers than in the other American wildernesses. I do not think there exists in the world as stupendous a village as the one which the prairie dogs have constructed for themselves in the plain that leads to the sources of the Ki-chi-è-qui-ho-no. This village is twenty-five miles in length, and is equally extensive in width, which, supposing it to be almost circular, makes a superficies of about 625 square miles. From these gigantic dimensions one can easily judge of the numbers of the interesting population that live there.

Villages of the prairie dogs are to be found extending from Mexico to the farthest boundary of the United States. In making choice of a site for the establishment of their colony, the prairie dogs always choose an uncovered and rather elevated spot, sheltered from inundations, and on which grows a stunted weed that is their usual food. It is to be supposed that this quadruped can live without water, for it sometimes takes up its abode in a locality where neither river nor spring is to be found for more than twenty-two miles around, and on ground where not a single drop of water can be obtained, even by digging a well upwards of 120 feet deep. So that the borders of these villages have, generally speaking, an aspect of aridity and desolation. Those little vandals add to this sad appearance by gnawing and devouring all round their dwellings every kind of vegetation ; they only spare a few flowers, the sight of which seems to please them,— such as the *Erigeron divaricatum*, the *solanum*, the *Ellysia myctagenea*, and two or three others of the same species.

The prairie dog resembles the squirrel in shape, size, and physiognomy : it has nothing in common with the real dog but its cry, which is very like barking. It burrows for itself sometimes to a depth of nine feet, and afterwards places the earth it throws up from the galleries within the form of a cone over its subterraneous abode. These galleries are generally from four to five inches in width, and frequently rattlesnakes and owls of a small species do not scruple to instal themselves in those spacious and commodious lodgings to the utter detriment of the lawful proprietors. In the fine season, the prairie dog seats itself during the greater part of the day on the summit of its dwelling, and then chatters with its neighbours in a most noisy manner. At the approach of a horseman, or of any dangerous animal, the first group that perceives the enemy barks in a particular way. Immediately the alarm is communicated from one to another, to all the citizens of the republic ; each raises his head, pricks up his ears with uneasiness, and gives an anxious glance around him : then begins a chorus of shrill barking ; an extreme agitation is seen to prevail throughout the village ; and again, as if by enchantment, all is silent, and the entire community has disappeared under the earth with the rapidity of lightning.

Towards the end of October, when the dogs of the prairies feel the approach of winter, they fasten up with straw and stems of flowers all the passages leading to their burrows, then they fall asleep until the return of spring. In the great northern solitudes of Texas, one rarely takes a long journey without meeting many republics of prairie dogs. The borders of the Ki-chi-e-qui-ho-no, in particular, contain several very considerable ones.
(*About 34°30′N; 101°30′W.*)

(The Abbé Em. Domenech : *Seven Years' Residence in the Great Deserts of North America.*)

Playa

SYRIAN DESERT

ABOUT THIS part of my journey I saw the likeness of a fresh-water lake. I saw, as it seemed, a broad sheet of calm water stretching far and fair towards the south—stretching deep into winding creeks, and hemmed in by jutting promontories, and shelving smooth off towards the shallow side : on its bosom the reflected fire of the sun lay playing and seeming to float as though upon deep still waters.

Though I knew of the cheat, it was not till the spongy foot of my camel had almost trodden in the seeming lake that I could undeceive my eyes, for the shore line was quite true and natural. I soon saw the cause of the phantasm. A sheet of water, heavily impregnated with salts, had gathered together in a vast hollow between the sand-hills, and when dried up by evaporation had left a white saline deposit ; this exactly marked the space which the waters had covered, and so traced out a good shore-line. The minute crystals of the salt, by their way of sparkling in the sun, were made to seem like the dazzled face of a lake that is calm and smooth.

(Kinglake : *Eothen*.)

Salt Sea : The Dead Sea

PALESTINE

ABOUT MID-DAY I began to examine my map, and to question my guide. He at first tried to elude inquiry, then suddenly fell on his knees, and confessed that he knew nothing of the country. I was thus thrown upon my own resources, and calculating that on the preceding day we had nearly performed a two days' journey, I concluded that the Dead Sea must be near. In this I was right ; for at about three or four o'clock in the afternoon I caught a first sight of its dismal face.

I went on, and came near to those waters of Death ; they stretched deeply into the southern desert, and before me, and all around, as far away as the eye could follow, blank hills piled high over hills, pale, yellow, and naked, walled up in her tomb for ever the dead and damned Gomorrah. There was no fly that hummed in the forbidden air, but, instead, a deep stillness—no grass grew from the earth—no weed peered through the void sand ; but, in mockery of all life, there were trees borne down by Jordan in some ancient flood, and these, grotesquely planted upon the forlorn shore, spread out their grim skeleton arms all scorched, and charred to blackness, by the heats of the long, silent years.

* * * * *

I bathed in the Dead Sea. The ground covered by the water sloped so gradually that I was not only forced to " sneak in," but to walk through the water nearly a quarter of a mile before I could get out of my depth. When at last I was able to attempt to dive, the salts, held in solution made my eyes smart so sharply that the pain I thus suffered, joined with the weakness occasioned by want of food, made me giddy and faint for some moments ; but I soon grew better. I knew beforehand the impossibility of sinking in this buoyant water ; but I was surprised to find that I could not swim at my accustomed pace : my legs and feet were lifted so high and dry out of the lake that my stroke was baffled, and I found myself kicking against the thin air, instead of the dense fluid upon which I was swimming. The water is perfectly bright and clear ; its taste detestable. After finishing my attempts at swimming and diving, I took some time in regaining the shore ; and, before I began to dress, I found that the sun had already evaporated the water which clung to me, and that my skin was already thickly incrusted with salts.

(*31°45'N; 35°30'E.*) (Kinglake : *Eothen.*)

Desert Lake: Lake Chad

FRENCH EQUATORIAL AFRICA

THE NEXT morning was more varied than the previous one. The river wound and rippled ; tributaries branched off to the lake ; and islands appeared. As we passed Djim Tilo, we saw the natives standing in two rows, swaying, the first row shaking their swords and the second their spears, as a sign of welcome. Our faithful Issein, F——'s interpreter, called out to them that we should be returning soon, and we glided on towards the lake, followed by their boisterous cries. Trees now began to appear on the banks, covered by thick blankets of liana ; they formed a kind of wall falling straight like a stage curtain from the heights into the river itself. F—— told me that in the forest posts, where every journey has to be made by canoe against these dense hangings, the traveller is soon exhausted. It was all new to me, though this particular kind of country did not last long.

In fact, the low banks were presently covered with tufts of papyrus and the leaves of ambacks. At every turn we expected to see the open water ; each time we saw an ever thinner line which was still the river bank. A number of fishermen came downstream in a row, mounted on horses standing on light wooden rafts. Only the torsos of the animals could be seen, their heads being covered. They were motionless, and seemed to be half-water and half-land creatures. After a while the banks became no more than beds of sand where the water penetrated. Occasionally clumps of plants appeared ; then the line of the horizon came into view, gradually opening out into a huge semicircular curve as we approached the mouth of the delta. We were intrigued by a strip of black on the water's edge ; when we came up with it, it moved, made a noise, and flew away. It was a mass of black and white gulls with red beaks, and they uttered hoarse cries. We had reached Lake Chad. The broad expanse of open and swirling water defended itself against the invasion of the river by a bastion of eddies. By now three-quarters of the horizon was taken up by a mass of yellow water, yellow as sand, yellow as the river, yellow as the mud and the sky. A world of ochre seized the eye and penetrated the nostrils. An enormous green crocodile greeted our arrival by clacking his jaws, and disappeared between two waves.

We struck bottom quite close to him. Two paddlers, without hesitation, jumped into the shallow water and got us off the sand. Pelicans, perched on the banks, watched us go up the Chari again, leaving the Lake to them.

It is difficult to explore Lake Chad properly. Either you must fly over it in a plane, in which case it appears—as I saw it three years ago—like a huge bed of greenish moss 40 times larger than Lake Geneva, from which you hear an occasional metallic splash of water ; or else you must cross it in a boat, and since the provisioning of our northern posts has to be made by road, crossing and especially landing are accompanied by considerable risk. Alternatively, you can go to Bol, which is on an island but which I was unable to reach. All the banks which are pointed out to travellers with the words " This is the lake " are merely the banks of distant reaches, tributaries, deltas, or dead waters. And you never know whether you are going to find the lake when you do reach its borders. This is what happened to me in the neighbourhood of Massakory ; all that was left of the reaches of the lake was a slimy ooze stinking of rotten fish. The lake dries up, moves about, fills up, empties, swells, lengthens, overflows and diminishes in the most mysterious manner. Tilho made a special study, for which he is celebrated, of the causes of these movements of the lake. From the accounts of Clapperton in 1824, Barth in 1852, Tilho and Audoin in 1904, and the Tilho mission in 1906, not to speak of the more recent works by the same author, some figures given for the size of the lake would seem to be as much as twice the figures given by others. The problem is to know whether the old measurements were arrived at by scientific observation, or whether they were estimates ; whether the rainy season was taken into consideration ; whether one or more years of exceptional drought or rain might have intervened. All these circumstances substantially change the appearance of the physical features of these parts.

What is known is that Lake Chad has a surface area of 24,000 square kms., and a depth of 19 feet. This is not very deep, and since its banks are very flat the least variation of water-level enormously increases its expanse. Even the wind, by causing surface currents, not only carries waves to the banks, but stirs up movements of mud and sand similar to the interior movements of swamps. Direct rains, and still more the rains that inflate the Chari and the Logone, farther south, bring an immense addition of water every year.

But the sun drinks up this water greedily ; so much so that from 1904 to 1908, for example, the liquid surface diminished by one sixth. After flooding N'Guigmi (14° 15' north) in 1907, the waters quitted the whole of the northern part of the lake and did not reach any greater height than the mouth of the Komadougou (13° 41' north). Later, however, N'Guigmi once again saw the return of the Lake below.

Amback, papyrus, water-lilies, bindweed and all kinds of reeds and aquatic plants have spread over Lake Chad and lent it its swampy appearance. This vegetation, stationary and floating, the shifting sandbanks, and the incalculable periodic movements of the water, give even the most experienced observers a headache when they try to make a map of the Lake area. Villages crop up on the islands, then disappear ; the islands themselves vanish. There is pastureland in the fields, then everything suddenly fades away, grass, white oxen and all, with their huge horns and arched foreheads, soft and spongy like cork. The Boudoumas build dykes, block up backwaters, plant gardens ; then the water floods over and everything is gone.

Lake Chad is more salt than the watercourses that feed it, and the degree of saltness varies according to the locality. Since it is not very strong anyway, the question is often asked whether the lake has a subterranean outlet.

(*13°N; 14°E.*)

(Pierre Olivier Lapie : *My Travels through Chad :* Translated by Leslie Bull.)

Salt Pan

SOUTH AFRICA

Six miles inland from Algoa Bay

ON THE evening of the seventeenth we encamped on the verdant bank of a beautiful lake in the midst of a wood of fruitescent plants. It was of an oval form, about three miles in circumference. On the western side was a shelving bank of green turf, and round the other parts of the bason the ground, rising more abruptly, and to a greater height, was covered thickly with the same kind of arboreous and succulent plants as had been observed to grow most commonly in the thickets of the adjoining country. The water was perfectly clear, but salt as brine. It was one of those salt-water lakes which abound in Southern Africa, where they are called *zout pans* by the colonists. This it seems is the most famous in the country, and is resorted to by the inhabitants from very distant parts of the colony, for the purpose of procuring salt for their own consumption or for sale. It is situated on a plain of considerable elevation above the level of the sea. The greatest part of the bottom of the lake was covered with one continued body of salt like a sheet of ice, the chrystals of which were so united that it formed a solid mass as hard as rock. The margin or shore of the bason was like the sandy beach of the sea coast, with sandstone and quartz pebbles thinly scattered over it, some red, some purple, and others grey. Beyond the narrow belt of sand the sheet of salt commenced with a thin porous crust, increasing in thickness and solidity as it advanced towards the middle of the lake. The thickness in the middle is not known, a quantity of water generally remaining in that part. The dry south-easterly winds of summer agitating the water of the lake produce on the margin a fine, light, powdery salt, like flakes of snow. This is equally beautiful as the refined salt of England, and is much sought after by the women, who always commission their husbands to bring home a quantity of snowy salt for the table.

We happened to visit the lake at a very unfavourable season, when it was full of water. About the middle it was three feet deep, but sufficiently clear to perceive several veins of a dark ferruginous color intersecting in various directions the sheet of salt. These were in all probability springs whose action had impeded chrystallization, and brought up a quantity of ochraceous matter. I caused a hole four feet in depth to be dug in the sand close to the edge of the water. The two first feet were through sand like that of the sea-shore, in which were mingled small shining chrystals of salt. The third foot was considerably harder and more compact, and came up in flakes that required some force to break, and the last foot was so solid that the spade would scarcely pierce it ; and one-fifth part of the mass at least was pure salt in chrystals. The water now gushed in perfectly clear and as salt as brine.
(33°40′S; 25°40′E.)
(John Barrow : *An Account of Travels into the Interior of Southern Africa, in the Years 1797 and 1798.*)

Great Salt Lake

UTAH

IN THE morning you wake to find yourself approaching the causeway, which takes you forty miles through (not across) the shallower part of the great Salt Lake. What it is exactly that makes these great salt inland seas a waking dream of desolation is more than I can say, but even in the glittering morning light which turned its waters into silver and clothed the surrounding mountains with a haze of tender blue, this lake seemed the solitude of solitudes, and if there could be water on the moon, one might think it a scene from moonland. Nothing lives in these dense salt waters ; there is no sign of habitation on the shores ; the wild duck which disport themselves in the brine and seem to like it are said to render themselves unfit for human company or consumption—which is perhaps why they do it. The scene is one of fantastic beauty, but it causes a slight shiver. (*41°10'N; 112°40'W.*)   (J. A. Spender : *The America of To-day.*)

Great Salt Lake

UTAH

AS SOON as you diverge from the valley of the Bear River, you immediately find yourself before the Great Salt Lake, which, with Lake Utah, constitutes one of the most curious features of the aspect of the Great Basin. They both lie eastward ; the first is saturated with a solution of salt, the second contains only fresh water.

The Great Salt Lake is seventy miles in length, and its height is 4,200 feet above the level of the sea. Its waters, as they evaporate, leave traces of salt all over the soil. The rocks that surround it are whitened by a saline substance, which forms into stalactites and incrustations that are often two inches thick. The composition of this salt is thus analysed :—

Chloride of sodium	... ...	97·80
Chloride of calcium	... ...	0·61
Chloride of magnesia	... ...	0·24
Sulphate of soda	... ...	0·23
Sulphate of lime	... ...	1·12
	Total ...	100·00

No fish can live in the lake, which is very shallow. Fresh meat left steeped in its waters during twelve hours can afterwards be preserved like salt meat, without requiring any other preparation.

To the east of the lake you distinguish an extensive plain partly covered with artemis, with mire, or with salt. From the centre of this kind of muddy bay rise numerous mountains, which appear like islands planted in a sea of saltpetre. Beyond this point commences the desert of the Seventy Miles ; a dreary, arid, and desolate district, covered with fragments of all sorts of articles, which the Californian emigrants left there with a view of lightening their baggage, so as to be less encumbered during the route.

Besides this plain, others more or less vast are also to be found on the borders of the lake ; they are covered with salt in a solid state, and most admirably crystallised over the primitive sand : other crystallisations some inches thick may also be seen glittering in the sun. Porphyry, metamorphic sandstone, gneiss, white marble, and dark calcareous limestone, form the principal components of the rocks that border the lakes. You may also perceive in certain places on the banks twelve or thirteen steps formed by the waters of the lake as they decreased; the last is at least 198 feet above the present level ; which would prove that in this spot exist subterraneous conduits through which the waters flow, at indetermined periods, into the lower basins.* The Great Salt Lake must have been formerly a vast inner sea which covered an immense extent of country ; as it withdrew, it left behind that dryness and aridity which now characterise the land. One of the most curious plants of this region is the one called the *Silk Plant* by the Americans, *Vache à lait* by the Canadians, and *Capote de Sacarte* by the Mexicans. Its root is milky and bitter, but its bark is used to make ropes which prove to be stronger than leather. The only birds that frequent these localities are pelicans, cormorants, cranes, herons, sea-gulls, plovers, ducks, geese, and a few swans.

The malediction of heaven seems to weigh heavily on this solitude, which reminds one of the desolate shores of the Dead Sea, where Sodom and Gomorrah were destroyed. To the east there appeared inaccessible mountain ridges, and blood-coloured rocks dotted with green spots ; on their flanks undulated dark clouds ; whilst thick vapours moved above their summits, like the smoke of a volcano upon an azure sky. Light mists, produced at twilight, hovered amidst its vague glimmer, and danced over the waters, looking like crape tinged with the most lovely pink ; this crape spread over the horizon a transparent veil that shed upon nature the charm of a faint light, which, as it gradually rose to the summit of the mountains, assumed a more sombre hue, an indescribably dismal appearance, that filled the soul with sadness and the eyes with tears. This immense valley, of a lugubrious and funereal aspect, recalls to mind that of Jehoshaphat, the

---

* The variations in level of the lakes of the Great Basin have been the result of changes of climate since the Pleistocene.

valley of graves. An imposing silence continually reigns around this deserted lake, which might well be called the " Lake of Death." On its sterile strand, on the porphyry of its banks, you never hear the patter of the rain, the whistle of the wind, the leaves falling from the trees, the chirp of the birds, nor the swallow's rapid flight through the air. All is calm and gloomy, like the vaults of a gigantic sepulchre. One would say that God, in a day of wrath, had cursed these solitudes on account of the crimes of their inhabitants, whose ashes lay mouldering for many centuries beneath the sands of the desert.

(41°10′N; 112°40′W.)

(The Abbé Em. Domenech : *Seven Years' Residence in the Great Deserts of North America.*)

INDEX TO WORKS FROM WHICH EXCERPTS
HAVE BEEN TAKEN, AND ACKNOWLEDGEMENTS

INDEX TO AUTHORS FROM WHOSE WORKS
EXCERPTS HAVE BEEN TAKEN

GENERAL INDEX

INDEX TO WORKS FROM WHICH EXCERPTS
HAVE BEEN TAKEN

The opportunity is here taken of expressing to authors, publishers and others the thanks of both editor and publisher for permission to include excerpts from those works listed here and still in copyright.

26

INDEX TO AUTHORS FROM WHOSE WORKS
EXCERPTS HAVE BEEN TAKEN

PRINTED IN GREAT BRITAIN BY GEORGE PHILIP AND SON. LIMITED, LONDON

McGill Univ., Montreal, Canada

Dir., Geog. Summer School

Tuition - 145
Reg.   -   35

Date Due

May 3 56			
Jul 12 56			